Nicholas Pocock, Nicholas Harpsfield

A Treatise on the Pretended Divorce Between Henry VIII. and Catharine of Aragon

Now first printed from a collation of four manuscripts

Nicholas Pocock, Nicholas Harpsfield

A Treatise on the Pretended Divorce Between Henry VIII. and Catharine of Aragon
Now first printed from a collation of four manuscripts

ISBN/EAN: 9783744747196

Printed in Europe, USA, Canada, Australia, Japan

Cover: Foto ©ninafisch / pixelio.de

More available books at **www.hansebooks.com**

A TREATISE ON

THE PRETENDED DIVORCE

BETWEEN

HENRY VIII. AND CATHARINE OF ARAGON,

BY NICHOLAS HARPSFIELD, LL.D.,
ARCHDEACON OF CANTERBURY.

NOW FIRST PRINTED FROM A COLLATION OF FOUR MANUSCRIPTS.

BY NICHOLAS POCOCK, M.A.,
LATE MICHEL FELLOW OF QUEEN'S COLLEGE, OXFORD.

PRINTED FOR THE CAMDEN SOCIETY.
M.DCCC.LXXVIII.

WESTMINSTER:
PRINTED BY NICHOLS AND SONS,
25, PARLIAMENT STREET.

[NEW SERIES XXI]

COUNCIL OF THE CAMDEN SOCIETY
FOR THE YEAR 1877-78.

President,

THE RIGHT HON. THE EARL OF VERULAM, F.R.G.S.

REV. J. S. BREWER, M.A.
WILLIAM CHAPPELL, ESQ. F.S.A., *Treasurer.*
HENRY CHARLES COOTE, ESQ. F.S.A.
JAMES GAIRDNER, ESQ.
SAMUEL RAWSON GARDINER, ESQ., *Director.*
WILLIAM GILBERT, ESQ.
JOHN W. HALES, ESQ., M.A.
WILLIAM OXENHAM HEWLETT, ESQ., F.S.A.
ALFRED KINGSTON, ESQ., *Secretary.*
FREDERIC OUVRY, ESQ. Pres. S.A.
THE EARL OF POWIS, LL.D.
REV. W. SPARROW SIMPSON, D.D. F.S.A.
JAMES SPEDDING, ESQ.
WILLIAM JOHN THOMS, ESQ. F.S.A.
J. R. DANIEL-TYSSEN, ESQ. F.S.A.

The COUNCIL of the CAMDEN SOCIETY desire it to be understood that they are not answerable for any opinions or observations that may appear in the Society's publications; the Editors of the several Works being alone responsible for the same.

PREFACE.

My attention was first drawn to Harpsfield's narrative of the Divorce by my friend the Rev. Joseph Stevenson, who mentioned to me some years ago the manuscript copy of it in the Grenville Library in the British Museum. Some time afterwards I made a few extracts from it, thinking it worth while to make known by publication the important parts of it which bear upon the history of the period, but I had no idea of publishing the whole document, and indeed had thought little more about the matter till Mr. Stevenson informed me of another copy of the work in the possession of Charles Eyston, Esq. of East Hendred House, Berkshire, of which he at once pronounced that it was superior to that in the Grenville Library.

Still I had not formed the idea of publishing the entire treatise till my attention was again called to its value by Lord Acton under the following circumstances. In the summer of 1875 I printed a paper which had been previously read at a meeting of the Bristol Branch of the English Church Union, in which I casually alluded to the story as told by Sanders of Mrs. Cranmer being carried about in a chest with breathing-holes during the time when the Act of the Six Articles was in force. I was not aware that that story rested on any other evidence than that of Sanders, whom it has been the fashion ever since the days of Burnet to disparage as eminently untrustworthy. At one time I was of the same opinion, but the more intimately acquainted I became with Sanders's work the more reason I found to change my judgment about him.

PREFACE.

Nevertheless I mentioned the statement as one which had been made by Sanders in contrast with a ridiculous remark made by the late M. Merle D'Aubigné apologizing for Mrs. Cranmer not being presented at court, on the ground that the ceremony was unnecessary, and probably might have embarrassed the pious German lady.

It was this reference to Sanders that drew from Lord Acton a remark which he made in a letter addressed to me soon afterwards, that the same story had been told by an independent and less suspicious authority, viz. Dr. Nicholas Harpsfield.

Soon after this Lord Acton sent me a copy of the concluding part of the second book of Harpsfield's treatise, which he had had printed from the Grenville MS. including all the historical part of that book, and I determined accordingly, after consultation with him, to publish the whole treatise if I could find a publisher willing to undertake the risk of the publication. Not being acquainted personally with Mr. Eyston, I applied to him through my friend the Rev. Thomas Bowles, vicar of East Hendred, for the loan of his manuscript, which was immediately placed at my disposal in the kindest way. I copied it out, and from that copy the present volume was printed.

But before I go any further it is here necessary that I should describe the four copies which have been collated for this edition of Harpsfield. The first, here designated (G), is that in the Grenville Library. It consists of 314 leaves. The first book occupies 115 leaves, the second 107 leaves, the third 92 leaves. It is in a small square folio size, about 10 inches by 7, apparently copied by two or three different hands. The marginal references have been occasionally omitted, and its copier seems in some cases to have used his own discretion in altering words which were to him unintelligible. The press-mark of this MS. is Grenville XXXI.

It is not paged or foliated. After the 64th leaf of the second book there is a vacant leaf followed by 42 leaves. It is in writing of the time of James I. and there are no catch-words at the foot of the page. Two of the earlier leaves have been transposed in the binding, fol. 4 being placed as fol. 8. In the third book the last page of folio 60 has only five lines, the rest being vacant and the writing continued in another hand on folio 61. A similar fault occurs at folio 72, the back of which is vacant, and the narrative is continued in a different hand on folio 73. The chief characteristic of this manuscript as distinguished from the other three is its frequent omission of the marginal quotations, and its occasional alteration of words on the authority of the scribe, with the view of suiting the sense better. Thus at the beginning of the Epistle to the Reader, p. 12, where all the MSS. vary, G makes the passage run most easily by omitting the word *said*. At the passage on p. 279, line 6, after the words *and truth it is*, there is in the MS. a break, and it goes on, on the next page in another hand, *it is that the stories;* and after this point the copy has been very carelessly executed. In another place the word *Charibdis* ends a page the back of which is vacant, the next leaf continuing *and Sylla*. It is inferior to all the others, and has not been collated for the first and third books excepting in cases where any difficulty arose in settling the text from the other three. It has however in a very few instances determined the reading which has been adopted when the collation of the other three left any doubt as to what was the true reading.

The second is that which in the New College Library has the press mark (311 B), being that which was seen there by Antony Wood, and from which he quotes. I have called it, N_1. It is 11 inches high by 7 wide, and consists of 322 leaves, every tenth of which is marked in pencil by a later hand. The back of folio 119 is entirely vacant, but has been filled up with marks resembling handwriting, the first page of the leaf leaving off with the catchword *creditt*, which begins the first page of folio 120. The handwriting is of the reign of Elizabeth. There is no apparent difference in the style of the handwriting before and after folio 119, and it is not easy to account for the omission of an entire page, except on the supposition that the writer began folio 120 before the earlier part of the volume had been entirely transcribed. The last page of folio 322 is vacant.

These two MSS. are closely allied, though neither is copied from the other. Probably both are copied from the same MS. inasmuch as, where there are omissions of a line or two from carelessness in the one, the same fault is found in the other.

These two MSS. are to be distinguished from the other two (E), Mr. Eyston's copy, and (N_2) the second copy at New College, with the press-mark (311 A). Of these the third, or Mr. Eyston's copy, is a small folio, the three books of which are separately paged, consisting respectively of 148, 175, and 145 pages. It was executed in 1706, as detailed in Mr. Eyston's preface, from another MS. which was not the original, and which at first I thought might be the identical copy which had found its way into New College Library and is called (N_2). This conjecture was soon found to be erroneous; the very great resemblance between them having to be accounted for on the principle of their having been copied from the same MS. and that a different MS. from that from which (G) and (N_1) were copied.

The agreement between these two, (E) and (N_2), is so very minute as to indicate that they were both copied with great care, but the numerous omissions of one or two or three lines where there occurred an homœoteleuton, which are in almost every case common to both, show that the MS. from which they were copied was carelessly executed. A similar remark applies to (G) and (N_1), which do not resemble each other so closely, but indicate by similar omissions common to both that they are probably copied from the same document. Had I had only (E) and (N_2) to compare, the text would have been very inferior to that which is now produced from a comparison of the four MSS.; and if a text had been made up from (G) and (N_1) it would have been still worse. One MS. of each set would have enabled me to produce a text nearly as complete as is here exhibited, as it was very rarely that a correction could be adopted of (E) from (N_2); but, after (E) had been compared with (N_1) and there appeared any difference, the agreement of (N_2) with either of them always pointed out which reading was to be preferred. And it was rarely necessary to refer to (G), which is decidedly the worst of the four, though here and there it has supplied a word or two which I have with some hesitation given the preference to and admitted into the text.

All the copies are executed by transcribers who in some cases did not understand the references; accordingly these have given a great deal of trouble. They have been preserved as nearly as possible in the condition in which it was supposed the author had written them; the additions within brackets having been supplied when there was a difficulty in finding the reference, or when it had been copied wrongly in ignorance.

A remarkable instance of this copying in ignorance occurs in the references to the two volumes in Latin and English which were issued respectively in April and November 1530, containing the opinions of the Universities of Europe which were favourable to the King. Those to the English book were always correct if for " pag." is read " fol." Those to the Latin were unintelligible, as they were transcribed from the original MS. which referred to the volume by the signatures at the foot of the page. Nothing would have been gained by perpetuating mere mistakes of a transcriber when it was certain how the author must have written his reference, but in all these cases the alteration has been included in square brackets.

It must not be supposed that the same account is to be given of the portions of the text which are thus included. These represent the important additions which do not appear in Mr. Eyston's MS. nor in the New College MS. which so closely resembles it, and which have been supplied from the other New College MS.; and I think in every instance, or very nearly so, these occur also in the Grenville MS. The text which follows then represents in general the text to be found in Mr. Eyston's copy, which, though the most recent of the four, comes more near to the original than any of the other three. No notice has been taken of the small variations from this text which have been decided upon after a collation of the other manuscripts, or of all three of them; but when, as very often it has happened, there has been a passage omitted both in (E) and (N_2), and the sentence or part of a sentence has been supplied from the other two manuscripts, the words have been inserted within square brackets. The similar cases of omission in (N_1) and (G) have not been noticed. Thus in page 13, line 7, the word *lately* appears, though it is omitted by (E), and has been added because of its being found in both (N_1) and (N_2), and so shown to be an accidental omission on the part of the transcriber of (E), as (N_1) and (N_2) are quite independent of each other; whereas on page 14, line 4, the word *glorious* is inserted within square brackets to show that it does not appear either in (E) or (N_2), but is probably the right reading as having been preserved in (N_1), though omitted by carelessness in transcribing from the copy from which it is supposed (E) and (N_2) were executed. Again, at page 16, line 13 from bottom, the words *writing of all others and contrary to the* are in (N_1) and (N_2)

but not in (E), whilst the words *and, as it was said, filthily abused the archbishop's niece, the which harlot, Waldreda,* have been omitted in (N_2) but appear in (E) and (N_1), two independent witnesses, and are therefore not in brackets, whilst the words *as his wife and companion* are bracketed as containing a variation from (E) which occurs only in (N_2), and are not so certain as if they had appeared in two independent copies. Again, at p. 205, where the word *pacyfied* was written *practised* in (N_1), no notice has been taken of the mistake, nor in other similar cases. In some of these cases a word has been admitted into the text when the sense did not absolutely require it, on the principle that in copying a MS. the scribe was more likely to have omitted a word than to have inserted it, though in two or three unimportant instances I do not feel sure that I have not adopted the least likely reading of the two between which I had to choose.

As regards the spelling it was found impossible to adhere to the usual rule of the Camden Society of producing an exact representation of the original. The variation of spelling in all the four manuscripts was so considerable that no near approximation could be made to that of the original. And it seemed mere waste of time to attempt to decide between the probabilities of the author having written *e. g. marveylous* or *mervelous,* where he probably would have varied his spelling, sometimes using one form and sometimes another. Nevertheless it will be found that some old forms of spelling have been adhered to, which may serve to indicate to ordinary readers what was the most usual mode of spelling at the time. And this practice has been observed principally as regards proper names and in the headings of the different sections.

The copy here presented to the public must be considered as taken from Mr. Eyston's MS. without much attention having been paid to the spelling of that particular MS. and no variation from it in other respects having been adopted except on the authority of at least one other manuscript, or except in the case of a reference being a manifest blunder owing to the ignorance of the transcriber of the meaning of what he was copying. When the spelling therefore varies from the ordinary spelling of the day, it may be inferred that the original is correctly represented. The marginal references of the original have in all cases been placed at the foot of the page, except when they have been inserted in the text, for which insertion there has been the authority of at least one of the manuscripts. But in Mr. Eyston's copy there were towards the end several marginal references written by himself, calling attention to certain striking passages or giving a short running analysis of the text. These have been left, as in his transcript, in the margin, though this may be thought some detriment to the uniformity of the appearance of the page, none of them occurring in the earlier part of the treatise.

Of the value of Harpsfield's treatise it would be needless for the present Editor to speak. His opinion of its value may be gathered from the immense trouble he has taken in transcribing it, and collating four manuscripts in order to render the text as complete as possible. But it may be worth while to call the reader's attention to the fact that much of what would have been pronounced as fiction fifty years ago if this manuscript had then been published has been amply verified by the publication of the State Papers of the reign of Henry VIII. the Records of the Reformation published by the present Editor at Oxford in 1870, and by Mr. Brewer's Calendar so far as it has reached. The Editor has unfortunately been precluded from referring to that calendar for any period subsequent to the year 1530; but it has been thought worth while to add a few notes at the end to show how trustworthy Harpsfield's quotations in general are. The next volume of that work when published will probably confirm many more of Harpsfield's assertions, for the author evidently had access to documents many of which have only recently been published, and probably to others which are yet to see the light. On the other hand certain slight mistakes of his have been noticed in cases where, writing from memory, he was not quite accurate.

Other quotations have been inserted at length in the Notes, which appeared to be likely to be interesting or to refer to works which the reader was not likely to have at hand. If the selection should be thought somewhat capricious by some, others may perhaps be glad to be saved the trouble of referring to books which they would find some difficulty in procuring.

NICHOLAS POCOCK.

5, *Worcester Terrace, Clifton,*
February 28, 1878.

TREATISE

TOUCHING THE PRETENDED DIVORCE

OF

HENRY THE EIGHTH.

A
Treatise of Marryage
Occasioned
by the pretended Diuorce of
King Henry the Eigth
from
Q. Catherine of Arragon
devided
Into three Bookes
written
by the Reverend & learned
Nicholas Harpsfield
L.L.D.
the last Cath. Arch-Deacon
of Canterbury.

It is a copy of a manuscript whose originall
was taken by one Topliffe, a Pursuiuant, out of
the house of William Cartor, a Catholicke Printer, in Q. Elizabeth's dayes, and came to the
hands of Charles Eyston, by the favour of
Mr. Francis Hildesly, R.S.J.
in Com. Oxon.

Transcribed by William Eyston,
Anno Dni 1707.

TREATISE TOUCHING THE PRETENDED DIVORCE OF HENRY THE EIGHTH.

To my well-beloved Son, CHARLES EYSTON.

DEAR SON,

As nature has given you a right to the inheritance of my estate, a competency sufficient to support the quality of a gentleman, so I design, as a mark of true paternal affection, to add to it my small collection of books; that, by adorning your mind with useful study, you may deserve that character more from yourself than ancestors. Amongst the rest I leave you this Manuscript. A particular good fortune threw it into my hands, which, had it nothing but the subject to recommend it, would be no inconsiderable value to a Catholic, because it lets him see 'twas *Interest* and not *Religion* began the schism, and that 'tis truly Conscience and not Obstinacy makes him, by still adhering to the ancient Church, stand obnoxious to so many laws. But, that your esteem may equal its value, I have thought proper to acquaint you first what I have found concerning the Author, next what reason there is to believe this Copy authentick, and lastly to whose kindness I am obliged for it, and upon what conditions I had leave to transcribe it.

The author I find to have been the Reverend and Learned Doctor Nicholas Harpsfield, the last Catholic Archdeacon of Canterbury, whose Life and character I have subjoined, as well to lay before you the virtues of an excellent man as to add authority to the Treatise itself. Therefore I need here say no more concerning him, but refer you to the following character.

This copy no doubt is authentic, because, comparing the first words of the same Manuscript, which Mr. Wood, in the character he gives of Doctor Nicholas Harpsfield, tells us is kept in New College Library in Oxford, I find very little, at least no material, difference between them as the words are set down by Mr. Wood. (Wood's Athenæ Oxonienses, part 1st, page 171, 172.)

The epistle of that in New College begins thus:	The epistle of our copy begins thus:
It is an old saying, etc.	It is an old true sad saying, etc.
The first words of the worke are—	The first words of our copy are the same, being—
Forasmuch as this matter is incident to the life and doings of Sir Thomas More, etc.	Forasmuch as this matter is incident to the life and doings of Sir Thomas More, etc.
The Note at the end of their copy is—	The Note at the end of our copy is—
This copy was taken from the original, which was found by Mr. Topliffe in the house of William, sometime servant to the said Doctor Harpesfield, who confessed that two *lines* of the said original were of his said Master's own hand writing.	This Copy was taken from the Original, which was found by Mr. Topliffe in the house of William *Carter*, sometime servant to the said Dr. *Nicholas* Harpesfield, who confessed that two *leaves* of the said original were of his said master's own hand writing.

Besides this, Mr. Wood thinks this Manuscript of so great credit, that, in the character he gives of the right Reverend Doctor William Warham, Archbishop of Canterbury (speaking of the advice that Prelate gave his nephew and godson, Sir William Warham, to beware of Thomas Cranmer, his successor), [he] quotes out of the second book this following passage, whereby we shall likewise find there is no material difference between the two copies.

The words of the Oxford copy.	The words of our copy.
If ever after his death any should succeed him *in the see of Canterbury* called Thomas, he should in no wise serve him or seek his favour *and* aquaintance. For there shall, *said* he, one of that name shortly enjoy this see, that shall as much by his vicious living *and* wicked heresies dishonour, waste, and destroy the same, as ever the blessed bishop and martyr, St. Thomas, did before *benefit*, bless, adorn, and honour the same.—Wood's Athenæ, part 1st, page 572.	If ever after his death any should succeed *in that see* called Thomas, he should in no wise serve him or seek his favour *or* acquaintance, for there shall, *saith* he, one of that name shortly enjoy this see, that shall as much by his vicious living *as* wicked heresies dishonour, waste, and destroy the same *and the whole church of England*, as ever the blessed bishop and martyr, St. Thomas, did before *beautify*, bless, adorn, and honour the same.— See this copy, book the second, page 98.

By comparing these passages together we see the difference between the two copies so little as might easily proceed from want of care in the transcribers, or from faults escaped in Mr. Wood's Athenæ. To satisfy myself, therefore, in that point I have, within this year and half, made four journeys to Oxford to compare a greater number of passages, but was always put off with this civil excuse, that the Librarian was at London, or somewhere else out of town, and had not left the key of the Manuscripts behind him. But, however, by what we have here compared with the passages set down by Mr. Wood, I conclude that our copy is no less authentic than that of Oxford, because they appear to have been both transcribed from the same original, which was taken from a printer by Topliffe when it was ready for the Press.

This printer was William Cartar,[a] who in Queen Mary's time had been Amanuensis to our Author, Dr. Nicholas Harpsfield; but when Queen Elizabeth came to the crown, and his master was clapt up in prison, he became a printer, and by reason of his printing several Catholic books (a crime no less than treason at that time) he was seized sometime in the year of our lord 1583 by this Topliffe, a famous pursueant and priestcatcher in those days, for which poor

[a] Bridgewater's Concertatio Ecclesiæ Catholicæ in vitâ Cartari.

PRETENDED DIVORCE OF HENRY THE EIGHTH.

Cartar was hanged, drawn, and quartered, upon the 11th of January following.[a] Amongst other books that Topliffe found in Cartar's house, the original of this manuscript was one, and the having in his hands and designing to print this seditious history (as the bench called it) was one of the chief crimes laid to his charge at his trial by Elmer, the Protestant Bishop of London, and Judge Norton.

Lastly, this Manuscript was lent me by Mr. Thomas Hildesley, R.S.J. in Com Oxon, uncle to your Aunt Eyston, who gave me leave to write it out upon this condition, that I should never lend it to any one so as that it may be transcribed by any body else, for he designs, if ever he lives to see the times more favourable, to print it. Wherefore I am obliged to lay the same Injunction upon you as he did upon me, which is not to print this treatise, nor to let any body take a copy of it, lest they should injure Mr. Hildesley, through whose favor and friendship I came by it.

What I have further to say of the Manuscript is, that it was written in Queen Mary's days, and had been printed too, had that good Catholic princess lived but a little longer. That Almighty God will bless and prosper you in this world, and make you eternally happy in the next, is not only the wish, but the hearty prayer of,

    Dear Son,
      Your most affectionate loving Father,
          CHARLES EYSTON.

East Hendred,
January 19th, 1706-7.

---

[a] Life of Mr. Edmund Ginninges, page 66, Concertatio, *ut supra*, pages 128, 131.

The Life and Character of Doctor Nicholas Harpsfield, the Author of this Manuscript, entitled A Treatise of Marriage, etc.

The learned Author of this treatise, Doctor Nicholas Harpsfield,[a] was borne in London, in St. Mary Magdalen's Parish, in Old Fish Street. When he was born, or of what parents he was descended, I have not yet met with, and all I can find of his relations is that he had an elder brother named John,[b] who was made Archdeacon of London and Dean of Norwich in Queen Mary's days, but was displaced and imprisoned for not owning her ecclesiastical supremacy.

Both the brothers learned their Grammar schools at Bishop Wickham's college at Winchester, from whence, having rendered themselves capable for the university, they were both[c] chosen fellows of New College in Oxford. After which, Dr. Nicholas having with great industry gone through all the parts of philosophy, he applied himself to the study of the civil and canon law, wherein he[d] became very eminent. In 1544 he was admitted Principal[e] of White Hall in Oxford, an ancient hostel or inn for civilians, upon part of which Jesus College now standeth; and in 1546 he was made the King's[f] professor of the Greek tongue in that university.

Upon the alteration that was made in religion in King Edward the 6th's days, he out of zeal to the Catholic faith left the nation, and in 1550 went into voluntary exile.[g] But in Queen Mary's

[a] Wood's Athenæ Oxonienses, 171.
[b] Idem, 151.
[c] Idem, ibidem.
[d] Idem, 173.
[e] Idem, ibidem.
[f] Idem, ibidem.
[g] Sanders de Schismate, lib. 2do.; Pits, de Illustribus Angliæ Scriptoribus; and Fuller's Church History, book ix. p. 143.

days, when he saw religion restored, and, having taken in Oxford the degree of Doctor of Laws, he went to the Court of Arches, where he had considerable employment.[a] In 1554 he was made Archdeacon of Canterbury in the room of Edmund Cranmer,[b] a married priest, and brother to the archbishop of that name. By the remissness of which two brothers Heresy had so spread itself throughout the diocese of Canterbury that Dr. Harpsfield was forced to use more than ordinary rigour to suppress it, which makes Fox, in his *acts and monuments*, charge him with cruelty, and he is the only historian that gives Dr. Harpsfield an ill word.

In the first Convocation of the clergy that was held in Queen Elizabeth's days our author was chosen Prolocutor. And when the clergy there assembled had drawn up a declaration of their judgment on some certain points of religion, which at that time were conceived necessary to be recommended to the sight of the parliament,[c] he tendered them to the bishops that they might present them to the parliament. But this declaration prevailed no further on the Queen or the House of Peers than to set forward a pretended disputation of Religion, which was ordered by them to be held in the Abbey Church at Westminster, on the[d] last day of March 1559, and third of April following, at which Dr. Harpsfield was pitched upon to be one[d] of the disputants for the Catholic cause. But because he and the rest of the[e] Catholics waived this dispute, apprehending (as may be supposed) some foul play designed in it by reason Sir Nicholas Bacon was appointed moderator or rather judge, a man (as Cambden tells us) little[f] versed in matters

[a] Wood, *ut supra*, 172.
[b] Idem, ibidem, et Somner, Antiquities of Canterbury, p. 322.
[c] Fuller's Church History, *ut supra*, book the ixth, page 54, et Heylyn's Reformation, page 285.
[d] Omnes, *ut supra*.   [e] Cambden's Elizabeth, Anno 1559.
[f] Idem, ibidem.

LIFE OF DR. NICHOLAS HARPSFIELD. 9

of divinity, and a bitter enemy to the Papists, and withal they being willing to take the Pope's advice how to comport themselves upon such an occasion, there being points of that consequence called into question which the church had never submitted to a debate without his holiness's leave and approbation ; and because Dr. White, bishop of Winchester, and Dr. Watson, bishop of Lyncolne, opposed it more than the rest, they two were sent[a] to the Tower ; and Dr. Harpesfield, and all the rest of the Catholic Disputants—Dr. Feckenham, abbot of Westminster, only excepted—were bound to make their[b] personal appearance before the Council, and not to depart out of the cities of London and Westminster until further order was taken with them for their disobedience. The July following he was deprived of his ecclesiastical preferments and imprisoned[c] for denying Queen Elizabeth's Ecclesiastical supremacy. But to what goale he was committed I cannot find, but by a passage I meet with in Fox's 2nd volume, 254, I conjecture it was to the Fleet, where finding himself incapable of attending his cure at Canterbury, or propagating the Catholic Religion by any other way than his pen, he endeavoured by that means to impugn heresy, and wrote several books. First, his—

Dialogi Sex contra Summi Pontificatûs, Monasticæ vitæ, Sanctorum, sacrarum imaginum, oppugnatores et Pseudo-martyres. Printed in 4to. at Antwerp, anno 1566, which book, because he durst not[d] put forth in his own name, being then in holt, he sent to his learned

[a] Idem, ibidem, et Baker's Chronicle.
[b] There were six others thus bound over, whereof three were bishops, viz. Dr. Bayne, bishop of Lytchfield; Dr. Scot, bishop of Chester; and Dr. Oglethorpe, bishop of Carlile. The other three were Dr. Cole, dean of St. Pauls; Dr. Chadsey, archdeacon of Middlesex; and Dr. Langdale, archdeacon of Lewes. See Fox's 3rd volume of his Acts and Monuments, page 980, London edition, 1641, and Stow's Chronicle, page 638.
[c] Fuller, *ut supra*, page 143, et Wood, *ut supra*, 171.
[d] Wood's Athenæ, 157.

CAMD. SOC.   C

friend Dr. Alan Cope (then an exile on the account of religion in the Spanish Netherlands, but afterwards a Canon of St. Peter's church in Rome), and desired him to publish it in his name, which Dr. Cope did, but lest the truth should be concealed, or Dr. Harpesfield be defrauded of his due praise, he caused[a] those capital letters to be printed at the end of the said book: A. H. L. N. H. E. V. E. A. C., hereby mystically meaning Auctor hujus libri Nicolaus Harpesfeldus, Eum Vero Edidit, Alanus Copus.

During his imprisonment he also wrote his—

Historia Anglicana Ecclesiastica a primis Gentis susceptæ fidei incunabulis ad nostra fere tempora deducta et in quindecim centurias distributa, a work[b] no less learnedly than painfully performed, which was published by Father Richard Gibbon, a Jesuit, and printed in folio at Doway, anno 1622; to which is added his Historia Hæresis Wickliffianæ, which he also penned during his confinement, as he did his Chronicon a Diluvio Noæ ad annum 1559, written in Latin verse. He composed several other things besides these in his younger days, as his verses, epigramms, &c.; and in Queen Mary's days this his *Treatise of Marriage occasioned by the pretended divorce between K. Henry the 8 and Queen Katherine.* In fine, after he had with great edification and patience suffered an imprisonment of near four and twenty years on the score of religion, he surrendered up his pious soul to Almighty God, dying in one of the goales of London, in the year[c] of our Lord one thousand five hundred and eighty-three.

To conclude his character, I'll set down what Doctor Pits sayth[d] of him:

Erat vir gravis et prudens, moribus candidissimis, integerrimâ

[a] Pits, *ut supra*, et Fuller's Church History, book 9th, page 143.
[b] Fuller, *ut supra*, et Wood's Athenæ, page 171.
[c] Pits, *ut supra*, et Fuller, *ut supra*, page 143.
[d] Pits, de Illustribus Angliæ Scriptoribus, Ætate 16, numero 1030.

vitâ, multiplicis doctrinæ, et Catholicæ fidei confessione constantissimus...... Erat .... Poeta ingeniosissimus, orator disertus, Historiarum peritissimus, linguarum scientissimus, in utroque Jure optime, in Theologiâ non vulgariter versatus, solide fundatus, omnium denique optimarum scientiarum panopliâ ubertim instructus. That is to say:

He was a grave and a prudent man, sincere and candid in his behaviour, of great integrity of life, of universal learning. He was a very excellent poet, an admirable orator, a critical historian, a mighty master of languages, most eminent both in the civil and canon law, and withal an able divine, being solidly grounded in these latter studies. In a word, he was an inexhausted fountain of all good literature. And is acknowledged even by his adversaries to have deserved well of posterity.

A Treatise of Doctor Nicholas Harpesfield's concerning the Marriage occasioned by the pretended Divorce betweene King Henry the Eight and Queene Katherine.

THE EPISTLE TO THE GENTLE READER.

It is an old true saying (gentle reader) that truth is the daughter of time ; for truly, though it be [never] so much darkened, suppressed, defaced, and trodden downe, yet it bursteth out at length and most resplendently casteth forth her light and sheweth herself most gloriously, yea, like as the palme tree, the more it is overlaid with weighty burdens the more it assurgeth, mounteth, and riseth up in height. So truth the more she is with crafty sleights hid and covered, with many lies and force kept down and oppressed, the more in tract of time she discovereth herself, the more she riseth and springeth up, and with mighty power beareth down all her adversaries and spreadeth herself abroad to the perfect notice of all the world without any partiality or respect of person be he of lower or higher degree (Esd. 2, cap. 4). Thus the patriarch Jacob, which thought he had utterly lost his son Joseph and that he had been, as his other sons informed him (Gen. 37, 46), devoured of some wild salvage beast, found him at length not only living but exalted and adorned with high dignity and honour. Thus was innocent Susanna, which was thought by all the people guilty of foul adultery and adjudged therefore to die, marvellously delivered. Thus were the marvellous subtle and crafty hidden sleights and traines of the priests of the Idol Bell, whereby they made the King and all the people believe that the said Idoll daily devoured great store of victuals, at length discovered and spied out (Daniel, cap. 13, 14). Thus were the Arians and Eutychyans, the Iconomages or breakers of Saints'

Images, and other heretics, whose heresies a great while in Greece and other countries, a great number of bishops under the colour of truth and holy scripture, and the emperors by force and violence, did defend and maintain, in time suppressed and overthrown, and the truth again openly received, embraced, highly advanced and honoured. But why run I to so far years and to foreign countries? We have even at home, lately to our great comfort, felt the might and strength of this Lady truth, I mean of the sincere truth of the holy Catholic faith, which, being these divers years injured, defaced, and abolished, is now by the goodness of God and our princes restored to her old honour and dignity; her adversary dame heresy with all her untruths gloriously discomfited and conquered, and among other one great untruth most dishonourable to the realm and to the person and state of our gracious Queen, which untruth hath occasioned all those other untruths, heresies, mischiefs (wherewith this realm was miserably overwhelmed), I mean that untruth whereby she was, after her most noble gratious good mother had above twenty years most lovingly continued in marriage with the King her father to the good contentation of God and all the realm, most wrongfully declared unlawfully born and illegitimate. This untruth also is (God be thanked) quite vanquished, overthrown, and put to flight with the Queen's enemies which most heinously conspired against her and her whole royal dignity. And she now most rightfully sitteth in the Royal Throne due to her vertue, to her noble birth, and due to her grace as the most honourable and lawful issue of King Henry the Eight and Queen Katherine. And so is she now by Act of Parliament and by the whole realm justly recognised, which recognition with the said Act, though it be sufficient to quiet, satisfy, and content any true, honest, and loyal subject (and so it doth), yet in as much as there remain abroad in men's hands divers books written as well in Latin as English containing much colourable matter to the defacing and defaming of the truth and of the honourable birth of our most gratious Queen, and her mother's marriage, whereby Dame Untruth hath hitherto made a [glorious] glittering pretence of the great injustice and unlawfulness of the said marriage, and hath or may perchance put some scruples in some light and unlearned persons which have or hereafter shall happen to read those or the like books; you shall therefore now presently (Gentle Reader) receive good matter to control and check the said untrue and lying damsel, and all her vain, peevish prating and prattling, neither doubt I anything, but as God hath sent our gracious Queen a glorious victory upon her enemies and hath openly advanced the truth and honour of her worthy undefiled and unstained birth, so after that you have read this our treatise you shall see and will confess also that the said lying dame with all her arguments, reasons, and foule shifts made and practised for the defacing of the said marriage, is victoriously conquered and spoiled of all her vain feeble defence and munition which she putt her trust in. The which labor we have with better will taken in hand, because this lady untruth touching the unlawful divorce was and is the very seedwoman of all the miseries and evils, of all the heavy and hateful heresies, which of late have most pitifully overwhelmed the realm, and was not as one saith *fundi sed regni nostri calamitas.* And therefore it is necessary that we and our posterity truly know the manner, form, and fashion of the said divorce, and the consequents thereupon, and what may be said to such reasons, wherewith the said divorce was set forth and maintained, especially seeing many men have thought and said also that the pretended justice of the said divorce to be the ground and foundation of their schisms and heresies. And have also said and thought that as the Pope and the Church were deceived in the said marriage, maintaining the same against the law of God and nature, so they did likewise uphold

EPISTLE TO THE READER. 15

many other wrongful opinions and grievous errors which they say were justly and godly by King Henry and King Edward reformed, amended, and abolished. To whom we answer that we are content to deal with them liberally, and, knowing the clearness and justice of the said marriage, to offer them more than we need, that is, that if they can prove that the said marriage was so detestable as was pretended, to confess that the church hath erred not only in that point but in such other as they charge the same withal; but in case it shall evidently appear (as I little doubt but it will) that this marriage was without the controlment either of the law of God or the law of nature, then have they just cause to fear and mistrust lest this new religion and such opinions as have of late been sown in England be (as they are indeed) far from all truth and directly against the Catholic faith, and lest for the just revenge of the said divorce God hath suffered this realm to be plagued and afflicted, as well otherwise as with such schisms and heresies as never were in this island before since it first received Christ his faith. Wherefore happy had it been for King Henry and the realm if he had never attempted to break and dissolve the said marriage, and had hearkened to the good, grave, and godly counsel of Sir Thomas Moore, and of the good learned Bishop of Rochester, and such other, or at least, after he had refused their wholesome counsel and most cruelly imbrued himself with their and other godly persons' innocent blood, had (especially after he was by the Pope excommunicated for his great offence) fallen with King David (with whom he had offended God in adultery and murder of innocent persons, and with the good Emperor Theodosius rebuked by St. Ambrose (Soz. lib. 7, 24) for his cruel act in putting as well guiltless as guilty persons to death) to repentance and penance, and thereby to have saved his poor soul as men do in great shipwreck their bodies, taking handfast of the mast or some board of the ship, therewith to be cast to land. But he (the more pity) did exasperate his fault with other greater faults, and after carnal adultery accumulated also spiritual adultery by schisms and heresies, to the utter undoing of his own and many a hundred thousand souls besides. He should have called to remembrance and might soon have found many antient documents and stories, as well of the unhappy success and end of such princes as entangled and dishonoured themselves with unlawful marriages, continuing in the same without any reformation, as also good and wholesome precedents of other, which at length advised themselves better and received their just and lawful wives again. What thing is more frequent and common in old monuments and in all men's mouths, than the destruction of Troy for the unlawful marriage of Paris, King Priamus' son? And have not we tasted, though not so great temporal, yet much greater spiritual smart for the unlawful marriage of King Henry? And yet the blindness of many (the more pity) hath been such, and they have been so insensible in [understanding and] soul, that they have thought and said that the King and the realm were much happy and blessed for the said divorce, which men seem to me much like to Dion Prusicus, an Historiographer, who, affectioned to his own country of Troy, contrary to the writing of all other and contrary to the belief of the whole world, writeth that the Trojans overcame the Grecians and not the Grecians the Trojans. Well let us leave such blind affectioned people, and let us show what befell to Lotharius, the French King, repudiating his lawful wife Thietburga; and to Guntherius, Archbishop of Cullen, whom the King put in hope that if the divorce took place he would marry his niece; and to Thietgandus, Archbishop of Tryers, which divorced the said King. Surely the said Archbishops were for that fact deposed by Pope Nicholas, and spoiled of all their ecclesiastical dignities and holy orders, and died out of their country in Italy like laymen. And the divorce being pronounced the King took not the said Archbishop's niece to wife but one Waldrada, and, as it was said, filthily abused

EPISTLE TO THE READER. 17

the said archbishop's niece, the which harlot, Waldrada, the king, for fear of the Pope's excommunication, for a time put away, but afterwards received her again [as his wife and companion], and yet pretended otherwise to Adrianus, the said Nicholas' successor, that he had kept the said Nicholas' commandment; yea, and being at Rome, took to witness thereof the holy body of Christ, which he there received, as did many of his nobles, in confirmation of his saying.[a] And, loe, the just vengeance of God fell upon him and them, shortly after consuming them all and the great army they had in Italy with a marvellous pestilence. The king might and should [also] have called to his remembrance, among other things, the examples of King Philip of France, the first of that name,[b] and of another king, Philippus Augustus, the second of that name, which both, although they had put away their lawful wives and taken other, yet for fear of the Pope's excommunication they reformed their faults and putting away their harlots received their lawful wives again. These good precedents of the repentance of the prophet David, of the emperor Theodosius, and of these two kings of France would God King Henry had followed, which thing as it is to be wished so now it cannot be amended. It remaineth now for us, lest any man be by the said books deceived, to justify the former marriage and to answer such objections as be laid against the same. But yet before we come to our whole and entire answer we think it good to advertise you that the books which we answer are in number five. The first and principal is the book made and printed here in England, both in Latin and English, in defence of the censures of the universities. The second author is one Egidius de Bellamera, that long before our time writeth of this matter. The third is one Marcus Mantua, a

[a] Vide hanc historiam in Chronico Reginonis, [sub an. 861].
[b] Paulus Æmilius, Historia Franciæ, lib. 3 et 6 [fol. 119, ed. Par. 1548].

CAMD. SOC.   D

learned lawyer of Padua, and one of our own time. The fourth is our own countryman, Mr. Robert Wakefeild. The fift is an English book without any author's name, called "The glasse of Truth." Besides all this we answer as well the Act of Parliament made the five and twentieth year of King Henry for confirmation of this divorce, as certain other statutes made afterwards for other marriages of the said king. We think it good also to give you here beforehand as it were a little taste how the said authors demeane and handle themselves in some part of this matter, whereby though you should read nothing else of our answer you might easily ayme that the matter cannot be very good and sound which is with such slight and wretched crafts handled and maintained.

First then here is to be considered upon what an absurd, ungodly, impious, and, as I may say, blasphemous foundation the principal patrons of the king's cause and of the [said] universities ground themselves, affirming that that marriage which was frequented by the patriarchs and select people of God before the law of Moyses and commanded afterwards by the same is of his own nature wicked, detestable, abhominable, with many such other foul names wherewith they slander the same, and finally against the law of God and nature, whose slanderous mouths Moses himself stoppeth, commanding, as I have said, to the Jews the said marriage. (Deut. cap. 25.) And, therefore, it is easy to perceive that this marriage is not against the Levitticall (cap. 18) law as they pretend upon vain imagination of their own heads, unless we will say that God's law is contrary to itself, yet they will seem to have hold of the New Testament, and then they bring forth the Corinthian that married his stepmother, or rather abused her, his father yet living, and of King Herod marrying of his brother's wife, his brother yet living. Now, every child may see that this argument hangeth very loosely and concludeth nothing against our case, yet they will seem to have the doctors of the church on their side, whereof the first and principal which they allege is Tertullian, who hath a wrong opinion and condemned by the church as an heresie, that it is not lawful for a christian man to marry twice, which heresy he maintaineth by a wrong exposition of the 18th of Leviticus whereupon these men ground their assertion. And yet, as bad a witness as he is, they durst not allege his whole sentence, but left out part thereof, which doth overthrow their said assertion. The next author that seemeth to make most for them is St. Gregorie, our Appostle, whom they do openly bely, saying that he thought this marriage could not be dispensed withal, whereas himself expressly dispensed with our nation for it, as appeareth by the very place themselves allege, and therefore they have craftily and falsely pared away that part that made directly against them. To the words of the counsel of Gregorie the younger they add these words (*It was agreed according to the word of God*) which are not there. They allege the Council of Constance touching Wickliffe for that which is not in the said Council to be found, and which Wickliffe never defended. They impute also to our great learned countryman John Bacon that opinion, which he did never maintain, in alleging Origen, Isichius, Hierom, Rodolphe, Hugo Cardinalis, and divers others, they leave out material words making against themselves. They cite untruly Irenius, St. Augustin, and St. Thomas. They make a definition of the law moral by the which their own definition it is evidently proved that this marriage is against no law moral. But that the commandment to marry the brother's wife is a very plain moral law. They make a long process that because we cannot marry our own sister therefore we cannot marry our brother's wife. But who doth not see that this collection doth nothing conclude? They make a plain false open conclusion that affinity of itself and his own nature is as strong a bar and impediment to marriage as consanguinity; one of their own chief principles is that a man cannot marry his brother's wife because she is one flesh with his said brother, which is manifestly untrue, for she is no part of his flesh after his brother's death. And generally this is to be observed, that all their collections, reasons, and arguments are so loose, so little coherent, and so impertinent, that they conclude nothing for their pretended purpose, yea all their chief authors, which they allege in the 3rd and 4th chapter, whereupon they would seem to build their assertion and to underprop therewith their ruinous edification, either speak nothing at all of the case or be directly against them, as we have severally and distinctly sepecified in each of them. This may for an Introduction serve for the said principal book made in Latin and afterwards translated into English, neither is the translator behind with his naughty foul shifts, corrupting even his master's book, which he translateth, putting in this word *God* which is not either in the said Latin book or in the original author St. Ambrose, secondly in mistranslating St. Augustine's words, translating *when shame drived them from it*, instead of *when Religion did forbid it*. Thirdly, for translating out of the said St. Augustine, for (*though it be permitted by naughty laws that brethren may marry their sisters*),—*although it was suffered by naughty and corrupt laws to marry his brother's wife*. Fourthly, whereas his authors write that St. Dunstane, Archbishop of Canterbury, excommunicated Earle Edwyn for marrying *cognatam*, that is to say his kinswoman, he hath translated it, for marrying his brother's wife. Fifthly, he belyeth our noble learned countryman John Bacon, saying that he was clapped and whistled out at Rome for maintaining this marriage, and withal corruptly translateth this word *Explosus* for clapped and whistled out, besides other places which I omit. But these are the most principal and notable, and such as corrupt and destroy the very meaning of the principal authors, and quite alter the case. Let us now give you also some little taste of the other writers, and how substantially and faithfully they demean themselves. As for Egidius de Bellamera [he] maketh nothing against our case, for the dead brother that he speaketh of left children behind him, wherein the case is shifted and altered from our case. And yet our said countryman John Bacon defendeth that the Pope may dispense even in that case. And Egidius himself (the dispensation being once passed) dareth not avouch that the marriage may or should be broken. And, good Lord, to what distress is he, with other learned men of that time, brought, going about to answer the said 25 chapter of Deut. which law they would fain make but a dispensation. But this it is too open and too manifest an absurdity, as we have at large declared. Wherefore Marcus Mantua is fain to help it with another shift, and saith it was a figure, which as we grant to be true, and therefore we are not now bound to that law. So there is no coherence in the world to conclude thereupon that either the Church may not ordain that this marriage may be lawful and received again as many other Judicialls may be, or that the Pope may not dispense with it, seeing it is forbidden by the only prohibition of the Church. Then followeth Mr. Wakefeild, and he the better to countenance his matter giveth the third exposition to the said 25 of Deuteronomy, and such as never yet was heard of either among the Christians or the Jews, saying it must be understood of the brother that died before he carnally knew his wife, adding for confirmation thereof a most open untruth, that Thamar that married the two sons of the patriarch Judas and was afterwards espoused to his third son Sela was then a virgin, which thing, though it were true, cannot infer that the said 25 chapter must be taken of the brother's wife being a virgin. He allegeth to prove that she was a virgin St. Chrisostom, but the book that he allegeth is no book of Chrisostom, but rather of some unknown author of the sect of Origen, and yet, as bad as his author is, he saith not that she was a virgin. He allegeth also for his purpose Lyra and St. Augustine which say no such thing. By the which you may ayme how groundly and pithily he proceedeth in so weighty a matter as this is, and especially that he rejecteth St. Augustine making against him, and maketh no account of him, and telleth us plainly that the Septuaginta and St. Hierom translate many things for holy scripture which are but their dreams. But our English doctor incomparably passeth all other for his new, fine, and far-fetched exposition of the said 25 of Deuteronomy, for he saith it must not be taken for the natural brother but of some other kinsman after the brother, and sendeth us for the proof thereof to the book of Ruth. But O the shameless impudency of this man, for, though there be no doubt nor never was but that it must be taken of the natural brother, yet if there were any such doubt there is no place of all scripture so open and plain to remove the same as the said book of Ruth. So each of these our four writers have a several shift to avoid the said 25 of Deuteronomy, and yet none of them all is anything to the purpose, whereby it appeareth how evil their cause is and how weak a foundation they build upon, which is that this marriage is against the law of God and the law of nature. We will yet shortly lay before you three or four places of the English dialogue, the author whereof so artificially handleth his matters, that if he had suffered his own authors, especially Innocentius and Isidorus, to tell their own tales, they had utterly overthrown all his intention. Besides this, he mistranslateth the words of the general Counsell of Constantinople, putting in for these words (*if they be not sent for*) *though they be sent for*, and thereby quite altereth the sense and changeth the meaning of the said Council; and, now content to mangle and maim the Catholic Councils which made against him, he craveth help at the Council of Antioch, kept by the Arians, such pretty proofs he picketh and prieth out. You have heard before how the chief patrons of the King's cause belied Wickliffe and the general Council of Constance. Now cometh this jolly fellow and addeth thereto another lie, which the said authors, whom he chiefly followeth, have not. He maketh also another lie, that the university of Paris and other learned men say that the hearing of this matter doth not pertain to the Pope. But the most loud and lewd lie of all is when he saith that there are few articles of our faith which are approved by more authentic authorities, by more probable, yea invincible reasons, by more laudable customs and usages, than the King's cause is. So much we have briefly touched concerning our said five authors, to give thee (gentle Reader) a short demonstration how substantially they have handled this matter. Set now to this the manner, form, and fashion how this matter was set forth and handled with many crafty and ungodly means. Sett to the dishonourable practises, as well for this as for other marriages of the King. Sett to the pityful, strange, and terrible events falling upon the King's other marriages after this divorce, and upon the King and the whole realm otherwise beside, with such other occurrents as you shall chance upon in perusing this our treatise, and then I suppose it will soon appear unto you that the King's marriage with Queen Katherine was good and lawful and acceptable to God, and contrariwise the divorce ungodly and unlawful and highly displeasing to Almighty God. As you may more fully and evidently understand by our said treatise following, which we have divided into three books, whereof the first containeth certain reasons and arguments that we have gathered to maintain and justify the said marriage, with the answer of the reverend father in God John Bishop of Rochester, a martyr, made to the said Latin book printed in England for the maintenance of the censures of the universities, which we have compendiously gathered out of a book made by him in Latin and never yet printed as far as we know. The second book containeth our own answer to the said Egidius de Bellamera, Marcus Mantua, Master Wakefeild, and the English dialogue, with an historicall discourse of the said divorce, and the manner and order of the compassing the same, with a declaration of the contents of certain letters sent by the King and Cardinal Wolsey to the King's agents at Rome, with our answer also to certain objections against the marriage of Queen Katherine contained in the said letters. The third and last book containeth certain discourses upon divers Acts of Parliament made as well for the confirmation of the said divorce as of the King's new marriage with Lady Anne Bulleyn, and touching the divorce also of the said Lady Anne Bulleyn, and afterwards also with the Lady Anne of Cleve; and sheweth the marvellous repugnancy of the said Acts with the former book made for the improving of the marriage of Queen Katherine, and sheweth withal the manifold plagues that fell as well upon the King's marriages after this divorce as upon himself and the chief procurers and promoters of the said divorce and upon the whole realm, besides with other several points therein accurringe as thou (gentle Reader) in perusing thereof shalt more at large see and understand.

The first book of the Treatise touchinge the pretended divorce betweene King Henry the Eight and Queen Katherine.

Forasmuch as this matter is incident to the life and doings of Sir Thomas Moore, and forasmuch as we have for causes before by us rehearsed obliged ourselves by promise for this Treatise, we are now to disburden and discharge us of the said promise, taking the matter in hand, and after some sort perfected and finished it. I say in some sort, for that I well know our small wit, learning, and ability will not suffer us to prosecute and sift this matter so finely, so exquisitely, and exactly as for the great weight and importance of the same it might and would be done. And would God Sir Thomas Moore himself [p. 2.], who as well for that of all men he was most ripe in the matter, as for his excellent wit and learning, could of all men most clerkely and most absolutely have done it, or some other more erudite person, had exonerated and discharged me of this my pains and labour, for I fear lest, for want of sufficient ability meete and correspondent to such a weighty enterprise, I may seem somewhat to have empayred not only the matter itself but the worthy doings and proceedings also of the said Sir Thomas Moore, for the justifying whereof we have purposely and principally taken this matter in hand, whereunto we are the more animated for that hitherto (as far as we could ever hear or see) there is nothing in the world done in the English tongue to satisfy the English nation or reader, neither yet in Latin, the one half of those things which we shall now bring to light; we will therefore first show you what the oath was that the said Sir Thomas Moore refused, and then afterwards the causes why. It is then to be understood that the 25 year of King Henry the Eight, as well the sentence definitive of divorce made and given at Dunstable by the

Archbishop of Canterbury, as the new marriage with the Lady Anne Bulleyne, was by Act of Parliament (1533) confirmed and [p. 3] ratified, as being pretended to be good and consonant to the laws of God. In the which Parliament it is notified that the former marriage with Queen Katherine was directly against the laws of God, which laws forbid the son to marry the mother or stepmother, the brother the sister, the father his son's daughter or his daughter's daughter, or the son to marry the daughter of his father procreate and born by his stepmother, or the son to marry his aunt, being his father's or mother's sister, or to marry his uncle's wife, or the father to marry the son's wife, or the brother to marry his brother's wife, or any man to marry his wive's daughter or his wive's son's daughter, or his wive's daughter's daughter, or his wive's sister; which marriages, although they be plainly prohibited by God's law as it is there pretended, yet they have at some times proceeded under colour of dispensations by man's power, which is but usurped, and of right ought not to be granted, admitted, or allowed, as the clergy of the realm in their Convocations, and the most part of the famous universities of Christendome, and many right excellent learned men by their private writings, have testified and declared. To this there is a proviso in the said statute adjoyned, that the article in [p. 4] this Act contained concerning prohibition of marriages in degrees mentioned in the Act shall always be taken, interpreted, and expounded of such marriages where marriages were solemnized and carnal knowledge had. Then was it further enacted that every subject should take an oath that they should truly, firmly, and constantly, without fraud or guile, observe and fulfil, maintain, defend, and keep to their cunning, wit, and utmost of their powers the whole effect and contents of that statute under pain of [imprisonment] misprision of treason.

Now remaineth for us, for as much as Sir Thomas Moore refused to take this oath at Lambeth, as we have before declared, to show that he had just cause so to do. In which our declaration we will pursue this order.

First we will shew that the marriage with Queen Katherine could neither ought by God's or man's law to have been broken and annulled, which thing being so there was then sufficient cause of the said refusal.

Secondly, putting the case that that marriage was justly and lawfully abrogated and infringed, we will show that even the second marriage was also unjust and unlawful, and then pardie was the refusal admittable and allowable. Now admitting [p. 5] that the first was justly voided and annhilated, and nothing to remain that might blemish and frustrate the second, yet are there other branches of the said statute such as for the which the said Sir Thomas Moore might lawfully repel and reject the tendering of the said oath. But here peradventure (gentle reader) upon the second and third point thou wilt not a little marvel and think the same inopinable and absurd paradoxes. Yet I pray thee stay thy [indifferent] judgment until thou hast thoroughly read and diligently weighed our whole discourse; and then I suppose thou shalt have more cause to wonder at the marvellous strange proceedings of those times than at my sayings.

Now for and touching the first point in the which the adversaries, to prove the invalidity of the marriage, allege holy scripture, counsells, and fathers, and divers universities, and the writings of divers private men in our time; the principal book of their said allegations and assertions being a book made here in England in Latin and translated into English; we shall first answer the most material points and authorities of the said book. What, say I, we shall answer? Nay, rather the Holy Bishop [p. 6] and martyr of Christ, John Fisher, Bishop of Rochester (who was imprisoned in the Tower with Sir Thomas Moore for the refusal of the said oath), hath already answered in his learned book, made also in Latin, against the said former book,[a] whose answers, albeit abridged for enlarging too much

---

[a] Printed at London 1530, in quarto, and translated into English and printed in octavo. Entitled in Latin Gravissimæ et exactissimæ illustrissimarum totius Italiæ et Galliæ Academiarum Censuræ, etc.

this our treatise, we intend precisely to follow, partly for the cause aforesaid, partly for that no man hath more deeply, more profoundly, and more exquisitely travelled in the matter, partly and chiefly also that our countrymen, which have hitherto seen no part of this book in English and perchance neither in Latin (for that I understand it is not as yet printed), may evidently see that the said bishop and Sir Thomas Moore grounded their refusal of the said oath upon no small and slender foundation. Now when you hear the said bishop speak, suppose that you hear Sir Thomas Moore also, not only for the oneness and conformity of mind that both were in touching this matter, but for that it is likely that Sir Thomas Moore had seen and read the said bishop's answer, and had otherwise most exactly pondered, weighed, and considered the forenamed book made for the divorce, and had conference (by the King's [p. 7] appointment), as well upon other books and writings as also upon this book, both with the Archbishops of Canterbury and York, with Doctor Fox, the King's almoner, with Doctor Nicholas, the Italian friar, who were all on the King's side, and with Doctor Wilson also, who was altogether against the said marriage, and for the refusal of the said oath was sent to the Tower, albeit he did afterward relent and condescended to the King's pleasure and will, having not the grace of like constancy that the other two had. Neither did Sir Thomas Moore commune with any man so much and so often of this matter as with Doctor Wilson, by all the which time of so often conference they were in every point of an opinion. Now among other things he diligently conferred with the said doctor all the laws and counsells alleged in the said booke, with the words of St. Augustine *de Civitate Dei*, with the epistle of St. Ambrose *ad Paturnum*, and the epistle of St. Basill translated out of Greek, and the writings of St. Gregorie, and other doctors, and the places of holy scripture withal. So much have we now interlaced that you may understand how much furnished and how ripe Sir Thomas Moore was in this [p. 8] matter, and that you may think that when you hear the blessed bishop's answer you hear, all under one, Sir Thomas Moore's answer also. The only answer to the which book, though it were matter sufficient to quiet satisfy and content any reasonable man in this question, yet shall we, to make all clear and sound and to put away all manner of perplexities that might incumber some men's heads, add thereto for a surplusage whatsoever other objection or matter worth the answering we find, either in any Latin or English book, for the justifying of the said divorce, with our answers thereto accordingly. In the answering of the [said] former book we will insert or intermingle nothing of our own, lest we might seem to do some injury to the sacred memory of the said blessed martyrs and their worthy doings. Now after these premisses let us in God's name commence the matter itself, wherein we will first lay before you certain motives and reasons which may seem sufficient to any indifferent affectioned man to prove that the King's marriage with Queen Katherine was good, and could in no wise be either by the law of God or man infringed. Certain it is then the King Henry the Eight had married one of the most noblest ladies, not only for [p. 9] her birth and parentage, being daughter to the worthy king and Queene of Spaine, Ferdinandus and Elizabeth, but also for her singular and excellent virtues, that was then living in all Europe. Certain it is, also, that he continued most lovingly with her about twenty years without any torture or scruple of conscience touching the said marriage. It must needs then be a matter of marvellous moment and weight that should induce and import a divorce between such excellent personages. It must be an impediment very certain, sure, and notorious, that should after so long time in such personages, in such a cause whereof Christ himself sayeth, *Quos Deus conjunxit, homo non separet*,^a sunder and break this knot. Let us then search what impediment of such great force may be in this marriage found. Was, trowe we, any impediment of man's law only that was able to undoe this knot? No, truly, for albeit there was an impediment of man's law and the law of the Church, yet all the adversaries uniformly agree that with any such impediment the Pope

---
^a Mathewe 19, Marke 10.

may dispense and may clearly extinguish the same. It must then be an impediment of more force than this [p. 10], and that must either proceed from the law of nature or from the law of God. Yea, marie, say they, both these impediments accurre in this marriage. So say they indeed, but this asseveration to every wise man is very strange and hard to be believed, and implieth a matter altogether unlikely, or rather impossible, that is, that neither our wise Solomon, King Henry the 7th, nor the noble King Ferdinand, no nor the Pope himself, with all their grave counsellors, their learned divines, and lawyers, could espie that impediment, especially the marriage being not covertly or in haste, but after long time, after grave and mature deliberation, contracted and solemnized, or if they did espy it that they would also heinously, as it were, conspire against the law of God and nature. And yet being a more wonder than all this, that in such an open and high injury in so grievous a contumely, done both to God and nature, either the knowledge of all Christendom beside should be so simple and grosse that no one man should perceive this injury, or their charity so cold that no one man all this while or privately or openly would find fault with this marriage. No not the Protestants themselves which had alienated themselves from the Pope and from the whole Catholic Church [p. 11]. This point well thought upon may easily persuade a man that there was no such great obstacle in this marriage as these men have at length found out, or rather make men believe that they have found out; for truly at the first hearing of the finding out many great and large countries which were first found and discovered and brought under the dominion of this noble Ferdinandus and his successors, about the time of contracting this marriage, (the which [great] benefit, I suppose, God would never have employed upon him if he had so grievously offended his law and the law of nature,) was at the beginning strange and incredible, even so the verity of this asseveration was, and yet is to the hearts and ears of all good and learned men much more strange and incredible; for such strange countries were found out, indeed, as it is now notorious to all the world; but these men's paradox after all this hurley-burley, and after so many foul shifts, is yet unfound, and such as to the world's end never will be found, nor yet had been attempted to be found; if ignorance, flattery, ambition, spite, malice, and envy, had not attempted to find out, if lechery had not embraced the attempt, if covetousness of the goods and lands of the church, if importune ambition of the one side, if [p. 12] feare of heavy displeasure of the other side, had not set forth and furthered the said attempt. But yet, say they, as well this as all other degrees of marriage before rehearsed and comprised in the book of Levitticus be repugnant to the law of nature and are naturally of all men to be abhorred. Howbeit if the law of nature be as Ulpian defineth that law that nature teacheth all living things, of which law I think the adversaries mean not, but rather of that law of nature that naturally all nations are governed and ruled by, which Ulpian calleth *jus gentium*, and the civilians call it *jus naturæ secundarium*, which teacheth indifferently all manner of people to reverence and honour God, to obey their country and parents, to defend themselves, to propulse violence and injury, with many other like things, and of the which *Cicero pro Milone* writeth *est enim hæc non scripta sed nata lex ad quam non docti sed facti, non instituti sed imbuti sumus*. If they accept either of these laws of nature they shall never justly maintain that the law of nature forbiddeth all the degrees aforesaid, for as much as many of them were in so many and so famous Commonwealths, even of such persons as were accounted the best for natural virtues and so long frequented that it were a hard thing to say that all [p. 13] they did against the mere law of nature or that fact shall be imputed to them of God in the day of judgment as a mortal and dampnable deadly fact. Queen Elisa, otherwise called Dido, married her uncle Sycheus,[a] which marriage the adversaries say is against the book of Leviticus. Alexander, King of Epyrus, married Cleopatra, King Philipp of Macedon's daughter, to whom he was uncle.[b]

[a] Justinus, lib. primo.
[b] Diod. Siculus, lib. decimo sexto [cap. 15].

Anaxandrides, King of Sparta, married his sister's daughter,[a] and the good King Alcynous, king of the Phæcenses, married his brother's daughter,[b] which kind of marriage continued long in the commonwealth of Rome;[c] a decree being made by the people whereby that marriage was made lawful, and seemed so to have continued until the time of the Emperor Nerva, who made a law to the contrary.[d] In all Thessalia it was lawful to marry the wive's sister. Deiphobus, one of Priamus' sons, married Helena, his brother Paris' wife. Helenus, Hector's brother, after the death of Pyrrhus, married Andromache, Hector's wife.[e] Eumenes, King of Pergamus, left both his wife and kingdom to his brother Attalus.[f] King Demetrius married with Cleopatra, his brother's wife; yea, among the Romans, Marcus Crassus married also after the same sort, as Plutarch writes, neither findeth fault with it.[g] But in case there be any man that will not be satisfied with the examples of these persons and countries and such like, which are able [p. 14] and sufficient to break and overthrow these men's assertion, let him [then] repair to holy Scripture, and to such people as God hath especially chosen and elected to serve him. And there shall he find divers precedents and examples which will subvert also the said assertion, as well after the time of the law as before, when men were most, yea, in a manner only, directed by the prescript rules of the law of nature. There shall he find that Amram Moses's father married his aunt Jochebed, which kind of marriage is forbidden in Levitticus. And yet the uncle is not forbid to marry his brother's daughter, neither in the Hebrew text nor in the Statute, albeit the degrees are in both equal, whereby the marriage of the aunt seemeth not to be against the law of nature. Neither will the answer of the adversaries serve, saying

[a] Herodotus, lib. 5° [39].
[b] Homer, lib. 7° Odis. [66].
[c] Plutar. in problem. Rom.
[d] Dionicius, Livius, lib. 4° Decn 1°, non multo post principium.
[e] Virg. Æn. lib. 3. [329]
[f] Pausan. lib. 1° [cap. 8], Livius [lib. 42, cap. 16].
[g] Plutar. in apophth. Eumenis, Justinus, lib. 36 [cap. 4], Plutarch. in vita Crassi.

that it is forbidden by the Levittical. law, though not by express words, yet by implication and meaning.

First, because the Patriarchs before the promulgating of the law of Moses frequented this marriage, as appeareth both in [Abraham marrying Sarah, daughter at least to his brother Aram, if she were not] Abraham's very sister, and in Nachor, Abraham's brother, that married the other daughter of Aram.

Secondly, in Othoniell, that married his brother Caleb's daughter after the promulgation of the law of Moses.

Thirdly, it appeareth by the continual use and manner of the Jews, who since the making of the law have and do use and practise the said marriage, as Nicol. de Lyra [p. 15] and Paulus Burgensis, men most expert in the manners, trade, and custom of the Jews, and also of the literal understanding of the Old Testament, do testify.

Fourthly, it appeareth that the law of nature doth not forbid all such degrees as the Levitical specifieth, for that as well in Thessalia, as we have said, and divers other countries, as even among the select and choise people of God, it was lawful to marry two sisters; yea, in that time that the law of nature did bear most and almost the only sway, the Patriarch Jacob married two sisters, both of them living. And if the adversaries will reply that God did dispense with him, truth it is so he did for having two wives at once (as a thing in the judgment of the most part of divines against the law of nature), but not for marrying two sisters, which is neither against the law of nature nor yet against the Levittical law, the one of them being dead, wherefore it may be well inferred that to marry the brother's wife after the brother's decease (both degrees being all one and equal) is not repugnant to the law of nature.

Fiftly, we say that these men's assertion containeth too much absurdity and cruelty, and that for the cause we shall now shew. We know by St. Paul that those that were no Jews, worshipping yet one God and keeping the moral precepts of nature, were saved, and contrariwise [p. 16] those that transgressed the said moral precepts were condemned. Now, will these men be so severe [Aristarches and] censurers as to condemn all these people violating no moral precept instilled of nature for this only marriage.

Sixtly, we say that the fathers in the Council of Orleans dispensed with the Frenchmen; St. Gregory, our Apostle, dispensed with our English nation; Pope Innocent the third with the Lyvonians, for some degrees prohibited in Leviticus, and even for the very marriage with the brother's wife, which they could not have done if these marriages were in so high degree destestable and against nature as these men pretend.

Last of all, we add that for our case it was not only permitted, but also generally commanded to the Jews, the which commandment God would never have promulged if the law of nature did stand so straightly against it as these men say it doth. Whereupon we conclude that nature doth not resist all the marriages contained in Levitt., or at least so precisely that none of those marriages may upon reasonable cause be tolerated and borne withal; for albeit some of them be such as the marriage is not avoidable and to be annihilated, but even of itself void and annihilated, though there were no other law of God or man to annul them, yet putting the case that the law of nature did forbid all those marriages comprised in the said Levitt., the prohibition [p. 17] were not of like and equal force in every degree, as it fareth with many other prohibitions as well of nature as of the law of God and of the law also of the Church. As for example, the very law of nature forbiddeth prodigality and outragious lashinge out of our goods. And yet the guilt of such a man holdeth and remaineth in force by law notwithstanding.

Neither is it lawful by God's law or the law of nature (as many learned divines write) to possess divers benefices with cure, yet the guilt of such benefices is not void and frustrate thereby. And to come to causes of marriage. He that maketh a single vow and that notwithstanding marrieth, offendeth God and the law, and yet his marriage is not to be broken. So he that maketh a privie contract of matrimony transgresseth the law, yet doth the matrimony hold. Again, he that maketh a bare promise to marry a woman without any present and formal contract, if he marry any other he offendeth God's law and the law of nature, yet doth not the said promise infringe the second matrimony. Even so it is with many of these degrees. But perchance you will demand of me which be those degrees that the law of nature doth so evidently, so directly, and so precisely undo and annihilate, and which be the other. To this demand, to make a full and resolute answer is a matter of some difficulty, by reason of diversity of opinions in this matter occurrent. Howbeit all [p. 18] resolve upon this point, that the marriage between the father and the daughter, the mother and the son, is of that straight prohibition which we speak of, and needeth no other prohibition to undo and annul the same. Now a great number of lawyers and divines are of this mind and sentence, that there is no other such straight prohibition by the mere law of nature in any of the other degrees, which marriage God also himself seemed in Paradise to forbid, saying, *Propter hoc relinquet homo patrem et matrem et adhærebit uxori suæ.* The marriage of other persons (say they) is wicked and detestable, not properly for the sole prohibition of nature, but by the prohibition of God's law given afterwards to Moses. Some other add the grandfather and the grandmother, the brother and sister, the father and daughter-in-law, the mother and son-in-law, but yet for the stepmother it seemeth she hath been dispensed withal, coming afterward to the faith of Christ, as we will hereafter show. Now touching the marriage of the rest comprised in Levitt., the prohibition of nature either is none at all, or not of such force and strength as it doth utterly destroy and overthrow the said matrimonies, which great difference and odds the adversaries should have weighed and considered, and especially, among other, for this cause. There is and ever was accompted a [p. 19] certaine kind of prohibition of nature even in these degrees that be out of Levitt., so far that even till the time of Pope Innocent III. the very seventh degree of consanguinity and affinity was such a bar to matrimony that it both withstood and forbade and did also undo the contract following. But ever since his time the impediment of the 5th, 6th, and 7th degree is and hath been removed, and now doth not pass the 4th. And yet both in the 4th and in the 3rd, and sometimes in nearer degrees in the line collateral, there is and hath been dispensations obtained. And this have I the more enlarged touching the law of nature, by reason that the adversaries, being in a manner driven from their other allegations, made thereupon at length a special demurre. Wherefore, albeit Sir Thomas Moore had heard many things alleged for the infringing of the said marriage by the law of God and the Levitt. law, and of some faults also pretended to be found in the Bull, yet had he never heard till after his return from Cambray that it should be in so high degree against the law of nature also, that it could in no wise be by the church dispensable, for at his return the King himself told him so, and laid the Bible open before him and read to him the words that moved his highness and other erudite persons so to think [p. 20], and asked him what himself thought thereon. But Sir Thomas Moore neither then nor at any time hereafter could find any such grievous and heighnous prohibition of the law of nature in the said case. Neither any man else shall ever find that will ponder the premisses, and that also which we shall hereafter more amply say out of the answers of the said Sir Thomas Moore's colleague and commartyre the blessed Bishop of Rochester, yet is this marriage, will they say, though not by the law of nature, yet by the law of God in Levitt. forbidden, and therefore the Pope cannot release and undo God's own prohibition.[a] But this assertion is not true.

First, for that the very same degree (as for one man to marry two sisters) is not as we have said forbidden.

Secondly, for that St. Augustine and the residue of the fathers, doctors, and expositors of scripture excepteth this our case.

Thirdly, and most of all, for that this marriage was not only permitted (as the said marriage of two sisters) but straightly commanded to the Jews.

[a] August. 61ᵃ quæst. in Levitticum.

Fourthly, for that this marriage was used and practised among the Jews as well before the law of Moses as ever since, and is also at this day as a thing not prohibited by Moses' law.

Fifthly and lastly then were the Levitt. directly and openly repugnant to the Deuteronomion, and one and the self same thing to one and the self same people both forbidden and yet commanded also; yea and then were there plain contradiction [p. 21] even in the very same chapter of the 18 of Levitt. wherein the Jews are commanded to keep the ceremonies, judgments, laws, and precepts of God. Now that this for marriage of the brother's wife was one of the said judgments, precepts, and laws is manifestly by the Deuteronomical book (cap. 25°), wherefore it will follow, as these men dress and drive their affairs, that if the said marriage be expressly forbidden in the 18 of Levitt. that the said chapter imployeth implacable and irreconcileable contradiction. And therefore we do necessarily infer that neither the Levitt. nor any other part of Moses' law withstandeth this marriage, and so is their great shootanckcr quite drowned, that they would fasten their assertion withal, that this marriage is not lawful by the Levitt. and so by God's lawe. So then if there occur no obstacle either in the law of nature or in God's law, then must the impediment rise upon man's law only, and the law of the Church, wherein that the Pope may dispense, none of the adversaries can or hitherto hath denied. And then standeth this marriage upon a good and sure ground. And this shall stand for our first reason for the validity of this marriage, yet this notwithstanding, that the notoritie of the manifest and open justice of our cause may more evidently appear to the reader, we will deal with our adversaries more largely and liberally, and will imagine [p. 22] the case (contrary to most open verities) that this marriage was expressly forbidden in the Levitt. and no permission or commandment in the Deut. given for our case, yet say we (and most truly) that the Pope's dispensation is good and available, and that for this cause, which shall serve for our second reason, Christian men are not bound either to the Levit. or to any other law of

Moses, as to the law of Moses given to the Jews, further than it containeth moral precepts proceeding from nature, to the which all Christian men be bound, though they be not in the Gospel. And the Jews with all other nations were obliged before the law was of Moses promulged, and to the which only, both in the time when Moses' law took place and now that Christ's law taketh place, the Gentiles were and are bound. For the precepts of Moses' law (as the precepts of Moses) did not bind other nations, unless it were such people as became Jews and professed their law, otherwise were the infidels bound upon pain of damnation to have been circumsized, and to many other things of the Jews law. Neither are we now more bound than they were before the coming of Christ, that is to the moral precepts only of the law. For it is a most sure principle and ground of our Christian belief, that by the death and uprising of Christ all the law of Moses is quite frustrated, abrogated, void, and annihilated. And instead of that which was but a shadow and figure the verity itself [p. 23] by the death and resurrection of Christ is substituted. The priesthood of the old law is now transposed and translated from Aron to Christ our Melchizedec (Heb. cap. 7), and therefore the priesthood being changed and translated the law also must needs be (Heb. cap. 8), as St. Paul saith, changed and translated (Rom. cap. 7°), the which abrogation of the old law (ad Galat. cap. 4°) St. Paul oft inculcateth, resembling us to a woman that by the death of her husband is discharged from his obedience. And to the sons of the free-woman Sara and not to the son of Agar bond-woman. This thing also was plainly decreed by the first the council of the Apostles kept at Jerusalem against those Jews that (Actuum, cap. 15°), being converted to the faith of Christ, contended that the Christians were obliged to the observation of Moses' law. Wherefore as touching the law of Moses (but only as I have said for moral precepts, which were in their strength and efficacy before the law, and yet be through the world) the 18 of Levitt. doth no more charge and bind the Christians than doth the precept of circumcision, the precepts of consecrating and ordering the priests of Aron, the precept that they should not sow their ground with two kinds of seeds or wear any apparel made both of wool and flax, and, to be short, the precept to offer in sacrifice sheep, goats, and calves, and such other things. For even of these and such like it is said:[a] These be my judgments and commandments, keep all my commandments, all my judgments, and do [p. 24] them, as it is written in the 18 of Levitt.[a] We must then, touching the said 18 of Levitt., have our respect and recourse to the law and rules of nature, and not to Levitt. as Levitt. or God's law, and to the Gospel to consider what degrees of marriage be by nature forbidden and what be not. As for the Gospel there is no commandment therein that is not the very precept of nature, except matters touching the sacraments and our faith, which are not natural but supernatural. Now for the degrees mentioned in the 18 of Levitt., I find in the New Testament no prohibition, but only in St. Paule,[b] forbidding the marriage of the stepmother, and in St. Marke that sheweth of the unlawful marriage of Herod with the wife of his brother Philipp. But both the father and the brother were yet living, as we shall hereafter more amply declare. And so these places are nothing coherent to the state of our present question. But what need we dwell and demurre upon this point any longer, seeing that whether all the degrees of the Levitt. be against the law of God or no it is nothing prejudicial to our case, which is not (as we have said) comprised under the said Levitt. precept, and so out of all check and controlment either of God's law or the law of nature, and so consequently upon reasonable causes capable of the Pope's dispensation? Wherefore the reader must not lightly be [p. 25] moved with the heinous and hideous exclamations which the adversaries ring into men's ears, crying out against the Pope for dispensing with the law of God and nature, which, as you have heard, is in both sides untrue. Now, for thy better instruction, gentle reader, and that thou shalt not mistake me or the said reverend father the Bishop of Rochester, I thought good to advertise thee that, after my

[a] Levit. cap. 3, 4, 8, 9.   [b] I° Corin. capite quinto et sexto.

judgment, the Pope cannot properly dispense with either of these laws. And albeit many writers avouch that he may, yet they seem not to use the word in his peculiar and exact signification, but to mean a declaration, an interpretation, both in the law of God and in the law of nature. And in this sense the said bishop seemed to take this word when he speaketh of the dispensing of the law of God and nature. Now, there is a great difference between interpretation and dispensation, for, when the Pope doth but interpret the case, then he sheweth that the case is not comprised under the meaning of the law. But when he dispenseth he sheweth the case whereupon he dispenseth to be contained under the meaning of the law. But then he dischargeth and delivereth the party with whom he dispenseth from the observation and bondage of the said law. As for example, albeit both the law of God and nature forbid theft, yet if a man for extreme necessity to save himself from starving [p. 26] do steal, the Pope doth expound it to be no theft and that the said party doth not offend the law. The law is made to bind all men in like. But, because there may a case occur that some one man or certain persons should be exonerated and discharged from the observation of the said law, the prince doth exempt and deliver them from the said bond, and this properly is called a dispensation. So, though the ecclesiastical law forbiddeth that any man should keep two benefices with cure of soul, yet may the Pope release a learned and a noble man from the bond of this law and dispense with him. Thus much premised touching the word dispensation. Let us now consequently declare what motives and reasons we have to prove that this marriage upon the Pope's dispensation is good and available, wherein, first, is to be considered the large and ample authority given to St. Peter and the Popes his successors in these words of Christ: *Tibi dabo*, I will give thee the keys of the kingdom of heaven. Whatsoever thou shalt loose upon earth shall be also loosed in heaven; which authority of loosing doth not consist of loosing and remitting of sin only, but in loosing and releasing also human and ecclesiastical laws and prohibitions.

Insomuch that he may dispense even with those things which the Apostles themselves have in the Church ordained, and with such things as have been decreed by any general council, yea, although there be especial proviso made in the said council that the Pope [p. 2] shall not dispense with any of their decrees, for the Pope hath his authority not of the councils but of God himself; wherefore, it followeth that, seeing this marriage is not interdicted or forbidden by the law of God or the law of nature, that the Pope by his dispensation may make it good and effectual to all intents and purposes. Now, putting the case that there were a great scruple and doubt whether both or either of those laws withstand this marriage (as the adversaries contend they do) and so consequently whether the Pope's dispensation be available or no, who can be a competent judge in this difficulty but the Pope himself? To whom only it appertaineth to discuss, resolve, and decide all great and perplexed difficulties rising upon our faith, or in matter moral necessary to be known for the training and ordering of our life, and especially in question rising upon dispensation. But, as Pope Julius gave out this dispensation, so Pope Clement upon mature hearing and discussing of the matter being brought in question gave definitive sentence for the validity both of the marriage and dispensation. Wherefore there remaineth no manner of scruple or doubt to be had for the same cause. And the King was bound to obey the Pope's sentence, unless we shall think the sentence of Christ's own vicar in the earth, and whom he hath furnished and adorned with the prerogative of so [p. 28] excellent and singular authority, shall now have less moment and weight with us than the sentence of the high bishop of the old law then had among the Jews. To whom, being a figure of this our high bishop the Pope, authority was given to determine and decide all hard, dubious, and litigious questions insurging upon Moses' law,[a] yea with commandment that those persons should suffer death that shewed themselves refractory and disobedient to his sentence. Thirdly, we say, that, forasmuch

[a] Deut. cap. 17.

as the adversaries themselves cannot nor do not deny but that the Pope may dispense with ecclesiastical and man's law, this dispensation must needs take place, namely, seeing it hath all such things as are requisite to such a dispensation; that is, a person able with sufficient authority, a just, a reasonable, and an urgent cause.

It is evident that the Pope is furnished with sufficient authority. And in this point there is no difference between princes and private persons, for in this respect all are equally subject to the Pope. Now, touching the justice, the equity, and the urgency of the cause sufficient to induce the Pope to dispense is open and apparent in the very bull itself. The greatest causes for any dispensation to be obtained in matrimony are wont to chance in the persons of great and noble princes. And such dispensation conduceth and profiteth more to the commonwealth than [p. 29] when it is granted to any popular or common person, and the Popes ought and are wont sooner to condiscend to release and remit the observation of the law to such personages than to other. Between the which two sorts there ought to be had great difference and a greater respect to the one than to the other. As for the worthiness and excellency of our personages, the one was the daughter of the noble King and Queen of Spain, Ferdinandus and Elizabeth, and the other the son and heir of our wise and famous King Henry VII. The justice, commodity, and urgency of the cause was so exuberant and great as a man cannot lightly imagine a greater; that is the keeping and conservation of peace, unity, and tranquillity between the two realms of England and Spain and other countries thereto belonging; which cause is expressly specified in the said Bull, and so sufficiently ableth and justifieth the same, especially with other clauses thereto adjoined, signifying that the Pope was moved and induced by other causes also, albeit they be not nor need not there be specified; wherein it is reason that we should think that he said the truth. Now, if Moses' law commanded the brother to marry the brother's wife dying without issue, yea and that to his perpetual ignominy, infamy, and shame if he refused to marry her, for private causes touching the wife and the husband [p. 30] deceased only, as that his family should not perish, that the poor widow might be provided for; and for the brother's comfort that he should not die sorrowful and comfortless for lack of children (which was the greatest grief and discomfort to the Jews in the world), and was somewhat eased when his brother's first child should by the law be counted as his own. That God himself, I say, for these private considerations commanded this marriage by an open law, may not, I pray you, Christ his own vicar on earth dispense with some certain persons, especially where, besides the private causes of comfort that the deceased brother may have even now of his brother's children, though not to be taken as his own, as it was in Moses' law; besides his private comfort for his wife to be made a Queen; besides his private comfort and heart's ease to see his brother exonerated and delivered by this marriage of a heap of mischiefs and miseries that might perchance otherwise have fallen upon him (for that the dead have some such care and respect it appeareth by the story (Luke 16) of the rich glutton)—may not, I say, Christ his vicar for the public and commonwealth of two so great realms, graciously dispense with this marriage? We say then, fourthly, that, considering that by the common and uniform opinion of all divines and canonists and the practice of the whole Church these many hundred years [p. 31] the Pope doth and may discharge and exonerate men's consciences and (as some term it) dispense with matters of much higher degree than this and of more weighty importance, there ought to be no manner of scruple taken for this dispensation. So doth he dispense with a *bygamus*, that is, admitting one to the clergy that is twice married, albeit St. Paul commandeth the contrary, and with a priest taken in fornication that should be deposed. Furthermore he exonerateth and dischargeth men from their [oath and from their] vow also, and in many other like cases, some of which cases touch very near God his own honour, as in our vows by the which we consecrate, devote, and dedicate ourselves to him and his service; the which vows and oaths God straightly commandeth us to keep; whereas in our case there is no such high consideration, yea none at all, but for the law of the Church, being as we have said a thing not forbidden by the New Testament, and by the Old both licensed and commanded. To this we may now adjoin our fift cause, which is, that forasmuch as there are some cases which the Pope cannot dispense withal, which are by the diligence and industry of divers writers (especially Durandus) specially noted and set forth, in the which our case is not comprised, this dispensation is by law effectual and available. Adding to this the sixt cause of no small weight and consideration that these noble personages [p. 32] had continued twenty years most lovingly in the said marriage without any repining and grudge either of their own or any other man's conscience against the same, yea that God had adorned and blessed the said marriage with a noble wise virtuous [lady] at this present our noble and worthy Queene procreated in the said marriage. So that if at the beginning there had been any impediment (as there was none) yet was it then grown to such a strength, force, and validity, as for any such impediment occurrent it ought not to have been in any wise infringed. Moreover seeing the common rule, which is, that, the act being vicious and nought at the beginning, cannot be by tract of time confirmed, in some cases faileth and hath his exception; how much more then shall we say it is so in our [own] case, notwithstanding the said presupposed impediment at the beginning? Surely the continuance of long time breedeth a great presumption that all due and necessary solemnities were at the beginning of the act interposed and observed especially in a case of matrimony. So that it is a much harder thing to unknit and undoe a matrimony with tract of time, with carnal copulation, yea with children confirmed, corroborated, and established, than it was to stay and lett it before it was contracted. Wherefore, any such surmised impediment to the contrary notwithstanding, to avoid the slander [p. 33] and manifold incomodities that thereof might arise, it was not to be dissolved and broken. For if it so sometimes chanceth that for shunning and avoiding of such slander, even where there occurreth no impediment, yet the matrimony to be contracted is stayed that it goeth not forward; how much the more then to avoid so heinous a slander, so grievous offence of men's minds, so great mischiefs as might of the said divorce have issued. This matrimony after such sort as we have said, enforced and strengthened, ought not in any wise to have been dissipated and dissolved. For the justifying whereof and for our seventh cause we will desire the reader to weigh and consider the plentiful, large, and exuberant authority that by the consent of all writers the Pope hath and ever had in the disposing, ordering, and dispensing of cases of matrimony of much more moment and weight than our present case is. Christ saith *Quos Deus conjunxit, homo non separet,* and yet hath the Pope decided, and the Church doth use, and hath of long time so used, that the wife and the man may with their mutual consent adhibited and foregoing enter into religion; yea, if the one parte enter into religion with the consent of the other, the Pope hath determined that the matrimony is infringed and dissolved. Again, if two contract matrimony with words meet and convenient [p. 34], yea, albeit the matrimony be afterwards solemnized, yet, if it be not consummated with carnal copulation, the Pope hath ordained and the Church hath so received it, that the one partie may enter into religion, and the other, left to their own will and arbitrement, to marry again if they will. Furthermore, albeit matrimony may not be contracted without apt and convenient words of the present time to induce present matrimony, but as a bare promise of affiance and betrothing, yet if the parties make but a naked and bare promise of affiance and betrothing without any present contract, and do after this carnally use themselves together, the Pope ordereth and the Church so observeth it, for present affiance and for a sure and stable matrimony that cannot be dissolved. Besides this, if a Christian man marry with an infidel the marriage is void, yet may the Pope upon a reasonable cause dispense with the same. Moreover, we say that the Pope hath and may dispense in some degrees that seem as hard or harder to be dispensed withal than our case; as for one to marry his uncle's wife, wherewith Petrus de Anchorano affirmed that the Pope might dispense in a case that chanced in a King's daughter of England. Again, the Pope may dispense with the uncle to marry his brother's or sister's daughter.[a] He may and hath also dispensed that a man may marry the woman whose sister he had before carnally known, as did *Martinus Quintus*, with great advice of [his] divines [p. 35]. Now, before this marriage that we intreate of, Pope Alexander the Sixt had dispensed with Emanuell, King of Portugall, to marry two sisters, the daughters of the said Catholick King and Queen Ferdinandus and Elizabeth, which marriage as it was not forbidden by Moses' law, so was it not commanded as ours was, and therefore the less doubt and perplexity therein is to be had. We will now adjoin our eighth and last cause, which is, That it is well to be considered that the precepts and rules for marriage are not constant, immutable, and invariable, as are the precepts of God's law and the law of nature. First, we find between the father and the daughter, the mother and the son, matrimony to be by God interdicted when he said *Propter hoc relinquet homo patrem et matrem et adhærebit uxori suæ;* other express prohibition of marriage we find none in holy Scripture till the time of Moses' law, whereby certain other persons be prohibited as well being of affinity as consanguinity to couple themselves in marriage; we find also that the Jews were forbidden to marry with any of the people of seven nations. But whether all marriages made against that prohibition were void and frustrate it is not very certain. After the coming of Christ, the law of Moses being repealed and abrogated, the Church was left to the state it was in before the law of Moses. Neither did it appear [p. 36] that Christ ordained any prohibition touching the degrees of marriage. Now did the Church not only renew and revive all the prohibitions of the Levitt., but the more to enlarge and amplify love, friendship, and charity, addeth many other prohibitions thereto. So that for many hundred years, even to the time of Innocentius the third, the prohibition of marriage ran

[a] Johannes Lupus de matrimo., et legit.

out in great force to the very seventh degree, as well in affinity as consanguinity. All such persons as without licence and dispensation contracted within any of these degrees were sundered and separated. But the said Innocentius, at the great and famous Council holden at Lateran, with the consent of the Prelates, as well of the Greek as of the Latin Church there present, abridged the prohibition to the fourth degree only, and quite cut away three degrees. And there be not a few well learned and godly divines that think it would not be far amiss that the fourth degree also were now by a General Counsell cut off and made lawful; provided that these oft and frequent dispensations in the other degrees might be cut off withal, wherein many craftily abuse the benignity and clemency of the see Apostolic; and, for that the said see sooner dispenseth with marriages contracted already and consummated with carnal copulation, than if they were to be contracted, do wilfully and for the nonce contract such unlawful marriages that [p. 37] they may the sooner obtain a dispensation. Whoso now will deeply weigh and consider the premisses may easily perceive that the said Sir Thomas Moore upon most just grounds of lawe and conscience did refuse the oath made and set forth for the confirmation of the said divorce. You will perchance say unto me (gentle reader), Sir, there is good appearance and probability of the cause as you have handled the matter, which as you have demeaned yourself might seem to be of some good force, and you might seem well armed with right good reasons and authorities, if that you were not for all that quite overthrown by the main and invincible power of so many counsells, of so many fathers, of so many divines and lawyers, yea, of seven of the most famous universities beyond the seas, besides our whole clergy at home. The names of which counsells, fathers, and other writers, and of the said universities set before the said book made for the King's divorce, do put thee perchance in some fear lest I shall not be able to bear so great an assault. But yet I pray thee take a good heart and fear nothing, for of very troth there is no cause. And this your fear (if you have any such) riseth much like as it doth often among the army to whom the Scurriers in the night with all haste some time bring word of a maine and terrible army of enemies approaching fast on? Yet when the day cometh, the place being viewed that they were suspected to be in, there is found nothing but a fair long hedge. The [p. 38] Reverend father and martyr John, bishop of Rochester, will so clearly deliver thee out of all this fear that you shall see not so much as one of these fathers to be against our cause; yea, which is more wonderful, you shall see them allmost all to stand stiffly and manfully against our adversaries and to propugne our side. The chief and principal arguments, reasons, and authorities which they bring for their assertion I will lay truly before thee, with the said bishop's answers. And that with as much brevity as I may for avoiding of tediousness, and over much enlarging of our book, adding nothing of our own but the penning, ordering, and placing only of them in such sort as they may best serve the turn, yet when we have abridged the said bishop's answers, we will say somewhat to the said universities, and to divers arguments produced by the adversarie parte, and touching divers other things wherewithal the bishop hath not meddled.

First then, and before all things, I must pray thee to have ever before thine eyes the very state of our question (that is whether the Pope may dispense with this marriage), and then to consider with thyself how fitly, how aptly, and how concludently the adversaries impugn the same. They say then that this marriage is directly against the law of God and the law of nature. The bishop denieth both twain, and yet sayeth that if they faile in proofe of either partie, the marriage [p. 39] is defenceable enough, for it may be that something be forbidden by the law of nature and yet not by the law of God. To have the property of anything is forbidden by the law of nature which made all things common, yet, because the law of God doth not forbid it, the law of nature bindeth no man. Some precepts there be of nature which be called primary and principal, and they ever do and at all times have bound. Some other there be which be called the secondary precepts, issuing out of the first, which do not bind but by some law of God and man. Again, something may be the precept of both laws, as to honour our elders, to pray to God bareheaded, and yet no man can say but that this thing is dispensable.[a] Wherefore, saith the Bishop, the adversaries must prove that this marriage is against both. And not that only, but so against both that no dispensation can take place. Let us now see how they prove either partie.

First, they say that it is against God's law both in the Old and New Testament; for the old they allege the 18 and 20 chapter of Levit. To this the Bishop answereth, that indeed the Levitt. forbiddeth in a generality to marry the brother's wife. But that general prohibition (sayth he), according to the mind of St. Augustine[b] and other doctors, hath a triple understanding. The one, the brother yet living; the second, the brother being dead, and leaving children behind him; the third, of the wife being [p. 40] refused and repudiated of the brother; and so is our case untouched in Levitt., neither can possibly be comprised in the same, being not only permitted but commanded also of Moses, in the Deut. (cap. 25). And he doth not a little marvel at the universities that had not as well an eye to the Deut. as to the Levitt., especially seeing that this marriage was frequented among the Jews even before the law of Moses, as appeareth in the two sons of the patriarch Judas, to whom Thamar was marryed (Gen. 38). And in case they would reply that Judas did therein according to the corrupt and naughty manners of the Cananites among whom he dwelt, he doth refell that at large, and sheweth very probably [c] that as many other things were put and written in the law of Moses which yet by the instinct and commandment of God the fathers that worshipped the true God used before, so was it also in this marriage, as he proveth by many authorities. And that it cannot stand with the justice of God to punish and plague this marriage with such grievous pains as be contained in the 18 and 20 of the said Levitt., and yet to command the same also, and

[a] Levit. cap. 19, p°. Corinth. cap. 11.   [b] Aug. q. 61, in Leviticum.
[c] Alphon. Abulen, cap. 38, gent. lib. ibidem, Hugo Card. ibidem, Chrisost. ibidem.

to say, as these men imagine, that for this kind of marriage the Cananites and other people were thrust out of their country, and yet to bring in their place the Jews that should by God's own commandment and by an ordinary law, use, practise, and observe the very said marriage. Neither that [p. 41] it could stand with the wisdom of God to be so contrarious in his laws, as for one and the self same case both to accumulate so terrible comminations, maledictions, and punishments for the breaking, and also so many large benedictions and promises of reward, wealth, and prosperity for the observing, of one and the same commandment. As it must of necessity follow if the same be forbidden in the Levit., and yet commanded in the Deut. law; neither could Moses justly and truly say to the Jews, keep and perform these commandments, for this is your wisdom (Deut. cap. 4) and your understanding in the sight of the people, that all that hear of these commandments shall say: Behold this people is wise and of good understanding, this is a great nation, and there is no nation so great. But, say they, the prohibition of the Levit. is general and nothing is to be added thereto, lest he that will add be found false and a liar. The Bishop answereth: If nothing be to be added, why did the divines and canonists of the University of Paris, and the divines also of the University of Bituricum, add carnal copulation, which is not in the Levit.? Neither is it a good consequent. This is simply and absolutely spoken in Scripture, therefore it must be also simply and absolutely taken as appeareth even in the said Levitt. where it is said: Thou shalt not work on the Saboth day; and [p. 42] Thou shalt not kill; for both some work may be done on the Saboth day, and naughty wicked persons may be put to death, with many like examples which the Bishop layeth forth; upon the which premises the Bishop well inferreth that the godly painted rhetorical conclusion which they make in the first chapter, that these prohibitions were hallowed and founded by God himself upon the fear of God, upon truth, upon justice, upon holiness, equity, concience, faith, &c., is plaine frivolous, and to no purpose; yea he returneth their collection upon their own heads, inferring that the commandment to marry the brother's wife was hallowed and founded upon justice, verity, holiness, fear of God, upon faith, and so forth.

The adversaries themselves saw full well that there was not so good hold upon the Levitt. as they did pretend. Wherefore the better to fortify their untrue assertion they run to the New Testament, and would faine take some hold thereupon. They say then first, that St. Paul did grievously excommunicate the Corinthian (1° Corin. cap. 2) for marrying his father's wife, saying that it was such a fornication as was not heard among the Paynyms; whereby he signified that it was against the law of God and nature that one and the selfsame flesh should marry and use one woman, and had therein respect to the prohibition of the Levitical law. And they will it well to be observed that both in this place and other writings [p. 43] of the Apostles, as in the Acts of the Apostles, chap. xv°. this word fornication includeth all unlawful marriages and filthyness forbidden in the Levitt. To this the Bishop answereth, first, that it appeareth by Nicholaus Goriam, Hugo Card., Glossa interlinearis, Theophilacte, Sedulius, St. Hierome, St. Chrisostome, and others upon the same place, yea by St. Paule himself, when he sayeth, I have written unto you not for his sake only that did the injury, or for his sake that suffered the injury, &c. (2° ad Corinth. cap. 7°); that the father yet lived; and by that also he writeth that it was such a fornication as was not heard of among the Gentiles, for to marry the stepmother (the father deceased) was often practised among the Gentiles, and seemed to be lawful among the Persians. And it may be thought that St. Paule had as well respect to the 22 of Deut., where this thing is forbidden, as to the Levitt., or rather to neither of those places, but to the very decalogue, where we are commanded to honor our father and mother. Howsoever it be, whether the father were living or dead, this place is not appliable against our case, which is the marriage of the brother's wife and not of the stepmother. And what shall the Levitt. prejudice us, though it forbid the marriage of the stepmother, seeing it doth not forbid the marriage we treat of? It is a world now to see how frivolously and [p. 44] how superfluously they busy themselves (for lack of better matter) with this word fornication. If this word compriseth all unlawful marriages mentioned in the Levitt. why did not St. Paule (2ⁿ Cor. 12) excommunicate also the other Corinthians, of whom he writeth that they had not done penance for their filthiness and fornication. And if this general word be so exuberant and plentiful in his signification, then may we infer that the said Corinthian had transgressed all those prohibitions mentioned in the said 18 of Levitt. As for the place of the Acts wherein the Apostles forbid fornication, it is only meant (as appeareth by all interpreters thereupon) that the Gentiles should keep no harlots, for they were in that opinion that simple fornication was lawful.

And thus you see how far and wide the adversaries rove from the mark and matter they should shoot at; nay, say they, we have for all this the very gospel on our side, wherein this marriage is expressly condemned, for so much as St. John Baptist (Mathæi 14 et Marci sexto) reproved Herod, telling him that it was not lawful to marry his brother's wife. And no doubt (say they) what interpretation soever we make that Herod's brother was living or no, St. John Baptist, that his words might have the more authority, grounded himself upon the commandment of God in the Levitt. binding as well the Gentiles as the Jews [p. 45]; for otherwise, Herod being no Jew, there was no law forbidding him to marry his brother's wife, albeit he had had of her ten children. And notwithstanding that St. John Baptist knew well enough that the Judicials and Ceremonials of Moses' law were by the coming of Christ expired, yet did he reprove Herod for this marriage; neither is it to be thought that he would have defended the authority of this part of the law, if he had thought it had been abolished and extinguished. Here first the Bishop sheweth by the mind of Albertus Magnus, Rabanus, Beda, St. Hierome, Origen, Eusebius, [Egesippus], and Josephus, that Philip Herod's brother was yet living. Wherefore this story nothing advanceth the adversaries purpose. And St. John had good cause, for this foul incest against the law of nature, to rebuke Herod, were he Jew or no Jew; yea, and so he had otherwise, though Philip had been dead, seeing he left a daughter, as appeareth by the gospel, and that he married Herodias, which (as Josephus writeth) took him to husband against the law of the Jews. Wherefore he might well reprove Herod for this fact. Howbeit it appeareth further in Josephus that Herodes Ascalonita, this Herod's father, married a Jewish woman, and was himself circumcised, and builded a sumptuous temple for the Jews, and of all things desired to be taken of them for a Jew; and therefore would, in his orations made [p. 46] to the Jews, call King Solomon and others his forefathers. How much more then is it to be thought that this Herod his son would be also taken for a Jew.[a] As for that these men would make the world believe that absolutely all Gentiles and Jews were bound to the prohibition of the Levitt. and not to marry their brother's wife, because St. John made no mention of any children, it is most untrue, for it is very certain that at that time many lived amongst the Jews that were borne in such marriages, and, among other, good Josephus, our lady the blessed Virgin Mary's husband, and many that had contracted also such kind of matrimony, whom doubtless St. John would have rebuked, as well as he rebuked Herod, if their marriage had been so detestable and damnable as these men pretend.[b] Whereas they say that St. John Baptist knew well enough that the Ceremonials and Judicials were vanished and wiped away by the coming of Christ. Truth it is he knew it, and yet no better than Christ himself, who, for all that, was circumcised, and observed also other rites, customs, and ceremonies of Moses' lawe.

[p. 47.] An answer to Tertullian.

The adversaries, not ignorant that neither the old nor yet the new Testament served their purpose (as you now perceive), the better to colour their matter, and to set a good countenance thereupon, heap

[a] Joseph. de Antiq. lib. 15°, cap. 14°.   [b] Euseb. lib. primo, cap. 7°.

Doctor upon Doctor. But I pray you mark well with whom they begin, and upon whom they make their foundation. And as you see them speed herein, so trust them for the residue. They commence then with Tertullian, whose antiquity they much set forth, and we deny it not, nor yet his testimony, but where he is worthily to be refused, as he is in this present question; for they allege him for this prohibition of Levitt.[a] whereby he went about to confirm and establish his heresy, for the which he is by the Church condemned, affirming that it is not lawful for a Christian woman (her husband being dead) to join herself again in marriage, and that by this reason, if she shall marry, either she must marry with a stranger or an infidel, and that the law forbiddeth, or with no stranger but with a brother.[b] But that the Levitt. forbiddeth; wherefore she can marry with no person. Who doth not see evidently how miserably Tertullian doth wrest and wring the Levitt. to detort [p. 48] it to the confirmation of his heresy? If a man would follow his vayne and humour in reasoning, it is death to prove that it is not lawful for any Christian man to marry at all. For the law forbiddeth us to reveal the filthiness of our sister, but all Christian men and women are brethren and sisters in Christ. Then as the Christian brother is forbid to marry his sister, so by the same reason and law the sister is forbid to marry any Christian, and, by Tertullian's own saying, to an infidel she cannot marry by the old law, and no more can she by the law of Christianity. Wherefore it followeth that Christian men and women are quite excluded from all manner of marriage. And yet, when all is done, Tertullian, as bad a witness as he is, and as much store as they make of him, he doth plainly overthrow their assertion, shewing in the same place that they out of him allege that Philip Herod's brother had a child by his wife, which doth quite alter the case from ours.[c] And, which is more and altogether for our advantage, that the law of Moses commanded in our case the brother

---

[a] In his book De Monogamia [cap. 7].
[b] Adversus Marcionem, libro 4° [cap. 34].
[c] Dicto, lib. 4°. In li. lati. [Signat. B. 2] col. 2, Anglice pa. 27.

to marry his brother's wife. But these men, lest they should be by their own author and allegation convicted, have full fairly and full faithfully quite left out in telling their Author's tale those words that made directly against them of the said commandment.[a]

An answer to St. Gregorie.

[p. 49.] Themselves by like saw that they should win little worship by Tertullian, and therefore they would fain reduble and redress this error and colour the same by the authority of St. Gregorie, which they do immediately conjoin, being a man for his high and excellent authority with like learning and integrity of the Catholic faith far above all rebuke and exception to be challenged withal. But yet (gentle reader) fear him nothing, but rather pity his case or rather their case that are brought to this shift, that they make St. Gregorie to speak, that he neither would, nor could, nor indeed spake, and pincheth and wringeth him sore to speak for them even in that place that he plainly speaketh against them. First they say that St. Gregorie was demanded of St. Augustine unto what degree Christians might marry with their [kinswomen, and whether they might marry with their] stepmothers and with their brothers' wives. Gregorie answereth that they may marry in the third and fourth degree but not in the second, as with cousin germans, which marriage, though the civil law permit it, yet he saith it is by experience known that no issue could come of that marriage, and the holy law of God forbiddeth us to [p. 50] discover the foulness of our cousins. Moreover for a man to marry his stepmother he saith it is a foul sin, and that it is forbid by the Levitical law to discover the foulness of the stepmother which hath one flesh with his father. He sayeth also that it is forbidden by the said Levitt. for the brother to marry the brother's wife, because she, being once joined with the former brother, is made his flesh. And for the reproving of the same fault St. John Baptist

[a] Videl. lib. 4°. [cap. 34]. Alioquin hoc permittente, immo præcipiente lege, quia si frater illiberis decesserit ut a fratre ipsius et ex costa ipsius supputaretur illi semen.

lost his head. He willeth also that the English people, which while they were infidels mingled themselves in such abomination, should be warned when they came to the faith that they abstain and forbear their carnal pleasure between man and wife, and that they believe and grant that it is a grievous sin to use it, and that they fear the terrible judgment of God lest they fall into the torments of everlasting pain. This is the summary effect of that they gather out of St. Gregorie. Then conclude they thus, It appeareth (say they) that St. Gregorie would not and thought he could not dispense with this marriage, no not with them that contracted the same while they were miscreants and infidels. Now for answer we say, that for the marriage of the stepmother, whether that marriage be prohibited by the Levitt. or no, it is out of our case. And as for the reason of the oneness of flesh between the father and his wife [p. 51], the brother and his wife, that the adversaries here speak of, and to the which the Bishop here largely answereth, we shall more aptly answer in another place. That one answer for avoiding of tediousness may serve for this place and many other like which the adversaries have accumulated to one purpose ; for the residue it is to be considered that Herod married his brother Phillip's wife yet living and having by her a child ; wherefore St. John Baptist did (as we have declared) justly and worthily rebuke Herod, and, being slain for the same, is and was ever taken for a blessed martyr. But on the other side, if Philip had been dead without issue, the law in this case commanding the brother to cople and match himself in marriage with the brother's wife, St. John could not justly have reproved Herodd nor could have been any martyr for that cause. Troth it is St. Gregorie speaketh nothing whether he were dead or living, whether he had children or no children. If he thought he were dead at that time, the common and uniform consent of all other writers standeth on the other side; if he thought he had no child the very Gospel standeth against him. What shall we then say to St. Gregorie? Forsooth this is to be considered as well in him as in [p. 52] many other fathers: That sometime the better to persuade the thing they take in hand, they are somewhat bold upon Scripture and draweth it to serve their purpose, as St. Gregorie doth here also, for the marriage of cousin germans, which is not forbid neither by the Old nor by the New Testament; wherefore these sayings of St. Gregorie must be gently and discreetly taken. But now, to come to the quick of the matter, these men for all their fair rhetoric saw well enough that when all was done St. Gregory stood all on our side. And therefore they craftily did cutt and pare off in uttering his answer the most pregnant and material point of the whole matter and tell us as his tale that which he said not but the plain contrary;[a] for he saith plainly that such as contracted such kind of marriage before they were christened should not be kept from the Sacrament of the Aulter, and the holy communion, which importeth also that he did not command them to be separated nor took their continuance in the said marriage to be a mortal sin, for then he could in no case nor would have suffered them (till they were divorced)[b] to have presumed to participate the high and holy mysteries. And as the sixt question of St. Augustine was to know what degrees of consanguinity and affinity were forbidden, so was the seventh[c] question whether [p. 53] those that were unlawfully and unhonestly coupled should be separated and kept from the holy communion of the body and blood of Christ; but these men have both suppressed St. Augustine's question necessary for the full understanding of St. Gregorie's answer, with all the most effectual part of the said answer. They have suppressed also the summary of the [said] 7th chapter, which is that such as be new converted to the faith being coupled in degrees of marriage forbidd, neither are to

[a] Nontamen pro hac re sacri corporis ac sanguinis Domini communione privandi sunt, ne in illis illa ulcisci videantur in quibus rebus se per ignorantiam ante lavacrum baptismatis astrinxerunt.
[b] Greg. tom. 2°, pag. 253.
[c] Septima interrogatio Aug. Declarari posco an sic turpiter conjunctis sit indicenda separatio et sacræ communionis deneganda oblatio. Tum sequitur summa, cap. 7° quod neophiti in gradu prohibito adjuncti nec separandi sunt nec sacra communione privandi; deinde sequitur cap. 7° responsum Gregor., Quia vero, &c.

be divorced nor to be secluded from the holy Maundy of the body
and blood of Christ; which thing implieth that this marriage is
neither by the law of nature nor the law of God so prohibited but
that it may upon reasonable and urgent grounds be dispensed withal,
which is the thing we affirm and ground ourself upon. Neither
doth St. Gregorie precisely say (as these men write) that if the
Englishmen so married and being converted did not abstain one
from the other they should have torments of everlasting punishment.
But to deter them from contracting such matrimonies, he putteth
them in fear only of the said punishments for their carnal pleasure,
which may be even in lawful matrimony so immoderate and excessive
that it may deserve the said punishments. Thus you see that the
author they most builded upon maketh [p. 54] most directly against
them, who doubtless if he had now lived would most highly mislike
of this divorce.

Answer to Pope Calixtus.

They go on now to prove by other witness that the Levitical[a]
forbiddings of marriage have in them the authority and majesty
both of the law of God and nature. The first witness is Calixtus,
but his testimony nothing appeareth or toucheth our case. For
it is of such marriages of kinsfolk as God's law and man's law con-
demneth and curseth. Our case is of affinity and alliance and of
such marriage as God's law commandeth and blesseth.

To Pope Zacharius.

Neither yet the testimony of Pope Zacharius hindereth us,[b] who
speaketh also of consanguinity and not of affinity, nor yet the gloss
by them alleged saying that the Pope cannot dispense in the second

---

[a] Calixtus ad episcopos Galliæ. [Conc. tom. i. p. 614.]
[b] Causa 30ª, q. tertia, Cap. Pitacium.

degree of consanguinity nor in the first of affinity. For it speaketh only of consanguinity and not of affinity, and that in the first and second degree, and yet confesseth that he may dispense in the second degree of consanguinity collateral; and answering to the chap. *Litteras, De restitutione spoliatorum*, saith that, though it be there denied that the Pope cannot dispense with [p. 55] the second degree, yet it is not to be simply and absolutely understood but that he cannot do it so facilely and easily.

To Pope Innocent the Third.

As little maketh against us Pope Innocentius but rather altogether for us *(Cap. Cum in juventute, De præsumpt.)*, for what is it prejudicial to our case or available to their purpose if he condemned as a grievous incest carnal copulation, especially of a Bishop with his niece? The said Innocentius was not ignorant that to marry the niece, which is the brother or sister's daughter, is not forbidden by the Levitt.[a] As little doth he hinder us when he sayeth that the degrees forbidden by the law of God cannot be dispensed with; for, as we have shewed, our case standeth not within the reach of the said prohibition, yea the said Innocent maketh altogether for us, and doth, as it were, decide our present question and controversy, not only declaring that our case may be dispensed with but in dispensing also with it himself.

To the Second Counsell of Tolledo.

We have now to consider certain counsells which the adversaries propound to corroborate their assertion. The first is their second counsell of Tolledo,[b] which can be of no great weight [p. 56], being but a particular counsell and that of eight only bishops. Again they dylate and stretch Moses' words further than Moses ever

---

[a] Cap. Litteras, De restitutione spoliatorum. De consanguinitate, Cap. De infidelibus. Cap. final. De divortiis.
[b] Can. 5to. [iv. 1734.]

thought, for, whereas Moses' prohibitions do not pass the second degree, they extend it even above the seventh. Besides all this our case is out of the said prohibitions. Neither is there any word in the counsell which denieth that the Pope may dispense with the said marriage.

To the Agathen Counsell.

But the fathers of the Agathen Counsell^a call it plain incest to marry the sister german, the stepmother, or the brother's wife. They forbid also those that be so foully coupled once to pray among the faithful until they repent and sunder themselves. But yet this notwithstanding, the adversaries if they had as meet it was they should [have] recited fully and sincerely the whole words of the counsell, they had eased us and answered the matter themselves; for it forbiddeth also and maketh plain incest for cousin germans to marry or for a man to marry with her whom any of his kindred hath before defyled and violated. Now, though by a private law all these marriages may be made incest, and incur the penalties appointed, yet will it not in any wise follow that they are so forbid by the law of God and nature as no [p. 57] dispensation of the Pope may mitigate, ease, and release the said prohibition, neither doth the counsell affirm any such thing.

To the Neocesarien Counsell.

No nor yet the Counsel Neocesarian saith any such thing, albeit it inflicteth grievous penalties upon the woman that marrieth two brethren, and to the man that marryeth his brother's wife. And, if the decrees of this Counsell be of such importance as no manner of dispensation can counterpeyse or overweigh them, then can no man before he be thirty years of age be made a priest; yet we see this point daily practised to the contrary.

^a Cap. 61º [iv. 1393.]

To the Counsell of Gregorie the younger.

Yea the Counsell[a] kept under Gregorie the younger forbiddeth the foresaid marriages as doth the Counsell before named, and doth aggravate the matter with terrible anathems and excommunications. Be it so, but yet all these excommunications would little fear any man unless you had of your own put in these words (It was agreed according to the word of God that, &c.). Indeed it was decreed in [p. 58] that Counsel that no man should marry with any of his kindred, yet this matter is daily dispensed withal. We do not for all that deny but that such persons as of self-will and obstinacy, without any lawful dispensation, contrary to the laws ecclesiastical, contract such marriages, may justly be excommunicated. Neither are all the decrees of this Counsell of such force that they admit no dispensation; for then the prohibition of this Counsell that none of the clergy should nourish and suffer his hair to grow long were indispensable.

To the Counsell of Constance.

If you peruse all the acts of this Counsell you shall find no such thing as they allege out of the same, nor no such heresy as they say the Counsell ascribeth to Wickliffe, that is, that all the precepts of the 18 of Levitt. were judicial only. No, neither Walden nor Woodford do impute any such error to him, but this only, that causes of divorce by reason of consanguinity and affinity are without any good foundation by man invented. Neither doth Woodford say that this article is utterly and absolutely condemned, but only if it be universally understood, for otherwise Scote and all his adherents were to be condemned of heresy, which affirm that among the Christians there is no degree of [p. 59] affinity by the law of God that stoppeth or letteth marriage, yea there be other of no small number which flatly deny that all the prohibitions of the Levitt.

[a] Cap. 2º. 21ª q. 3ª Cap. Nemo.

touching marriage be moral precepts, wherefore, though the proposition of Wickliffe in an universal sense be false, for some prohibitions be by God's law, some by the law of men whom God inspired, some grounded upon good and sufficient reason, yet in some particular sense it may be true.

An answer to the Conclusion of the Second Chapter.

I pray thee now (gentle reader), the premisses well remembered and considered, to ponder the epilogue of the 2nd chapter, and then thou shalt soon see that there is no coherence of it with the proofs by them before brought forth; only this will I now say, that the most gay, glorious, and glistering part thereof (That is, seeing natural inclination doth move us unto the observation and keeping of these forbiddings, seeing reason doth lead us, honesty stir us, &c.) doth rebound even upon themselves; for, seeing that God himself made and gave to Moses this Deuteron. law, seeing that the very instigation and inclination of nature moved the Jews to [p. 60] embrace and observe the same, seeing reason did force them, seeing the fear of God, the law of God, and of their neighbour did stir and excite them to observe this marriage, the censure of the universities, affirming that it is so straightly forbid by the law of God and nature that no relaxation thereof may be found at the Pope's hands, is of no manner of force, credit, truth, or authority. Now that all the parts of our epilogue are true you may easily perceive by that we have already declared and shall hereafter more at large set forth.

To Origen.

They hold on still and persevere in the confirmation and establishment of their untrue assertion and to the foresaid Popes and Counsells they accumulate the testimonies of divers other fathers.[a] But with

[a] Cap. 3° Anglice pag. 40, Latine [Signat. C. 4], Origenes sive Cyrillus, super 20 caput Levitt.

how good luck and to what effectual purpose you may soon judge by the first, which is Origen, or as themselves note it Cirill, who speaketh no one word of our case, as it will be evident to him that will take the pains to peruse the testimony here alleged, yea the rather maketh directly against them, and seemeth to take the said prohibition of Levitt. of such as marry with their kinsfolk's wives yet living, which [p. 61] thing may be gathered as well by this word *Dormire*, which signifieth in Scripture unlawful copulation, and by that he calleth it, Advoutry. As also for that he saith, *Turpitudinem nurus tuæ non revelabis, quoniam uxor filii tui est.* Thou shalt not discover the foulness of thy daughter-in-law, because she is thy son's wife, and doth not say *Quia fuit*, because she was thy son's wife. And therefore these men have full prettily left out these words, *Quia uxor filii tui est.*

To Chrisostome.

Put case Chrisostome thought it was no true story but a fable which the Saduces proposed to Christ of the woman that married seven brothers, and yet doth not he plainly say it is a fable, but that he thought so.[a] But what is that to the purpose, seeing that, even as they themselves allege, he speaketh not of the Levitt. but of the Deut. precept commanding the Jews to marry the brother's wife. And Chrisostome even in this very place findeth fault with the Jews that they kept this law no better. Could these men, I pray you, if they were hired thereto speak better to our part and cause?

To St. Basill.

Here is brought forth a long epistle of St. Basill ad Diodorum. But, as large as it is, it is very short for our matter, as little or nothing pertaining to our case. Troth it [p. 62] is that whereas the marriage of two sisters was by the fathers and by long custom before Basill's time forbidden, and that one making little account thereof went

[a] Homil. 71 super 22 Mathæi.

about to persuade men that the said matrimony was lawful because Moses' law did not forbid it, St. Basill, fearing lest this persuasion might tend to the breach of the law and custom ecclesiastical, straighteth himself as much as he could, and Moses' law withal, to prove by probable and colourable, and not by necessary concluding arguments, that even Moses' law did forbid the same. The contrary whereof evidently appeareth as well by the exposition of the Jews and of all Catholic writers, and by the perpetual practice of the Jews in marrying of two sisters, as by the plain words of Scripture, which forbiddeth a man to marry his wive's sister, his wife yet living; which words are superfluous and to no purpose, if he could not marry the said sister neither in his wive's time neither yet after; and if a man consider the epistle well he shall find that St. Basill chiefly resteth (for all his other apparent reasons) upon the law and custom ecclesiastical. Well, let it be forbidden by Moses' law, yet doth he not say that it is so straightly forbidden that no Pope can upon any reasonable cause release the said prohibition. And if he had so said, his saying should not reach to our case, which is not forbidden by Moses' law but commanded, whereof St. Basil speaketh [p. 65] not so much as one word.

To Isichius.

After this ensueth a long and a prolix testimony of Isichius,[a] wherein he exaggerateth and enforceth the grievousness of their sin that transgress the prohibition Levitical contained in the 18 and 20 chap. But yet all this exasperateth [and exaggerateth] nothing at all our case, which is without the list of these prohibitions. Yes, say they, for Isichius saith plainly that it is uncomely and as nigh to the life of brute beasts as can be for a man to be married or to meddle with his brother's wife, or his nigh kinswoman's wife, and that these things be not spoken only to the Jews, but to every man, woman, and child which intend to serve God. The Bishop in answering to

[a] Isichius, in cap. 18 et 20, Levit. [Bibl. Patr. Max. to. xii. 127, 141.]

this sheweth by divers ways and by the very words of Isichius, that he seemeth to speak not of marriages but of unlawful and foul carnal copulation; which thing we will leave to the readers own diligence to consider if he be desirous to know more thereof; we will now only by the way as of ourself note unto you that the English translator hath for the word *commisceri*, which signifieth *carnally to meddle* corruptly, translated *to be married and to meddle*. The Bishop also doth well note the corrupt dealing [p. 64] and conscience of the adversaries, that in so great and weighty a matter as this is have so unfaithfully and unsincerely demeaned themselves in the handling of Isichius, catching and patching a piece of his sentence, yea and even that but a parenthesis, and leaving out all the residue of the whole sentence as well foregoing as after coming. The which wholie set together doth plainly condemn the adversaries' assertion and doth justify ours. For be it that the 18 of Levitt. speaketh of prohibitions of marriages; be it that Isichius speaketh of unlawful marriages and not of unlawful copulation, otherwise with the nigh kinsfolk and with the brother's wife; yet, this notwithstanding, Isichius confesseth that, though the Levitt. forbiddeth to meddle with the brother's wife, yet by Deut. the brother, to relieve his dead brother and brother's wife from tribulation, adversity, and misery, was commanded yea and compelled to marry the brother's wife. Now if for this cause this marriage was given in commandment, may not the Pope, think we, to deliver great realms from battle, enmity, calamity, and misery, which might otherwise insurge, dispense with such noble personages for that marriage, which was by God himself for a less cause universally commanded to the Jews. And if that which Moses writ was not written only to the Jews but to all men [p. 65] that would serve God, then cannot this marriage be so abhominable as they make it, being by God himself commanded as Moses writeth.

To St. Ambrose.

As St. Basil, in Cappadocia,[a] for the marriage of two sisters, so St. Ambrose, in Italy, draweth and straighteth the law of Moses to

[a] Lib. 8 epist. 66 Anglice, pag. 51 Latine, [Signat. E, 1.] col. prima.

inflecte it to serve his good virtuous purpose against a nobleman who went about to marry his son to his daughter's daughter contrary to the law and custom of the Church, which nobleman took his chief hold of the law of Moses that did not forbid it. Now, St. Ambrose to averte and deflect him from this enterprise endeavoureth rather with somewhat probable and apparent than with pregnant and concluding arguments to prove that this marriage is against the law of nature and against the law of Moses. And that it is so well appeareth by that he saith that the marriage of cousin Germans is forbidden by Moses' law, being in the fourth degree, which degree the adversaries in reciting St. Ambrose do quite cut off as making directly against their purpose. Again St. Ambrose saith that it hath not been read that any man should take his neece to wife and call her his mate, and yet (as [p. 66] we have [before] shewed) Abraham married Sara, that was at [the] least his niece, and Othoniell with his brother Caleb's daughter. Neither was this marriage ever forbidd by Moses' law, as Nicholaus de Lyra and Paulus Burgensis and the common use and practice of the Jews do plainly testify. Yet let us suppose that it is forbidden; doth not St. Ambrose say even in the same epistle that some time this marriage hath been by special indulgence released to some certain person? And why may not the Pope then, upon good and urgent cause, release this also? Again, grant that it may not be released, as forbidd by Moses' lawe, what doth that hinder a dispensation in our case which by Moses' law was commanded, of the which our case St. Ambrose hath not one word. Now, as the Latin authors have by mutilation and detraction played no very honest part, so hath the English translator played the like part by addition and multiplication, shifting in this word (*God*) and translating (*if thou say it has been dispensed by God, &c.*) which words (*by God*) are neither in St. Ambrose nor in his author's Latin copy, but prettily by him interlaced to blind the reader withal and to make him believe that though this case be by God dispensable, yet is it not by man to be dispensed withal; the contrary whereof we have shewed [p. 67] in our arguments already made for the affirmative part. Neither did St. Ambrose mean of God, but of the emperor Theodosius, who had made a straight law against this marriage, for God neither needeth to dispense with this marriage which he never forbad or gave commandment to the contrary.

To St. Hierome.

What if St. Hierome[a] say that Sara was not Abraham's own natural sister and that even before the law of Moses this marriage was unlawful? We are not in hand to defend any such marriage; yet I pray thee (gentle reader) consider herein three things, the one that St. Hierome here striveth against an heretic, in which combat it chanceth often, as it doth to a man assaulted by his enemy, to take for his defence that weapon which is next at hand.

Secondly, that St. Hierome, whereof these men were not ignorant, writing upon Genesis, plainly avoucheth by the very words of Scripture that Sara was his own natural sister, and that Abraham therein did not offend, by reason there was no law then promulgated against this marriage.[b]

Thirdly and chiefly, that they have craftily conveyed out of sight the beginning of St. Hierome's sentence which they themselves allege wherein he declareth that [p. 68] Sara was at least Abraham's brother's daughter; and then it is not likely that Abraham would have married her if it had been against the law of nature as these men pretend. But if they had set in the whole sentence then had St. Hierome answered their own foresaid allegation brought out of St. Ambrose.

To St. Augustine.

There ensue four authorities fetched from St. Augustine,[c] whereof not so much as one impugneth the dispensation of that marriage

[a] Hieronymus contra Helvidium [§ 15].

[b] Quomodo inquit et Abraham sororem suam habuit uxorem; etenim ait vero soror mea est de patre, non de matre, scilicet fratris filia alioqui quale est ut Abraham, &c. ut in latino lib. Adversar. [Signat. E 2.]

[c] Aug. cont. Faustum, lib. 32º, cap. 8, 9, et 10.

which we are in hand withal. Faustus, the Manichee heretic, condemned both the Old Testament and the author of the same as naught and wicked. Now, to colour his wretched heresy, among other things he objected to the Christians, why they keep not the commandment of the Old Testament in marrying the brother's wife. These and such like (saith he) were the laws of the Old Testament, which if they were good why do you not keep them, if they were naught, why do you not condemn the author of them? St. Augustine answereth—That, albeit the Christians do not keep that marriage, yet thereof would it not follow that it was naught, and concludeth that though not carnally yet in a mystical and spiritual sense [fol. 69] the Christians did observe the same commandment. By the which answer he evidently overthroweth these men's conclusion that condemn this marriage as execrable and repugnant to the law of God. Neither doth St. Augustine speak any word that this marriage may not be by the authority of the Church received or dispensed withal.[a] Yea, say they, he saith in other places that the prohibitions Levitt. must be without all doubt kept in the time of the New Testament; we grant that the effect of them must be now kept for the most part but not for every part, neither St. Augustine so saith, but of certain things only there proposed. Now if we will grant that St. Augustine spake generally of all the commandments of the said 18 ch. it annoyeth us nothing, for we constantly say, and that with St. Augustine in the very third question before,[b] that our case is nothing comprised or controlled by the said 18 [chapter. Neither are the said precise words of St. Augustine pretended by the adversaries that the prohibition of the brother's wife, and all other prohibitions of the said 18] of Levitt. ought doubtless to be kept in the time of the New Testament in his book *de Speculo*. And St. Augustine himself rehearseth there many things of the law of Moses, as that adulterers should be put to death. That the spouse that is found deflowred and violated before she come to her husband should be

[a] Quas. 64 super Levit. et in Speculo.   [b] Quæs. 61 in Levit.

stoned to death, and such like, be not now in the Church observed. It is, moreover [p. 70], there to be considered that St. Augustine had not in his text those general words of the 18 of Levitt. *Uxorem fratris sui nemo accipiat*: Let no man take his brother's wife. As for the third place, if they had not used their old craft in mayming, mangling, and mutilating the Fathers' authorities it would have made plain against them, for the sentence is not as they rehearse it, but in this sort. As for other things,[a] which pertaining to virtue and good manners are not by any interpretation to be referred to any signification, but even as soon as they are once spoken must be done; surely such laws of God no man can doubt to be necessary, not only for the people, but even now to us also to form and frame our life by. Hereby St. Augustine would shew what part of Moses' law doth now bind us, and that is so much only as belonging to virtue and good manners, a man as soon as ever he heareth it knoweth that he ought to do according to the same. For such is the very law of nature, and that which the Schoolmen call morals. Now it is evident by that we have said and shall further say that the prohibition to marry the brother's wife dying without issue is not of that kind nor hath any such force. Touching the last place wherein they say that St. Augustine witnesseth [p. 71][b] that religion forbiddeth to marry our sister, he meaneth nothing else but the religion and law of Moses, before which there seemeth to be no written law forbidding this marriage. And St. Augustine, speaking of the marriage of nighe kinsmen, as the brother and such like, toucheth nothing our case, which he knew well was not forbidden but commanded by Moses' law.

To the Epilogue of the Third Chapter.

At length they adjoin an epilogue of the third chapter, which casteth forth a very jolly glistering lustre of many goodly illations

---

[a] Latin [Signat. E 3.], Ang. pag. 56, columna prima. Augustin. contra duas Epistolas Pelagii, lib. 3°, cap. 4.   [b] De civitate Dei, lib. 15, cap. 16.

of such things as either their fore-alleged authors have not at all, or make little against us; and for the most part for us, the particularities whereof the bishop discusseth and dissolveth. But for that they hang upon the authorities before rehearsed, I think it more tedious than necessary to repeat them.

To St. Anselmus.

They are now come to their fourth chapter, and, from the ancient authors and of most authority, to other of less antiquity and less authority, as themselves confess. The first of this rowe is Anselmus Archbishop of Canterbury [p. 72] as they say, for this his epistle is not found among his common epistles either printed or written,[a] but was brought over from Paris as a rare and precious jewel. The epistle (whosoever be the author) is very long, and yet nothing can be shorter for the adversaries' purpose, as having nothing making against this dispensation.[b] The question propounded unto him was of the degrees of consanguinity, and not affinity, and answer made thereto accordingly. Wherefore they have full properly shifted in of their own this word (*affinity*).[c] Whosoever be the author he doth somewhat boldly apply to his purpose Moses' law, as where he saith that Moses' law forbiddeth to discover our wive's foulness, whereas there is no such thing in Moses. But the foulness of thy wife and her daughter thou shalt not discover—meaning that one man should not meddle with the mother and her daughter. He bindeth men to the fift and sixt degree of consanguinity, and finally speaketh of such marriages as the filthiness thereof could in no case and for no just cause be healed and covered, which cannot be understood of this marriage, being by Moses commanded.

[a] In epist. ad quendam pium fratrem.
[b] Six leaves English in octavo, two leaves and a side Latine in quarto.
[c] Rogas enim me, prohibitio conjugiorum in consanguinitate qua ratione in ecclesia Dei tantam vim, &c.

[p. 73.] To Hugo Cardinalis.

It is not a little to be wondered that they would for shame allege this man,[a] who in the place by themselves alleged doth understand the prohibition of the brother yet living or deceasing with children, as he doth also other where. But yet he saith these be moral precepts I grant you, for it is a very moral prohibition that we should forbear our brother's wife, our brother yet living.[b] For the which cause St. John Baptist as he writeth did rebuke Herod; for otherwise it was lawful as he saith and by the law commanded.

To Rodulphus Flaviacensis.

Rodulphus also fully agreeth with the said Hugo.[c] I pray you now mark how they have corrupted the said Rodulphus' testimony, for when he had proposed an objection of two sisters married to one man (as to Jacob), defending the same because it was done before the law and then answereth to that case only: *Quanquam inquit hujusmodi matrimonia primis temporibus, &c.*[d] they adjoin his answer as though it had been generally made of all the prohibitions, yea, and not so content, alter and transpose his words and put for meddling, marrying [p. 74]; and quite pare off also these words that made against them, viz., not that it appeareth that the marriage (meaning of two sisters) was before the law unlawful and ungodly, &c.[e]

To Rupertus Tuitiensis.

Rupertus speaketh here altogether of nigh kinsfolk forbidden to marry, and not one word of our case, or any other prohibited by

[a] Hugo in 18 Levit. [b] Cap. 2 Levit. et super Mathæum.
[c] Rod. in Mathæum. [d] Super 18 cap. Levit.
[e] Tales nuptias lex prohibuit, non quod præcedens earum iniquitas appareret, sed quia earum abstinentia, etc.

affinity. And writing upon the said 18 chap. excuseth Abraham for marrying his own sister Sara, for that it was not then forbidden by the law.[a]

To Hugo de Sancto Victore.

Hugo de Sancto Victore[b] should have had a fair victory upon these men, and would quite have overthrown their assertion, if he had been truly and sincerely recited, for in the sentence they allege out of him they leave out two clauses of chief moment and weight; for whereas, after he had said that God in the first institution of marriage had forbidden two persons only to contract matrimony, that is the father and the mother, it followeth in all other he forbad no woman to contract the sacrament of matrimony.[c] This clause they rased out, as also afterward another; that is—Then that which by nature was lawful began to be by law unlawful.[d] By the which two clauses [p. 75], thus willingly and wilfully dismembered and mutilated, it appeareth that there was none of these marriages against the law of nature, but only between the father and his daughter, the mother and her son, which opinion quite overthroweth all these men's building. Thus as the whole sentence of Hugo maketh effectually for us, so is there no part of it that maketh anything against us.

To Hildeberte.

Hildebertus sayeth that the bishop of Roan in Normandy would not dispense with the unlawful marriage whereof he maketh mention.[e] I grant you. But that doth not abridge the Pope's

[a] Rupertus in 18 cap. Levit.
[b] Lib. 2º de sacramentis, parte 11, cap. 4 et 11.
[c] In ceteris omnibus nullam ulli ad sacramentum conjugii fœderandam prohibuit.
[d] Et tunc cœpit esse ex prohibitione illicitum quod fuerat ex natura concessum.
[e] Hildebert. Cenoma. ad Archiepiscopum Rotomagensem.

authority in dispensing, whereof he speaketh nothing neither of our case, nor of any case of affinity, but only of consanguinity.[a] Then have we a long process confirmed with divers authorities, that a man once handfasted and assured to a woman, and so likewise the woman to the man, may not, though there were no carnal meddling, marry, the man with his spouse's sister, nor the woman with her spouse's brother. Whereunto we need not greatly answer, but remit the reader to their own universities as to the divines and canonists of Paris, the lawyers of Angiewe, which hold the contrary opinion.[b]

To Ivo Carnotensis.

We have then the same eftsoones repeated out of Ivo,[c] and therefore one answer may serve both turns. But then have we many things accumulated to small purpose. As that a man cannot marry her whose sister he hath known carnally before. And against the marriage of the French King, which Ivo thought could not be dispensed withal and worthily, for it was plain adultery to superinduce any other wife, his former living. As little to purpose is the residue, wherein Ivo speaketh against marriages contracted against the prohibitions of the Church. But yet there is no word of Ivo that the Pope cannot dispense with any such marriage.

To Walterus de Constantia.

What author soever he be (being as yet commonly unknown) he is nothing prejudicial unto us, forasmuch as he doth not express the degree. Besides this, it seemeth by his own narration that the Pope had not dispensed with it, and therefore by good reason he requireth that the parties might be divorced.

[a] Ad episcopum Sagiensem et Henr. Archid. [Lib. ii. 14, et 2.]
[b] See their Ceusures prefixed before the Latin and English book.
[c] Ad Lesiardum episcopum epistola 240.

[p. 77.]   To Thomas de Aquino.

They are now in hand to prove their assertion by the Schoolmen as we call them, among whom St. Thomas[b] beareth a great sway, and is the first that cometh to hand. In the rehearsal of whose authorities they spend much paper and ink to little and slender effect. It shall be enough for us to touch that only which draweth anything nigh to the scope and mark of this question.[c] Concerning then the first authority, there is no mention made of our case, nor any part thereof, that may conclude the marriage that we defend to be contrarious to the law of nature; yea, it appeareth there, that there is no marriage, but only between the parents and children, of itself and immediately incident and repugnant to natural reason. The second place also runneth to that sense; that no other degree but the first only of the parents and their children is by the law of nature excluded. Now, whereas he saith there should be opened a great wicket unto the lusts of the body, except there were some restraint, and fleshly meddling forbidden among those persons which must be conversant together in one house; St. Thomas meaneth not of the restraint and prohibition of the law of nature, but of God's law.

The third place tendeth much to the same effect, and that [p. 78] more openly and distinctly than the other two. Wherefore to help all this, and their roving at large from their purpose, they would seem to shoot somewhat nearer to the mark. Therefore they shew us out of St. Thomas that affinity doth as well lett marriage to be contracted, and breaketh it after it is contracted, as doth consanguinity, and so it doth indeed, but by the constitution

[a] Anglice, p. 75, with the 5 leaves following. Latine [Signat. G. 4], being about 3 leaves in 4to.
[b] Thomas, secunda secundæ, quæst. 154, art. 9.
[c] In commixtione personarum conjunctarum aliquid est quod est per se indecens et repugnans rationi naturali, ut quod conjunctio fiat inter parentes et filios quorum est per se et immediate cognatio. Aliæ vero personæ, &c. 4 sententia Dist. 40, quæst. 3 et in tertia parte summæ, q. 54, artic. 9°.

of the Church only, which being set aside, there is a great disparity and odds between them. Wherefore a dispensation is sooner admittable in affinity than in consanguinity. The next and the fift place is, that infidels, though they be not bound to the law of the Church, yet are they bound to the laws of God; wherefore if they should marry against the degrees prohibited by God in the 18 of Levit. they must be severed and sundered after they be converted to the faith. This shott, loe, had hitt even the very mark, if this degree had been comprised under those prohibitions, which is not true, as we have already declared. Wherefore they shoot too far and too wide from the mark, as they do also in the sixt and last authority, wherein they shew that the Pope cannot dispense with God's law. Now, if we should on the other side heap on as they have done for their assertion such authorities as might for our part be deducted out of St. Thomas, our work would wax too big and too [p. 79] long. Wherefore their schoole Doctor, which they first allege, and who is indeed among and above all other of most deep learning, of most high virtue and estimation, there is nothing for their purpose, but rather that he impugneth them in the Allegations by themselves produced, we need not greatly fear any other that they shall hereafter allege.

To Altisiodorensis.

And that evidently appeareth even by their next author (whom they make to speak what pleaseth themselves) and followeth St. Thomas' conclusion before rehearsed: That by the law of nature the father and the mother only are excluded from marriage.[a]

To Petrus de Palude.

Yet they quit themselves well at length by Petrus de Palude, for indeed he, writing upon the Master of the sentences, saith plainly

[a] In quæst. de affinitate et consanguinitate.

(as they allege) that the Pope can no more dispense with a man to marry his brother's wife than to marry many wives at once, though God by special order and prerogative did in the old law dispense with both. But yet this seemeth not to be his stable, firm, and stedfast resolution, neither dareth he to avouch that all the prohibitions of the Levitt. are against the law of nature. [p. 80.] And saith, even in the said place, that the prohibition to marry the brother's wife is to be understood the brother yet living, and that for the same cause St. John the Baptist reproved King Herod. Howsoever it be, and whatsoever his opinion was at that time and that place, himself being afterward furnished and riped with greater learning and experience, and more years, when he had more advisedly digested and pondered the matter, writing upon the Levitt. sayeth plainly that this case is by the Pope dispenceable. And further that all degrees of affinity are now by the possitive and Church laws only interdicted and forbidden, though it be otherwise in consanguinity. And so that only witness that hitherto spake plainly and directly to their purpose is now quite gone from them, and so they are now to begin afresh.

To Johannes de Turre Chremata.

As for Johannes de Turre Chremata,[a] they might have found themselves answered even in that very place whence they fetched their authority; for, albeit he saith that the Pope cannot dispense with the degrees prohibited by God, yet he saith plainly that our case is not by God forbidden, but commanded; and what is it against us if [p. 81] the Popes Eugenius and Pius would not, and that the learned and wise men told them they could not, either dispense with the earle of Arminach to marry his own sister, or with the French king to marry his wive's sister. Concerning the former

[a] [Comment. sup. Gratiani Decreto, par 2.] Capite Conjunctionis [caus.] 35, q. 2 et 3.

case, I suppose it is not read that the Pope ever dispensed withal. Concerning the second, it may be they saw no good cause to move him. And that case, though it were not by the old law forbidden, yet was it not, as our case, commanded. And John himself saith that he heard that in [his] time the uncle was dispensed withal to marry the niece, albeit he saw no such dispensation. But, if he had lived since, he might have seen divers such.

To Antonine, Archbishop of Florence.

Our former answer to Johannes de Turre Chremata[a] will also satisfy for Antonine, affirming that the degrees prohibited by God admit and receive no dispensation. Yet is it further to be considered for him, that he willeth that in case any such dispensation be given out and matrimony carnally consummated, that for no consideration it be sundered and broken.

To Jacobus de Lausania.

The said Jacobus is here brought forth without any words or book of his, and it maketh no small matter, for [p. 82], whatsoever he hath otherwhere said, he serveth our turn, writing upon the Levitticus.

To Johannes de Tabiena.

We have nothing out of him but that these men told us before out of Petrus de Palude,[b] wherefore it is reason that he doth recant with his said master.

[a] Tertia parte summæ, Titu. de cognat. paragr. 2.
[b] In summa sua.

To Astexanus.

Astexanus[a] is also all under one answered already, in that he saith that the Pope cannot dispense with the prohibitions of God in the Levitt. seeing our case is out of that checke. And as our case is not checked by God's law, so neither is it by the law of nature, as may evidently appear to them that will read the same title whereof they bring this testimony.

To John Bacon.

John Bacon affirmeth that, touching the prohibitions Levittical for marriage, the Pope cannot dispense with the direct line ascendent and descendent, as the father to marry the daughter, or the mother the son. For this first degree is forbid by the law of nature. But, touching the second degree of collaterals (which is not forbid by nature), the Pope may dispense, especially with Paynims converted to the faith,[b] to whom the law of Moses was not given [p. 83], which declaration making against them, affirming that the Levitt. prohibitions did bind the Paynims as well as the Jews, these men have craftily pretermitted.

To Waldensis.

Yea and to Walden also speaking the like of the said Levit. prohibitions. And as for that he objected to Wickliffe we have already answered. But whereas he would have all the Levitt. prohibitions moral and against the decalogue, that saying hath no good foundation. For what part of the decalogue, I pray you, doth he infringe that marrieth his brother's wife, or his wive's sister? Consider all these parts of the decalogue by rowe as diligently and as nearly as

[a] In summa sua.   [b] 1, 4 Senten. distinct. 38.

you may, and yet shall you find no place there wherein to place this prohibition, unless you will understand it the sister and brother yet living, and then may you refer it to the seventh or ninth precept. But they say that Pope Martyn approved the sentence and judgment of Walden in this matter. Truth it is that he allowed and approved his works. But yet it will not thereof follow that he precisely allowed every particular thing contained in the said works, for there be many good and holy doctors that the Church hath and doth well like of their books, yet are there some [p. 84] points interspersed which the Church doth not [all the best] allow of. Now, where Walden saith that he breaketh natural honesty and shamefastness that discovereth the privic parts of his own flesh and blood, as it were the privities of a strange person, we answer that if we account all things to be against the law of nature that natural shamefastness forbiddeth, then should no man (were he never so honest) meddle with any woman at all, for that natural shamefastness concurreth in all such acts.

To the residue of the Scholastical Doctors.

To knit up the matter here be divers other scholastical doctors named which affirm (as it is alleged) that infidels being coupled in marriage against the law of God and nature if they afterward come to the faith must be separated and sundered. Be it so: yet neither they nor any other hitherto produced have proved that this marriage is against either of those laws.

To Johannes Andreas et Johannes de Imola.

If they hitherto have found no substantial matter either in the holy Scripture or in the Counsells, the fathers and the Scholastical doctors (as it is now evident to the eye) shall we think that they may possibly take any [p. 85] great benefit at the hands of the doctors and expositors of the canon law? No, surely, yet let us see what they have found, which is nothing else but what we have already answered unto, and now again is repeated out of Johannes Andreas and Johannes Imola,[a] who say that the Pope cannot dispense with degrees prohibited by the law of God. But where say they so? Forsooth in the expounding of a decree of Pope Innocentius who (as we have said) dispensed with our very case.[b] And John Andreas saith that our case is dispensable, and citeth for it the aforesaid dispensation of Innocent, yea Abbot [c] Panormitane expounding the said chapter saith that the same John Andreas affirmeth that the Pope may dispense with cases forbidden even by God's lawe.

To Abbott Panormitane and others.

And thus is Abbott also all under one answered,[d] who confesseth that a man cannot marry his brother's wife, unless the church dispense with him. Seeing then the Captains of the canon law be on our side they do but in vain object here against us Vincentius and the said Pope Innocent; which Vincentius is of this opinion, That the Pope may in all things dispense saving with the Articles of the Christian faith,[e] as Abbott reporteth of [p. 86] him and doth [not] mislike with him for it. To perfect and finish our answer to the fourth chapter we make a direct contrary to them, but yet a true conclusion, which is, that, the premisses considered, no man ought to approve and commend the determination of these Universities, which do hold and conclude that to marry her whom the brother departed without children hath left is so forbidden by the law of God and also by the law of nature that the Pope hath no authority or power to dispense with such marriages whether they be contracted already or are to be contracted.

[a] Cap. litteras, De restitut. spol.
[b] Cap. final. de divor.
[c] Jo. Andr. cap. Per venerabilem, Qui filii sunt legit.
[d] Dicto, cap. Litter. et cap. final.
[e] Ab. de concess. prebendæ, cap. Proposuit.

An answere to the fift Chapter.

We have now waded through the greatest part of the book and the chiefest and most principal proofs. And now are they come to their fift chapter, and to spin the matter very fine with a number of definitions of the law of God, of the law of God judicial, moral, and natural; and as the spider draweth out of her poisoned body matter very fickle and brickle to abide any brunte and insult, so have these men framed and drawn out of their own certain definitions of very small force; whereby they will afterward frame also reasons of like force of their own proper making and invention, to underprop and maintain the Censures [p. 87] and Judgments of the said universities, of the which we will answer so much as shall be effectual and material. And loe at the very beginning of their chapter,[a] besides a crafty sleight legerdemaine, there concur two notable untruths. A legerdemaine I say, for that whereas hitherto they have but in generality gone about to prove the Levitt. prohibitions to proceed both from the law of God and nature, now they frame their reasoning as though they had specially proved this for and touching the brother to marry his brother's wife. Two untruths I say accompany this legerdemaine. The one in that they say they have truly and faithfully shewed what holy writ, what the Popes and fathers, what the doctors and interpreters of holy scripture do judge concerning their case; whereas very few by them alleged once speak of this case, and many of them speak directly on our side. The other that they have most wretchedly and miserably mangled their own authors' testimonies. We will now then as compendiously as we may consider their said definitions.

The definition of God's lawe.

The law of God is the word or mind of God commanding things that be honest, or forbidding things that be contrary to honesty;

[a] Anglice, pag. 94; Lat. [Signat. I. 4].

which law the sacred holy [p. 88] universal Church hath of long time by her authority received and confirmed as either being sowed or planted in the reasonable creature of God by the mouth and spirit of Almighty God, or else shewed to him by revelation.

Albeit this definition is for many causes to be rejected, yet, because it nothing hindereth our cause, we will not greatly stick at it. This would be notwithstanding by the way considered, why these men shun the definition set forth by Gerson and Gabriell and commonly of all men received. Surely they feared lest the final cause which they ascribe should much annoy their purpose, for they do admonish us that the prohibitions Levitt. conduce nothing to the supernatural end and to heavenward, which is the principal regard and scope of the Christian law. These men saw well enough that, seeing Abraham married his own sister, Jacob two sisters, and the son of the patriarch Judas married his brother's wife, this kind of marriage did nothing hurt or hinder them but that they might atcheive and obtain eternal blisse; and therefore they quite cut off the said final cause. Now seeing every part of this definition doth and must needs agree with the law of God in the 25 of Deut. commanding the brother to marry his brother's wife, it followeth that this marriage, being by God [p. 89] himself commanded, cannot be a thing evil of his own nature, a thing execrable, damnable, detestable, with many such other foul names as these men do note it withal, and exasperate the matter heinously against us, which I would wish the Reader well to remember when he shall hear them to pour and vomit out their foul filthy rhetoric, and therein ryally to roule and revell against God's owne blessed commandent.

The definition of God's lawe judiciall.

They make three kinds of God's law, that is to say, morals or naturals, judicialls, and ceremonialls. Judicialls they define to be those which be statutes or pains, or at the least those which God in time past did answer unto Moses when he asked him counsell of the suits and controversies of the Jews. This definition we reject, and St. Thomas, whose authority they have set in the margent, saith not so but plain to the contrary; for whosoever will peruse his 105 and 106 question, where he entreateth of the judicialls, he shall find many that have no penalties appointed, especially where he rehearseth cases judicialls, which as he saith do appertain to domesticall conversation. As where the Jews are forbidden to marry [p. 90] out of their tribe, and the brother to marry his brother's wife, and that they shall not marry strangers, which last commandment is contained under no part of their definition, and so thereby is no judiciall. And then of what kind shall it be? for it is no ceremoniall or morall; wherefore they had need to set also a fourth member of God's lawe, and so then is their definition incomplete and insufficient.

The definition of the lawe of nature.

The law of nature, say they, is a general knowledge and judgment which God did grave in the mind of every man, to help him to form and frame his manners and living. If this be a good definition (as therein we do find no fault) [a] then must it of necessity follow that this marriage is not against the law of nature, and so is their next and principal foundation overthrown. For if the knowledge of these prohibitions be naturally sown and ingrafted in every man's mind, marvell it is that so many and so notable, learned, and virtuous men, and of so excellent and pregnant wits, could never espie this law of nature all this while, which these men, with their sharp eagle's eyes, hath now at length found out [p. 91], and, among other, their own only doctor, Petrus de Palude, which could not see that the Levitt.[b] prohibitions do naturally forbid marriage, but doth understand the prohibition that the brother shall not marry his

[a] Definitio legis naturæ quam S. Tho. probat in 4° senten. dist. 37, q. 3, et in principio opusculi de decem præceptis. [b] In Levitticum.

brother's wife, his brother yet living, which we grant to be by the law of nature prohibited. After this sort Franciscus(ᵃ) de Maaso, Alexander de Halis,(ᵇ) Symon de Cassia, Hugo(ᶜ) Cardinalis Glossa(ᵈ) interlinearis, Petrus(ᵉ) Blesensis, Rodulphus(ᶠ) Flaviacensis, Christianus(ᵍ) Druthmarus, Hahmo(ʰ) Episcopus Halberstatensis, and, beside many other, Albert,(ⁱ) worthily called the great, understand this prohibition; which Albert sheweth a pretty fit natural cause also why it is said that the brother should stir up seed to his brother, for, albeit the seed is not of sufficient efficacy to make the woman to bring forth, yet it is of sufficient efficacy to alter the qualities of the matrix. And for this cause the woman bringeth forth oftentimes a child resembling the first husband, if there be no long time between the death of the first and the marriage of the second, which thing may be also shewed by this; that if a man which is a leper meddle with a woman, and not long after some other man also that is whole and sound, this other man becometh a leper. And this Albert, with divers of these now rehearsed, doth [p. 92] affirm that Herod married his brother Phillip's wife, yet living. But, among and above all other, it is a marvellous wonder that St. Augustine could never espie that our case was by the law of nature prohibited, who giveth three understandings to the Levitt. precept; and our case is comprised under none of them all, of the which one is that this commandment is to be taken of the brother's wife, the brother yet living. Now, beside these so ample authorities and testimonies, our author, with sixteen good and substantial reasons, doth justifie and inforce the said understanding of the brother yet living, which for avoiding of prolixity I do pretermit. Some other ([and] that a great number) be that understand this prohibition of the brother leaving children after his death. And that this pro-

---

ᵃ Lib. 4, senten. Distin. 41, q. de affinitate.
ᵇ In summa Theol. quæst. 169.
ᶜ In Mathæum.
ᵈ In Mathæum.
ᵉ De gradibus affinitatis.
ᶠ In Leviticum.
ᵍ In Mathæum.
ʰ Super Marcum.
ⁱ In Mathæum et Lucam.

hibition is now grounded upon the laws and constitutions of the Church only, among whom is that excellent, holy, learned, and witted man Bonaventura; yea, the great learned schoolman Dunce, of singular high wit and capacity, affirmeth that now in the New Testament there is no cause why affinity should barre and stoppe marriage,[a] but for the constitutions ecclesiastical only. These and many other things which our author proposeth and proveth considered, a man would and might well think [p. 93] that, if there be in every man, as they say, though he be marvellous blinded and darkened, a certain prudence or common wit ingendred in him, graven in him by God his maker at his first creation. And this witt or reason they call natural light, and light of understanding, and the light of the visage of God, &c. And that there be written in the heart of man with the finger of God certain rules or laws of general justice, virtue, and honesty, &c. by the which every man may easily perceive (as they stoutly affirm) that this marriage is against the law of nature. A man may, I say, well think that some of the aforesaid authors, and namely St. Augustine, should have espied some part of all his life this clear bright Sunne of the law of nature, which thing, seeing he did not nor many other right excellently witted and learned, these men's gay painted process, set forth and enforced with so glorious, glistering, shining words, is void of all manner of truth, and containeth palpable absurdity, nor is able to move as much as a child of any good and competent capacity.

The definition of the lawe morall.

Of the law moral, first they say thus, Whatsoever is commanded of God in holy Scripture and is shewed unto us inwardly in our hearts by these foresaid general [p. 94] rules, or that in a good and formal reason followeth of them, or else that agreeth with them though it doth not follow of them. All these the divines call the lawes moral, which law they define and determine on this manner.

[a] 39 dist. arti. 2do, quæst. 4ta; 4ta sententia dist. 41, quæst. de affinitate.

The moral law of God is the word and mind of God commanding those honest things and forbidding those unhonest things which the natural reason of man, lightened with the light of the word of God, doth according to the rules and teaching of common justice or virtue teach us to do or leave, and which the same natural reason so lightened doth shew us that we be bound to keep them, although they were never commanded by none other law.

We have now heard a definition which yet these men dare not call their own, but ascribe it to certain unnamed divines, I cannot tell whom; wherein it is to be thought that either they do not all the best trust their own definition, or that there lurketh under this some unknown hidden crafty sleight. And marvel it is what they mean to reject such definitions as by most wise, witty, learned men have been delivered unto us, and to obtrude to us other, partly their own and partly fetched from obscure men, and of little or no estimation. Howbeit, seeing this definition doth nothing incommodate and hurt our cause, we will take it in good worth [p. 95]. For even by their own definition it will appear that the Levit. prohibition of the brother's wife taken in a general sense (as they take it, and contend it must be taken), is no moral law of God. And that will we prove by this reason. There is none never so slender a logicioner that doth not know that the thing which is defined cannot be truly and competently said of that thing to the which the definition [it]self is contrary. But this definition is contrarious and repugnant to the Levit. prohibition, generally and absolutely taken. Wherefore that thing that is defined which is the law of God moral cannot be verified of it. The minor we will prove after this sort. The said prohibition generally taken is not the word and mind of God shewed us according to the rules and teaching of common justice and virtue. [Ergo, &c. The antecedent also we prove after this sort. If the prohibition taken generally were commanded to us by the rules and teaching of common justice and virtue,] then could no man that were not void of the feeling and understanding of common justice be either ignorant or doubtful of the truth of the said prohibition. But this is a main untruth as we have already shewed, for that men of most excellent wit and learning did not take it in that general sense. Wherefore it ensueth of necessity that in taking and following the general sense [p. 96] of the said prohibition it is not the law of God moral. Let us now also try, examine, and discuss this clause and declaration made before their definition and see if there be anything that will weigh on our side. Whatsoever (say they) is commanded of God, &c. Let this stand as the major of our collection and argument. To the which we do accommodate and apply this minor. But the marriage of the brother's wife dying childless, God in the Canonical Scripture commanded, and the very same among the Jews by the rules of common justice, inserted, planted, and sett by God in every man's heart did follow, and that in a good and formal consequence. Ergo this precept was to them the law of God moral. The first part of the minor is by consent of all the interpreters of Scripture notoriously true; wherefore it remaineth for us to establish and confirm the second part thereof. And that will we do putting you in remembrance of a thing or two first; one is, that whosoever refused to marry his brother's wife deceased without children, this man so far as lay in him did a grievous injury to his brother. First, for that by his fault his brother's memory was delete and abolished among the Jews. Secondly he was spoiled of house and family. Thirdly he was disappointed and robbed of the portion of inheritance that was [p. 97] due to his succession. Fourthly himself was under the malediction and curse of the law. Fiftly he was deprived and spoiled of the manifold benedictions and blessings of the old law. Sixtly and last he was noted and infamed with the perpetual ignominy and shame of sterility and barrenness of children. The other is, that he that married his brother's wife did perpetuate and give everlasting continuance to his Brother's memory, he gave him succession, he established his house, he confirmed the inheritance of his family, he depulsed the shame and ignominy of barrenness and sterility, he did not exonerate him from the curse of the law, and procured to him the manifold benedictions and blessings of the same. And was there, think you, any man, while the state of the Jews continued, that did not most heartily wish both to enjoy the fruition of these commodities, and to be discharged from the said griefs and discommodities? who would not have employed all his best endeavour as well to have gotten those benefits as to avert and put away from himself these displeasures and discommodities? These two things premised, I frame this reason. Among other rules and precepts of common practice, there are two of no small strength and force. That is, to doe to another man that thou wouldest have done to thyself. And that thou wouldest not another man doe to thee, do not thyself to any other. Now, if any [man] [p. 98] of the Jews refused to marry his brother's wife (his brother dying without children) he transgressed and violated both these precepts, for both he did not that good turn to another which he would should have been done to himself. And that shrewd turn he did to another which he would not should have been done to himself. Whereupon it will follow that the said commandment to marry the brother's wife was agreeable to their own definition of God's moral law, for both God did command it in holy Scripture, and the same did flow out of the rules and precepts of common justice, or at the least might be by a formal and necessary illation deduced thereof, and was correspondent to the same.

Loe, good reader, whereas these men with all their long fine fetches and manifold arguments heaped one upon another could not yet nor never shall hereafter prove that this prohibition must be universally understood; we have proved by a formal and necessary illation fetched and deduced even from their own definition that it cannot nor may not so be taken. Now, if they will once descend and come down from their generality to any particular sense and understanding of the said prohibition, let them take what sense soever they will of those three that the fathers and doctors have embraced, and then shall none of those three hinder our case. This that we have now deduced in this fift chapter, I pray thee (gentle reader) well to remember, and then shalt thou [p. 99] see that all their arguments are very sophisms and sophistrie, as easy to be broken and overthrown as the spider's cobwebbe.

An answer to the sixt chapter.

Now shall we see by the sixt chapter why they have made such a muster of their definitions. And that is to make them a foundation to rear their untrue and false conclusion upon, that this marriage should be against the law of nature and law moral, which is their second principal matter. And truly if we should say no more than we have done already, especially in our short answer to the fift chapter, a man might soon be thereof instructed what to think and what to answer to all their brickle building upon their said definitions; yet as we have heretofore done so shall we now set before you (with as much compendiousness as we may) the chief and most material points that they gather for the maintenance of their purpose. They tell us then first that they have said enough of the light and troth of their two grounds, but yet they have quite forgotten to tell us which these two were, which defect the English Interpreter goeth about as well as he can to supply. Well, let us consider some of their proofs whereby they would enforce this [p. 100] marriage to be against the law of nature and law moral. First they are in hand with their old definition of the law of God moral, and rules of common justice and virtue, whereunto we need not further answer than we have already. After this we have a true but an impertinent process that the Levitt. booke is a part of Canonical Scripture; we do not controvert or strive for the credit or discredit of the book, but for the true or wrong sense thereof. But then have we a terrible thunderbolt shot against us out of Levitt.,[a] that is, that the said Levitt. doth forbid such things as of themselves are naught and against honesty, and that it calleth this marriage filthiness, a mischievous and accursed deed, abhomination, infamy, and a thing

[a] Latin [Signat. L. 1] Angli. pag. 106.

unlawful. Then are there rehearsed divers grievous pains, both temporal and spiritual, that this marriage by God's law is chastened withal, and how the Cananites were cast out of the country for this filthy marriage. Indeed we were in great danger if this thunderbolt did hit us or touch our matter; but God be thanked it cometh nothing near us. For, as we have and must still say, our case is not within the bounds and limits of any prohibition Levitical. And a strange marvel were it, if God should for this marriage thrust out the Cananites and other people and supply their place [p. 101] with the Jews, and yet give them in commandment under great penalties the very self-same marriage, for the which he took such vengeance upon other people. Wherefore, he that married his brother's wife among the Jews needed not to fear any of these threatenings and punishments before rehearsed, knowing full well that they should not light upon him for this fact, but rather the manifold benedictions and blessings of God for keeping and observing his commandment. Now, for as much as though the Levitt. calleth such things as are forbidden in the 18 chapter execrations and abhominations, some man might well say that those names, with all the punishments and threatenings put there, belong not to the first prohibitions of the said chapter touching marriages, but to the latter, which are of other greater faults. To avoid this objection there are many things said:[a] First, that the whole order and process of the said 18 chapter will not (especially being compared with the 20 chapter) suffer this exposition. The said 18 chapter is partly dissuasory, partly teaching. It teacheth the Jews of certain ungracious manners and laws and then dehorteth them from the same. Now, if the law-maker had understood the last end of the chapter, of the latter prohibitions only, he might seem to have fallen out from his purpose and to have forgotten in the last end of the chapter what he intended in the beginning. And seeing [p. 102] adultery [and the sin against nature was never lawful among the Cananites], by their incestuous and beastly marriages, why should we

---

[a] Latine [Signat. L. 2] Angl. pag. 108.

not think that the lawmaker did mean of the first prohibitions. Surely in the 20th chapter the last prohibition of all is that we should not marry our brother's wife, and straight after that followeth all these things the Gentiles and heathens have done. Wherefore all the precepts contained in the said 18 chapter are moral. And those grievous names and pains appertain to such as transgress any part thereof. To this might we answer with a few words as almost to all the residue, that our case is not included in the Levit. prohibition. But yet we will give some little taste what the Bishop answereth otherwise.

First he noteth that it is untrue that the state of the said 18 chapter standeth wholly upon dehortations but rather upon suasions and exhortations. You shall do my judgments saith God and my commandments. Again, Keep you my laws and judgments, and eftsoones, Keep my laws and judgments. So that the principal part of this chapter seemeth to rest upon this point, and then consequently it dehorteth from the rights, lawes, and customs of the Cananites. But this suasory and hortatory part these men do suppress and tell withal an untruth of the state of the chapter.

Secondly, here is to be observed, that seeing, as appeareth by the word Judicial before rehearsed, there be in this chapter some judicials, all [p. 103] are not morals, and truly, if there be any judicial, it is of the marriage of two sisters and of the brother's wife.

Thirdly, it is to be noted, that, if there were no judicialls in this chapter, then Moses should quite have forgotten himself bidding them to keep the judicials whereof he had made no mention in the said chapter.

Fourthly, it is to be marked that the greatest causes why the Cananites were expulsed out of their country be not (as these men imagine) those only that be in this chapter but many other more heinous than these mentioned in divers places of holy Scripture, namely in the 2, 8, & 20 chapter of Deuteronomie and the 12 of the booke of Wisdome.

Fiftly and last, this is to be observed that oftentimes the Old Testament exaggerateth and exasperateth matters with words of execration and abhomination and of such as shall perish from the people, which perishing these men take (but falsely) for eternal damnation, and yet the matters themselves are not ever of their own nature naught and damnable and against the law of nature. For it is said that he that eateth blood shall perish from the middle of the people, and Paulus Burgensis gathereth many like phrases, whereof few or none at this day do bind us. Now, if Adultery and the sin against nature were not among the rights [p. 101] and customs of the Cananites, why are they here rehearsed, whereby it appeareth that all things comprised in the said 18 chapter be not of one sort, force, and fashion? But the Counsell Agathense (say they), the Counsell of Toledo, Isichius, and many other fathers do extend these penalties to the said incestuous marriages.[a] And to your said Counsells and fathers we have [also] sufficiently answered, and these Counsells and Fathers do apply these threats, penalties, and punishments of the Levit. to all that marry within the seventh degree of consangunity or affinity. But yet it cannot be thereby gathered that all these prohibitions be against the law of nature. As for Gulielmus Parisiensis we find no such thing as they allege in his book by them named.

Nay, nay, say they, it well appeareth that this marriage is against the law of nature, for that there was never any nation so savage and beastly but thought that we ought this honour, duty, and reverence to our brother and brother's wife that we should refrain from their marriages. And therefore heathen poets, historiographers, and law-makers do speak against this kind of incest. But oh, Good Lord, where is due honour, duty, and reverence, that these men do owe to the holy sacred Scripture, and to God himself, that by these heathen poets and historiographers presume so far to disable, so shamefully to [p. 105] disgrace and

[a] Isichius et Rab. super 18 et 20 cap. Levitt.

infame this marriage which God himself commanded to his very chosen and select people; yet let us see how jollylie they prove their poeticall conclusion. Forsooth we have here for the proof thereof a Raggeman's Roll of Machareus, Caunus, P. Clodius, Tereus, Thiestes, and I cannot tell of what other monstrous names and persons that with grievous incest defiled their own daughters and sisters. Of our case there is not as much as one convenient example, as far as I can see, proposed. For as for Tereus and Thiestes, the former shamefully abused his wive's sister, his wife yet living, and Thiestes his brother's wife, his brother being yet alive. But if it would have pleased these men to have looked upon the commonwealths of the Lacedæmonians, the Athenians, the Persians, the Romans, and many other which our author reciteth (beside divers examples which we in the beginning of this Treatise have proposed), they might easily have found that these nations saw no such clear light of nature as these men have now at length spied out. Neither yet will it follow that because this marriage was afterwards by the Emperors forbidden that it is[a] either against the law of God or the law of nature. After this followeth a long process partly superflous and impertinent, partly [p. 106] false; That we cannot by the law of nature marry with our sister, and that this was one of the causes of the deluge in the time of Noe, that men abused their brothers' wives with abominable fornication. Whether it be by the mere law of nature forbid to marry our own sister there is somewhat already said. And our author here doth enlarge his proofs that it is not so straightly forbidden, which we do here omit, because that, though it were true that it is forbidden, yet it is impertinent and nothing concluding against our case. Neither is it true, that they allege of the causes of the deluge. For it appeareth by Berosus' own words that they[b] abused their brothers'

---

[a] Cod. de incest. nuptiis, Lat. [Signat. M. 1] Angl. page 113. Chrisost. in cap. 1º Math. homilia prima. Hieron. contra Helvidium. Ang. lib. 15 [de civitate Dei], cap. 16. Idem contra Faustum, lib. 22, cap. 35. Methodius Episcopus de causis diluvii.
[b] Berosus, lib. 1º de antiquitate.

wives in the life of their brother. Methodius also sheweth that they committed detestable abomination with their mothers, their sisters, with mankind, and very brute beasts also. Howsoever it be, their own authors speak of the marriage of our sisters and not of our brother's wife. Now our translator perceiving belike that his authors whom he translated roved far from the mark they should prick at, and that there was nothing to serve against this marriage in the authors by them alleged, thought it good by one shift or other to make the matter more apparent on their side. Wherefore, like an honest true dealing man, he hath in this so important and [p. 107] weighty a matter (as lightly hath not chanced in England) and in such a book as was made for the confirmation of the Censures given by the Universities, and for the full and perfect establishment of that cause, played such a part as well sheweth he trusted more by such vile practices to abuse the reader than to the goodness of the cause. I mean for that he hath translated St. Augustine very falsely in the sentence now following,[a] Which thing (meaning the brother to marry his own sister) the more old it is, insomuch it was done at that time only when necessity drew them to it, so much the more it was afterwards damnable (when that shame drew them from it); where he mistranslateth *when that shame drew them from it,* for *when Religion did forbid it;* which I especially note to you for that there hangeth the very material point of his Author's process upon it and a condemnation also of their conclusion, that it is against the law of nature for the brother to marry his own sister. For St. Augustine saith, Although this marriage was used for necessity at the beginning, yet afterward Religion did prohibit the same. And what religion I pray you but Moses' religion and the books of the law delivered him by God? So that before either this marriage was excusable (for the which as we have said St. Hierome [p. 108] excuseth Abraham) or not so damnable and detestable as these men infer it to

[a] Quod profecto quanto est antiquius compellente necessitate, tanto factum est damnabilius Religione prohibente.

be. Well this man hath not so craftily juggled nor so bleared our eyes but that we have espied his gales well enough, as well in perverting of this sentence as of another sentence of his immediately following. For where St. Augustine hath, *Etiamsi perversis legibus permittuntur fraterna conjugia*, although it be by naughty laws permitted that brethren may marry their sisters (for so it was among the Athenians, the Persians, and divers other countries), this man, that his author's process should not seem altogether void and impertinent from the matter, translateth these words thus: Although it was suffered by naughty and corrupt laws to marry the brother's wife, yet for all that, &c. Now that neither the signification of the words nor the mind and process of St. Augustine can bear this translation, it is so evident by the place itself, yea and by the residue of his own translation, that I will use no further needless confutation of this shameless impudence. The Adversaries,—seeing well enough that the Reader might think that this was but a slender and weak collection and deduction; I am forbid by the law of nature to marry my own sister, Ergo, I am forbid also to marry my brother's wife; therefore to help at this pinch, the Translator (as we [p. 109] have said), hath for the sister prettily conveyed in the brother's wife,—goe now [a] about to underprop and maintain the said argument with a certain reason of small force, as you shall now see. That is, if it be against the law of nature that any man should marry his own natural sister because it is not lawful by the law of nature to discover her foulness, and if he which marrieth his brother's wife discovereth the foulness of his brother, he shall break also the law of nature that coupleth unto him by marriage his brother's wife. Here may the Pope answer to them

First, that they have not yet proved that to marry the sister is directly against the law of nature, and that Moses forbidding this marriage propoundeth no such cause.

Secondly, he may say that they mistake this word foulness, which signifieth here the privy member as it doth in the 18 of Exodus,

[a] Augl. pag. 116. Latine [Signat. M. 2].

where it is said, Thou shalt not go up to my Aulter by steps lest thy foulness be discovered. And that when Moses sayeth, Thou shalt not discover the foulness of thy brother's wife, the Pope will answer that it is to be understood the brother yet living, all which time her member and vessel is the husband's, and that there is an unity of flesh between them, but not after his death, as we shall anon more largely shew. Now in the sister, as long as she is unmarried, it is her own [p. 110] member, and therefore not to be discovered by the brother.

Thirdly, he may say that, unless they can manifestly disprove the Authors that understand this prohibition (the brother yet living), by whom he may well uphold and defend his dispensation, they waste all their mind in vain.

Fourthly, he may say that, if they take this foulness otherwise, and for the dehonestation and dishonouring of the brother, yet, inasmuch as this marriage was by God himself commanded, and the brother much thereby, as we have said, relieved, holpen, and honoured, their collection is of no more force than a bullrush. Many other things also saith our author in subverting and infringing the foresaid reason, which we here now pretermit.[a]

Now, touching the maintenance of the said argument, they bring two reasons, the first that affinity doth as well break marriage as consanguinity. He will say it is untrue [and their proofs thereof too weak and insufficient. First, it is not true] that there be so many persons excluded from marriage by God's law in the one as in the other. For in consanguinity there be but five only; but in affinity seven, as may easily appear by the 18 and 20 chapter of Levitticus. Secondly, albeit it were true, yet it is but a waterish cold argument to say there be so many persons forbidd in the one as in the other. Ergo, affinity hath [p. 111] as great force to let marriage as consanguinity. Thirdly, he

---

[a] Levit. cap. 18 et 20. Causa 35, Quæstio 2. cap. Nulli, et cap. Quædam lex, et cap. Si vir, et cap. Sane, et Causa 35, Quæstio 5, cap. 3 Porro, et Causa 35, Quæstio 8, cap. 2, Hæc salubriter.

will say that their comparison doth halt, whereas they speak of degrees prohibited by the constitutions ecclesiastical and but of persons touching the Levitt. wherein is a main difference; for the diversity and variety of every person doth not vary and alter the degree of consanguinity or affinity. Otherwise the brother of the father only, the brother of the mother only, and of both should make three degrees. And likewise the sister. Fourthly, albeit there is one and equal distance of degree between the aunt, that is, the father's sister, and her nephew by her brother, as is between the uncle, the father's brother, and his niece by his brother or sister, yet Moses forbiddeth the first marriage and not the second. Fiftly, Moses forbiddoth the sister's marriage, whether she be of [the] father or mother only or of both, because she is of kindred. But my wive's sister, because she is of alliance only, he doth not simply and absolutely forbid, but only my wife living, nor my brother's wife but when he dieth with children. Now where they say that the Church was compelled to set the bonds of marriage both in affinity and consanguinity in like distance of degree, the Pope may marvel what they mean by that saying; perchance they mean that the fathers of the Church were compelled [p 112]: But to this they were not compelled either by the law of Moses or by the law of nature; wherefore it was but a mere positive law. They say now further, that, if it were not so as they conclude, the wise lawyers would have bound those persons of consanguinity unto a straighter bond of marriage than those persons that be only of affinity, and not both utterly in one and like degree. We say that if the fathers had spoken of one degree of malice, [then] there had been some appearance in their saying, for it should then have been as great malicious incest to marry with my wive's sister as to marry with my own sister, which is accedentlie forbidden by Moses' lawe. Wherefore, seeing the fathers did not speak or mean of any such degree of malice or naughtiness, but only of such degrees where all persons being of like distance or nighness to the stocke be accounted of one degree, this kind of reason is frivolous and sophistical and far unmeet for the persons of these learned men.

Neither do the words of St Augustine help them, saying that our daughter in-law ought to be taken of us as our own daughter, for he speaketh that of the daughter-in-law, her spouse yet living, for Sela, Judas' son, to whom Thamar was espoused, did then live. And therefore Judas could no more meddle with her than with his own daughter [p. 113]. Wherefore, their conclusion that affinity hath like force as consanguinity is not true; and, beside other things, the untruth thereof is easy to be perceived. For, that affinity borroweth and fetcheth all her force and strength of consanguinity so far forth that if the husband and wife have no kindred, then have they also none alliance. And, therefore, Bonaventura saith fitly, that consanguinity is a bond of itself, rising of the very natural blood as soon as the party is borne. Affinity is but an accidental bond, rising by marriage and fleshly meddling, which procureth the unity of flesh between the man and the wife as long as they live, and ceaseth with their death, and so doth not consanguinity. And, therefore, though the husband being revived cannot claim his wife again, yet the brother revived from death to life shall be of kin and consanguinity to his brother and others as he was before. Here also may be considered that we have before said, that, by the Judgment of Scotus and other, there is at this day no prohibition of marriage by reason of affinity but only in respect of the constitutions ecclesiastical. Wherefore we conclude against them—That, if we will absolutely consider the force and strength of the prohibition of nature, there is a [p. 114] greater prohibition in consanguinity than in affinity in letting or breaking of marriage. But, if we consider the Canons and Constitutions Ecclesiastical, we grant the force to be like and equal on both sides. But then this Argument is to be exploded and laughed at—By the law of the church, Affinity is as strongly forbidden as consanguinity—Ergo, the Pope cannot dispense with affinity, or the Pope cannot dispense with the brother to marry the brother's wife.

Now, touching their second reason,[a] they say it is very evident and plain; for he that marrieth his brothers's wife taketh his

[a] Latine, pag. 63. Angl. [Signat. M. 3.]

brother's flesh and blood to marriage, the which thing plainly is against the law of nature; for, seeing the husband and the wife be one flesh and blood, truly he that taketh his brother's wife taketh also the flesh and blood of his brother. And as for our brother, he is the flesh and blood of our father and mother, and that more near unto him than any of both their sisters because he is their own son. Therefore if it be forbidden by the law of God and also by the law of nature to marry our father's sister or our mother's sister or else the wife of our father's brother, or mother's brother, whose wives be but of affinity to us, and that only in the second degree, truly much more it should [p. 115] be against nature to marry our brother's widow, for the nearer that they come to the stocke and to be one flesh and blood, the more they ought to be forbidden. But our brother is more near unto our father (as is aforesaid) than is either of our uncles or aunts.

Here may the Pope also say that in this second reason two untruths are couched. The one that the wife is the flesh of the dead brother; the other that we are forbidden by the law of nature to marry our uncle's wife. Concerning the first, because this pretended unity of the flesh is their principal apparent reason whereby they would fortify their untrue assertion; and, because it doth often intercurre in their book, we will here make answer for the whole all under one. We say then that this unity is only to be counted while the husband and wife do live and no longer, for as long as they live, the wive's privie member is accounted his according to the saying of St. Paule. The woman hath no power of her owne body, but the husband.[a] And in another place he calleth this member the vessell or member of the man, saying, that every one of you may know how to keep his vessell or member in sanctification and honour. Now the husband being dead, it is no longer his member, and therefore no discovering of his foulness, but it is now the [p. 116] foulness of him that hath married her. Wherefore it is a conclusion among the divines, That if a man should be resuscitate from death

[a] Prima Corin. cap. 7º Prima Thesal. 4.

to life (as Lazarus was) he could not claime his wife again but with her own consent and by a new contract.[a] For it is most certain that death dissolveth the bond and knot of matrimony. St. Paule saith that the husband being dead the wife is delivered from the law and bond of the husband, and that she may marry where she thinketh good. So that, if in the intermediate time she should chance to marry any other, the party revived could not recover her to be his wife, though she would never so fain have him. Wherefore this pretended unity is no impediment to marry and it were the stepmother, as our author hath declared in answering before St. Gregories authority. Here also would be remembered that which we have declared out of Scotus and his adherents, that now the Judicialls of Moses being abrogated, no affinity doth lett matrimony, but only by reason of the laws ecclesiastical. Wherefore the Pope will and may deny that his brother hath married either his father's flesh, [or his brother's. The like answer will he make for the uncle's wife, which (her husband being dead) is no part of his flesh,] and therefore whatsoever impediment be [p. 117] by God's law he will say there is no impediment by the law of nature ; yea, he will say that before his time there hath been dispensation given out to marry the aunt, the very sister of the father, which was one flesh with him. And that therefore it may be more easily dispensed withal to marry the uncle's, that is the father's brother's, wife, neither will he grant that the nearer they come to the stock the more they ought to be forbidden. For the brother's daughter hath a more stable and permanent unity of flesh with her uncle, her father's brother, whether he be living or dead, than hath the brother's wife with the brother being dead ; and yet is not she (by the law of nature) restrained from her uncle's marriage ; nor by the law of God, as Petrus Paludensis saith. My wive's sister also is as nigh the stock as my brother's wife. And yet is she not forbidden to marry but while my wife liveth.

They add here a prolix declaration to prove this marriage against the law of nature, but in effect nothing else but that which we

[a] Henricus de Band. 3 q. 2.7. Them. in cap. 9 ad Romanos. Cap. 7 ad Romanos.

have [had] already, consisting and resting upon the Levitt. prohibitions and the unity of the flesh. Wherefore we will but touch only some special and material points. The rules, say they, of general justice and virtue be such as pertain to order and frame [p. 118] our manners, teaching us things to be followed or avoided even of themselves for the obtaining of everlasting blisse. Then they add that there is no man *but seeth* (the Translator, I cannot tell why, hath *but sayeth*) that the things which be forbidden in the Levitt. Laws be even such things. To this we answer that if they understand these prohibitions universally, St. Austine, with a number of [other] excellent learned men, never saw any such thing in the Levitt. In case they descend to any particular sense, then is this marriage out of the reach and compass of the Levitt. Neither is it to be forgotten that now these prohibitions appertain to eternal blisse, which clause, for all that, they left out of their definition in the fift chapter as we have declared. But who is there that seeth not this to be very false? For the rule of common justice, planted by nature in us, is not able to reach and compass things supernatural, and eternal felicity, the knowledge whereof cometh only by especial grace infused and celestial Revelation. Now, if every law that serveth to form and frame our manners be rules of common justice, then were many things in Moses' books moral laws, which be now abolished. They are then in hand how by the Levitt. no man should discover his father's foulness, because he is next of the kin, and they bring in Cham, Noe's son, and Reuben (Gen. 9 et 49), which examples every [p. 119] man seeth be far from the purpose. Neither the conjunction of blood nor the marriage is the principal cause why the son must abstain from his mother, or the daughter from her father (for during the marriage so must all other persons also); but for that the son and the daughter be not only of kin to the father and mother, but take their flesh of them immediately. And for this cause the son must forbear his mother, albeit she were a very harlot and he unlawfully borne. They frame also other false maxims and principles, as that the brother cannot marry the brother's wife, because she is one flesh with her husband, and he also one flesh with his brother. And that they that will be married must be two, and by marriage made one flesh. For I may, by this reason, as well conclude that I cannot marry with the widow that any man married after my brother's wife's death which was married to my brother before. [For this widow was one flesh with her husband, and he was one flesh with his former wife; and so by their reason one flesh with my brother.] Wherefore it followeth, by their conclusion, that I cannot marry with her, which thing is false, as appeareth by the Canons Ecclesiastical, and by daily experience. It is also false that those that must be married must be twayne and not of one blood, as appeareth in the marriage of the uncle and the niece and of cousin Germans, which are not forbidden by the [law] Levitt. Again they [p. 120] say that there can be no marriage between persons which be already coupled by natural love and friendship, which is not true, as appeareth in them which be of the fifth, sixth, and seventh degree of kindred, and may now lawfully marry though natural friendship remaineth in them still. Other things might there be said to some other allegations of the adversaries, which because they be of small force or answered already we do pretermit.

Yet have we another long declaration and a needless, that the moral precepts of the Old Testament be not abolished, which thing as we grant them, so we ever look when they will once sufficiently prove that our case is forbidden by any moral law of Moses. They argue as though Moses' law pertaining to love and charity and other virtues were not yet taken away. And surely by the course and drift of their reason, the Ceremonials and Judicialls should have at this day their force. And albeit there was no law of Moses which was not ordained for the exercise of some virtue, yet will it not follow that the same thing now is (as they say) either by express words commanded or else so confirmed that it may be understood, unless they mean by their confirmation certain general precepts of piety, charity, chastity, and other virtues. And yet in this so needless a matter, their owne [p. 121] authors be against their principal purpose, as appeareth in Scotus; for if the same things be moral [precepts now, as Scotus affirmeth, which were moral] in the old law, we say that, forasmuch as in the old law the prohibition of our case was no moral precept, that it is none also at these days. They cite besides Irenæus, St. Austine, and St. Thomas, and even their own authors, if they had fully and faithfully cyted them, would have made against them; for they leave out in Irenæus[a] what the precepts were which Christ did not annul, but extend and enlarge, that is—Thou shalt not commit adultery—Thou shalt not kill—Thou shalt not forswear thyself—of the which kind you well see our case is not. And in St. Austine[b] they leave out certain material words, as they did in the very same sentence before. For St. Austine speaketh of murder, theft, idolatry, false testimony, and such like things, which they pretermitting do craftily apply the residue of his words to their purpose; neither does St. Austine say, as they would have the reader take it, that the barbarous people did for honesty sake abhor this marriage. In St. Thomas[c] they have left out the beginning and ending of the sentence by the which it may easily appear to the learned what his meaning and mind was. Finally [p. 122] it is frivolous and untrue which they write that Christ did revoke and call back matrimony to the old state, because he abhorred marriages within the Levitt. degrees. For Christ did that rather to represse and abolish the immoderate licence and liberty of the Jews in repudiating and rejecting their wives and marrying other. Touching degrees of marriage, he speaketh nothing but only where he saith, For this a man shall leave his father and mother, and stick to his wife, and they shall be two in one flesh, by which words the parents are forbidden to marry their children.

Yet, after all this stir and business, they saw well enough that

[a] Irenæus, lib. 4. cap. 27.
[b] August. contra tertiam epis. Pelag. lib. 3. cap. 4. supra cap. 4.
[c] 1. 2. q. 104. articulo. 3°. Mathæ. 19. Mar. 12. Luc. 16. 1 Corin. 6, et Ephes. 5.

this marriage was not forbidden [but] by the laws of the Church only, and so was it dispensable. And if it were by Moses' law forbidden, the law was by Christ abolished. Wherefore these men will in no case the Levitt. laws to be annulled by Christ, whereof they render sundry causes of small effect, and therefore worthy of no long answer. Why should Christ, say they, annul and repeal the Levit. laws, the which, straight after, he would inspire to the fathers of the primitive Church to command them again. Whereto we answer, Why did he inspire to the same Church to burn frankincense, to purify women, to keep the four imbring days, with many other ceremonials and some judicials also, which judicials the Church may receive [p. 123], and revive each one again, as the interpreters of holy scripture do confess. They talk now to no purpose that we should not be exempted from the law of God, seeing that this marriage is not to be controlled by the same. And to as little purpose is it that they demand why these marriages were forbidden, if it were not for that the Church judged them marvellous foul, unhonest, and unclean, the filthiness whereof we might easily see by the very light of natural reason. Not so; for marriages were forbidden many a hundred year through the whole Church, even to the seventh degree of consanguinity and affinity, which be now lawful to all men in the fifth, sixth, and seventh degree, and were then also by the law of nature. And as for this marriage, God himself purified and made it clean, commanding the same to the Jews.

There it followeth, nor truly it needeth not, that our adversaries should demand of us, why Christ did not make express mention of the Levit. laws in the Gospel if he would have had them live and endure among us still after the synagogue and the old law was dead. It needed not, indeed, neither needed it anything for you to move this, which no man hath or will object against you. We have not nor will not cumber you with such void and frivolous questions. And yet we say, that if Christ had expressly commanded the [p. 124] Levit. prohibitions to be kept, you had been nothing the nearer to your purpose, seeing our case is no parcel of the said prohibitions. And as you might have spared this question, so might and should you also have spared vainly to abuse your own labour and the reader's in telling us that which no man denieth or requireth at your hands, and all from the purpose, That many things be forbidden by God's law whereof doth nothing appear in the New Testament.

We are at the length come to the Epilogue or conclusion of the sixt chapter, where you hear many jolly, fair, and large words, that these Levit. prohibitions be moral, and that this marriage is by them, by reason, by honesty, and by the law of nature forbidden. And yet this matter remaineth still as full and as fresh to be proved as though they had said nothing (as they have not, indeed!) to the matter itself and against the dispensation of this marriage. Wherefore, when you read this epilogue you shall find nothing but an heap of untruths accumulated, and by us already severally confuted.

An Answer to the Seventh Chapter.

In this seventh and last chapter the adversaries, as though they had sufficiently and evidently proved that this marriage were against the moral precepts of God's law [p. 125], go busily about to prove that the Pope cannot dispense with any such moral precepts. But we trust that there is no man so contentious and froward that will, after that he hath well considered that we shall now put him in remembrance of, be anything moved with these men's sophistry.

1 First, then, we affirm and avouch that this marriage was often practised before the law of Moses and under the time of the law, even to the very expiring and extinguishing of the same law.

2 Secondly, that it was a very precept and commandment of that law that the brother should marry the brother's wife.

3 Thirdly, that the reason of the said precept did ever continue and endure even from the beginning of that nation.

4   That these learned men do produce no grave author that testifieth this marriage to be by God's law forbidden.
5   Fiftly, it is evident that this marriage is neither in the New nor in the Old Testament forbidden.
6   Sixtly, that very grave and learned writers avouche that there is no stoppe or impediment against this marriage but the Church law only.
7   Seventhly, that some affirm it to be agreeable and conformable to the law of nature.
8   Eightly, that Moses did not forbid the like degree of affinity in marrying the wive's sister.
9   Ninthly, that it is certain that by Moses' law a man [p. 126] may marry his brother's daughter, which is nigh unto him by the line of consanguinity.
10   That in such case it hath been dispensed withal by the Popes.
11   Eleventhly, that our very case is dispensed withal and incorporated into the canon law. Cap. final, de divor.
12   Twelvethly, that many excellent famous writers be of this opinion, that, albeit it were forbidden by God's law, yet the Pope might dispense with it. Yet for all this (say they) that this is a moral precept of God, and therefore not to be dispensed withal. And there can be no case imagined for the breaking of such prohibitions for any profit or need or for regard of any slander or necessity. And many places of Scripture for establishing of this assertion are heaped up together. But we say to them, that there can be no precept more natural, nor more fetched from the very grounds and principles of nature, than for a man to restore that which he hath found to the owner. To restore to the party that which he hath committed to our custody to keep. To sanctify the Saboth day. Not to break our promise and vow made to God. And yet am I not bound to restore that which is committed to my custody or that I have found, to the party demanding it, if he will convert the same to the destruction of himself or his country. The law also in some cases doth discharge us if we work [p. 127] upon the holy

day.[a] And many men have had and daily have from the Pope a release from their oath and vow. Again, if a man slay one taken in adultery, it is manslaughter and against the precept of the decalogue,—Thou shalt not slay. Yet may a prince make a law that it shall be lawful for any man to slay such as be taken in adultery. How much more then may the Pope dispense in our case which was once generally commanded to the Jews. Neither doth authorities brought forth by them out of holy Scripture prejudice our matter, which intreat of God's commandment to be observed; for we have oft declared that our case is not prohibited by any law or commandment of God, which notwithstanding (as you have heard) are in some cases some time released. Now whereas they lay forth a great number of fathers and other authors, and another needless process that the commandments and precepts of God must without any excuse or shift be kept and obeyed (as we have said), some such cases be released; yet if we grant them their conclusion it hindereth us nothing, seeing this marriage (as before is shewed) is not forbidden by any commandment of God. Neither do their authors, Ciprian ([b]), Basile ([c]), Ambrose ([d]), Bernard ([e]), Isidorus ([f]), Pope Fabian ([g]), Urbanus ([h]), and Marcellus ([i]), speak anything against the Pope's dispensation but against such [p. 128] as transgress wilfully the laws of God or of the Counsells and Fathers. And as none of their authorities make directly and expressly against us, so some of them even in the places themselves allege make well for us. As doth St. Basille, saying God hath commanded, Keep this commandment that I give thee this day. Thou shalt neither add nor diminish and detract anything from it. Where is this written but in Deuteronomie? Whereupon it followeth that seeing

[a] Cap. final. de feriis et ibi Abb.
[b] Lib. 1° epist. 4ª.
[c] De regul. cap. 13, 15 et 20.
[d] De Paradi. cap. 12.
[e] Lib. de [præcepto et] dispensatione [cap. 3].
[f] 11 q. 3, cap. Is qui.
[g] Causa 11, quæstio 3, cap. 95, Qui omnipotentem.
[h] Causa 25, quæst. 1, cap. 6. Sunt quidam.
Causa 25, quæst. 1. cap. 12, Omnia.

this marriage is there commanded, this commandment is to be kept and observed. The rule also which they produce out of Pope Urbane doth well serve our purpose, which is that the Pope may make new laws in such matters as neither the Prophets nor the Evangelists have spoken of before.[a] As for Innocentius, he speaketh of consanguinity and not of affinity, and himself did dispense in our case. St. Thomas doth except our case also from the prohibition of God's law,[b] conforming his opinion to the opinion of St. Chrisostome, whose words he doth recyte. They do now bring forth a number of School Doctors on their side, that say (as they allege) that the Pope can in no wise dispense with the law of God and nature; wherein their impudency is much to be marvelled at, seeing it is very notorious that touching the principal point they are all directly against them. For Alexander de Hales understandeth the Levit. prohibition, [p. 129] the brother yet living. Scotus avoucheth that in the time of the Gospel affinity doth not barre marriage, but for the constitutions of the Church only. Richardus sayeth that the first degree only of the parents and children is by the law of nature prohibited. Albertus Magnus understandeth this prohibition of the brother yet living, and saith plainly that this marriage is consonant to the law of nature. Franciscus Maro agreeth with his master Scotus [and taketh the prohibition to meane of the brother yet living. Gabriel was an adherent also of Scotus], and is of his former opinion. Herveus confesseth that those precepts which be not against the law moral may be dispensed withal. Jacobus Almaine maketh our case no parcel of the Levit. prohibition. Bernard de Trilla is an author so obscure that the Bishop never read his name but in this man's book. Finally, Antonius willeth (as we have said) that this marriage in no case be infringed and dissolved if it be once dispensed withal.

But yet they have another fetch to prove that the Pope cannot dispense with this case, for, if he should, then should he change the

---

[a] Cap. Litteras de restitutione spoliatorum, Cap. final. de divor.
[b] 1, 2, q. 103 [art. 4.]

will of God, which thing we do not grant. For the Pope in such matters doth not change and alter the will [and mind] of God or of the maker of the law, but doth declare only in what manner of cases the maker of the law minded not to bind men to the law; for by reason of the manifold difference of the time, place, and other circumstances [p. 130] there ariseth such variety of cases in any law to be made that it is not possible for the lawmaker in so few words to comprise them all. Wherefore, as in all civil and profane laws there is a power left to the Prince whom they call the soul of the law to declare the Equity (and that they call the *Epieikeya*) of the same law, so was it behoofefull and necessary that in the Church one should be left after Christ his assention to moderate, declare, and expound such laws as appertain to the government of the said Church. And therefore Christ said to his vicar St. Peter, Whatsoever thou shalt loose on earth shall be loosed in heaven. Now seeing there is some controversy of this prohibition (though it need not, by reason this marriage is commanded by the Deut.), and of some other Levit. prohibitions, whether they be moral or no, some few men without any sufficient reason affirming them to be moral, and all the residue denying, where and by whom I pray you is this question to be determined? By the Universities? Nay, but by Christ his own vicar, whose determination, once promulged, bindeth as well the Universities as all other, which matter our author doth more at large a little after this place prosecute.[a] Albeit our adversaries would seem to make him a minister only, and a dispenser of Christ's Sacraments to his sheep and lambs, which he hath taken of Christ [p. 131] to feed with the learning of the Church and Gospel. But if he be only a Minister, why said Christ unto him, whatsoever thou shalt loose on earth shall be loosed in heaven; for as touching sacraments he cannot loose and revoke them nor dispense with them? No, say they, nor yet can he change the decrees of the holy Fathers; as saith Pope Zosimus. But we must remember that

[a] Vide Jo. de Turre Cremat. in summa lib. 5 cap. 107, quem cum cæteris author allegat.

it is one thing to change the old laws and make new, and another thing to dispense with those that be already made. If the decrees of the Fathers cannot be changed, why are the fifth, sixt, and seventh degree of matrimony cutt off? Now as for Pope Leo[a] he speaketh of no dispensation but of Anatholius, who of his own head went about to infringe the decrees of the Nicene Council. Damasus[b] speaketh of such as by their own private authority do frowardly and wilfully transgress the holy Canons, of which number he is not that hath a lawful dispensation. And, if he would not intermedle with such matters as the Council of Capua had in hand, it will not follow that he could not. And Pope Hillarie[c] is both for his modesty and wisdom to be commended that would have his decrees to be by a Council also confirmed, that they might bear the more authority; which thing took not away his authority to dispense with [p. 132] the said decrees; yet at length they grant that for an inevitable necessity the Pope may dispense with the decrees of the Church.[d] But this is no dispensation but the allowing of a fact past; wherefore necessity only, though it be evitable, is sufficient to procure a dispensation. And who can be a competent and convenient judge of this necessity but the Pope himself. For hard it were and almost impossible for every particular necessity to indict a General Council. Neither doth the Pope (as these men seem to take it) in dispensing give men leave to do against the law of God, but declareth only that in that case the law of God doth not bind, and in this sense Panormitanus avoucheth that the Pope may dispense with the law of God.[e]

Because now they cannot deny but that the common opinion of divines and Canonists is that the Pope may dispense even with God's law (in that sense that we have declared), thinking that this might stand as a great stumbling blocke in their way, they labour busily to remove it, but all in vain for our case. They say that

[a] Leo ad Anatholium.
[b] Damasus ad Aurelium Archiepiscopum.
[c] Ambr. epistola 79, lib. decimo.
[d] 1 q. 7, cap. Necesse.
[e] Cap. Libuit, De feriis.

the lawyers restrain this to two cases, The one when that one law of God is expounded and restrained by another, as this commandment— Thou shalt not slay,—is limited and expounded thus, that it is lawful to slay misdoers. Another case, when the Pope of a just and lawful cause and such as is without sin doth [p. 133] put to or take away some part from the law of God. As to this commandment, In the mouth or witness of two or three standeth all the proof, the Pope for a just cause useth sometimes to put more witnesses than two or three. And neither of these limitations (as they say) will help the Pope in our case.

For touching the first, albeit the Levitt. precept was restrained in the old law by the Deut., yet, because afterward the said restraint was taken away by Christ, the Pope cannot dispense with it now (Gregor. in Epistola ad cives Romanos) unless he would make us Jews; no more than he may ordain that we should keep the Saboth day and circumsition and other figurall things, of which sort this precept of Deut. was one. Against the which St. Paul speaketh and sayeth that Christ profiteth us nothing if we be circumcised.[a] And St. Thomas[b] with Joannes de Turre Cremata saith that when the Apostle doth publish the law of God it is not lawful for the Pope to dispense. The Pope also can take no benefit of the second case to dispense, because there can be found no cause lawful enough that should be without sin for the which he may dispense.

To your first case we answer, that, in doubt arising upon the Canons, we may stand to the judgment of the Canonists. But when they arise upon a matter of divinity we should rather hearken to divines. Now if there were [p. 134] no more cases to dispence withal than these two we should need no dispensation at all, for every man that were skilful in holy Scripture should soon know what were lawful; by the lawes of our realm he that stealeth an ox or a sheep hangeth for it, and yet this matter was never distincted by holy Scripture. Neither doth he offend against the commandment, Thou

[a] Ad Galat. cap. 4ᵃ et 5ᵃ.
[b] Thomas, Quod. 4, artic. 13º. Johannes, cap. Lector, distinct. 33.

shalt not slay, that executeth any man for the said trespass. And by as good reason or better may the Pope dispense with our case, wherein the Pope maketh us not follow the Jews' ceremonies and superstitions. And as in the old law this marriage was commanded to raise up seed to the brother, so may the Pope now, though not for that end and respect, but for a far better, dispense with this marriage. Neither did Pope Innocent when he dispensed with the Livonians for this marriage cause them to be Jews. Now for such ceremonials as were deadly, whereof St. Paule speaketh, as circumcision, choice of meats, and the like, the Pope cannot revive. Otherwise it is of Judicials, whereof this is one, the which the Church may bring in ure againe. Neither were the Ceremonial laws only figurall and mysticall but the Judicials also, as St. Thomas writeth, who sayeth that the Pope may dispense against St. Paules prohibition of bigamie, which prohibition he did not promulge without the Spirit of God [p. 135]. Concerning the second case by them proposed, we say that if under the old law, which was a law of rigor and severity, there was a commandment given for this marriage for the relief and ease of a few persons, much more for the ease, relief, and safeguard of two most ample realms may the Pope now dispense with this marriage; neither doth he that obtaineth a dispensation for this marriage commit any incest or other sin, nor doth dishonest or shame his brother, but doth honest and honour him. And many marriages be called of the Fathers unlawful and incestuous which now be lawful, as we have before declared.

Now for as much as by the uniform consent of all divines and canonists the Pope may do many things by the fulness and absoluteness of his power and authority, lest this principle might hinder their cause, they go about to give an understanding to it; but to say the truth rather to abridge, minish, evacuate, and exinanite the same as much as they may. And albeit they run on upon this matter even to the shutting up and ending of their book, yet three or four words may soon wipe away all that ever they have said. Their understanding then is that the Pope, notwithstanding his absolute and plenary power, can grant nothing contrary to the precepts of the Gospel. We answer that he hath granted no such thing in our case. Yet we [p. 136] will not deal so peremptorily and precisely with them but that we will unfold unto you the most effectual part of their needless proceedings; wherein they are fain to confess against themselves that it is not lawful for any man to judge of the judgment of the see of Rome, or to reverse or revoke the sentence of that see[a] by reason of the preheminence of the same. Yet for all that, say they, if the Pope do anything against the law of God and nature he is not to be obeyed, nor his excommunications, curses, or other punishments; which thing they would prove (among other matters) by examples fetched even from our own country, and stories, but handled with such faith and truth as they have handled the holy Scripture, the Counsells, and the fathers before; for Loe Laurentius, Archbishop of Canterbury, successor to St. Augustine, after that he had cursed King Edbald for marrying his stepmother, could not be moved by any prayer or request of the Pope, nor by dread of cursing,[b] to absolve the king till he had renounced and forsaken that filthy and incestuous marriage. Now if a man will look (as reason is) how they will discharge their credit, for this story, they will (as they do indeed) forthwith remit you to our countryman, William of Malmesbury. But yet, when you have with your best diligence perused his book, you shall find no such thing, nor yet in Henry [p. 137] of Huntingdon, though he wrote this story at large. And yet, if this story were true (as it is notorious false), it will not follow that, because the Pope cannot dispense with me to marry my step-mother, therefore he cannot dispense with me to marry my brother's wife, dying without children. For the first is forbidden by the Levit. law, and not the second.[c] The translator belike espying this their fair glass

[a] [Causa] 17, quæst. 4, cap. [29], Siquis, et [cap. 30,] Nemini.
[b] Gul. Malm. De Gest. Reg. Angliæ.
[c] Antonin. Floren. 2° volumine histor. Titulo 19, et Jo. Whetamsted in prima parte granarii sui. Equidem cum illum de quo agitur pœnitentem videro delicti, præceptis domini Papæ libens parebo sed ut ipse in peccatis suis taceat et immuuis ab ecclesiastica

of their own making, thought he might be as bold also upon St. Dunstane's story now following as they were upon St. Laurence, and might himself supply their supposed defect; forhe saw or might soon see that the example of St. Dunstane made [very] little for their purpose; thereby to induce the Bishops or any other of this realm for this our case to disobey the Pope. What if Dunstane would not at the Pope's commandment absolve the earl Edwine, whom he had excommunicated for marrying his nigh kinswoman? There was good cause why he should not, for he found the Earle disobedient, stubborn, and impenitent, as appeareth by St. Dunstane's own words to the Pope's nuncio. And it seemeth that he was excommunicated for breaking of the law of God, and not for breaking the Levitt. law, as these men pretend. But yet say they this marriage was unlawful. Be it so. Yet it doth not appear in what degree it [p. 138] was unlawful, neither that the Pope had dispensed with it, but rather that he was untruly informed that the Earle had put away his unlawful wife, and yet Dunstane would not absolve him. Wherefore St. Dunstane played the part of an honest man and a good and zealous bishop. Let us then now see what an inhonest part our interpreter hath played. The Latin book saith that the Earl was excommunicated for marrying his kinswoman, and so the matter is out of our case, which is but of affinity, wherein the prohibition is not so straight as in kindred. Wherefore the interpreter, to make the case agree and jumpe with ours, and to make the unlearned by this craft believe that if any man should now resist the Pope in this cause he should do it with as laudable zeal as ever did Dunstan, which indeed is his author's conclusion also; like a good grammarian and faithful interpreter, translateth that the said Dunstan did excommunicate and curse the earl Edwine for marrying his brother's wife, whereas every child trained anything in grammar knoweth full well

disciplina nobis insultet nolit Deus; et mox, Avertat autem deus a me ut ego timore alicujus mortalis hominis vel pro redemptione capitis mei postponam legem quam servandam statuit in Ecclesia sua Idem Dominus meus Christus Filius Dei Eduerus in vita Dunstani.

that *Cognata* doth not signify a woman allyed unto us, but our kinswoman, which the very etymology of the word sheweth; for *Cognati* are called *quasi simul nati*, whereas you wote well they that be of allyance be not of one blood with us, but are copled and lincked unto us by marriage only. Can a man suppose [p. 139] you think well of this matter that is set forth with so foul shifts? We have yet another example [also] to little purpose, of Grosshead,[a] sometime bishop of Lincolne, that would not for any the Pope's threats admit into his church the Pope's nephew; wherein, seeing he was by their own allegation an unmeet and a very ungracious person, he did full well and bishoplike. [But what is this to the purpose to provoke men thereby to dislike and] disobey the Pope's dispensation in this marriage, which was by God himself commanded to the people of the Jews?

But now you shall hear them set to these stories as mighty and as notable a reason, which though it be at large with long painted supervacancall words exorned and set forth, yet in effect it resteth upon an authority of Pope Urbane, saying that there be two laws, one public, another private;[b] and the public law is that which hath been confirm'd by the writing of the holy fathers; the private law is that which is written in men's hearts by the inspiration of the holy Ghost, as the Apostle speaketh of certain which have the law of God written in their hearts. At length they conclude that this private law must be followed before the public, and therefore a secular priest, inspired with the holy Ghost, following this private law, may go from his [p. 140] dioces into another to enter into a monastery, and to profess religion against his bishop's will and the decree of the fathers, notwithstanding it prohibiteth any priest to go to another diocese without the license of his ordinary. So a bishop, though the Pope be against it, may go to a straight manner of living and profess religion. To this, beside many other good answers, the Bishop saith that it is very dangerous to follow such private inspirations, under colour whereof the devil doth and hath

[a] Alii appellant Grosthead.   [b] [Causa] 19, q. 2, cap. [2] Duæ sunt

circumvented many men, transforming himself into the angel of light, as he sheweth out of Gerson." Now the Canon that Urbanus speaketh of was made to stay and represse infamous and naughtie men of the clergy, which, to procure the impunity of their naughty doings, fly to another diocese where they are unknown; for the avoiding of which inconvenience it was ordained that no man should be received into another diocese without the letters commendatory of his own Dyocesan Bishop, which decree or Canon, which Urbanus calleth the law public, it is no marvel if it do not bind a good and virtuous priest following the inspiration of the Holy Ghost, which Urbanus calleth the law private, but that he may least be lett from his holy purpose, go into [p. 141] another diocese to profess himself a religious man without his ordinary's license. This is the very meaning of Urbanus, which cannot in any wise be stretched to our case, for God himself hath commanded that no man break matrimony. And there cannot be in any man an inspiration of the Holy Ghost to break and dissolve the same. But this must needs proceed from an evil spirit, being contrary to God's own commandment

We are now come to the conclusion and shutting up of the book; which is farced with many untruths.

First, that they have by many reasons well and sufficiently shewed that the prohibition of this marriage standeth not by man's constitution, but is planted in man's heart by nature. If this were true then could it not be possible but some of those excellent learned men which we have spoken of should have had this natural knowledge? Nay, then, could it not be but that every man generally should by and by without any teacher by the privy and secret instinct of nature know this marriage to be unlawful, which is a thing too much absurd to be spoken or thought?

Secondly, they say that as nature planted this prohibition, so afterwards chastity and reverent shamefastness kept it before the

" Gerson in libello de probatione Spirit.

law, as though the Patriarch Judas, and [p. 142] other Jews before the law, that married their children to their brother's wives, were void of this reverend chastity and shamefastness. At which time this kind of marriage was necessary to keep in remembrance the difference and diversity of the tribes and families. They add further that our Lord shewed this prohibition to his chosen people by Moses. Full well said, for God himself commanded this marriage by a general law. They say, moreover, that the custom of Christian men hath from the beginning of the faith followed this marriage. But we say to this that it appeareth at the beginning of the faith, and in the first Counsell that ever was made by the Apostles, that Christian men were bound to no other thing but to abstain from meat offered to idols, from blood and things suffocated, and from fornication, which the Gentiles (as we have said) thought lawful. Wherefore, seeing it was neither forbidden to the Jews nor commanded at the beginning to the Christians, this marriage was then lawful we deny not, but afterwards by divers Councils it was forbidden, but with those the Pope may dispense. But then, last of all, they say that they have sufficiently proved that the Pope's authority cannot stretch so far that he may dispense with such marriages whether they [p. 143] be already made or to be made. This matter indeed is prettily proved of them which have not as yet brought forth as much as one author that expressly so sayeth, whereas there is no small number of divines and Canonists that say the plain contrary. And now we will (gentle reader) for thy better remembrance and confirmation make a short enterviewe of those authors which they have brought forth for their purpose which are chiefly contained in the 3rd and 4th chapter, whereof Origen is the first who maketh no mention of the brother's wife.

Chrisostome maketh mention, but he is all on our side.

Basile speaketh nothing of the brother's wife.

Isichius, though he be foully mangled and maimed, yet doth he affirm that the brother was by the law commanded to marry the brother's wife.

St. Ambrose speaketh of the niece and not of the brother's wife.

St. Hierome saith that Abraham married his sister Sara, though, where he wrestleth against Helvidius the heretic, he saith otherwise.

St. Austine against Faustus speaketh of this marriage, but on our side, and saith that although the Church doth not now observe the Deuteronomicall commandment yet that marriage was not damnable. But he speaketh more on our side in other places as we have shewed.

[P. 144.] Anselmus writeth of kinsfolk, and no one word in especial of the brother's wife.

Rupertus neither treateth of the brother's wife nor yet standeth otherwise against us.

Hugo, if his testimony had not been foully corrupted, had made full for us.

Hildebert and Ivo spake of kinsfolk and that indifferently of all within the seventh degree.

Walterus also doth the like.

St. Thomas hath nothing against our case.

Altisiodorensis, though he be evil favouredly handled and mangled, yet doth say nothing prejudicial to us.

Petrus de Palude, who in his youth said this marriage was indispensable, being furnished with more learning, years, and experience, revoked that his opinion.

Antonine, though he were deceived by Petrus de Palude, yet he constantly sayeth, that, the dispensation passed, the marriage cannot be broken.

Astexanus speaketh of prohibition of God's lawe, and that is out of our case.

John Bacon, if he had not been evilly handled and depraved, had made for us.

Woodforde doth except our case from the Levitt. prohibition.

Walden disputeth generally of the said prohibition, and not specially of our case.

[P. 145] Johannes Andreas and Abbot Panormitane, whereas they entreate of our case, stand on our side.

Nicholaus de Lyra doth ever except our marriage from the Levitt. prohibition.

Alexander's Decretal, well considered, doth, as we have said, nothing hurt our case.

And these be the authors whom they have in their third and fourth chapter alleged for the establishing of their assertion. Wherefore, seeing their own authors nothing serve for them, though they have foully and shamefully corrupted, depraved, mutilated, and mangled them to racke and wrenche them to speak on their side, there can no indifferent man say or think that they have well and sufficiently proved their matters, or that they can get (seek where they will), either at the hands of the universities or elsewhere, better help than they have gotten already.

Thus now (good reader) have you heard a full answer made by the reverend father in God and holy martyr the Bishop of Rochester, and by me faithfully extracted and abridged; the last only sentence, about a nine or ten lines, being unanswered either because he did not finish his book or that my copie [p. 146] doth lack it. Howsoever it be, there is no material thing in it to be answered, and therefore the answer may be the better spared.

Whosoever will now leisurely and attentively weigh and ponder these answers to the foresaid book made for the justifying of the King's divorce (though they be not for avoiding of too much prolixity so fully and exquisitely set forth as in the principal author) shall yet find good cause highly to marvel of the King's doings and of theirs, that either procured or consented to the same divorce. And shall evidently see withal that this good Bishop did not, upon any rashness or wilfulness, but upon a godly conscience, grounded upon sufficient matter and cause, refuse the oath delated to him for the confirmation of the same divorce. He shall consequently see the very same in Sir Thomas Moore also, who had diligently perused, weighed, and considered the book made for the said divorce, and every point thereof, and was very ripe and ready in these foresaid answers, and divers others that might be made to the same book. And had thereupon most lawful cause to reject the said oath, and was wrongfully for refusing the same imprisoned and otherwise grievously mulcted. Albeit now the foresaid answer and matter [p. 147] of the good and blessed Bishop be so full perfect and absolute in itself as there needeth nothing else to be adjoined in this cause, yet, because I intend to keep nothing back from thee (gentle reader) that may seem requisite to a more perfect and exquisite answer, especially in such things as the Bishop hath not meddled withal, and in answering such objections as by him are not touched, and such other things as perchance he had not seen, and whereof many chanced after he was put to death; the better I say to take away all manner of scruple and to strengthen the said refusal made by Sir Thomas Moore, I thought it very convenient to enlarge this treatise with our particular answers to the premisses also, which I intend to do concerning such books only as be yet come to my hand, of the which one is a counsell of Ægidius de Bella Mera, written long before our time, which the adversaries do allege for their side. The other is a counsel also of one Marcus Mantua, a learned man of our time and a professor of the Civil Law at Padua. The third is a little treatise in Latin made by our countryman Mr. Robert Wakefeild. The fourth and last is a little English book in form of a dialogue entitled *The glasse of truth*. To the which four books we shall make [p. 148] answer for so much as shall seem necessary or convenient, and shall comprise our said answer in the second book now following.

THE END OF THE FIRST BOOK.

The second booke of Doctor N. Harpsfield's Treatise of Marriage.

WE will then first begin with the said Egidius, and with the better will, because we shall have occasion to add and supply somewhat to the Bishop's answer touching our countryman John Bacon, of whom Egidius speaketh, whom I suppose the said Bishop had not seen. The which John Bacon was clapped and whistled out of Rome (as our aforenamed English translator doth translate the said Latin book) for maintaining that opinion that we do now. The cause whereupon the said Egidius was consulted resteth upon this point.[a] Bernard, the Earl of Arminach, desired Pope Clement the Sixt, that upon certain reasonable causes he might be dispensed withal to marry his brother's wife, who had by her two daughters living; whereupon great consultation was taken. Egidius wrote thereof a counsell and was himself of that opinion, that [p. 2] the Pope should not nor could not dispense therewith. There were also two doctors of divinity and five doctors of the decrees that thought the case was indispensable. Their chief grounds were these:

First, that it was forbidden by God's law. Thou shalt not discover the filthyness of thy brother. Now with God's law the Pope cannot dispense, for that the inferior cannot break the law of the superior. And the very case seemeth to be in the canon law prohibited. The reason of the which prohibition is that this act is against the fraternal reverence, and that nature doth abhor such copulation, by reason of the unity of the flesh, and that the civil law doth punish such marriages; which opinion also he saith Petrus de Palude did hold, of whose authority he maketh a special ground.

[a] Egidius, Consilio 1—8.

Furthermore it was said that this is a moral precept and so indispensable. For this prohibition is founded in a moral and natural reason that we should not discover our brother's filthiness. Beside this they say that this dispensation did nourish sin, and did change the whole state of the Church, which lyeth not in the Pope's power to do. Now that it nourisheth sin it appeareth by this, that it discovereth the filthyness of thy brother, which is counted a dishonest thing among men; and that copulation is called in the said 18 chap. incest and in the 20 a thing unlawful, and so it seemeth [p. 3] it was even before the law, and so an evil thing by that very law of nature. And that this dispensation changeth and altereth the general state of the Church it appeareth (say they) by this, that the Church at this day generally abhorreth this kind of marriage; and for that it hath not been seen or heard that such a dispensation hath been given forth but only in the chapter *Deus, De divortio*. They say further that affinity, which is the cause of the prohibition, doth even after the dissolution of the matrimony continue; and therefore the effect also doth continue, which is the prohibition of carnal copulation. This is a summary effect, the substance of all their reasons. The which, forasmuch as they may be easily answered by that we have already said, and for that it were but a superfluous and tedious thing severally to repeat every answer again, we will leave the most part of it to the reader's own diligence, but some part thereof as shall be most necessary and requisite we will now answer.

Touching then the said chapter *Literas*,—It was answered on the other side that it was not spoken asseverantly but opinionatively, and by the way of allegation; and that our case was not comprised under these degrees, and that the meaning of the said chapter is that those degrees cannot be dispensed withal, without a just and reasonable cause. But to this chapter we shall say more in our answer to [p. 4] Marcus Mantua. To the chapter *Sunt quidam* it was answered that there is a great difference in taking away the law of the Church and quite destroying of it; and in dispensing with the same in some certain case, the law generally remaining in force otherwise. It was said also that the said chapter was to be understood in matters of faith, which the Pope cannot alter and change. Whereas it was said that such dispensations had not been used in the Church; thereof is no certainty, neither will it follow thereof that it cannot be dispensed withal; and perchance either no such case happened or there was no just and sufficient cause to dispense with it.

Now among other that did hold on our side was Martinus de Salva, the Cardinall of Pampilona; for the maintenance of which side many things were alleged, and among other that, albeit in the second degree of consanguinity in the line collateral and unequall (as the uncle to marry the niece) it was not wont to be dispensed withal, yet upon a reasonable cause occurrent, especially touching the commonwealth, the Pope might dispense; and that Vincentius was of that opinion, and Tancredus the Glosse and Johannes de Savo and Hostiensis. It was then said that the Pope may dispense with the law of God according as we have before said of oaths and vows and such like. It was moreover said that men should not marry against these prohibitions of their own private authority, and not meant but that some might marry upon a toleration and dispensation; and that this dispensation is not against the mind of the law [which hath a condition implied, that is, unless it be dispensed withal, for it is sufficient to keep the mind of the law]. But the chief reason of all which the said John Bacon most rested upon, and by the which he defendeth our part, was, that this precept is either moral, judicial, or ceremonial. Then said he the judicials and ceremonials do not now bind us in the time of the New Testament. He made upon this a foundation that no precept of the Old Testament doth bind us at this day as a precept of the Old Testament; for if it be a moral precept it bindeth us by the way of nature, and if it were a judicial or ceremonial it bindeth us (as we have said) never a whit. And this was as I said but a judicial and no moral, for if it had been a moral it should have bound all men, and at all times. But this did bind but the Jews only, to whom it was given, neither did it bind them before the time of the law. And if it had been a moral precept it could not have had a law made to the contrary as this had in the 25 of Deutrinomie.

Finally it was alleged that the Pope had dispensed in this case. But these arguments the adversaries [p. 6] went about to dilute and solve; which solutions that most touch the effect of the matter we shall now declare unto you. Concerning the Pope's dispensations for oaths, vows, and such like, they said they were to be tolerated because the Church had tolerated and admitted them, and that the solemnity of the vow cometh but of the positive law. But then said they that the Church had not admitted this dispensation. And to this we answer that at the beginning, when the Pope did first dispense with oaths and vows, men might have made the same reason that these men make now, and yet the dispensation should have been of never the less value. And, whatsoever was in Egidius' time, the Church hath since admitted this kind of dispensation. For if the Pope may dispense with such things as so nearly touch God's own honour in such things as we have before specified, he may much more dispense in those things that touch but man only, and his dishonesty; though in very deed there is no dishonesty done to the dead brother (as we have shewed) if the brother marry his wife dying without children. Now, albeit the solemnity of the vow is as they affirm but positive, yet the power and efficacy of that kind of vowe is stronger than in a single unsolempe vow; for in a single vow there is but a bare promise, no man receiving [p. 7] the same nor the party presently executing the same. But in the other the party presently and actually giveth the possession of his body and soul to God and to divine uses, and his said promise is by a meet and convenient minister accepted.

To the chapter *Deus* they said that the Pope did dispense with the Lyvonians only being lately converted to the faith as God did with the Jews in the said 25 of Deut. and as he did before the law was given, and as he hath done and doth yet tolerate this marriage amongst the Paynims. For though it be a moral precept, yet God himself may dispense with it. But how insufficient this answer is it may easily be seen by that we have already said and shall hereafter more largely say in our answer to Marcus Mantua. Howbeit Egidius himself dareth not absolutely avouch this to be a moral precept, or that it did of necessity bind men before the law of Moses; but sayeth that natural reason doth so instruct us by a certain decency and honesty. But we have before sufficiently shewed that it is both decent and honest, yea and correspondent to natural reason, that the brother should marry the brother's wife dying without children. And therefore Egidius doth but gather [a] conclusion of his own head when he saith that albeit this precept were judaicall, yet because [p. 8] it draweth so nigh to a moral and natural precept God's mind was to astringe and bind the Church perpetually to it; which he saith doth so appear because the universal Church doth so receive and observe it in the time of grace. How chanceth it then that God himself did command this marriage (especially in our case) in the 25 of Deut.? as for Egidius' reason a man might make the like of the prohibitions in the fivt, sixt, and seventh degree of consanguinity and affinity which were in ure many a hundred year before the time of Innocentius the third; and yet that reason had been of no force, for both before his time those degrees were sometime dispensed withal, and ever since, the said prohibition is totally taken away. Now many degrees of consanguinity, which the Church hath dispensed withal, should seem to draw nearer to a moral or natural precept than this; for that consanguinity originally ariseth of nature itself, whereas affinity ariseth but of marriage and by reason of consanguinity; hereto may be added the judgment of many great learned men that no prohibition of affinity is mere moral, nor forbidden by the law of God, but only (as we have said) by the constitutions of the Church.

Howsoever it be with other prohibitions of affinity, this was not so straight but that it was once commanded by God himself, if the brother dyed [p. 9] without children. And therefore, though affinity remain between the said wife and her husband's brother, yet it enforceth not so far that the Pope cannot dispense with it. Beside, if this reason of theirs did hold, the Pope could dispense with no degree of affinity prohibited by the Church, which is evidently untrue. Wherefore there was no cause why John Bacon should be clapped and whistled out of Rome for his foresaid opinion, which his adversaries were not able to confute nor the patrons of this divorce, but rather that they and their adherents should be so served. And truly there was no such thing done, as this translator here mistaketh out. It is only a superficial trick of this man's own invention to enforce the matter the more before the eyes of the ignorant. Neither his own authors whom he hath translated say so, but only this. *Ad hæc Baconus Roma olim explosus quod diversam sententiam aliquandiu tueretur*, which may be Englished thus, *Furthermore Bacon was reproved and rejected long ago at Rome because he was for a season of a contrary mind and judgment*. And, although *explodere* doth sometimes signify to reject with clapping of hands, yet the whistling and hissing out is rather *exsibilare* then *explodere*, which most commonly is used in Cicero and other good authors to repudiate and reject [p. 10] without any whistling or clapping at all. Neither his own authors (as I suppose) took the word here otherwise; and if the translator would gainsay it then might a man ask of him, and of his authors too, what original writer they had for their discharge. They shew none, I am assured, [and as well I am assured] that they can show none of more antiquity and credit then is the said Egidius, who in very deed when he had rehearsed John Bacon's opinion said, *Sed omnes fuerunt contra,—But all were against him*, meaning of the said seven doctors; but here is no word of the wonderful and spiteful exaggeration of clapping and whistling. Yet will we go a little nearer to the said translator and his authors also. We say then boldly,

First, that he was neither whistled nor clapped out of Rome, nor else otherwise rejected for any such opinion as they lay to his charge, for he did not defend that the Pope might dispense with the degrees forbidden by God's law; as doth evidently appear in the said Egidius;

but he said, and that truly as we have declared, that the law of God given to the Jews by Moses ceaseth and doth not now bind us, further than as it containeth the law of nature and moral precepts, whereof he took this [(even as the truth is) to be none but a mere judicial.

Secondly, we say] that even Egidius himself, though he were of that judgment that the Pope could nor should not dispense, yet when he had once dispensed [p. 11], and thought he had lawfully done it, he would in no case that any man should disobey or resist him therein; which is fully enough and sufficient to fortify and strengthen this marriage that we intreat of.

Thirdly, we say that albeit the said Egidius and the seven doctors were in the better opinion, and John Bacon in the worse, and that he was indeed and perchance worthily clapped and whistled out; yet all this maketh nothing in the world against us by reason of the great diversity of that and of our case; for the said earl had two children by his wife, and so the 25 of Deut. doth nothing help his case as it doth ours. Neither the said chapter *Deus*, which are our two principal stays, whereof the said earl's brother could claim no benefit. Beside this it may appear even by John Bacon's adversaries that there was no urgent cause to dispense with him as there was in our case. So that these great odds and disparities do quite alter the cases; which thing the authors of the same Latin book saw well enough I suppose, and that the very said counsell made rather against them than anything for them; and therefore, though they use suspiciously this word *explosus*, and the other rudely and rashly translateth it clapped and whistled out, yet neither the one nor the other durst name either Egidius or any other original author. Neither will John Bacon's adversaries' [p. 12] answer to the said 25 of Deut. satisfy any learned man, when they say it was but a dispensation given by God himself, who may dispense even with the law of nature if he will; which we deny not, but then we say that this is no natural or moral precept. Now in case it were but a dispensation, yet if God did permit the brother to marry his brother's wife to raise up seed to him, and that his house and family should not be spoiled and destitute of an heir, though it were not certain that any such should follow (for both the second brother might be as unable to get children as the first, and the wife might be naturally barren); surely there may accurre even now as great or greater causes touching the whole public weal and so urgent, as they may seem able and sufficient to crave and extort at the Pope's hands some dispensation. Howbeit we boldly say that the said 25 of Deut. was no dispensation, but a mere positive law of God, as much binding the Jews as did any other law in the whole Pentateuch; and we do not a little muse that either the adversaries of John Bacon or our adversaries now, and these universities, especially of Patavium and Bononie, do make but a dispensation of it. But it is much worthy the marking and to be marvelled at, to consider what drift and shift the adversaries are driven to while they [p. 13] go about to illude and avoid the said 25 chap. of Deuteronomy; for, to go no further than to these four which we have now in hand to confute, each of them have their [several] fancy and dream for the taking and understanding of the said chapter. Well, we will turn over the residue for the while till their time come, and confute first the adversaries of John Bacon, with whom we are now in hand. I say then that Josephus, Tertullian, Isichius, St. Austine, and the residue of the old fathers, with the latter writers, as Rodulphus Flaviacensis, Albertus Magnus, St. Thomas, Lyra, and all other as well old as new expounding or writing of this place, take it for a plain preceptive law; and so also all the Jews do and ever have done and do practise it accordingly. Yea, Alphonsus and Lyra affirm that this same very commandment (with many other beside) was by mouth and tradition without writing given to the Jews before the law of Moses. And Moses himself, before the law was given in the Mount Sinay, saith, when there shall arise any controversy among the people, let them come to me for judgment that I may shew them the laws and commandments of God. This then being a plain and open commandment, it is too much absurdity to make this glosse, that it is but a dispensation. Then whereas a dispensation is but a gracious releasing to some [p. 14] certain person or persons of the common written law; they must shew us a commandment before, which was released. In the law of nature they can shew no such; but perchance they will say this commandment appeareth in the 18 of Levit. where the Jews were utterly forbidden to marry their brothers' wives; which commandment was in part released if the brother died without issue; even as if where the law of the Church doth forbid all marriages within the fourth degree the Pope should dispense with some certain persons to marry within the said degree. But this is too farre wryed and wrested. For albeit the law of Moses be now divided into five books, and therefore called the Pentateuch, and several names given to every book; yet was it originally written by Moses all under one tenure and order, without any such diversity and names of books, and the Deuteronomicall law, as principal a law as the Leviticall. Again, the Pope nor no man else maketh a dispensation by the way of a law; between which is a marvellous great difference; for the law bindeth, the dispensation looseth from the bond of the said law. The law hath respect to that which for the most part is good to be observed. But, because it may so chance that it were not good to astringe some certain person or persons to the strait observation of the same law, there must be somebody that must have authority in such cases occurrent to remit and release the observation of the said law. Now the dispensation commandeth no man to take it, and is not lyghtly gotten but upon special suit, and toucheth but certain persons. The law commandeth, and is made without any such suit, and toucheth all alike. For refusing a dispensation no man is shamed, dishonested, or punished. For infringing and disobeying the law, there is a punishment set, accompanied with shame and dishonesty, as it chanced to those that refused to obey the said Deuteronomicall law. For such a person was brought before the elders and judges to persuade and entreat him to marry his brother's wife; wherein if he stood stiffly and peremptorily, he and his house lived ever after in perpetual and public ignominie, obloquy, shame and dishonour. Now if a man will consider what a great punishment it is for a man to be beaten with public ignominie and shame, and what a great bond or bondage rather marriage is, and yet, this notwithstanding, that the brother should be put to this open shame for refusing to marry her whose manners and conditions he neither liked nor had cause to like; he shall soon perceive that this was not by the way of dispensation but by the way of a hard and [p. 16] severe law. Moreover as in any civil or politic commonwealth the lawmakers are not wont to be so overseen to make two laws, whereof the one should be but a dispensation of the other; so much less is it to be thought that God, in whom is infinite wisdom, or rather who is the very infinite wisdom himself, should make (and that all at one time) two laws, whereof the one should dispense with the other. Neither can it stand with his infinite divine wisdom and providence that we should once imagine that God should generally interdict all manner of marriage with the brother's wife, and yet by-and-by [relent from his former mind and remit part of the said prohibition, and that by] the way, form, and order of a commandment to the contrary. These things are too far out of square so to be taken. Beside this, if it be a dispensation of the written law, then must it follow that the written law is released to some certain person or persons and not to all. But this releasement is general to all the Jews; yea, it is a very commandment to the whole nation to observe and keep this marriage, and so dispensation it cannot be; unless they can assign me some other that are bound to keep this law, this dispensation notwithstanding. Yes, marry, saith Egidius and the other doctors, this law bindeth all men, though by God's permission the infidels have been and be now tolerated to do [p. 17] otherwise, which is but a slender and an untrue answer and contrarious to that they said before; for if this marriage (as they say) be forbidden by the law of nature, the infidels be not, nor never were exempted; and for such marriage, though there were no other law to the contrary, they might be justly damned. And, if it be a precept moral, all nations now be and ever have been under pain of perpetual damnation obliged to the said precept. But I would faine ask of these doctors how God of his justice can damn any man for this marriage, seeing that himself commanded the same to the Jews. I would fain know how this man should get such knowledge (especially knowing this commanded to the Jews and prohibited by no other written law) as he should or might understand that this marriage is so highly abhorred and detested of very nature as these men pretend it is. Surely this man's ignorance is invincible and therefore by God's justice not to be to him imputed. If now they will say that it is not against the law of nature, but yet against the law of God in the Levitt., our former answer will also serve, for how is it possible for the said man to persuade himself that the marriage is against the Levitt. [p. 18], seeing the very same is commanded in the Deut.? We add to this, that this is but a judicial law of God written to the Jews only, and did nothing bind any other country. Wherefore, seeing other countries were not under Moses' law, they could not be dispensed and tolerated withal for not keeping that law to which they were never bound. And so every way these men's answer of the toleration and dispensation of the Levitt. prohibition is sufficient. And it appeareth evidently that this was a mere binding law as was any other in the Old Testament. The premises well considered; if any man were disposed to follow the rhetorical humour and vaine of this translator he might here exclaim against the said doctors, and say that they were, for their absurd opinion touching the law Deuteronomicall to be a dispensation, worthy to be clapped and whistled out. But such flowers of eloquence I leave to the translator himself. Yet perchance you will say that John Bacon's adversaries might reply that he was foully deceived in affirming that case to be a judicial prohibition when the brother dieth with children, which is a plain moral prohibition contained under the said 18 chap. of Levitt. and nothing to be cased by the 25 of Deut.; whereunto we [p. 19] answer and grant that the said 25 chapter doth nothing help this case. We say further that whether John Bacon were deceived or no, it maketh nothing against our case. Thirdly, we say that it is not certain that either that case is contained under the prohibition Levitt. or if it be that it is a moral prohibition. Truth it is that in St. Austin's time there was a great doubt, as we have shewed, how that prohibition should be taken whereto three interpretations were given.

The one was of the brother that married the brother's wife, the brother yet living.

The second of the brother that died having children.

The third was of the wife that the brother had repudiated.

Now as in the first sort it is certain that it is a moral precept, so for the second and third there is no such certainty, and learned men be therein distracted and divided into sundry minds and judgments. As for the law of nature, all is one whether the brother die with children or without children. Wherefore, as it is not moral in the one case, so it seemeth neither in the other. Nor the Church hath yet definitively pronounced in what sense the said prohibition must be taken. And, therefore, there is great probability in John Bacon's opinion, and no cause in the world why to clap or whistle out or [p. 20] otherwise greatly to reject the said John Bacon's opinion, which surely was one of the learnedest men not only in divinity but universally in all sciences that our country brought forth either at that time or lightlie before or since. Wherefore both our translator and his authors too were greatly to blame to make so little estimate and account of his censure and judgment whom foreign countries had in great admiration; as appeareth as well otherwise as by Paulus Pansa, a learned man among the Italians, part of whose words tending to the commendation of the said John Bacon it shall not be amiss to lay before thee.

Si Dei Opt. Max. (inquit) penetralia adire suadeat animus, nemo accuratius essentiam ejus mandavit litteris. Si rerum causas, si naturæ affectus, si cæli varios motus ac elementorum contrarias qualitates discere exoptet quispiam, hic se officinam affert, Christianæ religionis arma Vulcaniis munitiora contra Judeos solus hic resolutus doctor ministranda tradidit, Messiæ adventum dilucidat, Antechristi aperit venturas fallacias, Mahumeti sectam prosternit, Scripturæ nodos solvit et ænigmata cuncta serenat et cet. And this shall serve for an answer to Egidius.

[p. 21]   An Answer to Marcus Mantua.

Now to come to Marcus Mantua; we say that there is some difference and odds whether we find the opinion of a lawyer in his ordinary reading and exposition of the law or in his counsels, for as Johannes Knappius, a notable learned lawyer, and Zasius' schoolmaster, was wont to say, Doctors sometimes in their counsels have an eye and regard to lucre and gain; yet if any man will say that among our English angels that flew so thick among the divines and lawyers in France and Italy, this man had his fingers and heart pure and clean as well from present receiving as from expectation of all reward, I will not strive with him. It remaineth then only to see and consider the weight and efficacy of his grounds, and withal to consider how substantially he handleth himself in going about to solve such arguments as we have at the beginning of this treatise made for the defence and maintenance of the dispensation.

His principal ground (among other) is the said chapter *Literas*, where the Pope himself confesseth that the [p. 22] see of Rome neither can nor yet is wont to dispense with the degrees by God forbidden, as Marcus saith; this is [in] the 18 of Levit. in the which chapter it is said *Uxorem fratris sui nullus accipiat, Let no man take his brother's wife*, and, *Thou shalt not discover thy brother's foulness*. How can the Pope then dispense with this? For by as good reason he may dispense with a man to commit adultery, murder, theft, and such like, and many other such things he is forbidden to do. And therefore he cannot dispense that a man should keep a concubine, or that a king having a barren wife may marry again. Truly it were an absurd thing to say that the Pope may take away the law of God, which he cannot do, nor yet the law of nature, but only expound it. And in such kind of marriages with which it hath not been wont to be dispensed, the children cannot prosper, as experience sheweth, and the master of the sentences confesseth. Johannes Andreas also saith that he read in the Cronicles of Azolinus de Romano, that the pestilent wars that were raised in Marchia Tarvisana in his time rose upon that, that kinsfolk married by dispensations such as were espoused to their kinsfolk. Again, whereas the [p. 23] Apostles and the fathers have by their sentence defined anything, the Pope cannot make a new law, but ought rather even to spend his life in the maintenance of the same. Now, although the Pope may upon a good cause dispense with man's law, yet can he not for any cause dispense with God's law, especially where there should be occasion of sin. These are his chief grounds and reasons, especially the said chapter *Literas*, which he doth divers ways inforce to his purpose and considereth these words, *All that is not of faith is sin*, after such sort spoken as though the Pope would have said it is indispensable. He doth weigh and ponder also the words of the said chapter, that they be *verba enunciativa principaliter prolata propter se*, principally and of set purpose spoken to intimate that the Pope cannot dispense against that chapter, *non autem narrativa*, and not words of mere narration, but such as do dispose. And if Innocentius had ever meant that the Pope might dispense in any such case, he would have said so, in that place, as he hath done in other places; but he said not so because he knew full well that his authority did not reach so far as to dispense with degrees prohibited by the law of God.

Now for [p. 24] answer to the said chapter *Literas*, if we consider no more, but this only, that this marriage is not against the law of God as we have sufficiently proved, this consideration alone were sufficient to wipe away all that the said Marcus hath said or might say touching the said chapter. Yet for more ample answer we say, that though the Pope naming in the said chapter degrees forbidden by the law of God might seem to mean the Levitt., yet it is to be considered that there be in the said 18 chapter some degrees directly forbidden by the law of nature; and in such it is true, as the said chapter *Literas* saith, and as we say also, the Pope cannot dispense with them. Some other there are which are prohibited only by the law given to Moses, which law, though it be now expired by the death of Christ, yet, because these marriages were once forbidden by the law of God and be now forbidden by the law ecclesiastical, the Pope did not use to dispense with them without just and urgent cause; and this is the very meaning of these words contained in the said chapter, when any degree of consanguinity is objected wherein the See Apostolic cannot or is not [p. 25] wont to dispense. And therefore whether the words of the said chapter be *enunciative* or *dispositive*, seeing our case is not comprised under any prohibition of God's law, it maketh no great force. Now, where it is said that all that is done against conscience is sin, there is nothing meant that this marriage is sinful or indispensable, but only that a man that knoweth his marriage to be within the degrees of consanguinity especially by God's law forbidden, cannot meddle with his wife, for otherwise he should do against his own conscience and knowledge. Nay, Pope Innocentius and this chapter also rather maketh plain for us.

First, for that it speaketh nothing of affinity but of consanguinity, as it appeareth as well in the question proposed to Pope Innocent, as in his answer to the same.

Secondly, for that he saith that a dispensation may be had for marriages prohibited by man's law, and that St. Gregorie in that case dispensed. Now that St. Gregorie dispensed with the Englishmen that married their brothers' wives we have already declared.

Thirdly and lastly, it can in no wise be imagined that this chapter meant of our case, seeing that the very same Innocentius did dispense with the same as we have declared.

And thus have we answered to his third reason and seventh reason also. Concerning his fourth reason, many a blessed man [p. 26] in the Old Testament was born in such wedlock and prospered notwithstanding full well. Yea, blessed Joseph, husband to the Holy

Virgin, Christ's mother, was borne in this kind of marriage. And there is as little doubt but that Christian men marrying their brothers' wives upon good cause, and by lawful dispensation, may now also as well prosper as ever did any of the Jewes, wherein we need not to runne upp to farre and old foreign years. I report me to the state of Spaine and Portugall, how marvellously and wonderfully God hath increased, fortunated, and blessed it, as well at home as especially among the heathens, since King Emanuell, by the dispensation of Pope Alexander the Sixt, married two sisters, being the daughters of the Catholic King and Queen of Spaine, Ferdinandus and Elizabeth, whose daughter also our worthy Queen Katherine was; after whose divorce England hath so evil prospered, and hath been so overwhelmed as it were with the ocean sea of most grievous miseries, that it pitieth and rueth every good man at the very heart once to remember the same. Johannes Andreas speaketh not of affinity but of consanguinity. And if there arose any such wars the fault was not in the dispensations but in the naughty and corrupt minds of troublesome people. Albeit, it might be true also that some Popes had not so diligent and careful [p. 27] considerations in giving out their dispensations, and in weighing the just causes thereof, as perchance was requisite. Neither doth it evidently appear in Johannes Andreas whether these marriages were dispensed with all or no. To the said chapter, *Quidam*, we say as we said before, that it is to be understood in matters of faith, as in the next chapter *Contra* also, according as the glosse in both doth declare. And as this our case is no article of faith, so is it not any article annexed thereto, as the said Marcus would infer it to be, no more than are other constitutions ecclesiastical that are dispensable, and often be dispensed withal. And as there is no prohibition of God's law, so of the same (being lawfully dispensed with) there riseth no manner of sin in the world, no more than doth in other cases that are daily dispensed withal.

Wherefore it is not true that is pretended in the seventh objection, that the Pope can no more dispense with this than with the vices named in the first objection. Betwixt all which and our case there is a wonderful difference, for they are straitly forbidden, both by the Old and New Testament, and our case by neither; yea, plainly commanded by the Old. This in effect is that which Marcus Mantua setteth forth, though with more ample allegations, for the defence of the contrary assertion [p. 28], which, as it is (as you have heard) but of small force, so let us now ponder what weight and strength his solutions bear, whereby he laboureth hardly to undo and infringe some of our reasons and arguments that we have at the beginning of the process laid forth for the establishing of our side. Among the which he putteth his first and most endeavour and force to overthrow our hould that we have upon the said chapter *Deus*, and upon the 25 of Deut.

In the first, Pope Innocent dispensed with our case.

In the second, it was generally commanded to the Jews.

To the chapter *Deus* he answereth, that the Lyvonians being lately converted to the faith were dispensed withall, least otherwise they might perchance revolt to their old infidelity. He saith that matters of faith, and the advancing of the same, be privileged above all other, and that in favour and furtherance thereof many things are granted which otherwise should not be granted, and therefore this dispensation ought not to be stretched and extended to other causes. Again, these men were copled in this marriage before they were christened, and therefore they might the better be suffered to remain in the said matrimony [p. 29]. Add hereto, saith he, that the special motive and final cause why this dispensation was granted was their new conversion, which cause ceaseth in us, being so long time past christened, and therefore the effect also should cease.

Last of all, he enforceth this chapter to this end,—That as for a just cause, and for the furtherance of faith, the Lyvonians were dispensed withal; so, by these words, *Ne tales sibi de cetero, postquam ad fidem venerint copulent, prohibentes*, Forbidding them that from thenceforth after they were christened none should cople themselves

CAMD. SOC. T

with such persons. He enforceth the said chapter, I say, that they might not now marry with such; no, not upon any just cause or any dispensation whatsoever, that the end of the chapter might be answerable to the beginning, and that which was granted in the former part should [not] be denied in the latter; for if we should construe the said chapter otherwise it would follow that God's open and plain law in the Levit. might be taken away with a new law, which thing must not be granted. And it is against the said chapter *Quidam*. To this we answer, that his chief and principal point wherein he still resteth of the Levitical prohibition is, as we have said, untrue. It is also untrue that this dispensation may not be extended [p. 30] to any other cause than that which is contained in the said chapter; neither this interpretation maketh any correspondency between the beginning and the ending of the said chapter. This is rather a better correspondency to say, that, as the Pope for advancing the faith among the new Christians suffereth this marriage, so, for some other equivalent or ample and urgent commodity touching princes and their whole realms, the Pope may suffer this marriage amongst the old Christians also; wherein to dispense, one Pope cannot prohibit another, no more than he can in other matters that be dispensable. For neither the opinions of the doctors, nor the Pope's constitutions, can bind the Pope or restrain his authority. And so the said law, *Quod vero et jus singulare*, taketh no place no more than in other princes that may extend their predecessors' or their own privilege to other persons and places, albeit the said privileges cannot be by any private authority otherwise claimed, challenged, or extended. And, although the Pope do forbid the said Lyvonians from thenceforth all such marriages, yet is there no word in the said chapter whereby Innocentius restraineth himself or his successors to dispense with the same. Now the consideration that these Lyvonians were married before they were christened maketh rather [p. 31] on our side than against us; for in case this marriage be directly against God's immutable law, as the said Marcus avoucheth, and against both the law of God and nature as the said patrons of the Universities have (as you have heard) stiffly affirmed; then could not Innocent, even by his own decision in the said chapter *Literas*, dispense with the said Lyvonians; for, speaking properly of dispensation, the Pope can dispense with neither of them, as we have said. We may now add to the premisses (and not without good ground and reason) that the Lyvonians married after this sort even after they came to the faith, and yet were by Innocentius dispensed withal. Surely I find such a dispensation or toleration seven hundred years before Innocentius' time, in a counsel holden at Orleaunce. The words of which council (which as yet I have not read in any that have written of this matter) I will fully and wholly lay before you, which sound in English after this sort.

Touching incestuous marriages, let these things which are already decreed be kept; yet so, that we think good for them that either now come to baptism, or that by the preaching of the priests have not before heard of the fathers' decrees, according to their lateness of their conversion and of their faith, so to provide that the marriages [p. 32] already contracted be not dissolved; yet, that from henceforth that which is by the former canons forbidden touching incestuous marriages be observed, that is, that no man presume under colour of marriage to cople himself with his stepmother, or with his brother's wife, with his wive's sister, with his cousin germaine or cousin germaine removed, or with his uncle's wife by the father's or mother's side. And in case any join and cople themselves in this incestuous adultery rather than marriage, let them be kept from the ecclesiastical communion until they separate and divorce themselves; yet this we think good to be added, that it shall be left to the bishop to weigh and consider touching such as be in his diocese copled after this manner, whether they fell into this unlawful marriage by ignorance, or presumed by wilful disobedience to attempt such things as be forbidden; for as they are to be holpen and relieved that ignorantly fall into the lapse, so against them that knew before the fathers' decrees, and yet contrary to their prohibition do in this sort join themselves, let the old canons in every point take place, and let them not be received to the communion till they have by separation and departing cured this adultery according as it is ordained; for in the law of God it is written, Cursed [p. 33] be he that lieth with his father's wife, with his wive's daughter, his wive's sister, or such like; whereupon it followeth that whom God hath cursed we cannot (unless they amend) bless. So far goeth the decree.

Loe, here is first to be considered that this marriage is tolerated, even contracted by those that were christened, which had not heard of the fathers' decrees.

Secondly, that this marriage was tolerated by them whose authority is far under the Pope's.

Thirdly, that hereby we may understand also what Pope Innocent meant in his dispensation with the Lyvonians (which you shall anon hear of) by these words, *for the infirmity of that nation.*

Fourthly, that even the mother-in-law is dispensed withal.

Fiftly, that it should lie in the bishop's power to examine and discuss whether this marriage was contracted by ignorance or no.

Sixtly, that it may appear by these fathers' decree that all these marriages be not so straightly forbidd that as well Christian men as other are bound to take knowledge of all such prohibitions, or that every man hath the knowledge thereof by very natural instinct without any teacher or instructor.

Seventhly, that these prohibitions bind us not by the virtue and strength of the law ecclesiastical.

Eightly, there is no distinction or difference whether the deceased brother knew his wife, or whether he left any children or no.

Ninthly [p. 34] and lastly, that though neither the cousin german removed nor yet the nearer cousin german be comprised in the Levit. law of God, nor yet the wive's sister, the wife being dead; yet these fathers call all these marriages adulteries, and do apply the Levitticall prohibition to such as were not there forbidden, but are only by the Church prohibited; which thing is well to be observed and noted for that the patrons of the universities do make such a business to prove that this marriage should be by the law of God and nature prohibited, because the fathers do call it incest and adultery, with such like names.

St. Gregorie, as we have said, did also dispense and tolerate this matrimony here in England, but whether it were with such as married after they were christened (as these bishopps did) I cannot so precisely avouch; it is possible enough and may be as it seemeth gathered out of his own words; for although he do speak of such as were married in infidelity, yet it may be gathered that he meaneth also of those Christians that had no commandment or instruction to the contrary. And, therefore, he writeth thus, *But all such as come to the faith are to be warned that they can do no such thing, and if they do they are to be kept from the communion* [p. 85] *of the body and blood of Christ, for as in those things which they have done ignorantly their fault is somewhat to be born withal, so it is mightily to be punished in them that are not afraid wilfully to trespass.* You hear that he requireth warning to be given, you hear that the fault may be somewhat tolerated in them that do ignorantly sin.

Wherefore the new Christians (this being no matter of faith) may justly pretend ignorance if they were wont thus to marry, and never heard of any prohibition to the contrary afterwards. Again, if this marriage be neither against the law of nature nor the law of God in the Old or New Testament, what fault can be laid to them that do marry after this manner while they are infidels? Wherefore, whereas St. Gregorie said that they which come to the faith should be warned to abstain from this marriage and understand it to be a great sin, it seemeth that it must of necessity be taken of such as married after they were christened and had warning to the contrary. Upon these considerations and even by Innocent's own words in the said chapter *Deus,* it may be inferred that these Lyvonians were thus married after that they had embraced the Christian faith. I will now recite [p. 36] unto you the words of the decree: *Because the Lyconians lately converted to the Catholic faith have a manner and custom dis-*

crepant from ours, we grant for the infirmity of that nation that they may continue in their marriages which they have contracted with their brothers' wives, so that they have contracted this marriage to stir up seed to the deceased according to the law of Moses, forbidding them from henceforth, after they shall be christened, that they couple themselves with none such. We say then that if the Lyvonians married before they were christened in this sort, the marriage being agreeable to their custom, conformable also to the law of God and nature, and forbidden only by the laws ecclesiastical, they had no need of any dispensation at all, and that the Church had nothing to do with it, nor could break it, according to St. Paul's saying, *De his quæ foris sunt, nihil ad nos.* But if they married after they were christened and so obliged to the constitutions ecclesiastical; then there needed indeed a dispensation to supply the fault and defect of their marriage, which seemeth here to be granted to the Lyvonians for their infirmity; which infirmity stood either in their infirm and weak knowledge of the manners, right, and custom [p. 37] of the Christians in marrying, or in their frailty, lest they should otherwise fall and return to their old errors again. Thus much now to the said chapter *Deus.*

Our other principal reason taken out of the 25 of Deuteronomy he would fain avoid, but it will not be. He telleth us that Scripture is to be expounded four ways, by the historical, by the allegorical or figurall, by the annagogicall, and by the tropologicall sense, and saith that this commandment is now to be taken not in the literal but in the figurative sense; and, seeing the verity is now spread abroad, the figure ceaseth. He declareth also what this figure is. But because it is more lively and originally set forth in St. Austine we shall shew you his words therein.

St. Austine therefore saith that this figure signifieth every preacher of the Gospel, which is bound so to travel in the Gospel that he stir up seed unto his brother departed which is Christ. And the seed must have the name of the brother that is departed, and therefore we are called Christians. Wherefore, saith he, doubtless, we be not now bound to keep and observe this law carnally by bodily generation, according to the old understanding and meaning, but after a spiritual meaning and by spiritual [p. 38] and ghostly generation; which saying of St. Austine is nothing against this marriage, and forceth no further, but that the figure is now fulfilled and that we are not bound to this commandment. But he doth not drive his argument to any such end that this marriage is now unlawful, or that it may not be used. For it is very certain and a received conclusion among the divines that the judicialls may be by the Church or by the positive law of any Christian prince revived and received again. There was a commandment given to the Jews that they should not seethe a kid in his mother's milk, which was a figure to signify that Herode for all his cruel murder upon the innocents in seeking for Christ should not slay him being an infant, as Chrisostome declareth; there was also a meaning in that commandment to induce men to shun cruelty, and to use mercy towards their neighbours. There was also another commandment given them even in the same chapter, where the brother was commanded to marry the brother's wife; that they should not muzzle the oxe's mouth while he was threshing the corn; whereby was meant that he that travelled in setting forth and preaching the Gospel should have his living by the same, as St. Paule himself expoundeth it [p. 39]. Again, this was a judiciall law amongst them, that if a man had by chaunce medlye without any prepensed mischievous mind slain a man, he might have refuge to certain towns appointed and save himself and life, and such were delivered and set at liberty at the death of the high bishop, whereof our sanctuaries have now a certain resemblance. Furthermore, if any man did disobey the high priest's sentence he should die for it, which was a figure and shadow of the high authority which our high priest the Pope, Christ's vicar in earth, should have and hath in the Catholic Church; which thing as it was figurative and yet taketh place at this day, so might also the former law touching murderers that were discharged at the high priest's death (which was a figure of our deliverance by the death of

Christ) be in some part of christendom revived, with many other judicialls, whereof divers are now incorporated into the canon law; and among all other this our case of marrying our brother's wife, especially if it so chanced (as it is possible) that in some country replenished with Jewes the said Jewes would come to the faith of Christ, if they were permitted, as they were wont to do, to marry their brothers' wives, so that it be provided they be not bound to this as part [p. 40] of Moses' law now obliging them. Wherefore as the fathers at the council of Orleance dispensed with the Frenchmen, St. Gregorie with us, Innocentius the 3rd with the Livonians, to marry their brothers' wives, notwithstanding this was but a figurative commandment, so might Pope Julius for the common repose and tranquillity of both so great realms and dominions dispense with these two so noble personages. Ye will here perchance demand of me, if this marriage may be by any means lawful, why is it not now commanded by the Church as it was by Moses to the Jewes, seeing that all the prohibitions Mosaicall touchinge marriage be by the Church restored and commanded? Which your demand, though that which we have said out of St. Austine may somewhat satisfy, yet for your better contention we will adjoin some larger answer.

We say then that the said prohibitions be upon very good grounds renewed, for, seeing one of the principal reasons why marriage is restrained between those which are of kindred and alliance is for the multiplication and increase of love, friendship, and charity in marrying other, being strangers in blood, and seeing that this love and charity is more increased and multiplied in the time of the New Testament than it was [p. 41] in the time of the Old, it standeth with good reason that now the said prohibitions should not only be revived, but other also should be cast unto them as there are. Again, natural reverence, obedience, and shamefastness, that we owe to our parents and other of our ancients, forbiddeth these marriages; which causes (beside other which we need not now recite), seeing they do take place now and have their force, the said prohibitions take also place and force. But it is not so in the commandment given to marry the brother's wife; for among other causes was that the brother deceased might continue his name and family by his brother's child (which should be counted not his brother's but his own), and that he might avoid the shame and infamy wherewith they were noted and beaten in the old law which had no children ; this reason I say ceaseth in the new law, as appeareth by so many thousands dedicating themselves to perpetual chastity, which with us are no infamous persons but counted most happy and blessed, and wynne thereby perpetual honour and renown; as Isaias the prophet did prophesy long before, *Non dicat Eunuchus, Ego lignum aridum etc., quia hæc dicit Dominus Eunuchis qui, &c. dabo eos in domo mea et* [p. 42] *in muris meis locum et nomen melius et filiis et filiabus, nomen sempiternum dabo eis quod non peribit.* Accordingly whereunto, Christ saith: *Sunt Eunuchi qui seipsos castraverunt propter regnum Cælorum. Qui potest capere capiat.* Math. 19. This was also another cause; for before the coming of Christ the true and sincere religion of God remained amongst the Jews only, and so with their carnal generation and propagation was propagated and spread abroad. And therefore God would not they should marry with strangers or out of their own tribe, and that the brother should marry his brother's wife dying without issue, which reason now ceaseth, christendom being spread so far and wide and into so many nations. This may serve for this demand.

Let us now return to Marcus Mantua, whose two solutions being removed out of the way, we have no need now long to tarry about the residue, being of smaller importance and almost hanging upon one string and already in a manner answered. If we tell him of the Pope's ample authority given to him by Christ himself, he telleth us again that yet he cannot dispense with God's law, especially when as occasion is given to sin. If we tell him that the Pope must interpret doubtful and perplexed cases [p. 43], especially any question rising upon a dispensation, he telleth us that there is no manner of doubt in the world but that this dispensation is against God's law. If we tell him that the Pope dispenseth usually in greater matters, as in oaths, vows, and bigamie, he saith the Pope may dispense against the Apostles' order, as in bigamie, yet not against God's own law; whereto we say, that, if he may release the order of the Apostle, much more he may release that order which neither by God nor his Apostles or Evangelists is commanded at this day to the Church.

As for vows and oaths he saith the Pope doth make but a commutation, redemption, or change to the better, which seem to be done by the will and sufferance of God, which thing cannot be done in this case for that God forbiddeth it, and it doth induce sin, and so do not the other. It were well answered if it were as well proved as spoken, but (as we have oft said) it is neither against God's will nor yet breedeth sin. And if the Pope may either dispense or commute those things which seem so highly to derogate God's especial honour and service, why should his authority be barred in this case which nothing tendeth to the infringing of any honour or service especially due to God [p. 44]? Now if we tell him that this case is not foreprised and exempted from the Pope's jurisdiction among such as be specially noted to be exempted,—Yes, saith he, marriages forbidden by God (whereof this is one) are exempted, and withal for that it maintaineth sin. The like answer he giveth to that we have alleged of the long quiet continuance with fruit of children of this marriage, and to that we have also alleged for the Pope's large and ample authority, and finally, for that we have alleged of the just cause, utility, and necessity of this dispensation. And so as it were with one salve he cureth all sores, and with one medicine all diseases of the eyes. And, albeit we might say much more to the overthrowing of his solutions, yet for the avoiding of supervacaneous tediousness we will cut off all such endless matters. But, forasmuch as he disableth the just cause of the said dispensation, and partly by such reasons as I have not otherwise yet heard or read, I will not let this scape altogether unanswered. He saith then that the causes whereupon the Pope groundeth his dispensation (that is for peace, concord, and tranquillity to be had between England and Spain) were not true, forasmuch as at the time that the dispensation was granted [p. 45] there was neither war nor just cause to raise any, nor no suspicion of any war toward. And so is the dispensation in that case as though there had been no cause expressed, and so grounded upon no cause, seeing the cause is not just, and so, consequently, the dispensation void and frustrate; or rather a false cause, and the dispensation given forth without mature consideration and deliberation, which is principally required in a dispensation ; and in such cases the Pope seemeth to be circumvented and deceived by the importunity of the parties. Wherefore, seeing the cause expressed and specified is of no force and disabled, the other cause, wherein the Pope signifieth that he was stirred and induced to give out this dispensation for other causes also moving his mind, is of much less force. Surely there is no manner of probability in this objection, neither any false cause in the world alleged. There was no allegation that there was any war between those nations, but rather to the contrary. And therefore postulation was made that for the continuance of rest, peace, and tranquillity between these realms this dispensation might be granted; and so it was accordingly, as appeareth by the Pope's own words by [p. 46] Marcus alleged. So there was a cause, yea, a true, just, and sufficient cause, expressed; and yet, if there had been none at all, it is a conclusion amongst the doctors of law that when the Prince granteth anything graciously against the law, it is to be presumed and presupposed that there is good cause why, which rule most of all should take place here where the Pope himself confesseth that he was moved by other causes also, whereby he seemeth to supply the defect of the former causes, if there were any. This just cause, I say, is the more here to be presupposed for that after a special there followeth a general clause. And if this lawful cause is to be presupposed in the doings of other judges, much more is it in the Pope for his high dignity and peerless prerogative, wherewith Christ himself hath adorned him. Yea, we say further, though there had been no cause at all, that the dispensation holdeth, and all things issuing upon the same, that notwithstanding. Neither can Marcus Mantua himself deny this; and therefore, yet once again he would shift away this matter with his old shift that this dispensation is amongst God's prohibitions, and therefore it can in no wise stand. Marvel it is now to me that either the Pope should [p. 47] be abused and circumvented by any surreption, or that this matter should be without forethinking and examination hoverly housled and shuffled up that did hang so long in suspense ere it was determined, and whereupon was so great and long consultation had, not only by the counsell and learned men of both the kings, but with the Pope's learned divines and lawyers at Rome also. But most of all I marvel of the pretty protestation that is here full properly devised; for he saith that the king never consented to this dispensation, and did protest the nullity of the same, and that all that he did in contracting the said matrimony he did it for a reverential fear he had of his father. He addeth to this that at the time of the espousing he was not of lawful age, and was also of tender age when by the persuasion of his counsellors he consummated the matrimony with carnal copulation, and saith that this protestation might even at the time when he sued the divorce releive him. But there was never any such just and sufficient protestation lawfully before any judge proved and presupposed, but not granted, that the king ever made any such protestation at all; yet could not this (after so many years) anything releive him, especially seeing his father was dead and himself was king, and of eighteene [p. 48] years of age, when he solemnized the marriage with all manner of royalty, acceptation, and congratulation, as well of himself as of all the realm beside; the said marriage being afterwards adorned and blessed with the fruit of a noble prince, himself never in whole twenty years together repining or grudging against the said marriage; so that it is a great wonder that all this while this protestation should lie lurking (as Marcus imagineth) in the king's heart, and, being as it were hot coals covered with ashes, should after so many long winters burst out into so hot a fire. This, [this] I say, is inopynable, incredible, and a very paradox which Marcus saw well enough, and therefore hath no other shift but to run to his old starting hole of sin, of God's lawe, which we have long ago stopped up. Thus I trust now that every indifferent reader will judge that this great learned lawyer hath brought nothing effectual against this marriage and dispensation. By whom and his allegations he may also ayme and judge all other lawyers of our time which have impugned his marriage, of whom he must not look for better stuff than he hath already found in Marcus Mantua.

An answere to Mr. Robert Wakefeild.

We have now next to say to Master Robert Wakefeild, one of the king's chaplains, and to see whether he may speed better with his divinity for the furtherance of the king's cause than Marcus Mantua did with his law. There is extant in print a little book of his in Latin, written of this matter against the said reverend father the Bishop of Rochester, and some book of his which I have not seen. The effect of the said book runneth to this end,—First, he saith that the whole weight of the king's matter dependeth upon the authority of the holy scripture, the certain and infallible truth whereof is (as he saith) in the Hebrew text, from whence, as from a fountain, as well the Septuaginta as the Greeke, St. Hierome's, and all other translations issued; for the confirmation of the which verity contained in the said Hebrew text he hath made a special book, and in his said answer to the bishop he findeth fault with our common Latin translation.

Secondly, for the matter and marriage itself, he sayeth it was a thing vitious and wicked, abhomination against God, execrable incest against nature, and a thing morally naught of itself. And therefore Pope Julius was an anatheme and accursed [p. 50] for dispensing with the same.

Thirdly, whereas the bishop said that these words, Let no man marry his brother's wife, which are in the Latin bible, were neither in the Hebrew, Chalde, or Greek text, Mr. Wakefeild goeth busily about to prove that they were in them all, yea in the Arabyc too, though not by express words, yet by the very sense, namely, if the brother departed had carnally known his wife.

Fourthly, whereas the said reverend father had alleged Origen and other that understand the said Levitt. prohibitions (the husbands yet living), he endeavoureth to prove that they are to be taken not only (the husbands yet living) but being dead also.

Fiftly, whereas the said reverend father for the defence of the king's marriage had alleged that the like marriage is permitted in the law of Moses, as for one man to marry two sisters, alleging the text as it is in our Latin translation; he taketh upon him to show first, that it is not so either in the Hebrew, Chalde, Arabic, or in the Septuaginta; secondly, he laboureth to prove that there is a great difference between these two cases, and that it is far worse the brother to marry the brother's wife than one man to marry two sisters; thirdly, he sticketh not venterously to avouch that it was not lawful, no not by Moses' law, for one man to marry two sisters, no, though the one were dead. We will now [p. 51] consequently answer to every parcel, so far forth as the necessary defence of our matter craveth at our hands, lest otherwise the work should grow excessive.

We answer, then, that both members of his first assertion are untrue; for the king's matter hangeth not so much upon the bare words of Scripture (which yet doth not forbid the same) as it doth upon the constitutions ecclesiastical, wherewith the Pope may dispense.

Now concerning the Hebrew and other texts (all due reverence thereunto presupposed), we say that the high divine providence is here to be marvelled at; for, while the Jews kept their right faith, the certain and infallible solidity of holy Scripture remained with them. Afterwards, when the Jews were repulsed for their infidelity, and the Greeks received to the faith of Christ, they enjoyed the same benefit and privilege in the New Testament; but, when they also began to sunder and cut themselves away from the body and unity of the Catholic Church, the said privilege for both Testaments remained with the Latin Church; neither is it to be thought that the said Latin Church, in the which the sincerity and purity of the faith doth now rest, and hath these many hundred years rested, had no authenticall scripture in Latin whereby to establish their judgments, censures, and decrees in matters of faith, and [p. 52] whereby (as by a sufficient authority) to subdue, repress, and convict the adversaries of the faith; wherefore there is no doubt but the Holy Ghost inspired to the hearts of the fathers at the Council of Trent to establish, confirm, ratify as authenticall, the common and vulgar translation of the Latin bible. We add now further, that albeit the canonical Scripture be perfect and sufficient in itself to all purposes, yet in the true taking of the same, whether men allege the Hebrew, Greek, or Latin, or any other text, we must follow and embrace that sense only which the Church hath from time to time universally received. And what text soever be alleged, we must reject all other interpretations that are contrary to the received understanding of the Catholic Church; for otherwise, by reason of the high deepness and profundity and obscurity of Scripture, and by reason of the diversity of men's wits, dispositions, and judgments, every man would or might frame a new understanding of his own, as heretics hitherto have done, and at this day (the more pity) most wretchedly do. Wherefore the said Mr. Wakefeild hath too arrogantly taken upon him to control (by reason of his some skill in the Hebrew tongue) the said reverend father and the common Latin translation, [p. 53], and to say withal that the Septuaginta and St. Hierome have translated many things erroneously which are no parcell of Scripture, but their dreams only, and to condemn and to contemn the profound learned scholastic doctors, calling them sophisters, for that they were ignorant of the tongues. And yet, for all his brag of the knowledge of tongues, he was scarce worthy for deepness of knowledge to carry their books after them.

Concerning the second point it were too tedious to add any more to that we have said already; and I pray God that himself be not accursed and smart sore for it, for so heinously and cursedly speaking against the highest magistrates of the Church and Christ's own vicar, for doing nothing else but that which he might lawfully do.

As touching the third point, he maketh a great but a needless stir, for whether those words be in the Levitt. [text or no, the bishop doth not nor needeth not make any great account, for our case is not comprehended under any words of the Levitt.] be they never so general. Surely in all translations hitherto out of the Hebrew, either of ancient time or of late, were they Catholics or were they Protestants, there is no such general clause as in the Latin text; and Nicholaus de Lyra sayeth that in the corrected examples it is neither in the Latin; but then saith Mr. Wakefeild that Lyra was not well advised nor was in his right witts when he so said. And yet St. Austin's Latine [p. 54] bible lacketh that clause, as we have before rehearsed.

And Mr. Wakefeild himself confesseth that it is in no other translation expressedly, but yet he saith it is there implicately, especially when the brother leaveth children, or when he hath carnally known his wife. But loe now (gentle reader) this man that hath been so high and so severe a censurer upon this reverend father, upon Lyra, St. Hierome, and the Septuaginta, and upon the Pope himself, doth now attribute so much to himself, as none of all these nor any other father or Pope, or any rabine among the Jews, hitherto durst, making such a gay glosse to the 25 of Deuteronomy as never was heard before. God by Moses commanded the brother to marry the brother's wife, if he died without children. Nay, saith Mr. Wakefeild, you must add thereto, so that she be left a virgin. But you [will] say it is not [so] to be doubted, but that Mr. Wakefeild hath good authority for him. That shall you see anone. But in the meanewhile he is driven to this shifte to crave help of Nicholaus de Lyra for maintenance of this strange interpretation, although otherwise he rejected him as a madman. And yet somewhat it were, if he had any handfast of him, which surely he hath no more than a man can take of a beardless man's beard. As much handfast hath he [p. 55] upon St. Austine. But St. Gregorie, sayeth he, writeth that we cannot marry that woman which our brother hath known, of the which unity he doth often talk, whereto we will say no more than we have said already before; nor hath St. Gregorie one word that the said 25 of Deut. is so to be understood. His last refuge is to Thamar, which (as he saith) was a virgin when she was espoused to Sela, and before she lay with his father Judas. This is a marvellous virginity indeed, she having had two husbands and being carnally known by both. She was first married to Judas' son, called Har, that played the foul part that Scripture speaketh of, the cause whereof was, as Lyra sheweth, for that he was immoderately affected to the pleasures of his body. And therefore he would not have his wife Thamar to conceive with child, lest that thereby her beauty should decay, and lest he should for the time that she was nigh to be delivered, and until the time of her purification, be constrained to forbear his unmeasurable greedy carnal lust. Now it may appear by the very text that his brother Onan knew her also, though he wickedly did let the procuration of children. But yet, he saith, Chrisostome so sayeth, which were surely greatly to be marvelled, our premisses being considered.

I have diligently [p. 56], for my part, perused the place quoted by Mr. Wakefeild, and yet I find no such thing, as indeed there is none such, nor yet Mr. Wakefeild himself ever found any such thing; yet, when I had afterward better bethought myself, I chanced upon a certain book of Homilies, interspersed among the works of Chrisostome, of whom Mr. Wakefeild seemeth to have taken this testimony, and yet doth he not call her a virgin but *castam*, that is chaste.[a] Now, I trow that Mr. Wakefeild was not ignorant of that which every young grammarian could tell him, that there is a virginal chastity and a matrimonial chastity. The virginal chastity—which is utterly to be unknown—she had not; the other she had, and therefore after she was once espoused to Sela

---

[a] Cum esset casta in meretricem se immutavit. Homilia prima in Matthæum incerto authore.

she lived chastely and continently until that Sela came to marriable years. And then, seeing that Judas kept not promise with her in marrying to her his son, feigned herself a harlot, and lay with Judas.

Now, if Mr. Wakefeild will say that yet this author took the said word *casta* for a virgin, it appeareth to the contrary, even in the very same author; whereas he calleth married women also *castas*, that do not defile their matrimony with adultery. Howbeit, if he had called her a virgin, yet it were to little purpose, as well for that it will not follow thereof that the Levit. must be so understood, as [p. 57] for that this author is not Chrisostome, nor any author of name or credit, but rather a very heretic or grievously thereof to be suspected, as Erasmus saith.[a] Is not this a very strange dealing in so weighty a matter, to frame such a new interpretation as hath not been heard in the Church, and to build it upon an heretical or very suspicious nameless author, and yet the same to have no such thing? But yet we have for the last shift, Rabbi Moses Nechmanides Gerundensis to uphold this assertion. Yet seeing Mr. Wakefeild hath shewed at least his wretchless negligence (I would wish he deserved not a sharper word of wilful perversity and corruption) in alleging Chrisostome, wherein it was easy to try out his truth and honesty, I cannot greatly trust him in alleging this Jew, which is not so easy to be had or understood; or greatly credit him if he had said that Thamar was a virgin, seeing that the residue of the Jews and Scripture itself are against him; for that which we have shewed out of Lyra, of Har, is the opinion of the Jews, as Lyra himself saith; neither doth it appear by Mr. Wakefeild's own allegation that he said so precisely, but only that Sela was but ten years old, and Har and Onan were but twelve, when they married Thamar; wherein, unless we hear what good [p. 58] grounds the said Moses had for his opinion, we may be at our liberty, for anything that I see, to believe at our leisure and pleasure, as also Mr. Wakefeild himself, if he will therefore infer

[a] In prologo dictarum homiliarum incerto authore.

(as it seemeth he doth) that Thamar was a virgin; for St. Hierome writeth that both King Solomon and King Achab had children when they were but eleven or twelve years of age. He sheweth also of a woman about his own time that had a child by a boy that was but ten years of age.[a] Let us now by the way of gratuity grant Mr. Wakefeild that she was a virgin, what probable illation can he make thereof that the Levitt. must be understood of the brother's wife that is a virgin? There is no manner of coherence in the world in this kind of argument. Yet, though Mr. Wakefeild be destitute of authority for upholding this his strange conclusion, he would seem to have some reason to strengthen it withal, and that is, that otherwise the law Levit. and the law Deut. should be quite contrary one to the other. And then he telleth us out of St. Hierome that God cannot be contrary to himself. We will anon ponder the weight of this reason, yet let us first consider the unlikeliness and absurdity of this new conclusion. She must be a virgin, saith he; yea, but how shall this be tried? If they should stand to the bare word [p. 59] or oath of the woman, so might she make herself a virgin or no virgin at her pleasure, and her new husband that hoped to find her a virgin might be fondly deceived, and the law withal as fondly eluded and mocked. If you will say the matter was to be tried by honest matrons, they might also be deceived. Quia manus et oculi obstetricum *sæpe falluntur*, and they might, either for favour or corruption to gratify the one party or the other, report otherwise than truth. Beside, it is not likely that the law meant there should be such a narrow search and examination in this case, being a law astrictive and preceptive. But, if it had been permissively only that the brother might marry the brother's wife, then perchance Mr. Wakefeild's interpretation might the better have been allowed.

Thirdly, it is to be considered that even now, among the

---

[a] In epistola ad Vitalem, Op. 132. And chroniclers report that there was a woman in France, about the year of our Lord 1311, that was delivered of a child, being but nine years of age. Mater histriar.

Christians, from Christ's time hitherto, it is hard to find any sort of examples (albeit some few there be) of married folk that have abstained from all carnal meddling. The first among all the Jews is the singular example of Christ his blessed mother, and good Joseph. Now this being a common law, commanding the brother to marry the brother's wife, and laws being not made for things that very seldom chance (as this case is, the husband not to know his wife), but for things that [p. 60] divers and often times do chance, as Pomponius, Celsus, and Paulus do write, it is not to be thought that the high wisdom of God would make a law for such a rare case.

Fourthly, and most of all, it is to be considered that every law is to be ruled, moderated, and expounded by the final scope and end of the said law. Now, as we have shewed, the reason of the law is that the brother should supply the brother's office and beget a child of his brother's wife, which should be accounted the dead brother's child and bear his name and succeed to him in his inheritance; which reason taketh place whether she be known, or not known, if she have no children; yea, it may appear by the very words of Scripture, *Suscitabit semen fratris sui*, And he shall stir up his brother's seed, that God meant that the brother should marry the wife of his brother, although she were known. As though he had said, If the husband, knowing his wife and leaving his seed in her, have yet no child, this seed shall be stirred up by his [other] brother surviving; and it chanceth sometimes, by reason of the said seed of the dead brother, that the child shall resemble rather the brother deceased than his own father. The natural cause whereof we have before shewed out of Albertus Magnus.

Sixtly, we find that, as the Jews write, in this marriage [p. 61] there were seven conditions to be considered, amongst the which one was that she should not marry in three months after her husband's departure, that it might be certainly known whether she had conceived child by him or no, and, if no such thing appeared, then the next eldest brother was bound to marry her. But none of them shew that there was ever any such practice or observation to learn whether she were known or no, and thereby to lett the marriage; which no doubt would have been noted among the other conditions, if there had been any such observation among the Jews.

Last of all, we say that none of the doctors and fathers of the Church, speaking and treating of this marriage, none of the expositors of the holy Scripture, expounding the said twenty-fifth chapter, have made any such exposition; and shall Mr. Wakefeild's gay glosse, that he hath now after these three thousand and five hundred years with his sharp sight pried out, bear down the authority of all those fathers and of such reasons as we have before rehearsed? Yet let us weigh how pregnant and concluding his mighty reason is, by the which he would underprop the said gloss. For otherwise (saith he) the Levit. and the Deut. should be contrary one to the other, and God [p. 62] contrary to himself, now commanding one thing, and afterward breaking the same commandment, the one law taking away the other. This were indeed, if it were so, a most absurd and intolerable inconvenience, and the very civilians, in their politic laws, seek many and hard expositions, and the same also is well borne withall rather than the law should be taken as contrary, and so the one to abolish the other, which is not to be thought but when of purpose they are made for that intent, and that otherwise they cannot be avoided. But, God be thanked, there is no such matter of weight why we should once imagine any force of such contrariety and implacable contradiction, unless we receive Mr. Wakefeild's new gloss, without the which the Levit. and the Deut. have friendly and brotherly joined together divers thousand years. For let him, if he will, make those words of the Levit. *No man shall marry his brother's wife* as canonical scripture as he can devise. Let him exasperate the matter with the grievous and loathsome terms that this marriage is touched and noted withal, both in the Latin, Greek, Hebrew, Chalde, yea and Arabic text too (as he saith it is, and whereon he is without any great need very copious), whereby he would faine enable, make good, and enforce [p. 63] his newfangled exposition. Yet, when he hath aggrieved and exasperated the Levit. prohibition never so much, it is nothing contrary (setting all Mr. Wakefeild's gloss aside) to the said Deut. precept as being not contained under the said prohibition. Let him make it as general as he will, for it is well to be noted that not only in the civil law, in the statutes of this realm and other realms, but also in holy Scripture, general words and laws are not ever so generally and absolutely taken as the words import, but are to be mitigated, temperated, limited, and determined according to the nature, condition, and quality of the persons, the things, and matters that be intreated of, the time and place, and other circumstances. Wherefore, though the testator bequeatheth all his corne, yet if he had before appointed some to be sold, that corne is not comprised in the general legacy. So whereas general license is given to men to appeal in all causes, yet such causes as cannot abide long tract of time but must with all maturity and celerity be expedited are excepted. In the which and many other causes we must not so much follow the general words as the meaning, for, as Celsus writeth, *Scire leges non est verba earum tenere, sed vim ac potestatem.* The said rule is also [p. 64] to be observed in holy Scripture, as where the Samaritan woman said that Christ had told her all that ever she did in her life. The words are not so largely to be understood, but for such things as Christ told her touching her husband. And where Jeremias saith, *All men are set upon covetousness,* and where Scripture saith, *All that ever moveth and hath life you shall eat,* and *All flesh hath corrupted his way upon earth,* with such other places, must not be so generally taken as they sound. Ezekiel also saith, *All the house of Israel is shameless and hard hearted,* yet sheweth he that there were among them, whose foreheads were signed with the sign Tau, which did weep and lament for the abhominations that were done among the people. Esaias crieth out that from the sole of the foot to the top of the head there was no health in the people, and yet he confesseth that there was some just men among them. All which places, with many like, as they imply no contradiction, no more doth this place of Levit.; with the Deut. the words of the which Levit. though they be never so general must have their restraint and exception according to the 25 chapter of the said Deut. Not as though the prohibition were once general and precise and afterward in part released; no not so in any case, for it doth not fare with the Levitt. and Deut. as it doth in the civil law and the statutes of our realm, by the which many things be first generally and precisely forbidden, as for apprentices, 7 H. 4, and afterward in part mitigated, 8 H. 6, and 11 H. 7. So for liveries in King Richard the Second's time, and in part released 12 Hen. the 4th. So for wares not to be sold to strangers but for ready money, 5 et 9 Hen. the 6, with divers like. The case, I say, is not so with these two laws of God, for at the making of those primary statutes these that were afterward specially excepted were comprised first in the general statute, but in the Levitt. the Deut. case was never comprised, which is as primary as special and as effectual in law as the first, and a declaration withal how the first is to be understood. And even by the civil law the former and the latter laws are to be considered the one by the other, *Non est novum*, saith Paulus, *ut priores leges ad posteriores trahantur.* And Tertullian, *Antiquiores leges ad posteriores* [*rahi usitatum est. Sed et posteriores leges*, saith the said Paulus, *ad priores*] *pertinent nisi sint contrariæ.* The later laws, saith Paulus, pertain to the first, unless they be contrary. Now that God's law is not contrary Mr. Wakefeild himself confesseth, Yes, saith he, they must needs be contrary if we understand the Deut. of the brother's [p. 66] wife once known, for the fact is against nature and abhominable. Indeed if they spake after this sort, the one, No man shall marry his brother's wife, the other, It shall be lawful for every man to marry his brother's wife, or the brother shall not marry the brother's wife dying without children, and if the brother die without children the brother may and must marry the said wife, here were open contradictions; but it were a plain blasphemy to imagine any such thing of God's law, and Mr.

Wakefeild when he is best awaked doth but dream that there should be a contradiction, unless we receive his newfangled fond fancy in the expounding of the Levitt. Neither the weight of the matter lieth either upon those bare words, *Thou shalt not discover thy brother's filthiness* or upon the general words, *No man shall marry his brother's wife*, as Mr. Wakefeild imagineth, but upon the true sense and meaning of both; which meaning (as we have oft declared out of St. Austine) is threefold, and our case contained under none of them all, and so clear out of the compass of the Levitt. As for any filthiness that Mr. Wakefeild imagineth in knowing the brother's wife (if there be any at all), it is for such commodities as we have declared [p. 67] rising to the dead brother and his wife, so covered, supplied, and extenuated as it is very small or none at all, for who shall call or think that to be filthy which God himself hath commanded?

Concerning the fourth principal point. It seemeth that the Bishop of Rochester in the said treatise that Mr. Wakefeild impugneth sheweth that among other understandings the Levit. prohibition might be understood of the brother marrying or misusing his brother's wife, his brother yet living, and so likewise of the other prohibitions also, and that he alleged Origen and others for that purpose. Mr. Wakefeild saith it cannot be so understood, and bringeth forth Philo, Josephus, St. Austine, and other, that seem to take this prohibition of the husband being dead, and goeth about to prove his assertion by the 20 of the Levit. where it is said that they that marry their brother's wives shall be voyde and spoiled of children. Then findeth he great fault with the *Septuaginta* for translating otherwise than it is in the Hebrew, and saith very impiously and wickedly that they have impiously translated *morientur absque liberis* for *erunt absque liberis*, that is, they shall die without children, instead of, they shall be without children. Now, saith he, if the brother lived it was plain adultery [p. 68], and the pain of that was death; yea, and we will say that so it was also in unlawful matrimony, as it appeareth in the said 20 chapter, in him that

married the mother and the daughter, commanding that they should
be burned; where it is ordained also that he that marrieth his stepmother or sister should die for it; unless he would understand it (the
husband[s] yet living), and then it maketh against him, and so it
doth winde him which way he will. For if to marry the brother's
wife be such foul abhomination against nature as Mr. Wakefeild and
the patrons of the universities do make it, why doth Mr. Wakefeild
find fault with the *Septuagint* for translating, *They shall die without children?* wherein they make rather for his assertion than against
it. And if there were a divers and less pain put for this marriage
than other, then doth it appear thereby that the fault also is less (as
indeed it is) whether the brother hath children or no children or
marrieth the wife that is repudiate. In which cases the marriage is
not against the law of nature, as it is when one marrieth his brother's
wife, the brother yet living, which is the third sense that St. Austine
and the other fathers do accommodate and apply to the Levit.;
which though the bishop in his book [p. 69] against the patrons of
the said universities doth shew by many a good father and doctor
and by manifold reasons that it may well be so understood, yet doth
he not dwell upon that point nor maketh any certain resolution
thereof. And this shall suffice for this point.

In the fift point Mr. Wakefeild laboureth to turn the bishop's
argument upon the bishop's own head. For where he had recited the
text as it is in the vulgar and common Latin translation, *Thou
shalt not take thy wive's sister (in pellicatum) to be thy harlott, nor
shall not reveal her filthiness while she is yet living*, this word *(in
pellicatum)*, saith he, is neither in the Hebrew, Chalde, Greek, nor
Arabic, no more than are those words, *No man shall take his
brother's wife*. Wherefore, if the bishop rejecteth the one, he must
also reject the other text. We answer that it is not material
whether the words be in the Bible in the one place, as we have
shewed, or out of the Bible in the other place, as we shall now
shew. And yet the places are not altogether like, for this sentence,
No man shall marry his brother's wife, and, *The brother shall not*

marry his brother's wife, seem not to be of like suit and form. For the first by reason of the generality seemeth to exclude all manner of such marriages, and so doth not the second, and therefore it implieth not the [p. 70] first. But the residue of the sentence touching two sisters implieth the very same that the words *in pellicatum* do, for a man cannot marry two sisters together but one must needs be a harlot. And so though these words *in pellicatum* do the more inforce that the said prohibition of two sisters is to be taken both of them yet living, yet, nevertheless, it is sufficiently expressed in the said prohibition by these words (*illa adhuc virente*), which clause, seeing that Mr. Wakefeild deemeth not to be in the Hebrew, Calde, Greeke and Arabic,[a] what victory or vantage could he have upon the bishop though *in pellicatum* were left out, for it evidently appeareth that one man may marry two sisters (though not at once) by Moses' law? Wherefore, seeing the degree is all one, the brother also may by Moses' law marry his brother's wife. Nay, saith Mr. Wakefeilde, to this there is some odds and the later case overpeaseth the first, for the later, saith he, especially if the wife were carnally known, was ever by the law of nature forbidden and the other permitted, and therefore God dispensed with the old fathers, as well that the uncle might marry the niece as one man to marry many wives or two sisters. As touching many wives it may be granted that it was a dispensation especially by God given, which marriage as many think is against the law of nature, and so are not the other two marriages by Mr. Wakefeild's own confession, and so [p. 71] need no special dispensation either for the law of nature or for God's law, by the which they are not forbidden, as appeareth in the Levit.

Wherefore we conclude that the marriage of the brother's wife is no more against the law of nature than the marriage of two sisters. Yet, saith he, there is a great diversity both for the law of Moses, which doth expressly forbid the brother to marry his brother's wife,

---

[a] Sororem uxoris tuæ in pellicatum non accipies nec revelabis turpitudinem ejus, illa adhuc vivente.

and doth not forbid one man to marry two sisters expressly, but by implication, as for the law of nature, seeing it is a much more foul thing for the brother to use his brother's wife, carnally known and to discover his filthiness, than for one man to marry two sisters, where there is no discovering of such filthiness; we deny every part of this collection, for the brother (as we have said) is commanded to marry his brother's wife, and there is no filthiness in this marriage, either by God's law, the same being by God commanded, or by the law of nature, the brother being now dead; yea, there seemeth no more filthiness by natural reason in the one than in the other, if there be any at all. For two sisters are by very nature one flesh and one blood, and by the strength and bond of the said natural blood are so coupled and knit together in unity of flesh that the said unity is not quite broken off by death. So that if the dead sister should be [p. 72] resuscitated, she should be accounted of the same kindred and degree to her sister and other kinsfolk that she was before. Now the brother and his wife are but secondarily and accidentally joined together by affinity and not consanguinity, and grow to an unity of flesh by carnal copulation, which unity is dissolved by the death of either party, so that the dead person being revived cannot claim the marriage of the survivant. Wherefore it must needs follow against Mr. Wakefeild that if there be any unnatural and foul act in either of these cases, that the unnaturalty and foulness surmounteth in him that defileth and deflowereth two sisters. Wherefore Mr. Wakefeild is fain to drive and shift the matter somewhat further, and to adventure so far as flatly to deny that by the law of Moses it was lawful to marry two sisters, though the one were dead. This strange assertion he would seem to maintain partly by the authority of St. Basile, of the civil law and law ecclesiastical, and by the discourse of certain reasons. As for St. Basile, the said reverend bishop hath already exonerated us of all charge in answering to him, which himself hath fully done in his answer to the patrons of the said universities, the effect whereof we have before rehearsed [p. 73], and therefore now will make no superfluous repetition. We grant that this marriage is forbidden both by the civil law and by the constitution of the Church; but then it is too loose an argument to infer thereby that Moses' law doth forbid it, or that, though it were forbidden by all three, the Pope cannot dispense with it, especially seeing by Mr. Wakefeild's own confession it is not against the law of nature. That it is not against the law of Moses it well appeareth by his words, by the which he forbiddeth a man to marry his wive's sister while his wife yet liveth, whereby by a received and well-allowed argument, called *a contrario sensu*, it followeth that his wife being dead the marriage is permitted. But then forgathering this argument Mr. Wakefeild maketh a great business against the bishop, and yet this his collection is conformable, not only to the letter of the text, but to the uniform interpretation also, both of all the Christian writers and the rabbins upon the same place, as also to the common practice of the Jews ever since Moses' law was given, even to this hour. Wherefore, if in civil and politic matters the rule of Paulus is well to be allowed, saying, *Minime mutanda sunt quæ interpretationem certam semper habuerunt* [p. 74], how much more then is it to be observed for the interpretation of holy Scripture. But this observation is of little force with Mr. Wakefeild, and he maketh very light of St. Austine and his interpretation, and shaketh him off with a, Whatsoever St. Austine saith, thy marriage is utterly unlawful;[a] yet will he render a great substantial cause belike why he doth arrogate so much to himself in this matter. He sheweth then a great marvel that St. Austine could not see so far and so deeply in this matter as this our new Vigilantius or rather Dormitantius thought he did see, that this argument *a contrario sensu* is but a fallable argument, and giveth an instance that Christ saith, It is not lawful to put away the wife except for cause of fornication, and to marry another; it will not follow, saith he, by an argument *a contrario sensu* that a man may put away his wife for fornication and marry

[a] In Leviticis Quæstionibus, Tale revera conjugium, quicquid dicat Augustinus, omnino illicitum est.

again. For as long as either party liveth they cannot marry again. This was well and truly concluded and [yet] no sufficient instance given against the bishop. For there be two things in Christ his saying, the one, in dismissing the wife which is not lawful but for fornication, the other, in marrying again. To the which the clause of fornication doth not reach or appertain [p. 75]. And therefore there can be no argument *a contrario sensu* deduced thereof, but yet of the former part full well, as for example, —It is not lawful (except for cause of fornication) to dismiss the wife. *Ergo, a contrario sensu*, for fornication it is lawful. So, likewise, a man cannot marry his wife's sister while his wife liveth. Ergo, if she be dead, he may marry her sister by Moses' law. Thus you see that Mr. Wakefeild's own instance reboundeth upon himself. And if any man would say, The said argument *a contrario sensu* might seem to reach as well to the marrying again as to the dismissing, we say, Nay, truth it is that the said place of St. Matthew seemeth somewhat obscure and doubtful, but then are there other places of Scripture that declare how this matter is to be taken, as Christ himself, in the 10 of Marke, and St. Paule also (p° Corinth. chap. 7°). Not I, saith he, but God commandeth that the wife shall not depart from the husband, or, if she depart, let her remain unmarried, or let her be reconciled to her husband. Beside this, the authority and practice of the whole Catholic Church doth evidently shew how that place of St. Matthew is to be taken. Now, neither Christ, nor St. Paule, nor the Church, helpeth Mr. Wakefeild's interpretation for the forbidding of the [p. 76] marriage of two sisters. And, though the Church forbiddeth the said marriage, yet doth not the Church teach, nor never did, that Moses' law must be so expounded, or that the same marriage was even in the time of Moses' law taken for adultery as Mr. Wakefeild doth. Well, this drift seemeth not to be very well driven by his divinity; he will, therefore, crave a little help at the lawyers' hands, and then he telleth us that the lawyers say that the argument *a contrario sensu* holdeth not when there followeth an absurdity in law. But let us hear what great absurdity this is. Marie, saith he, that one and the selfsame degree of consanguinity and affinity should be lawful and unlawful, commanded and yet forbidden. Then, addeth he, that seeing two sisters and two brothers being [in] one degree of consanguinity, and seeing that the brother is forbidden to marry the brother's wife, it were absurdity in law for one man to marry two sisters. Yea, but now both his divinity and law faileth him, for as we have oft said, and as it is most evident in the Deut., the brother was commanded to marry the brother's wife, if he died without children. And as the brother is forbidden even so is the sister also, and as the brother cannot marry the brother's wife yet living, so no man [p. 77] can marry his wive's sister, his wife being yet alive. Again, as the brother may marry the said wife, though she be carnally known and have also children, if they chance to die before their father, so may a man by Moses' law marry his wive's sister, though he had carnally known his wife and had also children; and so it is not true in this case that one degree was forbidden and not forbidden. But what if it were so? It were, saith he, a great absurdity in law; which saying is very untrue, for in very deed by the consent of all, as well divines as lawyers, one and the selfsame degree is by the Levitt. both forbidden and also permitted. The aunt is forbidden to marry her nephew, and yet the uncle is not forbidden to marry his niece, the degree in both being all one; and so both Nicholaus de Lyra and Paulus Burgensis, with other Christian expositors, do take the said Levitt. and the Jews also do so expound it and practise it accordingly. But then Mr. Wakefeild falleth a chiding and brawling with the said Nicholaus and Paulus, for that they took this for no inconvenience and absurdity. He might as well have fallen out with a number of the fathers of the Church and other learned men, and those two were very excellently seen [p. 78] in divinity and in the Hebrew tongue, and in the manners, customs, and rites of the Jews. The said Lyra doth not then only say that there is a difference between these two marriages, but sheweth a cause also. For to the aunt, saith he, the nephew oweth a certain natural reverence and subjection. And therefore it were not seemly she should marry him, and so thereby be subjected to him, and owe him awe and reverence as the wife is bound to owe the husband. But, to disgrace Lyra, Mr. Wakefeild saith that he is contrary to himself, and saith otherwise in the 18 of Levitt. and the 15 of Josue. Here a man might wish for more modesty and truth in Mr. Wakefeilde; for even in the said 15 chapter he resolveth as we have declared, notwithstanding he had proposed before some reasons to the contrary. Indeed, in the said 18 chapter, when he had shewed that we cannot marry our father's sister, so, saith he, matrimony is forbidden between the father's brother and the niece, because it is one degree, which his saying is nothing contrary to that which he otherwise said; for in the other places he meaneth of the law of Moses, where indeed it is not forbidden. In this place he seemeth to mean of the law of the Church, by the which the one marriage is forbidden as well as the other [p. 79], because both are in one degree. The foresaid conclusion of Lyra, Burgensis doth very well like, saying *Hæc expositio postillatoris efficax est et valida*, and saith further that the Jews commonly practise this marriage. And this Burgensis being, of set purpose, bent to spy and note the defects and faults of Lyra, would have, long ere Mr. Wakefeild was borne, spied out this contradiction if there had been any hold thereon. Yet is there one reason more, and that is that the law which removeth and forbiddeth the less incest forbiddeth also the greater. Thus he saith, and truly; but when he runneth to unfold his argument and to apply the same he proceedeth so obscurely and confusedly that it is hard to gather his mind and meaning. He telleth us that though the Levitt. did not expressly forbid a man to marry his own daughter or his sister by the father and mother, his niece by his brother or sister, or the uncle's wife by the mother's side; yet that all these marriages are implied in the prohibitions of the said Levitt. and saith it is even so with the marriage of two sisters. I grant that some of these be not by plain words prohibited, yet the said prohibition by force of reason and by very necessity is to be inferred. It is written in the Levitt. cap. 18 [p. 80], that no man shall come near to any woman of his kindred and flesh to discover her shame. If a man have any kinswoman at all, his own natural daughter must needs be his kinswoman, and so her marriage forbidden. Again, whereas the Levitt. expressly forbiddeth a man to marry his son's or his daughter's daughter, it followeth of a necessary illation that much more he is forbidden to marry his own daughter. Moreover there is an open plain commandment that no man shall marry his sister, whether she be his sister by the father's or mother's side, whether she be borne in wedlock or out of wedlock.

Wherefore necessity inforceth this understanding, that the Levitt. doth exclude a man to marry his own sister both by father and mother. As for my uncle's wife by the mother's side, though the 18 chapter of the Levitt. doth not forbid that marriage, yet the 20 chapter doth with express words forbid it. But it will not follow of these prohibitions that it is prohibited also by Moses' law to marry two sisters. And that Mr. Wakefeild saw well enough, and therefore he jumbleth in a blind false reason, that, as we cannot marry with our wive's daughter or [daughter's] daughter, which marriage he confoundeth I cannot tell how with the marriage of our own daughter or daughter's daughter [p. 81], so and much more, and as [he] termeth it *a fortiori*, we are forbidden to marry our wive's sister. He telleth us out of St. Hierome's translation (although otherwhere he findeth oft fault with it and with them which allege anything that is not in the Hebrew text, as this is not,) that it is incest to marry my wive's daughter? Let it be so. But yet by what good illation can he infer his argument *a fortiori*, I cannot marry by the law of Moses my wive's daughter. Ergo, I cannot marry my wive's sister, seeing that the one is by [the] express words forbidden and the other is not, but rather by a good reasonable construction of the words selfe permitted. If he will say the degrees be by God's law both of like, what if it were so? So are the degrees between the aunt and the nephew, the uncle and the niece, and yet, the former marriage being prohibited, the marriage of the uncle is not nor never was forbidden among the Jews, as we have before declared, neither is implied either by the words or meaning of the Levitt. as Mr. Wakefeild would have it. Beside this there is a great diversity; for, where a man marrieth with his wive's daughter's daughter, he representeth, as it were, a grandfather to her whom he marrieth, and therefore this marriage seemeth to be [p. 82] more unnatural than the other with two sisters, which are but in the line collateral, and not in the line ascendent or descendent. Wherefore the prohibition is not of like force, although they were by Moses' law in one degree.

But what do we so needlessly travel in this matter? For, albeit it were true that by Moses' law one man could not marry two sisters, yet had not Mr. Wakefeild obtained his purpose touching the marriage of the brother's wife, which is not forbidden but plainly commanded by the said law. And so have we sufficiently answered Mr. Wakefeild's book touching any material points belonging to this marriage.

An answer to a dialogue in Englishe called the Glasse of Truth.

There remaineth yet one book more whereto somewhat must be said, a book written in English in form of a dialogue, but without the author's name, whereby he provided that he needed the less to blush or be ashamed if he should hear of his folly again. He calleth the book *the Glasse of Truth*, but it is farced all with untruths, and his glass is so brickle that it will not abide handling or a true man once to look on it but that it will fall in pieces. The effect of which book I will now compendiously [p. 83] discover to you.

First, in his prologue he hath a special consideration for a divorce to be had that the realm might have an heir male.

Then, when he cometh to the matter, he maketh it so cocksure that he esteemeth there be few articles of our faith which be approved by more authorities, more probable, yea invincible, reasons, by more laudable customs and usages, than was the King's cause. But if you once call him to account of this so large, so bold, and so untrue asseveration, he will tell you that this marriage is forbidden by the law of nature and by the law of God, by the decrees of the fathers and counsells, and that the Pope cannot dispense with them. All which his proofs when you have well viewed them and examined, you shall find them none other in substance but such as he took out of the book that the Bishop of Rochester hath already confuted, as we have before declared; yet is he peerless in one point and hath (albeit in a little book) far overrun all them, and spied out that which all that were of counsell with the former book could never espy, that is, that in the said 25 chapter of Deut. this word brother must not be taken for the natural brother but for some other kinsman next after the brother. Then are there two other special points that he would prove, the one which the said patrons of the Universities hoverly touched [p. 84], but this man goeth directly and plainly to work, and telleth us that the Pope ought not to be judge in this matter, but that it ought to be heard and determined at home by the metropolitans and other bishops.

The other and the last is that Queen Katherine was carnally known by Prince Arthure. And all this is conveyed in a dialogue between a sorry doting divine and a sorry lewd lawyer, framing of their own heads new divinity and new laws ecclesiastical, and running as far a square from all good divinity and law and from the due [proof of the matter taken in hand, as they square and disagree from the due] observation and property of a dialogue. For loe suddenly while they two are talking alone together, forgetting that they were secretly friendly and familiarly talking, and thinking they had been before a great audience pulpited, the lawyer saith to the divine, I think there cannot be a better exhortation than you have given us all. Then the divine for his part saith, Wherefore now using the saying of St. Paul I do exhort you in our Lord that you his subjects, &c. And surely they have even as much forgotten themselves, and much more in the principal matter, as you shall [hereafter] better understand.

Concerning now the five points which we have gathered out [p. 85] of his book, to the second we will answer never a whitt more than we have done already.

To the first and third we shall now forthwith say somewhat. We shall reserve our answer to the fourth and fifte for a while and to a place convenient for the same.

Now, touching the first, we say that the author speaketh neither like a good Englishman nor like a good Christian [man]. Somewhat tolerable this talk had been in the mouth of some Frenchman or of some person of those countries where the female is barred from the title of the crown. But whereas many women have most nobly and most virtuously governed many great countries (the manifold examples whereof be in stories occurrent), and whereas, beside many other great foreign countries where the right of the crown devolveth to the woman, the Crown of England also for defect of issue male is entailed to the female—this discourse was not very seemly for an Englishman. Neither was it seemly for any Christian man to devise and practise ways for a prince whereby he might put away his lawful wife for lack of issue male; neither was it to be thought that God would fortunate and bless such an unlawful divorce with any happy issue male. And indeed so it fell out. For, albeit the [p. 86] divorce at length proceeded, yet had the King by the Lady Anne Bulleyne no issue male, and, though he had such issue afterward by another wife, yet had the realme thereby small comfort or commodity, as we shall hereafter more at large declare.

The next article we have to intreat of is of the exposition of the 25 of Deut. whereof you have had three expositions already, partly false, partly nothing to the purpose. Now shall you have another as bad as any of the other. He is in hand with the former exposition that we have confuted. That the said 25 chapter must be taken in a mystical sense and maketh a jolly impertinent process, telling us that we are not bound to the law Deuteronom. and cometh nothing nigh to the purpose and to our argument, which is not to deny that the said 25 chapter is to be taken in a mystical sense, or to affirm that we are bound to the same, but this only, that seeing this marriage was once commanded by God, and is not at this day forbidden but by the law ecclesiastical, the Pope is not restrained to dispense with it. This is the mark we shoot at, from the which our divine roveth a thousand yards and more. Wherefore if our wise lawyer that after this extravagant process answered the divine (By the faith I owe [p. 87] unto God you speak fully) had [set in for that word, *foolishly*, he had] answered him truly though not so smoothly and flatteringly. Neither yet was our divine altogether so ignorant but that he saw well enough that his former answer was too weak and too loose, and therefore goeth about with a more fond exposition of his own, which he took to be very mighty and strong, to make the whole matter fast and sure, as it were with a tenpenny nail. In the Levitt. saith he, this word (brother) must be taken for the natural brother, but in the said 25 chap. of Deuteronomie not for the natural brother but for some other nigh kinsman, and saith that many so take that place; and yet nameth no one person nor book, nor was able to name any of any authority and credit; for if there had been any such they could not have scaped the knowledge of the said universities, and of those which here in England made the foresaid Latin book, and conferred upon the King's divorce, which were the two archbishops of the realm, besides divers bishops and many notable divines and lawyers. Well, let us now see what this man with his sharp piercing insight hath found out. Let us see what proofs he hath for his new conclusion. Marry, saith he, it appeareth in the book of Ruthe, but yet he neither nameth chapter nor any word of the booke [p. 88]; and great marvel it were if there should be any such thing in that book, seeing the place of Deuteronomy so plainly speaketh of the brothers, calling them אחים, which word is also in the Levitt. *Turpitudinem uxoris fratris tui non revelabis.* The word is אחיך the very same word that is in the Deut. Neither will it help if perchance he would reply that this word (*fratres*), אחים in Hebrew, is not taken for the natural brethren, as Genesis 13, where Abraham called Lot, his brother's son, brother, saying, *Viri fratres sumus nos*, אֲנָשִׁים אַחִים אֲנַחְנוּ for albeit that be true, yet seeing one and the same word is both in the Levitt. and the Deut. we must either take it in both places for some other kinsman than the brother, and then is all the question at an end, and the Levitt. prohibition doth nothing serve for them against us, or else in both places we must take it for a brother and so understand the Levit. by the Deut. as it is the most congruent and natural exposition of all other to expound one place of holy scripture by the other. And so we say once again that this marriage is commanded by God to all the Jews, and that this word *Brother* in the said 25 chapter must be taken in his proper and natural signification as the Jews do take it and ever have taken it [p. 89]. For, among the seven observations which we touched before, this is one that they take the word for the natural brother, and say that, in case there be many brethren, the eldest is bound to take the wife of the deceased, and, in case there be no brother, then the law bindeth the next of the kin to marry her. Yet saith this divine that his interpretation is plainly to be proved by the story of Ruthe. As plain as he maketh the matter he telleth us nothing how it may be proved by that story. And to say the truth he is in this matter like [un]to the dog which (as the proverb is) drinketh of the flood of Nilus, and with haste runneth away fearing to be bitten by some serpent. Surely this divine that hath made so fond and strange an interpretation, and for the confirmation of the same avoucheth the book of Ruth, and as soon as he hath named the same flyeth away and dareth not abide, feareth belike to be stung of some serpent, and so it is indeed. Wherefore fie and double fie upon the impudency of this nameless and shameless divine. For it is so far off that this book helpeth anything his assertion, that, if he had purposely searched out all the places in holy Scripture to prove that the said 25 chapter must be taken of the natural brother, he could never have [p. 90] brought forth any one place so fit, so apt, and so necessary [concluding] for our purpose and against himself. And because our divine telleth us this as it were a celestial oracle *ex tripode Apollinis*, and that our ignorant doctor of law thinketh that this divine hath so profoundly declared the matter that he never heard (as he saith) the like, I shall unfold so much of the book of Ruth as shall pertain to this matter, and shall set our doctor to school again to learn his divinity afresh, and that no high solemn doctor of divinity, but even of a poor ignorant woman, which as ignorant as she was knew well enough, and so did all other women among the Jews, that Moses' law was to be understood even of the very natural brother. And, the more to repress and beat down this divine's shameless forehead, I will go no further than to his own story of Ruth, and to Nohemye, Ruth's mother. This Nohemy's husband, Elymelech, in the time of a great famine that raged in Judea, went to the country of the Moabites with Noemie and with her two sons Maacham and Chelyon, where he married the said two sons, the one to Orpha the other to Ruth. At length the said sons and her husband being dead she returned to Judea, and her said daughters-[p. 91]in-law brought her on her way and would needs have gone through with her and have dwelt with her in Judea (Ruth, cap. p⁰.), but she dehorted them and willed them to return. Turn again, saith she, my daughters. For what cause will you go with me? Shall I have any more sons in my womb that you may look that they shall be your husbands? Return, I say, my daughters, for I am now too far grown in years to marry; yea, if I might conceive this night and bear sons, if you would tarry until they should be marriageable you should be old women ere you married. Can a man in all scripture find a place more apt and fit to prove that the meaning of the 25 of Deut. was of the very natural brother? And yet is there one thing more here to be observed, that the said 25 chapter is to be taken not only of the brother by father and mother but of the uterine and half-brother also. With much ado Orpha returned, but Ruth by no means could be inflected and moved to break company from her mother-in-law, and in fine, after her coming to Judea, she married with

Booz, the next kinsman that her former husband had, saving one who gave over his title, right, and claim to Booz very solemnly before the elders of the [p. 92] city. Thus doth it evidently appear that, in case Noemye had any son living and marriageable, Ruth should and ought to have married with him, and that for defect only of such issue she married with the said Booz, which marriage our divine plainly confesseth is not against the law of God. But in case I were minded to be as frowardly disposed as he is, and to make this marriage indispensable, by reason of the mystical sense, as he doth for the marriage with the brother's wife, I might infer even by his own argument and by his fair figure that the marriage with any nigh kinsman of the brother departed could not now be dispensed withal. For St. Ambrose[a] maketh a mystical and an allegorical sense of the marriage of the said Booz. For the residue of this dialogue we will for a little time defer our answer, and will proceed to intreat of the Act of Parliament by the which the oath was tendered to Sir Thomas Moore, the principal ground of all this our treatise. But forasmuch as this Act passed not until sentence was given for the divorce by the Archbishop of Canterbury, and forasmuch as our purpose is in this treatise not only to set forth the reasons and arguments made for the furtherance of the said divorce with [p. 93] convenient solutions thereto, but also to shew the whole manner, fashion, and trade of the proceedings touching the said marriage, and as it were an entire full and perfect story of the same for the better instruction and riping of our posterity, we intend before we come to the said Act of Parliament to discover and lay before you, in as compendious a sort as we may, divers things that proceeded before.

The beginning then of all this broil (as we have partly touched already) proceeded from Cardinal Wollseye, who first by himself, or by John Langlond, Bishop of Lincolne and the King's confessor, put this scruple and doubt in his head. At the first hearing whereof the King, somewhat astonished, held his peace awhile, not

[a] De fide, lib. 3, cap. 5⁰.

a little marvelling at this matter so moved unto him. At length he answered thus: "Take heed, I beseech you, reverend father, and well consider what a great and weighty enterprise you take now in hand;" and, speaking much in the commendation of his wife, said that his marriage was allowed by the most learned and virtuous bishops of the realms of England and Spaine, and confirmed also by the Pope's authority, adding thereto [p. 94] that she had oftentimes sworn that she never carnally knew Prince Arthure, as well for his tender age as for the weakness and infirmity of his body. After a few days the cardinal assaulted the King afresh and with much more vehemency, being with him the said Bishop of Lincolne, who very earnestly, as one which (as he said) had a tender and special regard and charge above all other of the King's soul, for the safeguard of the same, did solicit him that he would suffer that the validity of his said matrimony might be well considered and examined according to right, justice, and equity. Thus say some of the Bishop of Lincolne; though himself (as we have shewed) denied that he was one of the first movers of this matter.

The King at length began somewhat to give ear and yield to these persuasions; whereupon, as though the divorce were now concluded and determined upon, the cardinal was in hand with the King that he would cast his fancy for to marry the French King's sister, late wife to the Duke of Alenson, a young virtuous lady. But the King resolved nothing with him at that time; neither was it long but that the cardinal was sent [p. 95] ambassador to the said French King, and it was thought that the King was moved for the marriage of his sister, and that it had gone forward, saving that the most virtuous lady had a special respect and regard that she would not marry the King to the great discomfort and undoing of Queen Katherine. When this practice of divorce came to the knowledge of Queen Katherine, little marvel was it she took it grievously even to the very heart, considering, after so long quiet and prosperous continuance, her great misery and calamity eminent, if the divorce should take place, as indeed it did, not many years after; which her unfortunable and unlucky chance, it was thought the main and great tempest, wherewith she was tossed and tumbled by the rageous insurges [of the seas] of the wind and water, and often driven from the shore before she could at the first coming out of Spaine arrive, did many years before bode and portend; and, as it hath been said, the Queen herself by reason thereof mistrusted ever and feared some unlucky and unhappy chance impending upon her. The Queen remaining in this great dolour, sorrow, and lamentation, the King did comfort her and willed her to bear all things [p. 96] patiently, saying that all that [which] was attempted tended only to the searching out and finding of the truth. Then was there nothing so common and frequent and so tossed in every man's mouth, in all talks and at all tables, in all taverns, alehouses, and barbers' shops, yea, and in pulpits too, as was this matter, some well liking and allowing the divorce, some others most highly detesting the same.

The King, that the matter might be more orderly and authentically heard, discussed, and determined, requested Pope Clemente to send purposely some cardinall into England, furnished with sufficient authority to end and decide that weighty matter; who sent the Cardinall Laurent[ius] Campegius, that had been legate in England ten years before, and did associate to him Cardinall Woolseye. There were in the meanwhile sent by the King divers learned persons, some to Italie, some to Fraunce, and among others Doctor Stockseley and Doctor Foxe, some into Germanie, as the Bishop of Hereford, to learn and know the censure and judgment, as well of private men as of whole universities. The King in the meantime licensed Queen Katherine to choose counsellors where she would, and she among other chose William Warcham, Archbishop of Canterburye [p. 97], and Nicholas West, Bishop of Elie, doctors of law, John Fisher, Bishop of Rochester, and Henry Standishe, Bishop of Saint Asse, doctors of divinity, with divers other, whereof some played very honest parts and stood stiffly and fast to her cause, some played the prevaricators, and fled from her to the King's side.

This Warrham was brought up in the new colleges of Wintone and Oxforde, a man, beside his great learning, of deep profound wisdom, and was lord chancellor of the realm before the Cardinal. Many ways were attempted to draw him to the King's side, and at length he fell in the King's high and grievous displeasure; and it was thought that he should be appeached of treason for concealing the matter of the nun, Elizabethe Barton, for his enemies had spread abroad rumours that he was privy to her doings. And Cromwell, that after the fall of the Cardinal grew in high estimation and credit with the King, scornfully and spitefully said that if the King would be ruled by him because he was an archbishop he should be hanged on high that he might with his heels bless all the world. Neither long after, either for grief and anguish of mind or for very impotent age, he departed out of [this] troublesome [p. 98] world; in whom this is to be noted, that, twenty years before any manner of conjecture rose of any such perilous world imminent as followed after his death, he would to his familiar friends and kinsfolk report that there hung over England such miserable calamity and wretchedness as since Christ his birth it never suffered the like, nor yet should suffer again until the coming of Antichrist; yea, he charged upon his blessing the right worshipful Sir William Warham, knight, his nephew and godson, being then a young gentleman and waiting upon him in his chamber, that if ever after his death any should succeed in that see called Thomas, he should in no wise serve him or seek his favour or acquaintance. For there shall, saith he, one of that name shortly enjoy this see that shall as much by his vicious living as wicked heresies dishonour, waste, and destroy the same, and the whole Church of England, as ever the blessed bishop and martyr Saint Thomas did before beautify, bless, adorn, and honour the same. This I heard not long since of the mouth of the said Sir William, who yet liveth. I have heard also certain credible persons that have reported certainly that themselves had heard other which foretold [p. 99] (many years ere it chanced) this dolorous doleful wretched world that followed upon this divorce.

So much have we enterlaced by the way by occasion of the mention of the said archbishop, who to ripe and instruct himself the better in this matter assembled divers of the most notable clerks and famous doctors of both universities at Lambeth, and there heard them reasoning and disputing touching this marriage.

The said Cardinal Campegius came into England in September, 1528, and the twenty-first year of the reign of King Henry the Eight, and, after that he had a while rested and reposed himself, spake with the King at Bridewell, where his secretary made an eloquent oration in Latin in setting forth and aggravating the great spoil late made at Rome, and the ransacking of the said city by the Imperialls, advancing highly the King's singular favour and benefits employed upon the Pope, the cardinals, and the whole city. Nothing was touched at this time openly of the King's great matter. But much and divers talk and rumour came abroad after the coming of this legate; neither would men spare to speak freely and frankly that the King, to serve his own appetite and pleasure more then for [p. 100] any just [cause or] impediment in his marriage, had procured the said legate to be sent for, that he might be divorced from the Queen, which almost universally was misliked, especially among the common people.

For repressing of the which talk, the King assembled at his palace of Bridewell, in the month of November, his nobility, judges, and counsellors, with divers other persons, to whom he declared the great worthiness of his wife, both for her nobility and virtue, and all princely qualities, to be such that, if he were to marry again, he would of all women match with her, if the marriage might be found good and lawful. But, her worthiness notwithstanding, and that he had a fair daughter by her, he said he was wonderfully tormented in conscience, for that he understood by many great clerks, with whom he had consulted, that he had lived all this while in detestable and abhominable adultery. Wherefore for the settling of his conscience and the sure and firm succession of the realm he did advocate this legate as a man most indifferent, and sayd that, if she by the law of God should be adjudged his lawful wife, there was never thing more pleasant [p. 101] and acceptable to him in all his life. He added, that at the last being of his ambassador in Fraunce, mention being made for his daughter's marriage with the Earle of Orleans, one of the most notable counsellors to the French King said it were expedient first to be well known whether she be the King's lawful daughter or no. This was in effect the King's oration. Our chronicles do write that the said doubt was cast in the counsel of Spaine also, after that the Emperor had agreed with our King to marry his said daughter.

Not long after this, both the legates repaired to the Queen, and told her that they were appointed by the Pope judges to hear and determine the controversy lately risen touching her marriage with the King, and to give a final sentence whether it were consonant to the law of God or no. The Queen at the hearing of this, being abashed and astonished and pausing awhile [at length spake thus]: " Alas, my Lords," saith she, " that now almost after twenty years there should any such question be once moved, and that men should now go about to dissolve and undo this marriage as wicked and detestable "—imputing the original of all her trouble to Cardinall Wolsey and to his [p. 102] deadly feud against the Emperor, whom he of all princes of Europe most maligned and hated, because he would not serve and content his immoderate ambition, aspiring to be made Pope. The Cardinal on the other side laid all the fault from himself, and declared that this thing chanced far against his will; he said he was by the Pope assigned to be a judge in this cause, and sware by his profession that he would, in hearing the same, minister justice and right indifferently.

The 28 of May following the legates sat solemplye at the Black-Friers, where the King by his two proctors, the Queen personally, appeared with the said four bishops and other of her counsell, refusing to stand to the legates' judgment as judges incompetent, and appealing from them to the see of Rome. The legates proceeded notwithstanding, and cited the King and Queen to appear again the 18 of June, upon the which day both of them made their appearance personally. At which time the King declared openly the great unquietness, vexation, and trouble, wherewith he was grievously cumbred for his marriage, so that he could scarce intend any matter touching the necessary affairs of his realm; wherefore he desired that the matter might be according to [p. 103] justice and right quickly and speedily determined. He commended also at that time the Queen's womanhood, wisdom, nobility, and gentleness. When the King had ended, the Queen made her protestation, and did put in her libels recusatories, and renewed her provocation, alleging the cause to be advocated by the Pope's holiness, *et litis pendentiam coram eodem*, desiring to be admitted for probation thereof, and to have a term competent for the same. Whereupon day was given by the legates till the twenty-first of the same month for their declaration of their minds and intentions thereunto. At which day both the King and the Queen appeared in person; and notwithstanding the said legates declared as well the sincerity of their minds and intentions directly and justly to proceed without favour, dread, affection, or partiality, as also that no such recusation, appellation, or term for proving *litis pendentiam*, could or might be by them admitted, yet she nevertheless persisting in her former mind laid in her appeal, which was also by the said legates refused; and they minding to proceed further in the cause, the Queen would no longer make her abode to hear what the said legates would [p. 104] further discern, albeit the King also requested and commanded her to tarry, wherein afterward she seemed to have some remorse of conscience, as it were for some disobedience towards her husband. And she reported afterward to some that were then of her counsel (by whom I had intelligence of it) that she never before in all her life in any one thing in the world disobeyed the King her husband, neither now would have done but that the necessary defence of her cause did force her thereto. Her proctor notwithstanding made answer for her and said that she would stick to her appeal. But the legates caused her to be thrice preconisate.

and called eftsoones to return and appear; which she refusing to do was denounced by the legates contumax, and a citation decerned for her appearance the Friday following to make answer to such articles as should be objected unto her.

The King upon this addressed his letters the 23 of the said month to Doctor Bennett, Sir Gregorie de Cassalis, knight, and master Peter Vanne, his ambassadors then resident in the court of Rome, of the premisses, willing them to have special [care and] regard that nothing should pass or be granted by the Pope's holiness which might either give delay or disappointment to the direct and [p. 105] speedy process to be used in his cause, neither by advocation of the cause, inhibition, or otherwise; but that, if any such thing should by the Cæsarients, or by the Queen's agents or other, be attempted or desired, they should diligently procure the stopping thereof, as well upon such reasons and considerations as before had been signified unto them, as by inferring the high and extreme dishonour and intolerable prejudice that the Pope's holiness thereof should do to the said legates, and also the contrariety both of his [said] bull and commission, and also of his promise and pollicitation passed upon the same; beside the notable and excellent displeasure thereby to be done by his holiness to him and his realm clean contrary to his merits and deserts; extending also the other damages mentioned in former writings apparent to ensue thereby to his holiness and the see apostolique, with the manifold and in manner infinite inconveniences like to follow of the same to all Christendome, and all other such reasons, introductions, and persuasions as they could make and devise for that purpose; putting him also in remembrance [p. 106] of the great commodity coming unto his holiness herein, by reason that, this cause being by his legates decided, the Pope not only should be delivered from the pain that he should in the time of his disease and sickness (to extreme peril of his life) sustain with the same, seeing it was of such moment and importance as it suffered no tract nor delay, but also his holiness should by such decision eschew and avoid all displeasure which he should not fail to have if it were or should be passed elsewhere. He would also they should inferre as the case required how inconvenient it were that this matter should be decided in the court of Rome, which then depended totally in the Emperor's arbiter, having such puissance near thereunto that, as it had been written by the Pope's own letters, their state and life there was all in the Emperor's hands, whose armies might famish or relieve them at their pleasure. He would further they should not forget the prerogative and jurisdiction royal of the crown of England by the ancient laws of the realm, which admit nothing to be done to the prejudice thereof; and also what danger they should incur that would presume to bring [p. 107] or present any such thing into the same. This was the effect of the King's letters.

Now, the said appeal notwithstanding, the judges proceeded and went still forward in hearing and examining the matter. Hot and fervent reasoning and disputation was there at home, hot and fervent suit was there at Rome, for the furthering of the said divorce. The summer drew fast away, and the King importunately called for expedition and full sentence of the matter. But the legates made no great haste, and Campegius pretended cause why they could not proceed until October following; whereof the King hearing, complained to the Dukes of Norfolk and Suffolk and other nobles of his counsell, which noblemen were in hand with the legates sitting the 30th day of July, that day or the next to give final judgment in the matter. Campegius swore on his honour and faith that he bare to the Church of Rome that the course of the courts there is at the end of July to suspend all matters until the 4th day of October, and that all judgments given in the mean season were void; wherefore he required the King to bear with him until that day (before the which they could sit no more), trusting that then they should make an end to the King's contentation.

The which answer did greatly offend [p. 108] the noblemen, and the Duke of Suffolk, giving a great clappe on the table with his hand, did swear that there was never cardinall that did good in England, and forthwith departed in great anger; with the residue of the nobility. The King, hearing of this, was wonderfully displeased and discontented, but much more a while after, understanding that Campegius was sent for to return to Rome with all speed, and that he provided for the said journey; who in September following came to Grafton to the King to take his leave, accompanied with the Cardinal of York, which was the last time that ever the said Cardinal of York saw the King, being shortly after cast in a premunire. For the King now had been in great suspicion that he had not dealt truly and sincerely in his matter and according to his expectation, and that he that [first] broached the said matter of divorce should in shutting up of the matter with crafty secret frustrations dally with him and delay and delude him.

The cause whereof (as some men think) was this. The King was now fallen into so deep love with [the] Lady Anne Bulleyn, that the Cardinall was certainly persuaded that, if the divorce should take effect, the King would surely marry with her, which marriage the Cardinall could in no wise fancy, and minded by all means [p. 109] possible to avert the King from it. Wherefore, when he saw that the matter should needs be removed to Rome, he wrought secretly by letters and messengers with Pope Clement (as it hath been reported and also by some written) to prolong and draw forth his determination for the divorce until such time as he had altered and changed the King's mind, and framed it according to his will and pleasure; whereof I can say nothing certainly. But this I find in the Cardinall's own letters, which he sent to the King's agents at Rome, and to the Pope himself, that he most earnestly travelled to have the said divorce with all speed and celerity set forth, and to stay the advocation of the said cause that it should not devolve from himself and his colleague to the court of Rome, and that he made his full account that the said delay and advocation would turn to his utter undoing, as in short space after it did.

Now, inasmuch as we have mention made of the King's and Cardinall's letters sent to the forenamed ambassadors, and withal sometime to Stephen Gardiner, that was afterwards Bishop of Winchester, and Sir Francis Bryan, knight; because there be many hidden secret [p. 110] matters in the same, and means whereby to procure and work the said divorce, and for that myself have seen the very originals, I think it convenient for the better furnishing of this historical and matrimonial narration, for the better satisfying of our promise and for the fuller instruction of our posterity, to unfold some part of the said letters.

And, albeit the King's doings and proceedings hitherto may seem somewhat tolerable and to have proceeded from a tymerous fearful conscience to offend God, and that he grounded all his doings upon the fear of God and to satisfy his blessed will and pleasure, as it was pretended; yet now, meethinke God saith as well to us as he said once to Ezechiell (capite 8°), " Dig a hole in the wall to see and behold the great abominations done in the Temple," which temple is every man's heart, and for this present matter the King's own heart. Let us, I say, dig the said wall; let us search and examine the secrets of his heart; then will at length many abominations appear. Then will appear the idols, which the King did secretly worship. And, least any man might think that I should too boldly and impudently intrude myself [p. 111] into the bowels and secrets of his bosom, his own letters and the Cardinal's letters, his own Acts of Parliament, his own doings and facts, have digged already to our own hand a great hole in the said wall, as you shall now and hereafter more plainly understand.

The King then sent to be his agents and orators at Rome the said Sir Francis Bryan and Master Peter Vanne, with instructions given them, in the which among other things they were charged to answer the Pope from the King, that he should have a good and vigilant eye to the Emperor's doings, and take heed how he did trust him or any of his promises for the restitution of his towns and pieces which were retained from him, or for the liberation of the cardinalls remaining in his hostage, especially minding to come in his own person into Italy with an army. He putteth also a jealousy in the Pope's head by the said orators, that it was to be feared least the Emperor would yet once again captivate the Pope and deprive him also, placing in his see Cardinal Angell, the General of the Observants, aspiring thereby to the monarchy of all Italy, and to have in his hands the possession of the see apostolic; for the shunning of which inconveniences and dangers the King certifieth [p. 112] that he had by his ambassdors opened the said dangers to the French King, and that they both thought it best that the Pope should indicte a general peace among all Christian princes, which they both were resolved and constantly determined to keep inviolably, yea and by themselves and their confederates to force the Emperor also to keep the same, in case he would attempt any thing to the contrary. But above all other things it was thought good and expedient by the King that the Pope's holiness should have a good and substantial guard about his own person; and, if the Pope did accept the said presidy, then to move him that the Viscount of Turcyne and Sir Gregorie Cassalis might be the principal captains of the said guard, which should be maintained at his charges and the French King's. Of this peace and presidy there is large mention made in divers letters sent to the said agents, which were also admonished to move and exhort the Pope, that, for the better enjoying of the sayd peace, he should personally resort to Nyce or Avynion or to some indifferent and apt place, whereto the Emperor, the French King, the Princes of Italy, and other might conveniently repair, upon the which voyage of the Pope concluded, [p. 113] then would the King send the Cardinal of York to be his lieutenant; provided ever that the King's great matter must have an indelayed perfection, for else the Cardinal would not put himself into hazard or take upon him that journey or travell toward any such convention till such time as the King's highness were before in good perfect surety of attaining his purpose.

Neither think you that this our declaration touching this peace and presidy is impertinent to our principal matter. For the very mystery thereof you shall now hear out of the Cardinal's owne letters sent to Master Secretary and Master Bennett, which words were written in cyphers and purporte this: "As you know, and as it was declared to you in counsell, one of the things noted to be much to the advancement of the King's cause was, that the Pope's holiness taking this presidye should thereby be brought to have as much fear and respect towards the King as he now hath towards the Emperor, and consequently be glad to grant the King's desire, though you were ordained to show the French King that it was done for his sake, and to the Pope for his," and indeed it was done for the benefit of the King's affairs. Yet to return again to our former instructions [p. 114] given to the said Sir Francis and Master Peter, the King's said orators; they were admonished to make no mention to the Pope at the first of his great matter, but to make demonstration as though the premisses were the charge committed unto them, for the which they were purposely sent in post. There was also in the said instructions an advertisement that the agents should perfectly and substantially instruct themselves against the coming of Master William Knighte, the King's principal secretary, of certain questions by the learning, experience, and knowledge of the best advocates [that] they could get in the court of Rome, to be retained of the King's counsell, and to be of his grace's part made sure by secret rewards, pacte, and convention, that afterwards they should not be allured or drawn to the adverse parte. The questions were propounded in form following, whereof I will shift no part of the King's owne words: "Whether, if the Queen, for the great and manifold effects that may ensue thereof, can be moved and induced to take vow of chastity, or enter in laxe religion, the Pope's holiness may *ex plenitudine potestatis* dispense with the King's highness to proceed thereupon *ad duas Nuptias*, and the children to be procreate in the same to be legittime; [p. 115] and, if it be a thing that the Pope perease may not do, standing such laws as be already written both divine and human, and using his ordinary power, yet whether his holiness may do it of his mere and absolute power, as a thing that the same may dispense in above the law, must perfectly and secretly be understood and known, and what president hath been seen of like matter, or how the court of Rome shall define and determine, and what it doth use or may do therein; so that it may perfectly and assuredly appear that no exception or scruple, question or doubt, can or may be found or alleged hereafter in any thing that may or shall be affirmed to be in the Pope's power touching that matter. Semblably, forasmuch as it is like that the Queen shall make marvellous difficultie, and in no wise be conformable to enter into religion or take vow of chastity, but that to induce her thereunto there must be ways and means of high policy used, and all things possible devised to encourage her to the same, wherein percase she shall resolve that in no wise she will condescend so to do unless the King's highness also do the semblable for his part,—the King's said orators shall therefore in like wise rype and instruct themselves by their secret learned counsell in the court [p. 116] of Rome, if for so great a benefit to ensue unto the King's succession, realm, and subjects, with the quiet of his conscience, his grace should promise so to enter religion or vow of chastity for his part, only thereby to induce the Queen thereto, whether in that case the Pope's holiness may dispense with the King's highness for the same promise, oath, or vow, discharging his grace clearly of the same, and thereupon to proceed *ad secunda vota cum legitimacione prolis* as is aforesaid. Furthermore, to provide surely to all events, as well *propter conceptum odium* as for the danger that may ensue to the King's person by continuance of his grace in the Queen's company (whose body his grace for marvellous great and secret respects is utterly resolved and determined never to use); if it shall be found and appear assuredly that the Pope may in no wise dispense with the King to proceed *ad secunda vota*, the Queen being alive in religion, but that she, being in religion or without, shall still be reputed as his wife, then shall the King's said orators perfectly inquire and insearche, whether the Pope's holiness may dispense with his grace upon the great considerations that rest herein to have *duas uxores*, and that the children of the [said] second matrimony shall be as well legitimate as those of the [p. 117] first, wherein some great reasons and presidents especially of the Old Testament appear."

And they are willed to advise the King's highness [upon the great considerations that rest herein] and the Cardinal of Yorke by post and in cyphers what they might know and understand in all and singular of the premises, foreseeing always, principally and above all other things, that in making of any privy search, conducting of advocates or learned counsell, offering of rewards or entertainment, or otherwise, they should use such high circumspection as the King's cause were not thereby published or known to the hindrance, slander, or impeachment of his highness's intent, using and proponing always the King's case as it were another man's.

There was also a charge given to Master Peter Vanne that, in case they found not the Pope so propice and inclinable to their desires as they looked for, he as of himself should apart say unto his holiness " Sir, I being an Italian, cannot but with a more fervent zeal and mind than any other study and desire the weal, honour, and surety of your holiness and the see apostolic, which compelleth me to shew unto your holiness frankly what I see in this matter. Surely, Sir, in case your holiness, continuing this particular respect of fear of the Emperor, do thus delay, protract, and put over the [p. 118] accomplishment of the King's so instant desire in this matter, and not impart unto his majesty therein bounteously of the treasure and graces of the Church and see apostolic, *quantum potestis ex thesauro ecclesiæ et ex plenitudine potestatis authoritate a Deo vestræ sanctitati collata*, I see assuredly that it will be a meane so to aliene the fast and entire mind, which his highness beareth to your holiness, as not only thereby his grace, nobles, and realm, but also many other princes, his friends and confederates, with their nobles and realms, shall withdraw their devotion and obedience from your holiness and the see apostolic, studying how they may acquite this your ingratitude in the highest cause that can be devised, shewed and, so long continued, with the semblable. And, therefore, Sir, at the reverence of

Almighty God cast not from you the heart of this noble virtuous prince, who finally cannot fail (the peace had with Christendome), nor may not long forbear to have in his puisance such a stay as may be able in the highest and largest manner to recompense his friends and to acquite the contrary."

The like charge was given [in general] to Doctor Stephen Gardiner, Sir Francis Bryan, and Sir Gregorie de Cassalis; to the which Sir Gregorie and Master Peter Vanne letters were [p. 119] sent from the King to make also, if need were, protestation and appellation *a non vicario ad verum vicarium Jesu Christi.*

During the pursuit of this great matter at Rome it chanced Pope Clement to fall very sick, and word was brought to the King, and for a time credited, that he was dead. Whereupon the King sent in all haste by post to his said agents there, by all possible means, by pollicitations of promotions spiritual, offices, dignities, rewards of money or other things, to procure and win the cardinalls' consent to choose and make Pope in his place the Cardinall of Yorke. And, in case the election were not like to fall upon the said Cardinall, then should there a protestation be made, being before couched and devised by Master Doctour Stephen Gardiner, and by the policy of Monsieur de Vauxe and Sir Gregorie to be set forth in time convenient; and thereupon the cardinalls of the King's side and the French King's adherents to depart the conclave, repairing to other sure place, that they with the residue of the cardinalls absent might proceed to election, any election that might ensue at Rome notwithstanding. And, to the intent the cardinalls should be the better animated to finish the sayd election to the King's desire, the said orators had charge given them as they saw [p. 120] good, to offer a presidie of two or three thousand men to be in the city for the time of the said election, which presidie, if they would accept, the King's orators should provide money for their entertainment. And all this was done (as the King's own letters purport) that the King thought that the making or marring of his whole matter and suite depended only in the advancement of the said Cardinall, whom the

King took to be assured to his cause and all at his devotion; but, if either imperiall or neutral were chosen, he had no hope that his matter should ever be conduced by authority of the see apostolic.

I here omit the importunate ambition of the Cardinall himself, writing a letter of his own hand (which original letter I have seen and read) to the said Doctor Stephen [Gardiner], to employ all his endeavour and wit for the sayd preferment to the apostolic see, and that he should spare no charges, promises, or labour. Not long after, though tidings were brought that the Pope was somewhat amended, yet, because there was thought some danger in him, instructions were given to the said agents, as they saw occasion, not to foreslowe to put eftsoones the cardinalls in mind of the said Cardinall of Yorke in case the Pope should die.

The Pope [p. 121] afterward being well recovered and the said presidie taking no effect, forasmuch as the Queen had appealed from the legates (as we have said), the King made marvellous instant suit that either the Pope would sign a Decretall drawn out for his purpose, or give a new commission to the legates, that they might proceed, all manner of appellations set aside, and that he would by his handwriting send word to the King that he would not advocate the matter to Rome; but nothing of all these things could be granted.

Many other things worthy of observation touching the suit of this matrimony are in the said King's and Cardinal's letters, which for eschewing of prolixity I pretermitt. I will now only talk of the brief whereof in these letters is very ofte and large mention, and no small adoe thereabout; the effect whereof, as also of all such objections as are made in the said dialogue touching the same, you shall now hear.

But first, for the more illustration of the matter and your better intelligence, it is to be observed that in the bull which dispensed with the said marriage there were divers faults found by the King's side; as that the cause of the [p. 122] dispensation should be false, wherein was pretended that the said dispensation was granted at the desire and prayers of the King (Prince Henry being then called) for peace and quietness between the realms of Englande and Spaine, whereas there was no war, nor likelyhood of war, or that the said Prince Henry being of no ripe age or intelligence (as being not yet twelve years of age) should for any such consideration desire any such thing. And whereas the canons so require, and the bull so saith, that the Pope useth the power and authority that God giveth him according as he weigheth and considereth the qualities of the persons, the causes, and of the times, how could the Pope consider the said Prince Henrye's qualities which he knew not, for there was nothing shewed of his young age, which is one chief quality to be considered and to be regarded in matrimony? Beside this, whereas this dispensation was granted for the continuance of peace and friendship between two princes, one of them (that is the King of Spaine) died ere the bull was put in execution; and so, the matter being whole and entire as it was at the beginning, if there were any cause it ceased and failed.

Again there [p. 123] was a clause in the said bull, that the King might by the said dispensation marry the said Lady Katherine *forsan cognitam*, as who saith, it may fortune knowne, which maketh a doubt of that thing which she knew well enough before. And thereby it may be well conjectured, saith the said dialogue, that she feared to tell the truth, least the Pope, perceiving that she had been known by Prince Arthur, would never have dispensed with this later marriage; or else indeed, if she had not been known, she needed not to have put in these terms at all. And thereby among other things the King's counsell thought that this bull was surreptitious and naught, because the true meaning of the supplication was not purely and truely declared in the same. The defects and faults of which brief are largely and amply contained as well in the instructions given to the King's said agents as in the legates' own letters sent to the Pope. The summary effect whereof, for so much as is meet for our purpose, we will faithfully lay before you.

The legates then, seeming (as it may appear by their said letters) fully resolved and determined to give sentence on the King's side, used all [the] means they could to get the [p. 124] Pope's consent thereto. They declare in their said letters written to the Pope in Latine that the King for his singular good devotion to the apostolic see, and for his excellent deserts towards the same, was worthy upon whom the treasure and favour of the said see should be most plenteously poured and employed. They declare what murmur and grudge was in England that the King's great matter was so tediously prolonged, and as well the people as nobles marvelled that men's ears could abide to hear that the Pope took upon him to dispense with God's law. In fine they shew that the rest, surety, and certain succession of the realm, that the quieting and settling of the King's conscience, depended upon the only hope to be delivered from that marriage, yea, and that otherwise the King and the realm would revolt from the Pope's obedience and devotion. And (to come to the brief we spake of) they shew that the matter being now hard in hearing, and many things so laid against the bull, both for the insufficiency and for the falsity of the causes therein contained, that albeit the cause of itself were dispensable, yet for the said defects the dispensation by law were void and annihilated. Loe the Queen upon a sudden procured an authentical copy of a brief (the original [p. 125] remaining in Spaine) signed with the Pope Julioe's the Second ordinary ring, sign, and seal in wax, to the great marvel and astonishment of the King, the legates and all other, the said copy giving out great and urgent suspicions that it was but a thing forged and counterfeited. It was a thing, say they, not once thought upon, and almost incredible, that even in the very opportunity of the time a brief should be brought forth touching the selfsame matter that the bull did, written and given out by the selfsame Pope, in the selfsame cause, to the selfsame parties, and even on the selfsame day, but yet with much more exact care, diligence, and consideration than was the bull itself, purposely made for the perpetual memory of the said dispensation. And it seemed to be a feigned and untrue matter, as well for the causes before rehearsed, as for that in divers principal and substantial parts it varied from the bull itself, and, being a thing that so nigh touched the realm of England, there was no copy of any such thing among the King's records nor any memory in any man's remembrance of any such brief either heard or seen in England; neither was it to be thought that the King of Spaine [p. 126] was more mindful, careful, and provident for the surety of this matter than was the King of England, neither that there was any man at that time of such sharp and pregnant wit that might think there should arise any controversy after so many years, and yet to be pacified with the exhibiting of such a brief only. Surely if a man should (say they) compare the bull and the brief together, he should soon espy that the bull was but a sorry, weak, feeble, and imperfect thing in comparison to this brief, which is so pregnant and absolute, that it exactly and curiously provideth for the clearing, extinguishing, and taking away all manner of doubts and exceptions that might be laid against the bull. Wherefore the said legates desire the Pope that, beside their other and former authority, their commission and power might be enlarged and amplified to compel King, Emperor, or whatsoever person in the world, by the censures ecclesiastical to exhibit and bring before them the said brief; and further, that, in case (the same being exhibited) the matter should come to such a straight and inexplicable difficulty that they should not be able to expedite and rid themselves out of it, and certainly [p. 127] to pronounce of the falsity or validity of the same, that then the Pope should call the matter to his own hearing, to the which they hoped the King would also condescend, provided that the Pope under his own hand would certify him before that he would once make an end of the matter to his contentation and desire; or, if he were not disposed to advocate the matter, that he should satisfy the King's desire and subscribe to a Decretall drawn out and sent with the said letters. Many causes also were alleged in the said letters why the Pope might proceed to the said divorce, and why also it was expedient that he should do so. And among others that it seemed by the framing of the said new brief that the adversaries themselves in a manner confessed that the bull was false and naught. There was beside, admonition given to the King's agents by all manner of means possible to try out the falsity of the said brief by the help of some scribes there that should view and search the records of Pope Julie and Pope Adryan, and that should view and consider also the other signets of Pope Julie, and confer them likewise with other prints and signets of the Popes' seals [p. 128] since, and of Pope Clemente, with ample rewards of present money or annual pension for the labour of the said scribes. The transumpt of the said brief was sent to the King's agents with a note of such defects and faults as the lawyers both spiritual and temporal at home had espied in the said bull, as of such suspicions and faults also as the Bishop of Worcester, being the King's ambassador in Spaine, had deprehended in the same.

Among other faults of the said brief, which pretended to agree with the original *De verbo ad verbum*, there was an error as well in the King's name as his father's, the Queen and Prince Arthures, whereby it was thought by the King's Highness and all other wise men in England that the said brief was feigned, contrived, and forged; for that no man of reason and experience could think that such express error and in so many places should pass the secretaries or chancery there, especially such a man of experience as Sigismunde was, that is said to have written the same, in whose writings no such error hath been found. And so far concerning the King's and the Cardinall's letters.

Let us then go forth and consider the order and manner of [p. 129] the residue of the King's proceedings concerning his marriage after the said Cardinal's departure. Before the which and after also, he sent divers learned men, as Doctor Stocksley, Doctor Lee, the Bishop of Hereford, and others, some to Fraunce, some to Italie, and some into Germanie, to procure the private censures and judgments of divers learned men, as also the public judgment of certain universities, for the disproving and disallowing of his first marriage. He sent also, after the said Cardinal was departed, Sir Thomas Bulleyne, Earl of Wiltshire, the said Doctor Stocksley, Bishop of

London, and the said Doctor Lee, his ambassadors, with others, to the Pope and the Emperor, intending to meet at Bononye, to the which place the said ambassadors came the Lent following; where they shewed unto the Pope, according to the charge given unto them, the private censures and judgments of a number of notable learned men and divers famous universities, and made great and humble instance that the Pope would determine the matter accordingly, who gently answered them that at his repaire to Rome he would thoroughly hear the matter and determine it as right and reason should require [p. 130]. They informed also the Emperor of these learned men's and universities' judgments, and he answered that if the marriage were repugnant to the law of God, and that the Pope should so find and declare it, he would hold himself contented.

Then was there the next year following, in the month of September, a proclamation that no person should purchase from Rome or use or put in execution anything in a year past purchased or to be purchased afterward, to the lett, hindrance, or impeachment of the King's noble and virtuous intended purposes, which proclamation was thought to be principally devised to put the Queen in some fear to take benefit of anything she had obtained or should obtain from Rome. It might also all under one serve against the Cardinall, in case he had or would procure any curse or other thing from the Court of Rome against the King to be restored to his former dignities, authority, and jurisdiction.

In March following there was a Parliament summoned, in the which certain lords spiritual and temporal of the higher house were sent with the lord chancellor to declare the said censures and judgments of the universities, which were openly [p. 131] read, translated out of Latine into Englishe. There were also a great number of books and writings of private men then shewed and exhibited, disproving the said marriage with Queen Katherine. In the month of May there were divers lords of the counsell sent to the Queen to Greenwich to inform her of the said censures and judgments, and that the Pope could not dispense with the matter, and to exhort her for the tranquillity and pacifying of the King's conscience to put the matter to four prelates and four temporal lords, and to give over her appeal, which she refused to do, as well then as being afterward in July requested to do the same at Eastamsted, after which time the King never saw her more, neither from the beginning of the suit did ever use her body.

In the mean season and the next year also, being the twenty-third of his reign, the Queen's marriage was defended as well in divers open sermons as also by printed books, especially [by] one made by Master Thomas Abell, the said Queen's chaplain; yea, in the Parliament holden in the beginning of the 24 year of his reign, one Temses of the Commons' House motioned the said House that they would make suit to the King to [p. 132] receive again the Queen into his company, for avoiding as well the bastarding the Lady Mary, his only daughter, as certain other great mischiefs that might happen. Whereof the King hearing, sent for Master Audeley, Speaker of the Parliament, and willed him to tell the said House that he did not a little marvel that, this being a matter touching his own soul and not determinable there, any of that House would so far intermeddle therein; and that he wished that the marriage had been lawful, for then never had he been so vexed and troubled with such torment of conscience, the grudge whereof rising upon the information of learned men and whole universities was the only cause that constrained him to forbear her company; adding that unless it were in Spaine or Portugall it had not been seen for one man to marry two sisters, especially the one being carnally known before; but he never heard of any Christian man beside himself that married the brother's wife, as a thing being of all nations highly detested.

In this mean season the King every day more than other cast his singular love and favour to [the] Lady Anne Bulleyne, and in the month of September of this year did create her Marchioness [p. 133] of Pembrocke, and gave to her one thousand pound land by the year, and passing to Calys the October following to speak with the French King, took the said lady with him, and after his return in the end of April did privily marry with her, and about a year after, perceiving her to be great with child, caused her to be proclaimed Queen, and at Whitsuntide following caused her to be crowned.

In the said 24 year there was holden a Parliament, and therein enacted that no man should appeal for any cause out of the realm to the Court of Rome, and an order appointed in the same how and in what manner appeals within the realm for matters spiritual should proceed. Among other things it was ordained that in all causes testamentary of tithes and oblations, of matrimony and divorces, then depending or that afterwards should come in contention, touching the King, his heirs and successors, kings of the realm, the partie grieved might appeal to the spiritual [prelates, to the abbots and priors of the upper house, and that the sentence of the said] prelates and abbots should stand for a final decree and determination, and the matter never to come in question or debate in any other court or courts. In this Parliament and in the [p. 134] Convocation House was great reasoning and many things alleged out of the Counsells of Chalcedon, Africk, Toletene, and others; that a cause or controversy happening or rising in one province should be ended and decided in the same, and that no patriarch should meddle with the jurisdiction of another, which were the chief grounds of this Act of Parliament; the which authorities with the like the said English dialogue allegeth, whereunto we shall hereafter answer.

The said statute of Parliament was intimated to Queen Katherine, and she moved to conform herself thereto, but, for all this notwithstanding, she would not relinquish her appeal. There was sent to Dunstable, Master Thomas Cranmer, Archbishop of Canterbury, associated with the Bishops of London, Winchester, Bathe, and Lincolne, to the which place the Queen was solemnly cited to appear and answer in a cause of matrimony. At length when she had been expected fifteen days and did not appear, the archbishop proceeded to the hearing and determining of the matter, and gave a final decree and sentence for a divorce between the King and the said Queen, and pronounced [p. 135] that the matrimony was against God's law. And yet after all this, the King sent his ambassadors to Nyce to commune with the Pope, which were the Duke of Norfolke, the Lord Rochford, brother to the new Queen, Sir William Paulette, comptroller of the King's house, Sir Anthony Browne, and Sir Francis Bryan, knights.

And likely enough it was that, though the King had attempted many things against the order of the Church, and had now in a manner abolished the Pope's authority, yet, if the Pope had confirmed and ratified his new marriage, that he would have returned again to his obedience, and would have redubbed and reformed all such attempts. But the Pope, when he understood how all such things as we have before declared had passed in England, was so far from any manner of confirmation of the said divorce that he accursed the King and the whole realm, the procuring whereof was imputed to Queen Katherine. And therefore the Duke of Suffolke was sent unto her at Bugden in December in the 25 year of the King, where he brake the order of her court, and discharged a great sort of her household servants, who, being sworn before to serve her as Queen, would [p. 136] not now serve her as princess dowager.

In January twelvemonth after, she departed at Kimbolton, and changed her woeful troublesome life with the celestial heavenly life, and, for her terrestrial ingrate husband, found a kinder and better and a celestial spouse, from whom she shall never be sequestrated and divorced, but reign with him in eternal glory for ever. At the time of her death she wrote a letter to the King of this tenour: "My lord and dear husband, I commend me unto you. The hour of my death draweth fast on, and, my case being such, the tender love I owe you forceth me with a few words to put you in remembrance of the health and safeguard of your soul, which you ought to prefer before all worldly matters, and before the care and tendering of your own body, for the which you have cast me into many miseries and yourself into many cares. For my part I do pardon you; yea, I wish and devoutly pray God that he would also pardon you." Then, after that she had commended to him her daughter, the Lady Marye, and her household servants, desiring him to be good to them, she shutteth up her letter thus: "Finally, I declare that my [p. 139] eyes desire nothing but only to see you." At the reading of which letter the King burst out a weeping. Her dead corpse was carried to Peterborough and there inferred.

Before she departed at Kimbolton, she had lyen two years at Bugden, passing her solitary life in much prayer, great alms, and abstinence. And when she was not this way occupied, then was she and her gentlewomen working with their own hands something wrought in needlework costly and artificially, which she intended to the honour of God to bestow upon some churches. There was in the said house of Bugden a chamber with a window that had a prospect into the chapel, out of the which she might hear divine service. In this chamber she enclosed herself sequestered from all other company a great part of the day and night, and upon her knees used to pray at the said window leaning upon the stones of the same. There was some of her gentlewomen which did curiously mark and observe all her doings, who reported that oftentimes they found the said stones so wet after her departure as though it had rained upon them. It was credibly thought that [p. 138] in the time of her prayer she removed the cushions that ordinarily lay in the same window, and that the said stones were imbrued with the tears of her devout eyes. I have credibly also heard that at a time when one of her gentlewomen began to curse the Lady Anne Bulleyne, she answered: "Hold your peace. Curse her not, but pray for her; for the time will come shortly when you shall have much need to pity and lament her case." And so it chanced indeed.

Now that not only the Pope but God himself cursed the King and the whole realm, it may easily appear by the manifold calamities and wonderful events, chances, and miseries that happened as well to the realm, which we have not so much read of as we have smartingly felt and sorrowfully seen, as to the King himself, whereof we shall speak in place convenient. We are now then come to the 25 year of the King, and to the Act of Parliament then made, and the oath therein ordained for the confirmation of the said divorce, upon the refusal of which oath delated to Sir Thomas Moore and for the justifying of his doings therein resteth and principally dependeth all this our treatise.

[P. 139] The chief grounds of this statute are three.

The one, that the Pope cannot dispense with God's law; which (speaking properly of dispensation) we grant.

The second, that for the brother to marry the brother's wife is directly against God's law; which, as we have abundantly and sufficiently declared already, is untrue.

The third is, that the most famous universities beyond the sea, beside our own at home and the whole clergy in their Convocation, and besides the private writings of many learned men, have determined that this case is indispensable, especially considering that the Queen was carnally known by Prince Arthure.

We will now first answer concerning our own universities and Convocation. Whereto we say first, that, for decision of matters of controversy especially depending in suit before the Pope and upon the Pope's own facts and doings, as this is, neither the universities of England, neither the Convocation of the clergy, be competent and lawful judges. Then we say that the matter, touching the Prince himself, and being of so great weight, the judgments of such universities and Convocations, as be his own subjects, cannot well seem to be of sufficient authority against [p. 140] the party grieved, for that men commonly are ready to gratify their Prince, either for winning of his gracious favour or to avoid his heavy displeasure.

We say thirdly, that especially at this time their doings were most to be suspected and justly to be refused as not proceeding from free, sincere, and stable judgment, the whole clergy being fallen into the King's high displeasure and into a premunire for recognising Cardinal Wolsey as the Pope's legate; the province of Canterbury, for recovering of his favour, being driven to disburse to the King a hundred thousand pounds, besides the province of Yorke, which did contribute for the rate. Beside that, they had given over their pastoral authority, which God had given them, and bound it all to the King's will and pleasure, not able now to make any decree ecclesiastical for the governing of their flock without the King's will and consent; and, to be short, fallen into a plain schism. Wherefore it was as easy for the King to overthrow this brittle and frail clergy as it is for a lusty, sturdy, strong man to give his adversary a fall in wrestling, whom he hath long kept in prison, with coarse and thin diet and hard lodging withal [p. 141]. And surely, unless it had been for the King's fair promises on the one side and fear of his high displeasure on the other [side], it would have been long enough ere the universities and clergy of their free and frank will would have condescended to the said divorce. It is not unknown how earnestly the proctors of both the universities [and clergy] were laboured, and what rewards they had to travel and work with the Convocations of the said universities to get their consent and seal. And it is not unknown how oft it was denied; and that, when all was done, it had not been obtained if partly some men had not shrunk out of the way for fear, and the very opportunity of the time had not been purposely espied when such men were away as were known would gainsay the matter. It is not unknown what a number of learned men and virtuous preachers openly spake against the said divorce, what a number of learned men did publicly in the universities stand with the Queen's marriage, as Doctor Kirkham, Doctor Roper, Doctor Holyman, Master Moreman, Master Bayne, with divers other, of the which men and their doings many things might be here inferred worthy [p. 142] of observation and immortal remembrance. But I will now only declare of two poor friars, and of the noble and excellent virtuous learned man, my Lord Cardinal Poole.

There was then among the Observant friars at Greenwich a man of good house and family called Peto, who had relinquished the brittle, bright, blazing lustre of the world to serve God devoutly

and entirely in the said house; which Peto, having more regard
to the [health of the] King's soul and the public wealth of the
realm than to the safeguard of his own body, having occasion in a
sermon he made to entreat of King Achab, said: "This King Achab
would needs give ear to the false prophets, which did circumvent
and deceive him, and would not hearken to God's own prophet
Mycheas, whom he pained and pinched with hard diet and straight
imprisonment," which story he accommodating to his purpose did
tell the King to his face: " Sir, I am the Micheas that you deadly
hate for prophecying and telling you the troth; and, albeit I know
that I shall be fed with the bread of tribulation, yet that which
God putteth in my heart I will frankly speak." Whereupon with
many persuasions he dehorted the King from the [p. 143] divorce.
Among other things, " Your preachers" (quoth he) " resemble the
400 preachers of Achab, in whose mouths God had put a lying spirit.
But I beseech your grace to take good heed least, if you will needs
follow Achab in his doings, you incur his unhappy end also, and
that the dogs lick your blood as they did his, which thing God
forbid."

What moved this father to speak these words God knoweth; but
that so it came to pass, a very strange event did afterwards shew.
For at what time his dead corpse was carried from London to Windsor
there to be interred, it rested the first night at the monastery of
Syon, which the King had suppressed; at which time, were it for
the jogging and shaking of the chariot or for any other secret cause,
the coffin of lead, wherein his dead corpse was put, being riven and
cloven, all the pavement of the church was with the fat and the
corrupt putrified blood dropped out of the said corpse foulie embrued.
Early in the morning those that had the charge of the dressing,
coffining, and enbalming of the body, with the plumbers, repaired
thither to reform that mishappe, and loe suddenly was there found
among their legs a dog lapping and licking up the King's blood as
[p. 144] it chanced to King Achab before specified. This chance one

William Consell reported, saying he was there present and with much ado drave away the said dog.

The King being thus openly touched out of the pulpit, though he were wonderfully exasperated, yet he digested and dissembled the matter, providing, notwithstanding, the next Sunday, which was Palm Sunday, that one of his chaplains, called Courrant, should prettily play home the said friar Peto, who was in the mean season gone to a provincial chapter of the said Observants, then kept at Canterbury. But, lord, what a stir that Currante made against that poor friar, being absent, and what nicknames he gave him! At length, as though he had now full conquered him, he began to triumph and insult upon him, crying out, "Where is Miser and Micher Micheas? where doth he now micher? He is run away, for that he would not hear what should be said unto him. Belike, he is somewhere lurking and musing with himself by what means he may honestly recant."

There was at that time among other in the roodclofte adjoining to the [p. 145] pulpit a reverend grave virtuous friar and father, called Elstowe, who, being much offended with this great Golias' bragge, answered out of this said roodclofte, "Forsooth" (quoth he) "Micheas is gone abroad, not for any fear of you but for the affairs of our house, and to-morrow will he return. In the mean season, loe, I will be another Micheas, and do offer myself upon the loss and peril of my life to avouch and prove by the holy Scripture all that he hath said, and do offer myself to stand against you (being one of the 400 false prophets) before any indifferent judge." Many other things he would have [then] spoken, and much ado there was to stay him. At the hearing of this the King was cast into a great choler, and in a great heat commanded that these friars should be conveyed thither where he should never hear more of them. After a day or two they were called before the Counsell, and after many rebukes and threats a nobleman told them that they deserved to be thrust into a sack, and to be thrown and drowned in the Thames;

whereat Friar Elstowe smiling, " Make these threats " (saith he) " to the courtiers, for as for us we make little accompt, knowing right [p. 146] well that the way lieth as open to heaven by water as by land." Of this sermon and answer my self have heard the said father Elstowe report. In fine they were banished; neither they two only, but all the Observants also, because they were of the very selfsame judgment and could not find in their hearts to smooth and flatter the King with his false prophets. But see the providence of God; for as they were the first that at the commencement of the schism were banished and exiled, so, the same being pacyfied by our gracious King and Queen, they were the first of all other that were called home and restored after twenty-four years to their old and dear habitation.

It would be a long story itself alone to discourse of all the like occurrents, and upon the free and liberal talk and great constancy that many other great learned men used, opposing themselves for the honour and duty they did bear to God, the King, and the realm against this divorce.

But the chief and most notable captains were the Bishop of Rochester, Sir Thomas Moore, and the Lord Cardinall Poole, of the which Cardinall the very course of our matter inforceth us here somewhat to enlarge; who, seeing that the King was fully bent to go through with his divorce, and not liking the same, and therefore [p. 147] loth to be a meddler therein, procured licence to go beyond the seas; yet could he not quite shake off the matter, for the King sent unto him, being at Paris, letters willing him to procure the learned men's consent there toward his new marriage. But he modestly excused himself as one unmeet for lack of learning and experience for such a purpose. Neither yet could he with this answer quite rid his hands; but yet he gained so much, which was somewhat to his contentation, that the King did associate unto him a colleague whom Master Poole was well content to suffer to dispatch those affairs all alone, himself in the mean season remaining quiet and nothing intermeddling. After one year's abode at Paris he repaired again into England. Then were there that counselled the King to assault Master Poole and by all means possible to draw him to his side, suggesting that being such a noble, young, virtuous, excellently well learned gentleman, if he were once assured to the King's side he should draw to the same a great parte of the nobility. The King liking well of this counsel foreslowed nothing that might win Master Poole to his parte, offering him (if he would advance and further his [p. 148] intended marriage) the choice of the Archbishopric of Yorke and the Bishopric of Winchester, both being then vacant; and for this respect he kept in his hands many months, first, the B[ishopric] of Winchester then of Yorke. Master Poole's brethren and kinsfolk wonderfully travelled with him to condescend to the King's desire, which loved him so tenderly, least otherwise his refusal might be the total ruin and overthrow of him and all their family; to whom he answered, "What, will you have me do against my conscience? Well, well, I will notwithstanding devise some means to content and satisfy the King," whereof the King hearing was not a little glad. Master Poole in the meanwhile humbly and instantly besought God to direct and govern his doings in this matter, that they might be conformable to truth, right, and justice, and to his blessed will and pleasure. At length, thinking he had now found a meane both to serve and satisfy his own conscience and the King's will and pleasure withall, he repaired to the court to speak with the King; but, when he was once come into his presence, he was suddenly so touched (by God's own providence as it is credible) that he could not, if his life had stood on it, a great while utter one word. Afterward, when [p. 149] he came to himself and recovered his speech, he spake quite contrary to that thing which he was determined to have spoken, and showed the King very plainly and openly that he wonderfully disliked of the divorce. Whereupon the King, much moved and changing countenance, put his hand upon his dagger, as though he would have strucken him, but yet he did no hurt. Howbeit he reported afterward that he was so highly offended with Master Poole's talk that he had thought to have slain him as he was in his talk; but yet, considering with what lowliness and humbleness and with what signification of love and duty the said Master Poole uttered his mind, and thinking surely that Master Poole did not hate him, he did forbear to lay hands upon him. [And] after this, when Master Poole had somewhat recovered the King's good will and favour, he got licence to repair again to foreign countries, thinking that the next way whereby to keep himself from intermeddling in that matter which he fancied not. And so a great while he did nothing interpone himself nor meddle therewith.

But at length, when he heard that not only the new marriage was passed, but that the King also had arrogated to himself the name of the Supreme Head [p. 150] of the Church, had abolished all the authority of the apostolic see of Rome, had suppressed all the monasteries, had put to death the Bishop of Rochester, with Sir Thomas Moore, with the Carthusians and other learned men, then wrote he a most eloquent book in Latine, and sent it to the King, wherein he most sharply rebuked him of the said and other enormities, and most gravely exhorted him to penance and to reformation of the said enormities.

But to cut off all other matters we shall now shew you one thing in the said book worthy of good observation touching this our present matter. For whereas King Henry the Seventh put to death Edward, Earle of Warwick, King Edward's brother's son and the Cardinall's uncle, a man most innocent, yet in respect that he was the only heir male of King Edward's house, and feared least to set up him in the royal throne there might be some stir and business against his posterity, loe the said Cardinal Poole, notwithstanding the great injuries done to his family by the said King, the Cardinall (I say), whose family King Henry the Seventh most feared, defendeth even his succession, his posterity, his niece and son's daughter; and against whom (I pray you), even against her own [p. 151] father, which contrary to the law of God and the realm, and most of all against the expectation of the said father, would disinherit her and dishonour himself as it were by open proclamation, declaring and proclaiming himself to all the world to have lived in grievous incest about twenty whole years. If a man would now well weigh and ponder the great noble blood, the sageness, the wisdom, the virtue, the high learning and dignity of this Cardinall, he should find him one such as Homer speaketh of, one instead of many, one I say able to countervail, yea, to overpass, and it were an university or two, of light, worldly, wavering, inconstant, fearful, ambitious men.

Here might we interlace to this our narration many other stories worthy of eternal memory, which we now will pretermitt, least we may seem to overlade this volume; yet we cannot choose but call to remembrance the blessed memory of Powell, Fetherston, and Abell, who were hanged, drawn, and quartered the 32 year of the King, as well for defending and maintaining the said lawful marriage with the King and Queen Katherine (the which was made treason the 24 year of his reign) as for denying [p. 152] the King's new supremacy. At which time, day, and place there was a marvellous strange sight and spectacle; for as these died for the Catholic religion, so were there then burnt three Protestants, Barnes, Gerat, and Hierome, for heresy; so that our new religion, as it disagreed with the Catholics, so did it disagree also from other Protestants.

But to return to our former matter; you will perchance say, "Well, howsoever the matter went with the King's subjects in England, there is no manner of sinister suspicion against the universities and learned men beyond the seas, but that they were most indifferent." Let them be as indifferent as you will; yet that they had no sufficient ground of their censures and judgments we have sufficiently declared before. And whether they were clear and void from all evil suspicion otherwise, let the world judge. This I am sure that I have heard a doctor and countryman of our own that said he was joined in commission beyond the seas with others about these affairs, report that he full well knew that mules were well laden with English angels that flew far and wide among the learned men of Fraunce and Italie. Of whom a man may say [p. 153], as Appollonius saith of certain of the sect of Montanus, that would needs be counted prophets, If we can prove that they took rewards surely they are no prophets. For therefore Johannes Cochleus wrote against this divorce. Our countryman Master Morison doth grievously inveigh against Cochleus for that book, and saith that he did not write it for the zeal and love of justice and truth, but stirred up with malice, envy, and hatred against the King, and for other corrupt affections; whose accusation the said Cochleus refuting, protesteth and most religiously sweareth and taketh God to witness that this accusation was untrue, and that he was not solicited either by the Pope or Emperor to write, nor anything at any time to him promised in their name for any such doings. Howbeit he saith he was on the other side promised no small reward in the year of our Lord 1531, if he would either himself write against the [said] marriage or procure some such censures and judgments from some universities of Germanye as had proceeded from the [said] universities of Fraunce and Italie. Yea, the very Lutherans were solicited and earnestly [p. 154] moved by the Bishop of Hereford (not without fair liberal promises as was to be thought) to give their judgment for the setting forth of the divorce, whereto they could by no means be induced. No doubt they would fairly and easily have condescended thereto, had it been for nothing else but to spight the Pope, if they might have chanced upon any plain and evident place of Scripture to make any foundation upon. It is also here to be considered that the French King was mortal enemy to the Emperor, and joined with the King of England to further the new marriage to the uttermost of his power.

There was also a privy conference, as at large appeareth in the King's and Cardinall's letters before by us mentioned sent to the King's agents at Rome, between the two Kings to make a league and confederation against the Emperor, joining the Pope in the same; so that the Venetians for the cause aforesaid and the French King also, as well for those causes as for that he was in some hope a while that the King would marry his sister (as it was thought), were well contented and careful also to procure that their universities and learned men might gratify [p. 155] the King of England. And yet for all this, things passed with great difficulty and very hardly, especially in the most famous university of them all and among the divines of Paris; whereof after long tossing and turmoiling fifty and three were found that thought the marriage unlawful and indispensable, yet were there forty-two among them of a plaine contrary mind. Then were there five other that, though they did not resolve one way or other, yet they thought the matter should be remitted to the Church to be determined, wherein in effect they concluded for the validity of the former marriage; and so remained but six persons in the whole to make the King's side overweigh the other.

Now, if the five universities of Fraunce, both the doctors of divinity and the decrees in the university of Paris, the university of Biturs, the divines and doctors of law of the university of Aniowe, presuppose that the matrimony should be good enough in case Prince Arthure did not carnally know Queen Katherine, which thing, I trowe, is not so fully proved as the case requireth, as we shall hereafter shew more at large; so that if there were no carnal copulation the greater number of the said universities [p. 156] be on our side. Well, be it that the King to his great charges and cost, and to his dishonour withall, got the censures of the universities of Paris, Orleans, Aniewe, Bitures, and Tholouse in Fraunce, of Bononie and Padua in Italy, where are, I pray you, all the other universities, either of Fraunce or Italie? where are the universities of Ferrara, Florence, Pisa, Senes, and other in Italy? Where be the universities of Salmantica, Toledo, Valentia, and others in Spaine and Portugall? Where be the universities of Germany and of other adjoining thereunto? of Polonia, Bohemia, of Denmark, of Colyn, of Lovaine, of Basile, of Cracovia, of Erford, of Franckford, of Friburgh, of Hafnia, of Heidelberge, of Hinglestade, of Lypsia, of Prage, of Rostock, of Vienna Austriæ, of Tubinga, of Wittenberge? I speak nothing of our neighbours of Scotland and their two universities.

Now, if the number of universities be so material that it carryeth with it the right and truth of the matter, who doubteth but that the Pope and the Emperor, if they had been disposed to work that way, might easily have procured treble or quadruple number of the said universities, as also of the private writings of sundry men for the confirmation of the [p. 157] first marriage; for the tuition and defence whereof many learned men have wrote their minds, both divines and lawyers, upon mere zeal of the truth only, without any solicitation of any man or hope of any reward at all, and among other Johannes Cochleus, that we spake of before, who made a very notable and learned book, which as yet it was not my chance to see. Whereof the great clerk Erasmus liked well, and said that, if he had been so well instructed and riped in the matter as Cochleus was, he would have been so bold upon the King as to have dissuaded him from the divorce. And the said Erasmus was wont merrily to say and write to his familiar friends that he would that Jupiter should have two Junoes rather than he would take away one from him. Whereby he showed his disliking of the [said] divorce.

Howbeit this wise godly Emperor saw full well that this was but an [implicate and] inexplicable endless labyrinth, and well knew, (as being a very Catholic Prince,) that, albeit the censures of learned men and of universities be of great weight, yet when there remaineth any perplex question and of great importance touching our faith or manners, the decision and determination thereof hangeth not upon them but upon the Pope or some general council, whereof the Pope is [the] head, [p. 158] unto whom God by his promise hath obliged himself to inspire them and infallibly to direct their doings, and hath not obliged himself to any private man or to any university, yea, or to any private synode of any one country, which have divers times failed and erred in such matters. It is the apostolic see of

Saint Peter that is the sure rock whereupon we must build. It is that see or some general lawful counsell [which] without the Pope's consent taketh no force, that must decide and determine such matters. It is, I say, the see apostolic that hath this special peerless prerogative given of God, that it never yet failed nor shall fail in her definitive sentence touching the direction of our faith or life; for, if it had, then had the universal church, which resteth upon the authority of this see, been deceived, which is too much absurdity to grant.

Now again for these universities, whereof the Parliament maketh [a] great accompte, why should not the censures of all learned men even of the said universities, which have written at that time, when there was no cause of any sinistrall suspicion or affection to be gathered against them contrary in this matter, to these men, as appear in their books, bear more sway with us than the [p. 159] suspicious testimony of these men given out at such a suspicious time? But, as we have showed, it appeareth well enough the said universities had but slender and light grounds to build their censures upon; yea, I will and dare boldly say that a number of them have full cordially repented their light, rash, and unadvised judgment, as well for the matter itself as for the miserable ruin and decay of true religion and faith, which incontinently happened in this realm after the said divorce.

And thus much may now serve for the universities. You will perchance say that the said censures may the better be borne withal, and the divorce also in case there were any carnal copulation in the former marriage, whereupon as well the said [former] book of dialogue as the statute grounded itself. For the proof of which copulation many reasons are producted in the said dialogue, with mention of the Pope's brief made for the confirmation of the bull; of the which brief we have before showed what faults were found therewith, and what great labour was made to infringe and disable the same. Wherefore, least any scruple or doubt before moved touching either the said bull and brief, or the said carnal copulation, may cause the reader to misdeem and mislike the said dispensation, we will now [p. 160] repulse and remove all such objections.

First, then, touching the false and insufficient cause that they pretended the bull to be grounded upon, we have said sufficiently in our answer to Marcus Mantua. The residue that we have declared out of the said letters and instructions is of little weight. Wherefore, though perchance lack and defect of convenient and sufficient intelligence and understanding might be presupposed in some other common and private person, yet in such a princely person as King Henry was, so well brought up and instructed in good learning as he was, and endewed with so good a wit and capacity as it is notorious he was, it cannot be thought or judged but that he, although he were (as is surmised) but twelve years of age, did well understand the contents of the said dispensation and the commodity and benefit that should come to him and his posterity and to both the realms by the said dispensation and marriage. And therefore it was no need that his age should be otherwise notified and expressed to the Pope than it was. And although he was not informed of his age in the said supplication [yet] it is likely he knew it otherwise. And [p. 161] forasmuch as he knew [that] he was the son and heir to King Henry the Seventh, he considered well enough the chief and principal quality of the person according to the purport of the dispensation. Furthermore, putting the case that he was so young and tender of years, or so weak and infirm of judgment, as in very deed he knew not nor understood what the matter meant; yet like as if the parents contract matrimony for their children being under age, and they coming afterward to age confirm the same, the marriage is good; so and much more if the parents for the wealth of their son obtain any dispensation, it is enough that the son afterward do ratify the same by his express word or deed, though at the time of the obtaining thereof he had no full intelligence of the matter. Less reason is there to infringe the dispensation by the death of the King of Spaine. For the dispensation was not made to him nor for any personal respect of him, but of him, his successors, and realm. It was made to King Henry and Queen Katherine, who both were living when the bull was put in execution. But saith the divine, " This [p. 162] clause (*forsan cognitam*) hath marred and vitiated the bull for lack of the pure and sincere demonstration of the fact." But yet I must ask the divine, or rather the lawyer (for the divine here taketh upon him that part which was more apt and seemly for the person of the lawyer), how he proveth either by his divinity or law that if a woman would crave a dispensation to marry her husband's kinsman she must needs insert whether she knew her husband before or no, which thing is to be [pre]supposed in married persons being of convenient age and health, and having conversation in bed and other places at liberty for the act, as even a little before the lawyer had told him. I find in the law, (for I trowe a man may pore long enough in the Bible ere he find the case,) that if the law require a certain quality to be put in the supplication, the omission of this quality doth vitiate and destroy the supplication. As if a man obtain a dispensation for a spiritual living, and doth not declare whether it hath cure of souls annexed to it or no. I find also that if a man obtain a dispensation to marry his kinswoman or wive's kinswoman he must insert the [p. 163] degree. But of this clause I find no necessity to insert it. Again, I find that the suppression of the final cause moving the Pope to dispense doth vitiate the rescript or dispensation, and not the suppression of the cause impulsive. Women are forbidden to plead other persons' causes before a judge. The final and principal cause of this decree was to repress the impudencie of women, and that they should not, contrary to the shamefastnes that becometh that sex, intermeddle with other persons' matters, or by their resorting to the judicial places run into any obloquy or danger of their chastity as Accursius noteth. The cause impulsive moving the prætor to promulge this edict was the uncomely, importunate, and unshamefaste behaviour of one Calphurnia; and yet other women, be they never so temperate, sober, and discreet, are barred from pleading. Now the final cause stirring the Pope to give out this dispensation was not for that Prince Arthur had not known Queen Katherine. If he had any respect that way and to any such cause it was but the impulsive cause, the defect whereof maketh not the dispensation vicious and surreptitious. If the divine will say yet would the Pope have been [p. 164] loather to grant the dispensation if he had been truly informed of any such carnal copulation, I answer that this difficulty should rise to the Pope, either because the law doth require such specification or upon some good reason. That the law doth require no such thing we have already shewed. As for reason (if there were any) the greatest were for the cause of the unity of flesh between the brother departed and his wife. But we have also declared sufficiently that all such unity is dead and extincted with the person deceased, and by this reason there could be no manner of dispensation given to any man to marry any of his kinsmen's wives. We add further that it is a rule that he that will impetrate and obtain anything of a prince is not bound to make mention of that thing which though it were expressed would not hinder the impetration. And therefore, though the lack of holy orders be a matter of great weight in obtaining a benefice, yet if in the supplication there be no mention made thereof the dispensation is good and effectual. Much less then needed she to say in her supplication, whether she were carnally known or no, especially in this kind of marriage, which by the old law was commanded to the [p. 165] brother surviving, though the dead brother had known carnally his wife. Yea, and in her supplication these words (*forsan cognitam*), though they do not imply absolutely the one or the other, yet implicately they imply both. And therefore it might be gathered by the Pope as well that she was known as that she was not. Wherefore it may also probably be inferred that Pope Julius that gave out this dispensation would also have given it out, notwithstanding the said carnal copulation being certainly to him known. Howbeit presupposed, but not granted, that the bull for those words were defective and insufficient, yet this insufficiency and defect and all other surmised defects are plentifully supplied by this brief. Unless therefore our lawyer and divine can frustrate and undo this brief, all things are sure and sound. But they meddle nothing with this point. Wherefore we will see what may be said to the objections contained in the said letters of the King and Cardinall. The presumptions that be gathered to enforce the forgery of this brief (as that there was no copy thereof in England, and such like, as we have before rehearsed) are not of such weight as should induce any indifferent judge [p. 166] to mistrust the same, for they are easily to be eluded and avoided by other as vehement and much more vehement. For:—

First, there was no cause why any such brief should be forged, the dispensation bearing sufficient strength of itself.

Secondly, though there were no necessity, yet was there some cause why it should be for a more cautele procured, and it were no more but to avoid such calumnious exceptions as have been laid against the bull.

Thirdly, in case it had been any forged matter since Pope Julius' time it were easy to be espied, seeing that all such seals at the death of every Pope are stamped and broken. Yet you will say, let it be Pope Julius' own seal, there is such express error in it that it doth utterly frustrate, exinanyte, and annul the benefit and validity of the said brief. Nay, truly that is not so, for it is a received rule in the civil and common law that if it be sure and certain that it is the party that was meant, error of the proper name doth not vitiate a rescript or dispensation. It was also decided by *Auditores Rotæ* that the acceptation of a benefice vacant is good and vailable, if there be certainty of what benefice it was meant, though there be an error in the name of the [p. 167] person deceased. Well, will our divine and lawyer say, if the brief be good and of any force, then must the Queen at length give over her long hold whereto she so stiflly and hardly leaned, that she was not carnally known by Prince Arthure. The contrary whereof is as well by many other reasons and arguments, as especially by the said brief clearly and plainly proved. It remaineth then for us to view and examine their arguments, of what importance they are. The lawyer then in the said dialogue concludeth as a certain troth that in married persons of [a] convenient age conversant together there hath been carnal copulation. We grant it is so to be presupposed, but yet the plain contrary oftentimes proveth true. I repeat me to the very profane stories [a] in the which we read that the famous harlot Phryne lay all night with Xenocrates the philosopher, whom she could by no means provoke to satisfy her lust, and reported afterward that she lay with no man but with a stone all night. The like continence he used with Lais, that was brought him unawares to his bed. I report next Ammon,[b] that continued with his wife many a year, both remaining virgins. I report the Emperor Henry [p. 168] the First and his wife Cunigundis that continued still a virgin. And to draw nearer home I report me to St. Etheldreda, whom we commonly call St. Audry, that continued with King Egfride her husband a virgin (Beda, lib. 4, cap. 19), which thing some of our stories shew also of King Edward the Confessor. But the most notable president of this kind of chastity is the virginity of our blessed lady, mother of Christ, and married to good Joseph. Neither the law concludeth it utterly for a certain and infallible truth, but saith it is *violenta et certa suspitio*, it may be otherwise and often it is otherwise. Yea, say they, this violent suspicion is enforced also by the very confession of Prince Arthur, whereof some persons of great house have deposed upon their oath and of their own hearing. But we say the denial of such a noble and virtuous Queen may and doth countervaile any such deposition. Nay, saith the lawyer, it is open in law that in this case the husband's confession is to be preferred to the woman's denial. But if the man in talk only and upon a youthfull courageous bragge saith any such thing to his companions (as did Prince Arthur, if he spake any such words at all), here the woman's judicial denial shall overweigh all [p. 169] such extra-judicial bravery, no nor the

[a] Drogen. Laer. lib. iv°. de vit. philos. in vita Xenocratis.
[b] Socrat. li. 4°, ecclesiast. hist. cap. p. 18 [al. 23].

man's oath shall overpoise the woman's denial if she dispose for her virginity with the hands also of honest matrons, and I do well allow the lawyers' saying in this dialogue that the husband's judicial confession making for the marriage is to be preferred. But here the husband's extra-judicial confession is extraordinarily brought forth to break the marriage that had continued twenty whole years without any gainsaying, without any sinister suspicion or grudge of conscience. The other conjecture that the nomination of King Henry to be called and taken as Prince after his brother's death was deferred for a month and more, is not so vehement and strong as the divine would inforce it, but rather maketh somewhat for us. For if it were deferred (as he saith) because it was thought she was with child, as that suspicion proved untrue, so might also the other of the carnal copulation. Wherefore we conclude that there is much more to be deferred and attributed to the judicial denial of so noble and virtuous a Queen than to the extra-judicial affirmation (if there were any) of her husband, especially the said denial being confirmed and upholden [p. 170] with many probable circumstances beside. For Prince Arthure was but fourteen years of age, and very weak, tender, and sickly beside. Wherefore it is like that either by the counsel and advice of his father and his physicians, or for very necessity and conservation of his health, he was constrained to forbear that act, or if he did attempt any such thing he was unable to satisfy that office. Beside this and beside their own confession, she best knowing of all the world her own case, offered also to bring forth witness of good credit by whom she certified her parents how the case stood between her and her husband in this point.

The greatest of all is, and such as should seem able to answer all this quarrel of copulation, that King Henry himself confessed to the Emperor that he found her a virgin, as the Lord Cardinal Poole said to him in his book before mentioned. In case all other things fail will the divine say, Yet the very brief which had this word *cognitam* without *forsitan* did plainly showe and prove that she was known. And seeing herself produced this instrument she had no colour left, but that she must needs be [p. 171] judged by law to confess all the tenor of the said instrument. This were somewhat indeed, if either the King or the legates had accepted the instrument for good and lawful. But they took it (as we have declared) for a thing corrupted, false, and forged; and therefore it seemeth not convenient that the party should take benefit by this instrument which he hath rejected and disallowed. It were somewhat if the Queen had not made a special proviso and protestation, that she did not produce that instrument but so far forth that it made for her purpose and no otherwise. This were somewhat, if it were not a rule that words enuntiative do prove no further between the parties than the necessity of the act that is in hand doth induce, and to the effect of that which is principally in hand. And therefore if a man do challenge a wife and bringeth forth a public instrument, in the which they call themselves man and wife, and in the which appeareth a gift made to her, that in [the] law is called *donatio propter nuptias*, yet because the instrument was not principally made to prove the marriage, these enuntiative words do not prove them man and wife. This were, I say, somewhat if the Queen had been the plaintiff and had grounded [p. 172] her upon this brief. But now she is defendant, and bringeth forth this instrument only by the way of exception for the establishing of the bull and dispensation, and for the enervation and evasion of her adversaries' intention, and therefore seemeth not by producing the same to confess all the contents of it, no more than he that maketh exception seemeth to confess all the contents of the exception, no more I say than if I should claim a woman and she should answer me, I do not confess myself to be your wife, and if I should, yet is there such kindred betwixt us that you cannot enjoy me. By the which exception, as she doth not confess me to be her husband, so the Queen avouching the bull to be good and sufficient, and if it were not to be supplied by the brief, seemeth to confess but so much only as serveth to the principal matter; which is, that though it were true that a dispensation which hath a false and insufficient cause is not good, yet the Pope afterwards confirme it, it is good; as it is indeed. And to this end as the principal was the brief producted, and not for all other matters that were but incident.

Finally, this were somewhat if it were not against all law, reason, justice, and equity, that this word [p. 173] *cognitam*, which was set in purposely to remove all doubt, scruple, and quarrelling that might (as now it hath) ensue upon this word *forsitan*, and to maintain and fortify the bull and this marriage, should now overthrow both, and yet the brief itself to be nothing but false and forged as they say. But that there was no such forgery or nullity of the said brief the King's own doings and letters may abundantly answer and satisfy any man. For after all this great and troublesome stir against this brief, after all the great search at home, at Rome, and in Spaine to find out sufficient matter of falsity and forgery, after all this fervent and hot [asseveration of the said falsity and forgery, after as fervent and hot] suit that the original should be brought forth into England or to Rome, suddenly all this heat waxed so cold that the King in his instructions given to Dr. Bennett gave this advertisement: *Proinde dicti Oratores nihil procurabunt de aliquo rescripto compulsionali vel mandato de Brevis exhibitione hic vel istic, sed potius silentio et tacite impediant quicquid pro Brevis expeditione agere voluerit Pontifex.* Again in the lord Cardinal's letters to Mr. Dr. Stephen and others are these words: "And furthermore you shall in any wise [p. 174] dissuade the Pope for sending either by his Nuncio to be sent into Spaine or otherwise for the original brief; and if the Nuncio be already passed, having charge to speak for the sending of the same to the Court of Rome, then to find the means that a commandment be by the Pope's holiness sent after him not to make any mention thereof. Whereby it doth evidently appear that they did dispaire to prove any such falsity or nullity, and that the production of the said brief should be a most assured confirmation and supplement of the defects of the said bull, (if there were any,) to the utter and total ruin and destruction of the King's intention, as himself confesseth in his letters to his said agents.

Now, because the said divine and lawyer do make such special account of carnal copulation, [and that the statute also notably resteth upon the same; if we should grant the said copulation,] I see no cause in the world why it should prejudice this marriage, and I am assured they neither have nor shall be able to shew any sufficient reason or cause. As for that which they have now alleged, that the Pope would not have granted the bull if he had known any such, or that he could not for their old reason of the unity of the flesh, we have already answered. And so now at length with much ado [p. 175] we are passed as it were the tossing, turmoyling, tempestuous sea of this busy troublesome question of the validity or invalidity of Queen Katherine's marriage, and have at large proved that it was good and sound both by the law of God and man. And consequently that Sir Thomas Moore upon just and sufficient causes did refuse the oath delated unto him for the confirmation of the divorce, and was wrongfully imprisoned and without sufficient and just cause condemned to the said imprisonment, and to lose and forfeit his goods and the use of his lands.

THE END OF THE SECOND BOOK.

The third book of Doctor N. Harpsfield's Treatise of Marriage.

WE will now, as well to satisfy our promise as to shew the great abundant goodness, clearness, and justice of the said Sir Thomas Moore's cause in refusing the foresaid oath (which is and was our principle scope and mark), add for a surplusage that putting the case the said marriage were not good and sound, yet that the said Sir Thomas Moore did not deserve to be so hardly dealt withal, no, not by their own statute; and that though the said marriage were nought, yet that he had good motives, causes, and considerations to refuse the oath put unto him. First, then, we say that the act punisheth none but [p. 2] such as being commanded obstinately do refuse to take the oath in contempt of the act. Now that Sir Thomas Moore's refusal did not proceed from any such wilfulness, obstinacy, or contempt is evident, as well by that himself was ready to swear to the commissioners that he did it not for any self-will or frowardness but only upon mere conscience, as for that when the commissioners pressed him with obstinacy, saying that he would neither swear nor yet shew the cause that moved him to forbear the oath, he was ready to open the said causes (the King's license and favour thereto obtained), which could not be granted him. And what man can justly judge his refusal to be wilful and obstinate that was builded and grounded upon such foundations as we have rehearsed, such as the adversaries never could nor never shall be able to answer? Again, that he did nothing for frowardness and self-will, or in contempt of the law, it may plainly appear to be seen by this, that the law once made, yea, and long before, he put away all such books as he had in his keeping made by other men against the divorce. And after the statute passed he never [p. 3] opened his mind what he thought in that matter [or what he would do in that matter] to any man living, no not to Doctor Wilson or the Bishop of Rochester, craving it at his hands. Furthermore he declared before the commissioners that he did not reprove other men's doings and oaths, but left all men to their conscience, and himself to his own conscience. Beside this he told his daughter, Mrs. Margarett Rooper, that the oath which was offered unto him was not agreeable to the statute, and that they were not by their own law able to justify his imprisonment. And albeit he might have found in his heart to have sworn to the succession (as indeed he was content, so he might have had the oath framed otherwise), yet might he not, nor any man else with a safe conscience, take the oath in such generality as it is [there] propounded, that is, that they should truly, firmly, and constantly, without fraud or guile, observe, fulfil, maintain, defend, and keep to their cunning, wit, and uttermost of all their powers, the whole effects and contents of [all] the Act. For then every man was bound to defend that [p. 4] the Queen was carnally known by Prince Arthure, which was very sore and hard. Then were all men bound to defend that all those marriages there specified had been dispensed withal. And yet was it never read or heard that the father, mother, or brother were dispensed withal. Now in case any man will say that the statute doth not precisely speak or mean that all those degrees were ever dispensed with, but some of them, which could not be, being all by God's law prohibited, this determination (as we have amply declared) is not true, especially for marrying of two sisters, and in our present case for the brother to marry the brother's wife. And we have shewed before that some of these degrees have been dispensed withal, especially by our own apostle St. Gregorie. If men were bound to defend every branch of the said statute, then were they bound to defend that Thomas Cranmer, Archbishop of Canterbury, was a competent and lawful judge in giving sentence of the divorce; which is directly contrary to all laws and orders ecclesiastical, for the matter was depending in the court of Rome, to the which the Queen had appealed. But [p. 5] then our lawyer in the dialogue taketh the matter mightily upon him, and utterly protesteth that the cause might, yea, and ought to be, heard at home in England and not at Rome; and so entereth into a long process against all law and reason, and with such wresting and writhing, such wrangling and mayming of the holy councils and the ancient fathers, that it would pity a man to consider his wretched dealing, and cause him, though he otherwise liked well of the divorce, to mistrust and mislike the same. And because this is one of the principal grounds of the statute, that the matter was lawfully and rightfully heard and determined by the said Cranmer, and because in the said twenty-fourth year there was great and solemn reasoning and disputation, as well in the Parliament as in the Convocation, whether the matter might be heard and determined in England, upon this and like grounds and authorities that this lawyer bringeth forth we will lay before you his said authorities and then solute them accordingly.

First of all he layeth forth certain canons (Canon 6) of the Council of Nyce. The old and the antique custom, let it be kept throughout Egipt, Libia, Pentapolic [p. 5], so that the Bishop of Alexandria have the power of them, for there is a like custom of the city of Rome. Likewise at Antioch also, and other provinces; let their customs and privileges be kept within their churches. What in God's name is there here that maketh for this lawyer's purpose or against ours? Is there anything here that barreth those that be under the patriarch of Alexandria or Antiochia to appeal to the see apostolic of Rome, or that in great or weighty matters the Pope may not intermeddle if they be brought to him by appeal out of other far countries, or that the matter may or ought to be taken out of his hands by any inferior person or persons. No, truly, nor can the council so say, unless the selfsame council should be contrary to many other general councils, and to the very use, practice, and rules of the church; yea, and to itself also, for the fathers of the said council decreed that such things as were passed in a former

---

^a Episcopi in magnâ synodi Nicænâ congregati non sine Dei consilio permiserunt prioris synodi acta in alia synodo examinare. Athan. Apol. 2°.

synod might be discussed and examined again in another council especially called by the Pope. Wherefore if any bishops that were under [other patriarchs had appealed from the synod of] other patriarchs or bishops to the Pope (as Athanasius, Bishop of Alexandria, Paulus, Bishop of Constantinople, and many [p. 7] other did, oppressed by the Arrians), the Pope might and did hear their cause, as Pope Julius did the cause of the said Athanasius and his colleagues, calling before him to Rome the Arrians, and finally restored the said Athanasius, Paulus, and other to their bishoprics whereof they were deprived.[a] Even so Flavianus, the Bishop of Constantinople, was outrageously oppressed by Dyoscorus, and other heretical bishops, at the council of Ephesus, made a libell of appeal and delivered it to Pope Leo, his legates being there present; whereupon, according to the [said] Nycene decree, Leo procureth a new synod, and moveth the Emperor Theodosius for his help and assistance therein. Yea, the very canon alleged by the lawyer overthroweth his intention and strengtheneth ours; for else let any of his adherents tell me how they understand these words (For there is a like custom in the city of Rome), whereof the sense seemeth no other but that whereas there was certain people of Egypt that would not recognise the Bishop of Alexandria for their patriarch, this Counsell maketh a decree against them, and adjudgeth them to the said patriarch, giving this reason of their decree [p. 8], that the Bishop of Rome was wont so to judge the matter, which is a plain testification of his authority above the other patriarchs. Beside this, when they will that the privileges and customs be kept at Antioch and other places, it must needs be that most of all places they would have the customs, privileges, and prerogatives of the apostolic see of Rome to be kept; among which this was one, that the party grieved in any matter ecclesiastical might appeal to that see, as we have already shewed, and shall bye-and-by shew more abundantly; which privilege doth nothing disturb or hinder the

[a] Quod autem post appellationem interpositam hoc necessario postuletur Canonum Niceæ habitorum decreta testantur, &c. Leo Epistola 25, ad Theod. August.

ordinary jurisdiction of the bishops in all other cases at home. It is read also in an epistle of Pope Innocent's in this wise. If any trial of cause, business, or contention arise among clerks and laymen, or between clerks of the higher or lower degree, whatsoever they be, it pleased and hath been ordained that, according to the Nycene council, all the bishops of the same province be gathered together, and so the judgment of the cause to be finished and have his full end. Here playeth our lawyer the [p. 9] forger and foyster rather than a good and sincere lawyer's part. He playeth the part of a crafty juggler, which as with a pretty legerdemain he conveyeth things out of our sight so doth this man also full prettily convey from the reader's eyes the name of Victritius Rathamagensis, episcopus, to whom Innocentius wrote that we should not espy how he conveyeth his gales, for if he had once told us to whom this epistle was addressed, and that thereupon we would have looked upon the epistle itself, then should we have soon espied the lumpish and foul hands of our juggler.

First we say, then, that the place himself allegeth maketh nothing against us. Yea, Innocent himself intermeddleth with the matters and controversies of other countries [farre off], and writeth that the fathers decreed by the sentence not of a man but of God himself that matters and controversies of countries [a] farre off should not be wholly decided and ended before they were brought to Rome, and there that which stood with right and justice might by the see apostolic be confirmed. And to whom doth Innocent[a] write this but to St. Augustine [p. 10] and other bishops of Africk, which desired that he would ratify and confirm such things as they had decreed in their synod? And who placeth those writings of Innocent among his own works but the said St. Austine? And who doth highly allow this answer but St. Austine? He made answer (saith he) unto us of all matters as right required, and as it was behovefull for the bishop of the see apostolic. Hath not this lawyer, then,

[a] Ad omnia nobis ille rescripsit eodem modo quo fas erat atque oportebat, Apostolicæ sedis Antistitem. Epistola 106.

made a pretty gloss to gather that which cannot be gathered out of the text? This interpretation is finely spinned (as the spider spinneth her cobweb out of her own poisoned body), not out of Innocent's text but out of the lawyer's fantastical head. But what if his own text without craving any further aid of Innocent doth utterly overthrow him? As surely it doth, and as certainly as the poor widow Ruthe hath before overthrown his other mate and companion the divine. I will therefore rehearse you the whole and entire sentence of Innocentius. If any matter or controversies arise (saith he) among the clergy, either of the higher or [p. 11] lower degree, let them according to the Counsell of Nyce, the bishops of the said province being together assembled, be finished and ended; neither let it be lawful for any man (the privilege of the Roman Church, to the which in all causes reverence and authority is due, reserved) to relinquish and go from those priests that in the said province by God's will do govern his churches to fly to other provinces. In case any man presume so to do, let him be sequestered from the office and function of the clergy, and let him be accounted of all men worthy to be punished as one that hath done wrong and injury. But in case any matters of great importance be in hand, let them, after the bishops have given their verdict and sentence, be brought to the apostolic see as the synod hath decreed and the good custom doth require. So far Innocentius. And what synod doth he mean but the synod of Nice, as doth appear by that we have brought forth of Athanasius and Leo, as he a little before meant also when he spake of the fathers in his letter to the Africans.[a] He allegeth beside, Isidorus, that the matters of every province must be ordered and dispensed by the same, or by a Counsell of the same province, as it was ordained in the council of Nice. Whereto we need answer no further than we have done. But yet why doth our lawyer suppress that the said Isidore a very few lines before writeth? The authority (saith he) to indict councils is by a

[a] In præfatione conciliorum.

private power committed to the see apostolic. Neither have we read that any synod was ever taken for good and sufficient that either was not called by the authority of that see or confirmed. What doth Isidore now help our lawyer? Where is now his mighty protestation? Where is now the authority of our domestical synods and Convocation that the said statute of the 25 year grounded itself upon? Did the Pope ever indict them or ratify them? There followeth then a decree of the council of Constantinople, which hath nothing but that which seemed to be derived from the Nycene Counsell, and conformable to the same. But did not Pope Damasus meddle with the Patriarch of Constantinople and the bishops that were subject to his obedience? Yes, truly, and according to his letters sent unto them they assembled together in a synod at Constantinople. Was not Constantinople subject to the see of Rome? Yes, [p. 13] truly, as our Apostle St. Gregorie[a] testifieth, and Eusebius the bishop there, and the Emperor himself did recognise. Yet to wrest this Counsell that it might somewhat sound to his purpose, our lawyer saith: But if it chance then to be called out of their administration, let them not go for other ordinances to be made, or for other dispensations ecclesiastical; which words, though they were in the Counsell, as they be not, were not yet to be taken of the Pope calling the bishops out of their diocese (as this lawyer would wrest them) by reason of the special privilege annexed to that see, as we have shewed. The words of the council[b] are these: But the bishops, unless they be called, let them not pass their diocese to ordain any priests, or to do any other function ecclesiastical. Is not this a handsome interpreter, think you, that translateth for *If they be not called—But if it chance them to be called*, turning a negative into an affirmative, and thereby preventing and destroying the whole sense and meaning of the general Counsell. Surely of this

[a] Nam de Constantinopolitana ecclesia quis dubitat eam sedi Apostolicæ esse subjectam. Grego. li. 7, Epistola 36.
[b] Non vocati autem episcopi ultra suam diocesim non accedant propter ordinationes faciendas vel propter alias dispensationes ecclesiasticas. Tom. 1°, Conciliorum.

place there can be no more inferred that which our good lawyer would infer than if I should infer,—The Bishop of London can neither make grants nor exercise any episcopal jurisdiction in the diocese of Lyncolne [p. 14] unless he be called. Ergo, the Archbishop of Canterbury or the Pope cannot call before them upon any appeal the said Bishop of London. He addeth now further the Counsell of Chalcedon, which containeth the very same that we had before out of the Nicene and Constantinople council; consequently he bringeth forth the fathers of the Aphrycan council that allege the said Nycene canon against Pope Celestyne, and wrote to him thus: That any legate should be sent as from your holiness' side, we find it not ordained or decreed in any Counsell or fathers. What then? The king himself sent for Legate Campegius, and desired that our Cardinal might [be] associate with him. And therefore the said fathers help the lawyer nothing. Yea, the said fathers might easily have found that decree that they deny to be found in the [great] Counsell of Sardica of 300 bishops kept not long before their time, and where were present a great number of bishops of Affricke,[a] in the which Counsell it was decreed that a bishop being condemned in any Counsell might appeal to the Bishop of Rome, and that it should be in his choice to renew and hear his cause again, or to confirm that which was [p. 15] adjudged before; either to remit the matter again to be heard in the said province, or to send some legate to the province furnished with his authority to hear and determine the matter with the provincial bishops. He heapeth on also the seventh Counsell of Carthage and the Milevitane Counsell, which both tend to one end and scope, that there should be no appellations made out of Affricke. Whereto we answer that the see apostolic of Rome seemeth not to be comprised in the said prohibition, which, as we have declared before, is ever in such matters excepted and privilegiated. And if any man will say that they meant of that see also, then we say that a particular Counsell of one nation cannot impair and abridge the special prerogative of

[a] Athanas. Apol. 2, contra Arian.

the see apostolic, confirmed (as we have shewed) by the chief general Counsells. Lastly, we say that, seeing these Counsells of Carthage and Milevitane were confirmed by Pope Innocent, as Pope Celestyne [a] doth testify, this is no prejudice to the Pope's authority to receive appeals from other countries, to whom he hath granted no such privilege or confirmation, no more than it is [p. 16] that other countries should not receive the Pope's legates because the Pope of old time granted to our Kings of England a privilege that they should not be bound to receive any legate from Rome unless themselves would accept him. There is yet left one Counsell more (so copious is our lawyer in his Counsells) and that is Antiochenum, which is left for the last case, and to make up all; which was no lawful Counsell but a conventicle and conspiracy of heretical Arrian bishops, meet patrons for this lawyer and divine, who being called to Rome for deposing of Athanasius durst not (well knowing their own naughty and reprovable doings) appear there, and therefore were taken for plain wrongers and slanderers of Athanasius, and he was restored again by Pope Julius to his bishopric. [b]

These now be his Counsells and proofs whereby he would maintain that this matter should be heard at home, and upon the which he buildeth his mighty and sundry protestations, which is (as you have heard) quite overthrown even by his own Counsells and authorities. And yet, as though he had made a great conquest, he [p. 17] threateneth the Pope very sore, that in breaking and violating these canons he had broken and violated his solemn oath, whereby he professed to keep the canons, for the which, seeing he could not dispense with himself, he cannot dispense with other. And after many superfluous false and heretical conclusions, which we pass over to avoid tediousness, at length he answereth the whole matter out of Innocentius all on our side, concluding that though the Pope may not dispense with God's law yet he may (as necessity and utility shall require) dispense with man's law, which is the

[a] Celestini ad Episcopos Galliæ, Epistola 3 ; *vide* Aust. Epistola, 90, 91, 92, 93, 95, 96.   [b] Athanas. Apol. 2.

thing that we also plainly avouch, affirming that there is no bar of God's law against this marriage. Yes marry, saith the divine, it is plaine against God's law, and it was an heresy of Wickliffe condemned, to say that the prohibition Levit. to marry the brother's wife was made by man and not by God. Wherefore seeing he is to be taken for an heretic that holdeth the contrary, this matter is not disputable but already judged and concluded. It is a common saying that it is pity to belie the very devil. Why should this man then belye Wickliffe though he were an archheretic, and not only Wickliffe [p. 18] but the general Counsell also of Constance, yea, and his own masters also, the patrons of the universities, out of whose book he took this assertion? But this geare is very suitable, for as they were bold to tell the matter otherwise than it is in Wickliffe or the said Counsell (as we have before out of the [said] bishop of Rochester's book declared) so is this man as bold to report the matter otherwise and much worse than his masters did. For they say not that Wickliffe affirmed that the Levit. prohibitions were made by man and not by God, but that they were judicial. Now were the judicials of the Levit. as well made by God as the ceremonials or morals. Neither is there (as this divine would make us believe, the more to exaggerate the matter) any special mention in the Counsell of marrying the brother's wife. And if there were, what is that against us that say and so prove that our case is not within the compass of the Levit. prohibition, which is to be understood where the brother dieth without children? If the Counsell had condemned this interpretation, then had the divine spoken somewhat to the purpose. Now he runneth and roveth [all] at [p. 19] random, and our conclusion is as far off from any condemnation made by the said council as he is from the knowledge of a good and learned divine and from the office of an honest true-dealing man. But to return where we left. Albeit he hath sore wounded his own cause by the Counsells and testimonies which himself allegeth to prove, that this matter might and ought to be determined in England, yet goeth he on further and layeth more untruths to the former, saying that the universities of Paris and Orlyans and a great number of clerks in Italy said that the Pope did wrong to enterprise to hear this matter at Rome. What a shameless forehead hath this lawyer, for albeit they misliked of the marriage yet there is not one either university or private writer that ever I read or heard of that held this opinion. I find in Marcus Mantua a Counsell whereby he goeth about to shew that the King was not bound to appear personally at Rome; but for removing the matter from the Pope there is not one word; albeit (as I said) he hath given himself so foul a fall, yet goeth he on further and animateth the subjects plainly to resist the Pope's doings and proceedings [p. 20] in this matter, calling it a prejudicial injury to the realm, and a pernicious example for all Christendome, and that we should not pass for the Pope's excommunications in this matter. Then lasheth he forth many authorities and examples, and among other of St. Laurence, Archbishop of Canterbury, rehearsing it otherwise than it is in William of Malmesbury or in Henry of Huntingdon as his master did before him, as we have declared out of the Bishop of Rochester's book, unto the which authors we now add Bede himself (Beda, li. 2, ca. 6), whom the said two storyers do follow. Whereupon we may infer that whosoever otherwise rehearseth this story, and after such sort as these men do, they tell an unlikely and uncredible tale. For either the King remained in his error and idolatry still and minded to continue still his unlawful marriage, and then were he a madman that would think the Pope so mad that he would in this case threate cursing upon St. Laurence unless he did absolve him, or the King himself repented of his said relapse and incestuous marriage, and then is it as incredible (considering the case of the tender and young faith in England) that St. Laurence would be so stiff and [p. 21] stubborn in reconciling the King, to the present danger and to the utter rooting up of all the faith of Christ so lately planted. [Howbeit] he reciteth also the examples of St. Dunstane and Robert Bishop of Lincolne, already answered by the said Bishop [of Rochester]. Howbeit in repeating the story of St. Dunstane, he calleth the woman there mentioned the earl's nigh kinswoman and not his brother's wife, as did the translator of whom we spake before. We conclude then,—Albeit the King's marriage otherwise had been unlawful, yet, until such time as they had been lawfully and justly separated by a meet and competent judge (which was not the said Archbishop but the Pope himself), the King and the Queen (the said statute notwithstanding) were to be taken for man and wife, and the King might have been by the censures of the Church compelled to receive her again. Yea, I will now plead another way. I will not urge and press them with the Pope's singular and extraordinary authority throughout all Christendom. I will dissemble that excellency and prerogative for a time, and yet will I affirm that this process at home against the said marriage was not good nor lawful, but should [p. 22] have been heard and determined at Rome by the Bishop of that see. For, as it was notorious that there were certain other patriarchs in other places of Christendom, as of Alexandria (which had 1,000 bishops underneath him), of Antiochia, of Hierusalem, of Constantinople, so is it notorious that all the west and Latin Church was under the Bishop of Rome, not only as the universal bishop of whole Christendome but as a patriarch also of the said Latine and west Church. And therefore, as great and weighty matters that could not be ordered by the Metropolitans and their synods were ended by the patriarchs of the said countries to whom there was recourse by appellation, so, though the Archbishop of Canterbury might as rightfully hear and determine this matter as any other as metropolitan and primate of England, yet, by reason of the Queen's appeal (which might have held by law, though the Pope had been only patriarch), the said archbishop could not interpose himself and meddle with the matter; for such appeals to the patriarch from such as were subject to any of them were practised and counted [p. 23] good and lawful above a thousand yeare agoe, and since are confirmed by the most famous general Counsell holden at Laterane. We add to this that the King had provoked and appealed from the Pope to the general Counsell, and then, if the said archbishop intermeddled after the said provocation, his doings were derogatorious not only to the dignity of the patriarche but to the supremacy of the Pope and to the authority also of the general Counsell. So on every side the jurisdiction of the archbishop was either none at all or justly declined and suspended.

We will yet, all this notwithstanding, use some more free and bountiful dealing with the adversaries. We will imagine with them that there was good cause of a divorce, and that the judge also was competent; yet for all that we affirm that Sir Thomas Moore had most just cause of refusal of the said oath, and could not with safe conscience before God ratify and allow all the contents of the said statute, and among other that clause of the statute where it is said,—We, your subjects, both spiritual and temporal, do purely, plainly, constantly, and firmly accept and approve and ratify for good [p. 24] and consonant to the law of Almighty God, without error and fault, the marriage solemnized between your Highness and your lawful wife Queen Anne. This clause, I say, neither Sir Thomas Moore, neither any other man so fully instructed and ripe in the matter as he was, could, without offence of conscience, approve and ratify, for three great errors and faults that were in that marriage.

The first whereof was that the King was married to [the] Lady Anne Bulleyne long ere there was any divorce made by the said Archbishop [of Canterbury]. The which marriage[a] was secretly made at Whitehall very early before day, none being present but Mr. Norris and Mr. Henage of the Privy Chamber and the Lady Barkeley, with Mr. Rowland the King's chaplain, that was afterward made Bishop of Coventry and Lichfield. To whom the King told that now he had gotten of the Pope a lycence to marry

[a] The clandestine manner of King Henry's marrying Anne Boleyn, and the faults in the said marriage.

[a] This and the few following marginal references were made by the transcriber of the manuscript.

another wife, and yet to avoid business and tumult the thing must be done (quoth the King) very secretly; and thereupon a time and place was appointed to the said Master Rowland to solemnize the said marriage.

At which time Mr. Rowland being come accordingly, and [p. 25] seeing all things ready for celebration of mass and to solemnize the marriage, being in a great dump and staggering, came to the King and said—" Sir, I trust you have the Pope's lycence, both that you may marry and that I may join you together in marriage." "What else?" quoth the King. Upon this he turned to the altar and revested himself, but yet not so satisfied, and troubled in mind he cometh eftsoones to the King and saith—" This matter toucheth us all very nighe, and therefore it is expedient that the lycence be read before us all, or else we run all—and I more deep than any other —into excommunication in marrying your grace without any baynes asking, and in a place unhallowed, and no divorce as yet promulged of the first matrimony." The King, looking upon him very amiably, " Why, Master Rowland," quoth he, " think you me a man of so small faith and credit, you, I say, that do well know my life passed, and even now have heard my confession? or think you me a man of so small and slender foresight and consideration of my affairs that unless all things were safe and sure I would enterprize this matter? I have truly [p. 26] a lycence, but it is reposed in another sure[r] place whereto no man resorteth but myself, which, if it were seen, should discharge us all. But if I should, now that it waxeth towards day, fetch it, and be seen so early abroad, there would rise a rumour and talk thereof other than were convenient. Goe forth in God's name, and do that which appertaineth to you. I will take upon me all other danger."[a] Whereupon he went to mass, and celebrated also all ceremonies belonging to marriage. This is, then, one error and fault. For, though the first marriage were not good, yet could not the King marry before the sentence of divorce, unless he should have [had] two wives living all at one time. But

[a] This Doctor Rowland's surname was Lee, and for performing the ceremony was made Bishop of Lichfield. Wood's Athenæ Oxonienses.

now let us dig another hole or two in the wall with Ezechiell, and then shall we see two other great filthinesses and abhominations.

The one was, that the said Lady Anne Bulleyne was precontracted to the Earl of Northumberland, and that the King himself was certified thereof, as I understand, by a right worshipful man that did learn it of one that knew most of all the secret affairs of the said earl [p. 27]. The other and last is, that, if the marriage with Queen Katherine were not consonant with the laws of God, surely this marriage with Queen Anne was much more discrepant to the said laws. If there were a fault and error in the former, it was much more in the latter. If it be against God's law to marry that woman that my brother hath known, much more is it against God's law to marry with her sister whom myself have known. For, though the law of God doth not command men to marry their wives' sisters, yet it doth not forbid them. But to marry the brother's wife if he died without children, the brother survivant, was commanded by Moses' law. Then as much difference as there is between the thing that is commanded and the thing that, though it be lawful, is not commanded; and how much difference there is between my own body and flesh and my brother's body and flesh; so much difference is there, I will not say in fault (for to marry the brother's wife by lawful dispensation is no fault), but between fault and error surmised in the first and the true fault and certain error in the [p. 28] second marriage. For now, to be plain with you, the said Lady Anne was sister to her whom the King had carnally known before. Wherefore, after that he minded this divorce, and had a while some comfort thereof, he laboured to the Pope to have a dispensation to marry that woman whose sister he had carnally known before, as the said Lady Anne Bulleyne declared herself to the Lord Cardinal Poole, and the said Lord Cardinal objected it plainly to the King in the book wrote against the said marriage and supremacy. Yea, I have credibly heard reported that the King knew the mother of the said Anne Bulleyne,[a] which is a fourth

[a] King Henry is said to have known carnally the Lady Anne Bulleyn's mother.

impediment, and worse than the precedents; of the which impediment Sir Thomas Moore was not by likelihood ignorant, and seemeth to touch them or such like in these words which he wrate in the Tower, among other things, to Dr. Wilson,—Finally, as touching the oath, the causes for which I refused it, no man wotteth what they be, for they be secret in my own conscience, some other peradventure than those that other men would weene, and such as I never disclosed unto any [p. 39] man yet, nor never intend to do while I live. Put now, gentle reader, a strange case, and as it were a paradox, that the first marriage was never good and sound from the beginning, and that the second was good and sound, yet say we still that Sir Thomas Moore had good cause to refuse the oath contained in the statute, especially for the last part of the same, and for the provisoe therein contained. Provided always (saith the statute) that the article in this Act contained, concerning prohibition of marriages within degrees mentioned before in this Act, shall always be taken, interpreted, and expounded of such marriages where marriages were solempnized and carnal knowledge had. Well, as bad as this provisoe is, it is so provided by the King himself, and by the whole Parliament, that, in case Queen Katherine were not known by Prince Arthure, she was unjustly divorced. And then surely stood the King's case upon a narrow point, as upon the only carnal copulation, which was a hard thing to prove, as we have before declared. Now, this provisoe partly giveth a very false, pernicious understanding to the Levitt. and partly it is otherwise, at least very [p. 30] defective. Their understanding, I say, is false whereby they make it free for a man to marry not only his brother's but his father's or son's wife, so she be not known. The defect is, that, as this false understanding is wrongly applied and specified, so is there another true and necessary understanding of the Levitt. at least suppressed, that is, that we should not marry with such women as our kinsfolk have married, but neither with such also as our kinsmen have carnally known without marriage. Now whether it was meant to make this kind of marriage free I cannot certainly say, but that either it was so meant or the true meaning for certain purposes for a time dissembled, it may somewhat appear by that which hereafter we shall declare. In the meanwhile we will say something as well to the express meaning of the statute as to the defect. I will then, concerning the said defect, bring forth two or three testimonies and reasons, and so proceed to the express proviso. Let us hear then what holy Scripture saith, which reproveth the father and the son that use one woman. Let us hear the Agathense Counsell, which calleth such marriage plain incest where one [p. 31] marrieth a woman that any of his nighe kinsmen have known before. Let us hear St. Gregorie, our apostle. Truly, saith he, it is not nor shall not be lawful for any man to marry that woman that his kinsman before hath married, or hath otherwise by unlawful copulation defiled her. It is plaine incest, it is abhominable before God and before all the world. And it is, saith he, decreed already by the Fathers that incestuous copulation should not once be accounted under the name of marriage. Wherefore, by the decrees of the Church, if my brother hath known any woman, and I (through ignorance of the fact) marry with her, we must be separated; and if a man will thoroughly and deeply consider and view the 18th and 20th chapters of Levitt. he shall find that we are as well forbidden to marry those persons there named, that our uncle, brother, father, or son have carnally known without marriage, as when they had married them. For whereas this reason is given,— Thou shalt not discover the foulness of thy father's wife, for it is the foulness of thy father; thou shalt not discover the foulness of thy [p. 32] father's sister, for it is thy father's flesh, and so the like in other persons; the same reason of the unity of the flesh taketh place where my brother or any other kinsman knoweth any woman without marriage. For whatsoever woman my father, my son, or my brother knoweth, they are one flesh with the same woman, albeit she be a very harlot, as well as with their own wives. And therefore St. Paul saith— *Qui adhæret meretrici unum corpus efficitur* —he that cleaveth to an harlot is made one body; and it is a received conclusion among the divines and casuists that affinity (which you know letteth marriage) is contracted as well by unlawful copulation as by marriage; which conclusion doth stand with natural reason. For matrimony hath two scopes or ends; the one is to beget and bring forth children, the second is the participation and communion of mutual life, and of the procuration, ordering, and dispensing of domestical affairs, and touching mutual offices and duties to be done one to the other. Now, though this second end taketh place but in those only that be married, yet doth the first end take place [p. 33] in all manner of carnal copulation whereby any procuration of children doth ensue. Whereupon I infer this conclusion,—Matrimony, in that respect that it hath corporal copulation for the bringing forth of children, doth cause affinity. But in unlawful meddling there is also like carnal copulation. Wherefore it breedeth and causeth also affinity.

Wherefore as matrimony is a bar, so is also carnal copulation without matrimony. And by the [very] civil law, and in the time when the Emperors were not yet christened, Alexander the Emperor made a law against such as married their fathers' concubines, saying it was a dishonest and irreligious marriage, and that they which did so did commit the crime of adultery.

Now the provisoe is so open against all law of God and the Church, and so offendeth all chaste ears, that it pitieth and rueth me at the very heart when I hear or read of this perilous provisoe, whereby I may marry not only my brother's, father's, or son's spouse, but his very wife, contracted to him by formal and pregnant words of the present time, yea, though the marriage were solemnized, in case there were no carnal knowledge; in the refuting of which impure and unchaste proviso, if I be the longer [p. 34], I trust the reader will bear with me as well for that it is necessary he be thoroughly instructed in this matter as for that he shall have an answer all under one to a like unchaste statute made seven years after. For as here it is provided that I may marry with my nighe kinsman's wife being not known, after his death, there it is so provided that if any man were betrothed to a woman, yea, though the marriage were solemnized, yet, if before the consummation, the woman were minded to play a lewd naughty part and to forsake her husband, or likewise the husband to forsake her, either she solemnized and consummated matrimony with another husband or he with another wife, the first marriage was frustrate and void. This is such a provisoe that the honest and charitable ears of the very Paynims could never abide to hear of. I cannot marry (saith Ulpiane) my father's spouse, though properly she be not my step-mother. As contrariwise my spouse cannot be married to my father. If this were the law of the Paynims agreeable to the law of nature [and honesty, promulgated by them that were only directed by the law of nature], by natural reason and by honest civil policy, what a heinous heavy hearing it is to hear or read such a statute made in a Christian realme! Neither will [p. 35] it avail to say that there is no affinity in this case. We grant you. But there is an impediment which the law calleth *publicæ honestatis justitia* that doth break all such matrimony foregoing, [and letteth also the matrimony following,] yea, this prohibition grounded upon public justice and honesty (which, as you see, the very Paynims by the only light of nature did observe) is so strong that albeit I contract spousals which of themselves are void and annihilated as being contracted with some of my nighe kinswomen, or contracted by me, being a religious professed man, yet cannot my kinsman marry with her. So much for the spousals.

Let us now consider the case where there is matrimony either contracted or solempnized, wherein is less doubt than in the former. And let us first inquire whether the very substance of matrimony standeth in carnal copulation or in the bond and knot of mind in persons married; and whether the said mutual consent be a sufficient cause to make a sure, true, and indissoluble matrimony; wherein it is first expedient to hear how marriage is defined. Matrimony, then, is a coupling and conjoining of the man and the woman with a continuance of individual conversation and living together [p. 36].[a] Well, then, what maketh this knot? the consent and unity of mind or the carnal copulation? Surely the consent of mind, as the notable lawyer Ulpiane saith—*Nuptias non concubitus, sed consensus facit*. Wherefore if there be a bequest made to a woman when she is married, the condition is fulfilled when the husband hath once contracted marriage with her and brought her to his house. And the civil law that forbiddeth a man to marry the wife of his kinsman deceased taketh place though she be a virgin. The [a]foresaid rule is also upholden by natural reason, for as in buying and selling and other contracts those obligations and contracts are made by the mutual consent only of the parties, whereof it is said nothing is so agreeable to natural equity as that the owner's will (meaning to transfer his goods into the hands and power of another man) be accomplished, so this contract and bargain of matrimony, whereby each party transferreth the power of his body to the use, will, and pleasure of the other, is by this mutual consent made and accomplished when the one saith, "I take thee to my wife," and the other answere, "I take thee to my husband." By the which words, though it be not expressed, as it needeth not, is implied too the said authority one [p. 37] to use the other's body, and the contract of matrimony is perfect of itself, though they do not presently practice the said authority. Even as there is emption and vendition contracted as soon as the parties be condescended upon the price though there be no money presently defrayed, no nor no earnest given for it. Now it is a rule, not only of the civil law (as we have said), before Christ his time, as well as after, but even the sure, constant, and certain rule, also of all the fathers and Counsells, of all the divines and canonists received of the whole Church that the consent and not the carnal copulation maketh the matrimony. According whereunto writeth St. Ambrose, *Defloratio virginitatis non facit matrimonium, sed pactio conjugii*. So saith Isidore, so saith Chrisostome, so saith St.

[a] Matrimonium est viri mulierisque conjunctio individuæ vitæ consuetudinem retinens. Ca. Illud, De præsumps. Magister senten. et alii, Distinct. 27.

CAMD. SOC. 2 I

Austine. And, therefore, there was true matrimony between Joseph and our Blessed Lady the Virgin Mary, as St. Austine writeth. To the which Joseph the angel said " Be not afraid to take thy wife." Yea, so seemeth St. Paul to say when he writeth— I do not command, but our Lord, that the wife shall not depart from her husband, and if she depart that she remain unmarried; by the which place it appeareth that though [p. 38] they be separated and use no such copulation yet the marriage remaineth, for if, after the said copulation, abstinence from the same doth not dissolve matrimony, it will follow that if before they ever meddled together (the better to apply themselves to prayer) according to St. Paul's counsel they had been agreed never to meddle, it should be a good and true marriage. Neither is it once to be doubted but Adam and Eve were man and wife in Paradise, and yet they had there no carnal copulation, and it was there said to them, They shall be two in one flesh. And if you would hold the contrary opinion that carnal copulation were required, then should the matrimony of those that be barren be no marriage, for carnal copulation is referred to generation, whereof they are destitute, and yet certainly their marriage is good. Again, if there be a contract made of present matrimony with a woman though the marriage be not consummated nor yet solempnized—if it chance another man to contract and solempnize matrimony with her afterwards, yea, and to consummate the same, yet by the consent of all writers and by the determination of the whole [p. 39] Catholic Church the second matrimony is void and the first doth stand. Furthermore, the inward end of a sacrament is to sanctify men by grace. Now the sanctification in the sacrament of matrimony happeneth not by the act of carnal copulation but when both parties give their consent before the priest (as I take it to be the truer opinion), or as other say, whether the priest be present or no. We add now, for the better exposition and explanation of the said Levitt. that King David had to his wife Abisaig, whom, as it evidently appeared, he never knew; and yet, because Adonias, one of King David's sons, went about to marry her, it was one of the causes why King Solomon put him to death, which marriage (as Lyra saith) is against the Levitt. law. And this exposition is the more to be marked, because himself was a Jew and (as some men think) born in England before the Jews were expulsed, and was most skilful as well in Holy Scriptnres as in the manners and customs of the Jews. By these reasons and examples it appeareth that the substance of marriage standeth, not in carnal copulation, but in consent. Against which, though nothing can be objected of any force, yet if they shall seem to any [p. 40] of our adversaries too weak and feeble we will bring him other witnesses and that such as he will not nor can well deny. I mean the patrons of the King's cause in the book before by us refuted. For, loc, to prove even the very same conclusion that we make, they bring forth Hildebertus, that the brother cannot marry the brother's wife, though she were not known. They bring forth *Consilium Triburiense* and the example of the said Adonias with some other things that we have alleged. They bring forth Ivo, which saith that one man cannot marry two sisters, though the first be unknown. They bring forth Pope Alexander the Third which had rather suffer Henry, a citizen of Papie, to be perjured than that he would take upon him the authority to dispense with him for his oath, by the which he had bound himself to marry a maiden to his youngest son which had been made sure before to his eldest son now being departed. Yea, they conclude that it is so far forbidden by the Levitt. law to marry the brother's spouse that it is plaine indispensable. If this be true, why have they made these and other cases of the marriage of such as were espoused to any of our kinsmen not only dispensable, but, by this new proviso, lawful to all men without dispensation. If they will say they were deceived, why did the King and Parliament trust [p. 41] them in the residue ; if they were not deceived in their former opinion, why did they so soon revolt from it. It appeareth, surely, in this and other matters, that as the violence of the wind carrieth away the shipp to and fro in the raging sea, so these men were tossed and carried now hither, now thither—not whither right and justice, but whither the King's and other men's pleasure did drive them. And, surely, I credibly understand that there was one of the noblest men at that time that married a gentlewoman which was before betrothed to his son. Now, whether this provisoe was made to serve his and some other men's appetites and turns, I cannot certainly tell. But you will, perchance, say that the Parliament had some good reason and authority on their side, of which kind, as yet, we can find none. Surely, among all the books, either in Latin or in English, that have come to my hands of the King's marriage, or otherwise have been written by any of our countrymen, I find no such thing as much as once touched, saving in Mr. Wakefeild, who, with a word or two, understandeth the said 25th chapter of Deut. of the brother's wife not known, to whom we have already answered. Yet, the better to satisfy thee (gentle reader) and the more fully to rype thee in the matter, the [p. 42] chief and principal arguments that may seem best to serve for the contrary opinion that I could otherwhere find, I will now set forth, and the solutions of them withal. I find then in effect three reasons and three authorities that may seem to sound to the contrary of our opinion. The first reason is deduced from the nature of the union and knot which is in matrimony, which union is this,—*Erunt duo in carne una*—they shall be two in one flesh. But this union is not but by carnal copulation. Again, if a man would regard the scope and end of matrimony he shall find that it is either to have procreation of children or to stanche and remedy the heat and fervour of concupiscence, and neither of these ends is obtained but by the said carnal conjunction.

The third reason riseth upon the signification which is implied in matrimony, for it signifieth and representeth the conjunction and unity between Christ and his Church, in that he took upon him our humanity. Now this conjunction and unity is not nor cannot be resembled but by the said fleshly copulation. Set now to these reasons the authorities following:—

First. Of St. Austine, saying, There is no doubt but that woman doth not pertain to matrimony [p. 13] with whom it cannot be shewed that there was conjunction of the sexe. Then, saith Leo, whereas the society of matrimony is so ordained from the beginning, that, beside the conjunction of the sexe, the marriage hath not in it the sacrament of the conjunction of Christ and the Church, it is not to be doubted but that that woman doth not pertain to matrimony with whom it is shewed that there was no matrimonial ministry. To these may be adjoined the authorities of Origen, that saith that our lady was called Joseph's wife because it was thought she should be his wife, and of St. Hierome and St. Gregorie that will not call our ladie's marriage nuptialls.

Last of all, though Alexander the 3rd decreed that a precontract should not be voided by a contract and carnal copulation following, yet it seemeth that there were some of his predecessors that decreed to the contrary. *Quamvis (inquit) aliter a quibusdam prædecessoribus nostris sit aliquando judicatum.* In this then resteth the very pith of such things as may be objected against our conclusion and assertion. And to say the truth they seemed even to Gratian himself so weighty and effectual that they made him stagger, and judge that there was no true marriage [p. 44] between our blessed lady and Joseph. Howbeit he had not deeply and considerately weighed and pondered the matter, and hath the whole consent of all divines and canonists concurrent against him. For the better understanding therefore of this matter and of our solutions following, one thing is well to be considered, which is that there is in matrimony, as in every natural thing, a double integrity or perfection. The one standeth in the very inward nature and as I may say in the essence of the thing; and this is the substantial and primary perfection, as for example of fire, of a knife, of an house, and of other things. The other perfection is that which respecteth and importeth not the substance of the thing but the operation and use of it, and this is the secondary perfection by the which the thing achieveth and obtaineth his scope and end, as the end of the knife is to cut, the fire to heat, the house to dwell in. Now the knife is a knife though it never did nor shall cut, the house an house though it be desolate and not inhabited, the fire is fire though it were (as they call it) *in vacuo*, where it should heat nothing. The lack of due consideration of this caused Gratian to err; for if we consider the [p. 45] first and principal and the essential integrity of matrimony, so doubtless it riseth and is perfected by mutual consent only. Howbeit if we consider the second perfection, which is not essential but accidentary, so doth carnal copulation perfect and consummate matrimony. Now Adam, saying, *Erunt duo in carne una*, meant of both perfections.

Concerning the second reason, it is to be observed that the end of a thing doth not pertain to the essence and substance of the same thing, as may appear by the examples before by us recited. Wherefore, though matrimony hath not that end which respecteth children, yet is it true matrimony and a true sacrament, and doth not lack the other end and scope of mutual habitation and communication of all duties and functions domestical, as St. Austine sheweth, *de bono conjugali*. As for the remedy against concupiscence, it is in double sort, the one which, by grace and virtue of the sacrament, is given them before any [carnal] copulation, that is that they may when they please use the same; the other is the very actual using and exercising of the said act, whereby a man contenteth and followeth his concupiscence to avoid other [p. 46] filthiness that might follow. Now (as we have said) this act is no essential part of matrimony. As for the said objection, Hugo, alleged in the King's own book, shall answer; whose words, as they are in the printed book translated, you shall now hear. Although, saith he, that the woman with whom it is known that the man had no carnal meeting doth not pertain to that sacrament or holy mystery which Paule calleth a great sacrament, that 'is between Christ and his church or company of faithful Christian people, yet verily it pertaineth to another sacrament or holy mystery, the which is much greater, that is between God and man's soul. For what? if it be a great mystery that is in the flesh, is it not as great a mystery, yea, and much greater that is in the spirit? for the flesh doth nothing help; it is the spirit that quickeneth and giveth life. Therefore it is true marriage and the very sacrament of marriage, although there never followed no fleshly adoe, yea, to speake better, both the marriage and the sacrament is so much the truer and the holier, inasmuch as there is nothing in it whereof chastity should be ashamed, but whereof love may rejoice and [p. 47] glory. For if God by Scripture be well called spouse of man's soul and the soul again the spouse of God, forsooth there is something between the soul and God whereof this thing that standeth in marriage between man and woman is the sacrament and image and likelihood and holy sign and token. And peradventure (for to speak more plainly in this matter) the very company that is kept outwardly in marriage according to the promise that each made to other is the sacrament and sign or token. And the thing itself of this sacrament is the love of minds of one to the other which is kept between them in this bond of company and league of marriage. And again the same love and favour in their minds, the one to the other, is the sacrament and token of that love and charity by the which God joineth himself unto man's soul inwardly, by putting into the soul of his grace and by sending into the soul part of his holy spirit, by the which the soul is made one spirit with God. Therefore the fleshly coplinge which before the sin of Adam was in marriage an office or virtuous deed and after the sin it was granted in the same marriage for a remedy, so both times it is putt unto marriage, but so that it is with marriage, but [p. 48] marriage hangeth not of it. For true marriage is before any fleshly meddling; and marriage may be holy without any such thing. It should be doubtless not so fruitful if such meddling were not, but marriage is much cleaner if no such thing be in it. For that after sin, fleshly meddling is suffered in marriage, it is rather of great sufferance and compassion lest the vice of concupiscence and lustiness (which, after that sin, was rooted in man's flesh) should contrary to all honesty and without measure break forth and flow abroad in every place without any regard, if there had been no certain place provided by the law where it may be lawfully received. Wherefore the very true, perfect, and full marriage is the same company, conversation, and living together which is consecrate by the league or bond of spousage or promise that one doth make to the other, when both of them by their free and willing promise do make themselves debtors the one to the other, and do willingly bind themselves by covenant that from henceforth the one will never depart from the other to the company of none other person while the other is alive, nor that they will never divorce themselves nor break off from this company that now is [p. 49] between them. And if so be it that unto this covenant and agreement of conversation and company together there be put to also in the first meeting a covenant and bargain of carnal meddling, then the man and the woman be afterwards bound the one to the other of duty to this fleshly meddling. And if peradventure at the making of the marriage this carnal coplinge be remitted on both partes by the vow and consent or promise of them both, afterwards they be no more debtors the one to the other for this thing. For that thing which by equal consent and agreement was remitted of both partes and confirmed by their vow and promise, it cannot be justly required afterwards of either of them. And yet for all that the sacrament of marriage standeth even in this case stedfast and sure; whereas the carnal copulation is neither cause of the virtue and goodness of it when it is there, nor cannot take away the virtue and perfectness of marriage if it be not there. And therefore this only consent and agreement of their minds is thought to uphold and continue this unparteable conversation and living together. And this consent was ordained for this cause, that this company of the one with the other, the which was begun between them by [p. 50] this consent and agreement, should not be suffered to be broken at any time so long as they were both alive; the which delaration of Hugo doth withal salve the authorities adduced out of St. Austine and St. Leo. For as himself answereth to these places, (albeit he did not attribute the said authority to St. Austine,) they speak of the second and accidentary perfection, without the which, albeit there is not fully represented the signification how Christ hath espoused our human nature, being incarnate, yet is there a true matrimony and a true sacrament resembling and signifying the said unity of Christ with us, as we have said, in love and charity. Howbeit other answere also may be made to the said authorities, as it may appear to him that will read the works of the said Hugo. As for Origen, St. Hierome, and St. Gregorie, though they say that there was not (*nuptiæ*) marriage between Josephe and our blessed Lady, thinking that that word properly appertaineth not but there where is carnal copulation, yet do they not deny but that it is a true sacrament.

Finally, that which is alleged out of the said Decretall, *Licet*, is of small force. For though it be said there they did judge otherwise, yet it is not to be taken that they did judge [p. 51] so by any judicial act or public decree and judgment; for there was never none such seen or heard of in the Church, but *they judged* is spoken as we commonly say *I judge so*, for *I think so*. It was but a private opinion of some without any final and public determination, which was ever in the Church to the contrary. Whereof it followeth that, the premisses duly considered, Sir Thomas Moore had just cause to refuse the said oath, as had also his blessed colleague the Bishop of Rochester, and [if] it had been but for the said provisoe only. And if they had died but for this branch only, they had died for a truth as well as if they had died for the maintenance of the first marriage, as partly they did, being the original quarrel made against them, wherein they said as truly to King Henry as ever did St. Paule the apostle reproving the Emperor Nero, or St. John Baptist reproving King Herod for their adultery. And if they had suffered for the same cause only, they had suffered, as I have said, for a truth (though the words seem to sound to the contrary) as well as the said St. John Baptist did. St. John Baptist said truly, because as we have declared, King Herod married Herodias against God's law [p. 52] and man's law, his brother, her husband, yet living. But, as he said to King Herod, Thou canst not marry thy brother's wife, so, if King Henry had then lived and reigned among the Jews, he would have said to him, Sir, your brother's wife, that you were commanded to marry, and that you have now by the law of Moses married, you cannot lawfully put away. Now, though this marriage be against the constitutions ecclesiastical, yet the Pope having once dispensed with it, and the impediment of the positive law taken away, if St. John had lived in our time and realm, he would have said to the King,—Sir, thy brother's wife, whom for the maintenance of peace and tranquillity of thy self and thy realm thou hast by the procuring and consent of thy wise father, with the consent and allowing of thy wive's father King Ferdinandus, and the learned virtuous men of their realms, and with the ratification also beforehand of Christ his own vicar on earth the Pope, married, thy wife with whose marriage neither at the beginning nor in twenty years continuall habitation thou didst or couldst find any fault; thy wife, I say, whose marriage God himself hath with fruit [p. 53] of a most [noble] virtuous lady confirmed and ratified, thou canst not now (without incurring God's high displeasure) reject, and marry another. Thus would St. John Baptist have said; and for so saying, and for their grave and godly admonition, the said bishop and Sir T. Moore have suffered imprisonment and other injuries, and in a manner death also. And the said St. John Baptist, if he had been in our time living, would have been wonderfully discontented with the King and with the patrons of his cause, for so shamefully abusing his name and authority for the furtherance of the divorce. For, as I have said, the said story of Herod is shamefully abused, and applied to that which St. John neither said, nor meant, nor thought; for he never spake nor meant (as these men pretend) of our case. And, as he never meant any such thing, so God neither could nor would of his justice have punished Herod for this kind of marriage which himself commanded. But Herod, even for this marriage, with his unlawful wife Herodias, and with her young, wanton, dancing daughter,

was notably punished. For, as for Herod, Aretas the King of the
Arabians, whose daughter he had repudiated [p. 54], not suffering
this injury, did fiercely set upon his realm, miserably wasting and
spoiling the same, victoriously discomfiting Herod's whole army.
In fine, he was with his harlot Herodias and for her sake thrust
out of his kingdom, by the Emperor, and banished to Vienna, in
France, as Josephus sheweth (Lib. Antiquit. Jud. cap. 18 et 19).
But of all other, the death of this dancing, devilish damsel, which,
at the instigation of her mother, required nothing for her reward
but St. John Baptist's head (as the Gospel telleth), is most worthy
of observation. And, as his head, at this cruel wanton's petition,
was cut off, to his great glory and perpetual renown of glorious
martyrdom ; so was her head also, to her everlasting shame, by the
marvellous providence and vengeance of God, cut from her shoulders, not by any sword, or by man's hand, but (a wonderful strange
thing to read or hear of) by force of the very ice; for as she passed
in the winter time afoot over a river marvellous hard frozen, loe
suddenly, contrary to all likelihood,[a] and to the expectation of all
men, the ice under her feet brake, and by and by was she drowned,
all saving the very neck, which did hang between the great pieces
of ice [p. 55]. The head thus being above, the body beneath in the
water, wagging and removing to and fro, did represent and exhibit
a marvellous spectacle and a strange kind of dancing. At length,
after long agitation of her body, her head, by the force of the
great cold and frost was first frozen, and then, afterward, by
the violence of the ice congealing together, quite cut off from
her body. Now, as this strange punishment had not light upon
Herode if he had married according to the law of Moses, his
brother dying without children, so, truly, if King Henry had put
from him his first wife and married another, agreeable and conformable to the law, will and pleasure of God, the hand of God had
never so heavily and so terribly fallen upon him and his second
wife; yea, and his other wives also, as afterward it did. For surely

[a] Nicepho. Ecclesiast. histo, li. i. cap. 20.

God doth not leave the rod of the wicked upon the lot of the righteous, least the righteous stretch forth their hand to wickedness. Now, in case [that] there be any man that, after he hath read all that we have said in this matter, will think that either the first marriage was naught, or the second good, we must work with him another way, and use toward him another but a more sensible persuasion, which he may [p. 56] (unless he be as unsensible as a man that will put and hold his finger in the hot fire and say the fire burneth not) feel even at his finger's end. We affirm, then, that God hath so plainly and wonderfully testified on our side, and against the second marriage, as he cannot lightly more plainly, unless we will have him personally to come down and [to] tell us how grievously he was offended therewith. God, I say, hath poured such vengeance upon the King himself, upon his new wives and new marriages, upon the chief procurers of the same, yea, and upon the whole realm (as the horrible events thereof since ensued have shown), that we have been wonderfully thereby at home astonied, plagued, and afflicted, and have been (as the prophet saith) a reproach to our neighbours, a scorn and derision to all that are round about us. And surely, among all other things, it is to be wondered or rather to be pitied that the King, having no better ground and foundation than he had (which how weak and futile it is, and how it is overthrown even by the authors producted by his own patrons we have already shewed) would needs yet proceed to a divorce; and that with so many ungodly and undue means as now, the hole being [p. 57] digged in the wall of the temple, do foully and shamefully appear, and against so many and marvellous impediments, not only of the first marriage, but others also that lay in his way; and that he would be so bewitched that, to have this divorce go forward, he laboured and would not stick (as we have declared) to have taken a dispensation of the Pope to have two wives at once, and to promise to enter into religion, so he might be discharged of Queen Katherine by her like profession, and himself afterward released by a dispensation of the said vow; and that he sought to be dispensed to marry with her whose sister he had carnally known before; moreover that he would marry her whom himself knew to have been before betrothed to another man, yea, to marry her whom himself credibly understood to have lived loosely and incontinently before; for Sir Thomas Wyatt,[a] the elder, understanding that the King minded to marry her, came to him and said, Sir, I pray your grace pardon me, both of my offence and my boldness. I am come to your grace of myself to discover and utter my own shame; but yet my most bounden duty and loyalty that I owe to your grace, and the careful [p. 58] tendering of your honor more than of my own honesty forceth me to do this. Sir, I am credibly informed that your grace intendeth to take to your wife the Lady Anne Bulleyn, wherein I beseech your grace to be well advised what you do, for she is not meet to be copled with your grace, her conversation hath been so loose and base; which thing I know not so much by hear-say as by my own experience as one that have had my carnal pleasure with her. At the hearing of this, the King for a while being something astonyed, said to him, —Wyatt, thou hast done like an honest men, yet I charge thee to make no more words of this matter to any man living. This story have I heard the the right worshipful merchant Mr. Anthony Bonvise rehearse, which thing he heard of them that were men very likely to know the truth thereof. Could any enemy the King had wish him a greater plague than, with such exceeding immoderate outrageous appetite to have this woman to his wife, so pitifully to have been blinded, and so wilfully and so headlong to have precipitate himself to such a danger. But now behold on the other side the tragical event of this marriage so long pursued, and at length, after so many [p. 59] dishonourable means, compassed. She had not continued with him many years but that himself and the whole parliament[b] were faine to declare and notify to all the world that his marriage with her was plain against the very law of God, and that it was never good and lawful from the beginning; and pardoned all that ever had spoken against it, and so in effect

[a] Sir Thomas Wyatt goes to the King and acquaints him with his familiarity with the Lady Anne Bulleyn.

[b] The parliament declare the marriage with Anne Bulleyn null and void.

confirmed (though unawares and by another meaning) the opinion and judgment of the said Bishop of Rochester and Sir Thomas Moore. Thus then, as the King put unjustly from him his lawful wife Queen Katherine, so was he by the mighty hand of God constrained to put from him also the said Lady Anne, and to be divorced in her lifetime from that unlawful marriage. And who gave the definitive sentence, trow you, that this marriage was never good? Who, but one that was the chief [minister] incenser and solicitor of the first divorce? Who, but one that was the chief counsellor and worker in the book made for the infringing of the first marriage? Who, but one that was made purposely Archbishop of Canterbury for the good service he had done and should do for the breaking of the first marriage? Who, I say, but even he that gave sentence also definitive against the said first marriage? [p. 60] This, this, I say, is the mighty and just judgment of God, that by what meane a man sinneth by the very same to plague him. What an astonishment and wonder was it for us at home to see it, and for all the world beside to hear, that after all this importunate suit to get her to his wife, the King caused her by parliament to be condemned as a foul detestable adulteress, and consequently to be put to death for the same, as one that had in her most abominable and detestable, filthy carnal desires confederated herself, not only with others named in the said parliament, but even with her own natural brother, George Bulleyn, Lord Rochford, as the said parliament also testifieth, by the which parliament it was made high treason to defend the said marriage with the Lady Anne to be good and lawful.ª So by the marvellous providence and vengeance of God, this woman which at such time as with her playing, singing, and dancing, she had best opportunity, never ceased (as the other dancing damsel that craved

---

ª By the which parliament it was made high treason to defend the said marriage with the Lady Anne to be good and lawful. [This note, which seems like a continuation of the previous marginal references made by the transcriber of the Eyston Manuscript, appears in the other copies of the manuscript and is therefore probably to be ascribed to the author. N. P.]

St. John Baptist's head importunately) to crave the good bishop's and Sir Thomas Moore's heads, which thing at length, to their immortal glory, she compassed ere the year turned about, to her perpetual shame and ignominie, lost her head also, as did the foresaid dancing [p. 61] damsel.

Oh what a strange and unlucky thing was this for the King to put away such a noble, virtuous lady, and of such an honourable royal blood, and his true, most loving, chaste, tender wife, for such an incestuous woman, being in all other qualities beside so far inferior to her, as she was in very chastity itself. It was no marvel if the King tenderly did weep at the reading of the letters she sent him at the time of her death (as we have before declared), who died the same year [and] not many months before the said Lady Anne, but in great diversity of merits and honour. You will, perchance, now ask me what was the cause that the King's marriage with the said Lady Anne was never good? Surely the true cause was that the King married her, his true wife living, and so had two wives at once, which is by the civil law a thing infamous. If you will reply that that was not the cause that the King and the parliament found, I grant you; and the more pity. Wherefore seeing that, as well many other things, as the strange event of the marriage of the Lady Anne Bulleyne, (which were able in a manner to extort this confession of the King) did little work with him to induce him to recognise his former fault, the hand and plague of God did hang still full heavily upon him, especially [p. 62] to plague him with marriages wherein he had most offended. If the King had (as good reason it was he should have done) considered with himself and examined his own conscience, why such unhappy and unfortunate luck happened to him in this and in his other marriages following, and had said *Quare venerunt hæc mihi?* wherefore are these things come upon me? Surely he might soon have found it was the very hand of God upon him for his unlawful divorce, and other his naughty doings following thereupon, and that the prophet's answer was as well made to him as to the Jews—*Propter multitudinem iniquitatis tuæ revelata sunt verecundiora tua, pollutæ sunt plantæ tuæ.*

If he had, I say, narrowly discussed his conscience, he should have found himself to have been one of that sort of men that pretended to be very inquisitive to know God's will and pleasure, and yet when they know it did the quite contrary, as it evidently appeareth the King did in refusing the good and wholesome counsel of the Bishop of Rochester and Sir Thomas Moore and others touching his said marriage. If he had well examined himself he should have found that he was of that sort of men which did not receive the discipline of God, and [p. 63] whom God did smite in vain, and by his scourges were nothing amended; which discipline of God whereby he was chastised for his first unlawful divorce, if he had received, and had acknowledged and amended his former fault by convenient repentance, especially after the great discomfort and dishonour he took by the said Lady Anne Bulleyn (by whose marriage, which of all things in the world he most desired, God most grievously plagued him as he useth by His high wisdom and justice to punish and beat us with our own disordinate desires and appetites) he had avoided many great plagues which lighted upon him afterwards, namely, in his other marriages also, whereof we shall hereafter intreat. But now being in hand with the Act of Parliament which destroyeth and annihilateth the King's marriage with the said Lady Anne, we think it convenient and meete for our purpose and for the reader's better instruction, somewhat to consider and ponder upon the said Act. It is then to be understood that in this Act the Levitt. degrees be both rehearsed and forbidden, as they were before in 25 year, and the said Act of the 25 year with [p. 63] all clauses, articles, and provisions therein contained, were repealed, annulled, made frustrate, and of no effect; so that the proviso contained in the statute of the said 25 year, that the prohibitions of marriages should be understood where marriages were solempnised and carnal knowledge had is now this 28 year of no force. And it was very well and worthily done to revoke the said provisoe, for such causes as we have above shewed. And it was as well done to set in this statute of the 28 year a certain understanding of the said prohibitions, in such form as now followeth.

And furthermore, to delate and declare the meaning of these prohibitions, it is to be understood that if it chance any man to know carnally any woman, that then all and singular persons being in any degree of consanguinity or affinity, as above written, to any of the parties so carnally offending shall be deemed and judged to be within the cases and limits of the said prohibitions of marriage; all which marriages, although they be plainly prohibited and detested by the laws of God, yet nevertheless at some times they have proceeded under colours of dispensations by man's power, which [p. 65] is but usurped, and of right ought not to be granted, admitted, or allowed. The meaning of this prohibition is here in some part well added and declared. And the other declaration made in the provisoe in the 25 year is well and advisedly detracted and abolished. I say in some part, for as it is true that we be forbidden to marry with any of the persons there prohibited, by reason of the former marriage of any of our kindred, so are we forbidden also to marry the same persons if any of our kindred without marriage have carnally known any of them. But as all those marriages be not so precisely forbidden by God but that some of them may be dispensed withal; and as the marriage of the brother's wife is not comprised under the said prohibitions (as we have at large declared) when he dieth without children, so is it not true that carnal copulation had by any of those persons with any woman is so great an impediment [as cannot be dispensed withal. Troth it is that there is an impediment] by the law of the church to marry any such woman, but then that impediment is not of like force for all such persons; and the impediment that proceedeth from the church only is capable of a dispensation. But if you will ask me why either the said provisoe is now taken away, and this [p. 66] new understanding as to this statute adjoined for the said provisoe, I can make no direct answer. It might serve some man's turn then, were it the King's or any other, whereof the cause I cannot yet attain unto. But this new understanding directly toucheth the King's own cause, and so nighe toucheth it that if it had been added in the statute of the 25 year, as it is now in the 28, it had quite marred all the rest, and utterly destroyed the King's marriage with the Lady Anne Bulleyne, which the said statute went about to confirm and establish; which secret mystery cannot be discovered, but that we must dig a hole in the wall with Ezekiell, for you must remember (as we have told you out of my Lord Cardinal's book) that the King had carnally known the [said] Lady Anne's sister before marriage with her, which kind of marriage standeth by this new understanding so directly against God's law as it may be by no man dispensed withal. Now this clause of the meaning of the said prohibitions being now put in, when the King would break the said marriage, and left out before in the other statute, wherein he would have his said marriage to be counted good and lawful, doth greatly enforce the said Lord Cardinall's [p. 67] declaration to be true. And here the wonderful providence of God is to be noted, that hath so marvellously wrought and suffered the King to fall into such palpable blindness, that he would (and that under the pretence of God's holy word) put away his wife, for that she was carnally known of his brother, and yet marry her whose sister himself had carnally known; which fact is as we have declared in a worse degree than the former. Wherefore when I consider this and other the premisses, I cannot be induced to believe that the King upon conscience only, and for avoiding God's displeasure (as it was pretended), but rather to satisfy and serve his bodily pleasure and appetite, pursued this divorce. And his mind being thus depraved and corrupted, and seeking the furthering and advancement only of his own corrupt will, he found like doctors and like prophets, who, preferring his sensual appetite and their own worldly advancement before God's blessed will, accommodated their answer to his carnal corrupted desire. For as the prophet Ezekiell[a] writeth to such as have filthy

[a] [Homo, homo de domo Israel qui posuerit immunditias suas in corde suo, et scandalum iniquitatis suæ statuerit contra faciem suam, et venerit ad prophetam ut interroget per eum me, Ego Dominus respondebo ei in multitudine immunditiarum suarum. Ezech. cap. 14º.]

corrupt cogitations in their heart, and yet pretend to seek and search and understand [p. 68] God's pleasure, and to be directed by the same, God sendeth false prophets to make them a suitable answer, to feed and maintain their corrupt humours, as it chanced (the more pity) to this King also. But yet, as I said, mark the providence and also the just punishment of God, which, seeing that the King (the premisses notwithstanding) would needs go through with the second marriage, brought him to this distress that he was fain to break off the said marriage that he had by so many dishonourable means procured; yea, and that even for the same cause for the which he put away Queen Katherine; which no doubt was one, though a more secret cause than other, both of this new understanding of the said prohibitions, and of the divorce also. And thus are you answered withall of your demand asking what was the cause of this divorce. But I cannot certainly affirm that either this cause or the other, that is, that he married the said Lady Anne, Queen Katherine yet living and not judicially divorced, was openly before the said Archbishop of Canterbury (for saving the King's honour) exposed. It appeareth that there were certain true, just, and lawful impediments alleged before the said Archbishop sitting judicially [p. 69], and confessed by the said Lady Anne, for the which the said Archbishop definitively pronounced that the said marriage was never good, nor lawful, but utterly void and of none effect,[a] which her confession is most commonly taken to be that she confessed how she was bretothed to the Earl of Northumberland before she was married to the King.

We are now passed two divorces, and the third is even at hand, whereof we will now intreat. We well remember that in the 30 year of the reign of the said King there came into this realm, in the month of September, Duke Frederick of Bavarie, the Palsgrave of Rhyne, and the Marshall of Duke John Fredericke, Elector of Saxony, with other, and concluded a marriage with the King and Lady Anne, the Duke of Cleves' sister. We remember also (being then by chance present) with what great triumph, with what a goodly

[a] It was upon something that the Lady Anne Bulleyn confessed to Cranmer which made him pronounce the marriage unlawful.

presence of nobles and gentlemen called from all parts of England, and after a most gorgeous sort furnished with horse and men, she was most honourably received by the King himself at Blackheath the 3rd of January, and married[a] the 6th of the same month following. And yet for all this solemnity, ere six months were fully passed, she was by the synod of the whole clergy, and by the parliament, divorced from him, and the marriage found to be of no force or strength, and both the King and she put at liberty to marry at their pleasures, with a declaration both of her part and the King's that the King never knew her. But some disliking and discontentation began with the King of her before he met her at Blackheath, upon what cause I know not. This only I have credibly heard, that himself being disguised and unknown, saw her and spake with her at Rochester, and lay there all that night, and in his return by water from Gravesend told the Lord Fitzwilliams and Sir Anthony Browne, Crumwell hath deceived me. Indeed the said Lord Cromwell was the greatest sollicitor, procurer, and contriver of the said marriage, and even about the same time that she was divorced, for his reward, and to bear her company in her adversity, when she lost the King's favour and her marriage, he lost the same time, not only the King's favour, but his head withal. The said Crumwell was informed by the Queen, that the King could not do the husband's duty to her, whereupon (I ask pardon of honest ear to tell it) he[b] counselled her to handle the King's privities, and to stir and excite his carnal lust, which the King highly disliked, and had also of her and of her honesty some disliking, and understood by her that it came by Crumwell's counsel. Now ere the said parliament was done (which ended the 24 of July, in the 32 year of his reign), the King had provided himself another bedfellow, the Lady Katherine Howard, and she the 8 of August following shewed herself openly at the court as Queen.

I think, gentle reader, you are now desirous to hear the cause of this divorce, especially because it is not specified in the said parliament, nor otherwise commonly known; it is not, indeed, specified

[a] King Henry marries the Lady Anne of Cleves, but from his first seeing her dislikes her.

[b] Cromwell's advice to Queen Anne of Cleve upon the King's dislike.

in the said Acte. But there was another Act made in the said parliament, by the which a man may see the cause as it were light by a glymsinge day hole. Well we have once again a new Katherine. Would God she had been anything like to the other, yet, as unlike as she was, the King never made any more foul means to put away the other than he used to come by the marriage of this, though the matter was not so long a contriving. For now, being taken himself for the head of the Church of England, both in causes spiritual and temporal it was easy[a] for him to find men both spiritual and temporal, ready to advance all his intended and desired purposes; but [p. 72] yet these matters were wrought in as secret manner as could be to keep the very true dealing and meaning of this divorce from the knowledge of the common people. Howbeit good and wise men saw well enough how things passed, and were sorry to see or [to] hear them so pass. I mean of an Act made in the said parliament wherein we must dig two great holes in Ezekiell's wall to see the great foul filthiness lying and lurking within it. We had a rule before in the book made for the King's divorce from Queen Katherine, that carnal copulation is certainly to be presumed between two married persons of lawful age conversant together and able to do the act. Well, I will not curiously sift this matter; but I say albeit it never were so true that the King never knew the said Lady Anne, yet was the King her lawful husband, and the marriage with her solemnized. This block they say lay in the way, therefore it must needs be removed. Well there is a fair and jolly remedy found ready at hand. For though the foresaid former understanding of the prohibitions Levitt. be taken of marriages solemnized and consummated with carnal copulation was abrogated, though to break [p. 73] the marriage with Lady Anne Bulleyne a precontract was of such force that marriage with carnal copulation

[a] [This word is distinctly written *rath* in the Eyston MS. and in N_1, which generally agrees with it. The whole line between *temporal* and *ready* has been omitted by an oversight in copying in N_2, which was therefore not available for correcting it. But there can be little doubt of the reading.]

and children following could not undo the same, yet now to make this marriage good with Lady Katherine, all precontracts, all solemnizations of former marriages lie in the dust, and only carnal copulation with a new marriage beareth all the sway. So that now if another jolly wooer could so work with the bridegroom that he could by craft or force win the possession of her before her first husband have known her, and then wed her and bed her, the first husband might go shake his ears for any means he shall have, or for any wife that ever he should recover. For if he should have claimed her he should claim her but by the Pope's law, wherein he had usurped to himself authority against God's law; wherefore this law must needs be abolished as a branch of papistical doctrine. But if we will follow and pursue this rule, and put away all things set forth by the Pope, we shall shortly leave no part of Christ his faith but that it shall be abolished, which the Pope hath and doth set forth, from whom as well in the time of the Brittaines and King Lucius, by Pope [p. 74] Eleutherius, as afterward in the time of the Saxons by St. Gregory in the time of King Ethelberte this island received the Christian faith. Howbeit were there none that set forth this rule but Popes? Yes, certainly there was many a good Council and many a good father, as we have before more largely declared, and that even by the book set forth for the maintenance of the King's first divorce, the authors whereof were (as it proved soon afterward) no great friends to the Pope. And as Papistical a doctrine as they make of it here, this Act was repealed by his own son King Edward, and the Parliament of those persons then assembled (which were no papists), upon divers inconveniences intolerable in manner to Christian ears and eyes, following thereupon; women and men breaking their own promises and faiths made by the one to the other, so set upon sensuality and pleasure, that if after the contract of matrimony they might have whom they more favoured and desired, they would be contented by lightness of their nature to overturn all that they had done before, and not afraid (in manner even from the church door and marriage-feast) the man to take another spouse and the spouse to take another husband [p. 75], more for bodily lust and carnal knowledge than for surety of faith and troth, or having God in their good remembrance; contemning also many times the commandment of the ecclesiastical judge, forbidding the parties having made the contract to attempt or do anything in prejudice of the same. And this have we alledged out of the very words of the statute. Wherefore I say that the said statute of precontracts was put for a *Lesbia Regula* as they call it. And a pitiful case it is when men's manners and doings shall not be applied to the law and directed by the same, but the law shall be applied and directed by the sensual and wilful pleasure of men ; and whereas laws were wont to be made for the times and things to come, to make a law to undo things already well passed, and the laws of the whole Catholic church withal. And yet all this shift will not help, for albeit it had been true that for some good cause the King's marriage with the said Lady Anne of Cleves was of no force or strength, and that he was at his liberty to marry again, yet of all women could he not marry with the said Lady Katherine, for that she was [p. 76] within the fourth degree of consanguinity to the Lady Anne Bulleyne. And as it wast true that by the laws of the Church he could not marry with the said Lady Anne Bulleyne though his former marriage with Queen Katherine had been (as was pretended) against the law of God, even so, though he might lawfully at this time have married, yet could he not marry the said Lady Katherine, as we have said. There must then needs a remedy be found to remove this impediment, which was facylely and easily found ; for these prohibitions saith the statute be no prohibitions of God's law, but Papisticall, and made to get money by, to keep reputation to the Pope's usurped jurisdiction. Under these colours of degrees of kindred or affinity between cousin germans, and by colour of carnal knowledge of any of the said kin or affinity before, in such outward degrees and by reason of such precontracts there was much detestable adultery, to the utter destruction of their souls and the provocation of the terrible wrath of God upon those places where such abhominations were used. Whereupon it is enacted that no reservation or prohibition (God's law [p. 77] excepted) shall trouble or impeach any marriage without the Levitt. degrees. If there were as much truth in this as there is tragical (but needless) exaggeration it were somewhat to be borne withal. If there be no prohibition in marriage but the Levitt. why doth St. Ambrose so vehemently forbid the uncle to marry his niece, which marriage is not controlled by the Levitt.? Why do the patrons of the King's first divorce go about to strengthen his cause thereby? If there be no other prohibition why doth St. Gregorie, why doth St. Ambrose, why doth St. Austine[a] so greatly disallow the marriages of cousin Germans? Why do his said patrons allege these authorities? Why doth the Counsell Agathense, brought forth also by the said patrons, make the marriage of cousin Germans, yea, or to marry a woman which any of our kindred hath carnally known, plain incest, as doth also St. Gregorie, whose testimony we have before rehearsed? If there be no other prohibition of marriage than the Levitt. why did the King make such a stir, and troubled, as I may say, Heaven and earth, to break his first marriage with Queen Katherine—which was not (her husband [p. 78] dying without children) checked by any of the Levitt. degrees? Luther,[b] also and other of his sect be in this wrong opinion that there is no degree forbidden but that which is contained in the Levitt. And yet is he of a contrary mind to our statute and thinketh that the brother is not forbidden to marry his brother's wife dying without children, or any man to marry his wive's sister after the death of his wife. If all things be lawful that are not forbidden by God's law, why are so many things and so straightly forbidden by the statutes and laws of this realm which by God's law are not prohibited? If you will say—God's law commandeth us to obey our

[a] Quod fiebat cum consobrinâ pœne cum sorore fieri videbatur. Aug. de civitate Dei, li. 16, cap. 15.
[b] Lutherus in sermone de matrimonio.

kings and princes and their laws, so doth he also give us as straight or straighter commandment to obey the rulers and prelates of the Church. " Obey," saith St. Paul, "your prelates, for they watch as such as shall give a reckoning for your souls." And Christ himself saith—" Let him be taken for a Publican and for an Ethnicke which doth not obey the Church." And went not Luther about by the like reason of the liberty and freedom of the Gospel (whereupon the statute groundeth itself) to [p. 79] spoil the secular magistrate of all due honour and obedience, as he hath before spoiled the ecclesiastical? Whereupon shortly after the horrible tumults and rebellions of the Anabaptists against all civil magistrates terribly and dangerously infested, vexed, and spoiled Germany. The great Counsell of Laterane, whereat were present 70 archbishops, 412 bishops—as well out of the Greek Church as out of the Latin—beside 800 abbots and priors, after long advisement and [upon] great grounds and considerations, did cut away the prohibition of the fifth, sixth, and seventh degree of consanguinity and affinity ; giving a commandment that all other degrees should be straightly observed ; which their decree was confirmed also by the Emperors of the East and West Church being there personally, and by the ambassadors of the King of England, and of other kings of Christendom there present. And do we now think that the Parliament of this realm, being but one member of the whole Church, may break this decree ordained by this Great Council representing the whole Catholic Church. Surely we could no [p. 80] more do it than the City of London may lawfully infringe an Act of Parliament or make a law of their own to bind the whole realm; unless we will think that there was no more danger, to serve and satisfy the King's sensuality, to make a law as well to disanull the King's former marriage as to enable him to marry that woman which, by the law of the Church, he could not marry. Then it was for the Court to obey his commandment in powlinge their heads, himself powlinge his own first for example, which commandment he gave the said year that he not only powled

St. Peter's head, but as much as lay in him did cut it quite off and put it upon his own shoulders, which was a very ugly sight, and a heavy thing to hear of. I mean when he banished St. Peter and his successors' authority, and took the supremacy in all causes ecclesiastical upon himself. It appeareth that the Parliament made no greater account to feed the King's gross and corrupt humours to change and abolish such laws than the courtiers did to powle their heads, who to content and satisfy the King's carnal pleasure and [p. 81] his impotent sensual appetite would break these two ancient laws of the Church, the one of precontracts, the other touching the marriage of cousin-germans. Yea, there is, beside these two, one other ecclesiastical law received and practised ever since our English nation was christened, as well in England as in all other countries throughout the whole Catholic Church, abrogated and abolished by this statute, as may be well gathered by the tenure of the same. I mean of the ecclesiastical prohibition touching the marriage with our godson or god-daughter and such like knit to us neither by consanguinity nor affinity, but by spiritual cognation. Whether this prohibition were taken away and frustrated by reason of some impediment of such spiritual cognation occurring in this new marriage with the Lady Katherine (as it is likely) I certainly know not; but of this am I right certain, that it was [a] pitiful and woful hearing and sight to hear of and see so many laws of the Church concerning matrimonial matters by this one statute to be so unadvisedly infringed and overthrown [p. 82]. And again, to see the great inconstancy and contrariety of the King and his Counsellors, as well for some points a little before rehearsed as for this point also. For in the book made for the disproof and disannulling of his first marriage with Queen Katherine there was another manner of account made of ghostly and spiritual cognation, as you shall now perceive by the words of the said book. Pope Zacharie (saith that book) answereth in this manner to Theodore, Bishop of Tisyn or Pavye, asking counsel of him whether that the god-daughter might be married with the natural son. Thy holy brotherhood (saith

Zacharie) knoweth right well that our Lord did command Moses, saying—" Thou shalt not discover the foulness of thy father, or mother, or sister, for it is thy own foulness." Seeing, therefore, that we are commanded to abstain from our own kindred carnall, much more it is convenient that we should with all straightness beware of her that is our father's daughter spiritual.

Thus far out of the said book. If this be true, and if we be as much and [more] bound to keep [p. 83] this prohibition of spiritual kindred as the prohibition Levitt., why doth the Parliament so severely forbid the one (which is of less force) and so loosely permit the other which is of greater force ? Yea, why doth the statute sunder and break the marriage with the brother's wife dying without children (which is not forbid[den] by Moses) and suffer this marriage which hath a stronger and straighter bond (as it seemeth by Pope Zacharie) than the Levitt. prohibition. But you will say Pope Zacharie was deceived. It is soon said, but was the Emperor Justinian above 200 years before him [a] deceived also, with the residue of the Christian men of that time, which Emperor straightly did forbid the said marriage, and even by the same reason that Pope Zacharie did. *Ea inquit persona omnino ad nuptias venire prohibenda est quam aliquis a Sacrosancto suscepit Baptismate; cum nihil aliud sic inducere potest paternam affectionem et justam nuptiarum prohibitionem quam hujusmodi nexus, per quem, Deo mediante, animæ eorum copulatæ sunt.*[b] We add hereunto that as we take the nature and name of man by carnal propagation [p. 84], so by the sacraments of the Church (especially by baptism) we take the name and nature of spiritual grace and of God's children ; wherefore as by the very instinct of nature there is a let and impediment of marriage by reason of carnal generation between some persons, so is there by the force of spiritual regeneration, which no doubt the Church hath promulged by the instinct and inspiration of the Holy Ghost. And, surely, the terrible punishment that God once sent to one which had defiled his Ghostly

[a] Incepit regnare anno 527 vel ut quidam 528.
[b] Cod. de Nuptiis, Leg. Siquis.

daughter (the like whereof I never read sent to any that [had] violated his own natural daughter) may somewhat persuade a man that it is as grievous, or a more grievous crime, for a man either to marry or to defile the said ghostly daughter than it is to defile his own daughter, which was that the party wretchedly died within the week, and that when he was buried there burst out of his sepulchre, in the sight of all the people, a fire which horribly consumed his flesh—bones and all—with the very earth that was cast upon him. Lord, what terrible torments did his wretched soul suffer in the other world whose dead carcase was so horribly devoured in this world.

This thing [p. 85] chanced not long before we were christened, and is written by our Apostle, St. Gregory. Now, if this law of Justin had been but a civil and politic law only of the Roman Commonwealth and no law and custom ecclesiastical, then might the Parliament have been borne withal as having authority to ordain and establish meet and convenient laws (as the time requireth) for the well ordering and governing of the civil and politic state of the realm. But, seeing the whole Church is but one body and we but one small member of the same, it lay not in the hands and power of the Parliament to change, alter, and abolish the law and custom of the universal Church. Yet, let us for the present falsely imagine that Pope Zacharie was deceived. What! was the whole Church also all this while deceived that so religiously and devoutly, before his time and ever since, abstained from such marriage? or was the Holy Ghost deceived that teacheth and instructeth the Church? or was Christ deceived that biddeth us to obey the Church and to take them that disobey for no better than Publicans and Ethnicks? Surely it is a strange and marvellous matter that this impediment should be taken for so great to make a countenance to the undoing of the [p. 86] King's marriage with Queen Katherine, to set forward the marriage with the Lady Anne Bulleyne, and now to undo the marriage with the Lady Anne of Cleves, and to countenance the new marriage with Katherine Howard, and to be taken to be of so little force and strength. Beside these great inconveniences and absurdities touching marriages permitted by this statute let us now consider and add a number of other. Whereas, then, the said great Counsell of Lateran cut away of seven, three degrees of consanguinity and affinity, leaving the four other untouched, and giving great charge to all people straightly and inviolably to keep them, neither durst to abridge or diminish any of them; albeit, upon just cause occurrent, it had sufficient authority to do it. Again, whereas long before our Apostle, St. Gregorie, bearing with the infirmity of our nation lately converted to the faith, was content for a time to suffer us to marry in the third and fourth degree of the line collateral, but in no case in the second, as to marry the cousin-german (as the King's own book made for his first divorce allegeth and groundeth itself much upon it), behold our Parliament, now almost a thousand years after [p. 87], having no authority to intermeddle in such ecclesiastical affairs, namely, to abolish and abrogate the decrees and customs of the Universal Church, hath arrogated so much to itself that it was made thereby free for all people to marry in the third and fourth, yea, and in the second degree, and all to feed the fleshly humour and sensual appetite of one man. Yea, if we will measure the matter by the words of the said Parliament, there is made open a wicket to greater absurdities and wickedness. For, whereas, by the said statute all marriages are made free which are not impeached and prohibited by the Levitt. behold an ugly sight and swarm of foul filthy absurdities. For the Levitt. prohibition doth not exceed the second degree, no not in the line ascendent or descendent, neither in all of that line expressly excepteth the said degree. Wherefore, by the tenor of this statute, a man might have married with the wife of his son's son's son, yea, with his son's son's wife, with his mother's father's wife, with his grandfather's wife, with his grandfather's mother, with his father's mother, with his wife's mother's mother for any express prohibition in the Levitt. to the contrary; which marriages with the like are forbidden [p. 88], not only by the decrees and customs of the whole

Church, but even among the Jews at this day, and taken for incestuous. Yet, to advance the marriage of the King with the Lady Katherine Howard no account was made of any prohibition but the Levitt., as though we had been Jews and no Christian men, and yet were we worse than the Jews, which (as I have said) observe divers prohibitions that be not expressly in the Levitt.; but then is there a causeless quarrel picked against the Popes that they made such restraints, and the Parliament objecteth unto them that they made those restraints of marriages for their own private lucre. But it well appeareth that such restraints be not made by the Popes only, but by general councils also, and are religiously and obediently to be observed of Christian men; and that they are not to be counted any marriages which are contracted to the contrary, though they be not by the Levitt. or any other law of God (to the which this Parliament hath only respect) forbidden. For, as we have shewed before, the Levitt. doth not bind us now as the law Levitt. but only as it hath the force of the law of nature in it. So that it remaineth in the [p. 89] only power and authority of the Church either to restrain and abridge, or to amplify and enlarge the said prohibitions; as it did indeed, many hundred years ago, enlarge them even to the seventh degree, and doth at this day to the fourth degree. For it standeth with very good reason that as the secular magistrate may forbid certain bargains and contracts to his subjects, and infringe them when they be made, as of such as be in their nonage; and as the father hath authority to irritate and break the vows and oaths of his children under age, so the Church also should have free power and authority to dispose and ordain of the ability and disability of persons in contracting the sacrament of marriage; and for the honour of God, for the behoofe and common profit of the Church, and for the advancing of honesty and decent godly order of the said Church, to frustrate and break all such marriages as be contracted contrary to her prohibition and decrees. Whereas, now they speak of the Pope's private lucre, if they had so great regard to their gain and lucre as is here pretended, they would never have abridged the prohibitions in the 5, 6, and 7th degree, whereby through [p. 90] dispensations they might have made a marvellous great mass of money if they would have sought gains that way. Howbeit the least part or nothing at all of that gain riseth to them, but rather to their scribes and other officers. And in case they had therein moderate gains for the maintaining of [their] ordinary charges, there was no cause so heinously to exasperate the matter. And if their gains were immoderate and excessive, there was no cause to find fault with the law, which was good of itself. Beside this, it is not unknown that the King himself had his share appointed to him even by Act of Parliament (anno 25, cap. 21), after he took upon him to be head of the Church, of such money as was paid for dispensations of matrimony and other causes ecclesiastical. We say, moreover, that it is worse for a man to break good laws to serve and satify his sensual appetite, especially having no authority to break and disanull such laws, than to make good laws and dispense with them, though there rise some gain thereby. Wherefore all this revelling against the Pope's covetousness was needless, and was but a shadow for the time to colour and cover and to countenance the King's sensual and unbridled [p. 91] appetite to serve his own carnal pleasure, which divers times princes prefer before the fear of God and their own honor. Wherefore it shall not be all out of the way to shew the like practices of some other princes in these matters only that we be in hand with (I mean of marriages), and to make a countenance of a general law made for the behoofe of the people; whereas in very deed the final scope was to serve the prince's own turn and his only desire and pleasure. For this cause we have had before so strange an interpretation of the Levitt. degrees. For this cause we have now a new, and unknown, and unchaste doctrine of precontracts, and a new, unknown, evangelical liberty of marrying cosen-germans. This policy used Valentinian the emperor, who minding to advocate to himself another wife besides his first, made a law that it might be lawful to marry two wives. And when he saw the people (which ever liketh liberty and dissolute living) fall to wiveing apace, then took he also his second wife Justina. Howbeit this difference there is between him and King Henry; that King Henry first practised the matter himself out of hand, providing [p. 92] himself a new bedfellow, and was content that other men should follow, which some did with such intolerable disorder and dishonesty, that his son was faine (as we have shewed) to repeal this statute. Now what should I speak of the licentious liberty that divers princes have usurped in this case? Antiochus, the son of Seleuchus King of Syria, married his stepmother Stratonica.[a] The Emperor Antonio Caracalla married his stepmother also. She was a very fair woman, and being on a certain time present with him, opened a great part of her body, as though it had happened by negligence or chance. To whom the Emperor said, I would if it were lawful. Why, saith she, if ye will it is lawful. Are ye ignorant that you are an Emperor, and a person that should make laws for other men, and not to be ruled by other men's laws, which words set him in such a fervent furious heat that he openly married her. Caligula the emperor married his own sister.[b] Darius, Artaxerxes' son, the King of the Persians, whom the Scripture calleth Assuerus, married his father's concubine Aspasia, and by the just punishment of God lost his kingdom (Justinus, li. 10). Thus when princes [p. 93] be once enflamed with outrageous lust and pleasure, there is nothing can stay, allay, and mitigate their fervent heat, but to attain their immoderate desire they do violently break (as a great beast or bird doth the spider's cobweb) all laws of God and of his holy church, and few of them remember the worthy saying of the godly emperor Theodosius, (Cod. de legibus et constitu. leg. 4), *Digna vox est majestate regnantis, legibus alligatum se Principem confiteri, adeo de authoritate juris nostra pendet authoritas. Et revera majus imperio est summittere legibus principatum et oraculo præsentis edicti quod nobis licere non putimur aliis indicimus.* If King Henry had well remembered and

[a] Valer. Max. lib. 5°   [b] Sueton. li. 1° cap. 24.

followed this lesson, he would not have dissolved and broken so many ancient laws of the Church to serve his sensual appetite; neither he and the realm had run into so many foul errors (I say nothing now in other causes) in matrimonial causes only as we have spoken of before, whereof the principal and capital we will now repeat unto you. As that the Levit. law bindeth now the Christians as much as it did bind the Jews; that the Pope can dispense with no part of that [p. 94] law; that it is forbidden by the Levitt. that the brother may marry his brother's wife dying without children; that the said marriage is against nature; that a man may put away his wife and marry another before any sentence of divorce be given; that a man may marry his father's or son's wife if she be not carnally known; that a man may marry the woman that his father or son hath carnally known; that a marriage contracted, yea and solemnized, may be broken by a latter marriage with carnal copulation; that a man may marry with his cousin german, yea, and as we have said, with the wife of our son's son, with his mother's father's wife, with his grandfather's wife, and such others as we have rehearsed which are not (as we have declared) prohibited by the Levitt.; that carnal copulation with any of the kin or affinity as be not forbidden to marry by the Levitt. is no bar of marriage to other being of the said kin or affinity; that we may marry our godson or goddaughter, and such other as we are knit and linked unto by spiritual cognation, which, and some other errors in matters matrimonial, have risen in and [p. 95] upon this unlawful divorce of Queen Katherine. Now, as the King brought in and allowed these and such other errors, so in his time sprang there also other great errors in causes matrimonial (so dangerous a matter it is to open once the gap to errors and heresies) which he would fain have repressed, and yet could not do it so fully as he desired, albeit for fear of his laws they were not publicly defended. Yet as soon as he was once dead they violently burst out, and were openly embraced and allowed, and his laws made to the contrary abolished.

Then might men read books and hear it preached that if the wife were an adulteress the husband might marry again. Then was it ordained by such commissioners as the King had appointed to make laws ecclesiastical, that, if the husband were three or four years away and not known where, the wife might take a new husband. Then was the heretic Jovinian's old lesson renewed, that the religious and virginal chaste life and the life of married men should be alike rewarded. Then were Wickliff's pestilent heresies concerning marriage revived. And, although the patrons of the King's first divorce made a great business against the other side that they should maintain in matrimonial causes Wickliff's heresy condemned by the Council of Constance, yet (as we have declared) that was altogether untrue, and (as we will now declare) the King and themselves afterward partly maintained, partly gave occasion to the maintenance of such errors. For when they made such an impure understanding of the Levitt. that a man might have married, as we have said, his father's or son's wife being unknown; and when they made an Act of Parliament that the latter marriage with carnal copulation should break and infringe the former marriage solemnized, it appeareth plainly that their opinion was (for other good ground have they none) that the substance of marriage rested upon the conjunction and copulation of the bodies and not upon the conjunction and copulation of mutual consent and unity of minds, which error we have before at large overthrown. And it was one of the errors and heresies of John Wickliffe, as were also other renewed in King Edward's time for the marriages of priests and religious persons, which were made lawful by Act of Parliament, but by all Fathers and [p. 97] Councils, yea and by Holy Scripture itself, most severely condemned; at which time it chanced otherwise with us than it did in St. Hierom's and St. Austin's time in Rome and other places. For, albeit the said Jovinian never durst teach and publicly defend this filthy doctrine of the incestuous marriages of priests and religious, but taught only, as we have said, that there was no more reward in heaven for the single life than for the married, yet was this doctrine so abhorred that he could deceive no persons, unless it were a few silly poor women (*August. de heresibus.*) But now in our time that the [wickedness and] iniquities of the Amorreans are ripe and grown up to the very full, it is rather contrary, for of the religions professed women (which is the frailer sex) few or none have married, but of priests and religious men (which ought to have been more constant and severe) great numbers have (the more pity) run out of their cloisters and out of the true Christian faith withal headlong into this incestuous marriage. Yea, both our archbishops gave this virtuous example, and led this holy harlot's dance, whereof one, the Archbishop of Canterbury, was married in King Henry his days, but kept his woman very close, and sometime carried her about with him in a great chest full of holes, that his pretty nobsey might take breath at.[a] In the meanwhile it so chanced that his palace at Canterbury was set on fire; but lord what a stir and care was there for this pretty nobsey and for this chest; all other care in a manner was set aside. He caused that chest with all speed to be conveyed out of danger, and gave great charge of it, crying out that his evidences and other writings which he esteemed above any worldly treasure were in that chest; and this I heard out of the mouth of a gentleman that was there present, and knew of this holy mystery. His brother also, the Archdeacon of Canterbury, was likewise married and kept privily his woman, and being thereof examined by Dr. Thurlby, that was afterward Bishop of Ely, and had commission from the King for the examination of such matters, sware upon a book that he was not married,[b] and indeed he might truly have sworn that he was never lawfully married. But what a pitiful case was it to see old doting lecherous priests and bishops of 60, 70, yea, and of 80 years of age, run a catterwawling, among whom one Holgate, Archbishop of York, a man about four score years of age, which had been a religious man also, married a young girl of fourteen or fifteen years of age, and yet for three causes she never was his wife;[c] the one for that he had

[a] Archbishop Cranmer kept a wench in a chest, which Dr. Harpsfield, the author of this treatise, avers from the mouth of a gentleman present.

[b] Edmund Cranmer, though married, swore he was not married.

[c] Archbishop Holgate was a Gilbertine prior of Wotton, and master of the Order of Sempringham. See Wood's Athenæ, vol. i. col. 160.

been a religious man and had solemnly avowed chastity; the second for that he was a priest; and the third for that she was betrothed to another man, and by very force kept from him, as I have heard the party myself confess, and complain in this Queen's time, and that he intended to procure process out for him. But whether the Archbishop's death or some composition stayed the suit, or to what end the matter came, I know not. Against these kind of marriages^a and maintenance of the same King Henry, in his latter days, made very sharp laws, whereupon many so married put over their women to their servants and other friends, who kept them at bed and board as their own wives. And after the death of King Henry they received them again (as love money) with usury, that is, the children in the mean season begotten by the said friends, whom they took, called and brought up as their own, as it was well known, as well in other as in Browne, Archbishop of Dublin. It would now pity a man at the heart to hear of the naughty and dissolute life of these yoked priests, led with other also beside their pretended wives, wherein the women were nothing behind for their parts, and to hear of the strifes, contentions, and debates that were among[st] them; among others there was one in Kent, which all to beat her yokemate with a washbeetle or battledore, upon whom he complained grievously to the Judges at the Sizes, and, the more to exaggerate his injury, shewed them openly the said battledore. Many like stories and frays were daily heard of at that time, and many of these women would say to the said priests, being reproved of them for their vicious living,—Why, knave, thinkest thou, if I had been an honest woman I would ever have married with thee? These and many other inconveniences, absurdities, and enormities, even in matters and causes matrimonial, fell upon this poor realm after and by occasion of the King's divorce with his first lawful wife Queen Katherine, which I thought good here briefly to adjoin as not altogether to our principal purpose impertinent, which is among other to discover and open the hurt, damages, and enormities

^a The shameful confusions arising from priests marrying.

chancing [p. 101] to this realm after and by the said divorce, especially in causes matrimonial.

But now let us return again to intreat of the King's marriage with the said Katherine Howard. You have heard what ungodly and dishonourable means he used to work and compass her marriage by putting away divers ancient old laws and customs of the whole Catholic Church upon a surmised ground of carnal copulation. But who can tell (for the grossness and indisposition of the King's body) whether he ever knew her or not ? Surely there concur some conjectures whereby it may be surmised he did not know her, or at least it might so chance. Then if it were so, either the Lady Anne was his wife still (no carnal copulation following which should break marriage before solemnised with her), or as he left the Lady Anne, even so for the same cause or reason he might have left Queen Katherine too, and upon some lusty hope or courage to take the third wife also. Who can think that such practices and means can ever take any good success, or that God will bless such marriages with children or otherwise! No more, surely, did he this marriage, but [p. 102] hath as well by this as by the former turned the King, as it were, into a salt stone as he did Lot's wife, following her concupiscence, and made him a spectacle, I say, for all men to the [very] world's end to wonder at. For behold, after he had been divorced from three wives and had put one of them to open shameful death, God did send such a tempestuous hurling wind that it brake and blew up by main force the brickle bush wherewith the King would have stopped (for the better countenance of his marriage) two foul gaps at once—the one to make his former marriage naught, the other to make his marriage following good. I mean of the Act of Parliament touching precontracts and marriages within the fourth degree. The cause and filthiness of which Act every man shortly after did see. God, I say, did send such a raging wind and so poured his vengeance upon this marriage that shortly after forced the King quite to break it off, to his great discomfort and dishonour, and to her pain and shame for ever. For she was found an harlot before he married her, and an adulteress after he married her. Whereupon she was, 'ere one full year and a half [p. 103] passed, condemned by Act of Parliament, which had so dishonorably a little before confirmed the said marriage; and shortly after put to death with one Thomas Culpeper and Francis Dyrcham, with whom she had incontinently and filthily used herself. So you now see to what end, by the wonderful hand and ordinance of God, the King's other marriages miserably and pitifully came, after he had once repudiated his first lawful wife, Queen Katherine, of the which marriages many other things here might be enlarged, and, among the residue, that for such sorrowful events of this marriage the King's suit and wooing was especially by the Duchess of Millane and Loraine refused and rejected, which is a very wise [and] virtuous lady and niece to the Emperor Charles, who had granted his good will to the same; and she, being earnestly urged and pressed why she refused to be [the] Queen of such a goodly realm, made answer—" I like not to be wife to such a husband that either putteth away or killeth his wives." And were it for her good chance or for her wisdom and foresight she seemed therein to have taken the best way, and [p. 104] to have sped better than the lady that supplied her room, for she afterward married, though not with a King, yet with the noble Duke of Loraine, to her great honor, contentation, and quiet. But how the Lady Anne of Cleve sped, to whom the King afterwards became wooer, we have already declared. This Duchess of Loraine was late here in this realm, and came purposely to see her cousin our gracious Queen and Mistress; and at her abode here had great liking of this country, whereof she said she might have been once Queen if she would.

Mr. Wriothsley, that was afterwards Lord Chancellor of the realm, was sent by the King purposely to the said Duchess to procure the said marriage. There was in his company, among other, his brother-in-law Mr. Knight, to whom the Duchess made the answer which we have before rehearsed, as himself afterward reported. Some men in these marriages would mislike, if there were nothing else, the multiplication of so many wives, which, in a great Prince, seemeth, to many men's judgments, a very unseemly thing; and truth it is that the stories of the Grecians report that Nicholaus, the Patriarch of Constantinople, excommunicated [p. 105] Leo the Emperor for marrying four wives,[a] though at divers times, which his fact I do not now intend to defend. But, Lord, what would he have said or done; yea, what might he justly have said and done to the King's marriages which we have not rehearsed. Some would also think it a thing worthy to be considered that God would not suffer the King to continue with his other five wives little more than half the time that he continued with his first lawful wife. Some would say that it were to be observed and marked that, of all the five wives which he afterward did marry, he had but two children, the one a male and the other a female. Some would also here say that it is greatly to be wondered at and pitied that, whereas among the Romans for five hundred years together there was no one man found that was divorced from his wife, now there should be found a King of England that should be divorced from more wives than were all the Kings his predecessors put together for five hundred years before ; yea, for a thousand, even from the first Christian King, Ethelberte. And yet, Spurius Carbilius, that made the first divorce, was reproved for his so doing of the very Ethnicks, though his wife were [p. 106] barren, which was the cause of his attempt. But the King repudiated Queen Katherine having a most noble, virtuous daughter by her. But I leave these and such other considerations; and must now say that perchance which to some men will seem strange, and yet it is most true. There is yet remaining one other marriage whereof we have spoken nothing which hath done more hurt to England than all the other. You will now perchance reply and say, Sir, what mean

Zonaras in annalibus, tom 2º.

ye so to say, how can this be true? By his last wife Katherine Parr he had no child ; other wives he had none but such as you have spoken of, saving Lady Jane Seymore, whose marriage God did bless, sending a goodly male child, Prince Edward, which was King after his father, unless you mean for that he was cut out of his mother's belly, which is but a slender cause for you to make such a grievous exaggeration. I mean indeed of that marriage, though not specially for the cause before rehearsed. Albeit, that mischance also might be accounted among the other great discomforts and misfortunes of his marriage that she should also die, though for [p. 107] the safeguard of the child, in such a manner as she did; yea, the child to be born, as some say the adders are, by gnawing out the mother's womb, might seem to some man a sorry heavy boding and prognostication to England, as it chanced many hundred years before to the Romans by the like birth of Julius Cæsar. It might seem, I say, to be a sorrowful boding of the grievous and terrible mischief that under his reign did afterward chance—that very nature seemed to be loth and as it were to abhor of his coming forth into the world. I say they were most terrible and horrible to be heard or spoken of among Christians, which we (the more was our misery) both heard, saw, and felt. If any man be disposed let him exasperate as much as his wit and cunning will serve him all the mischiefs and miseries that chanced to England in all those long raging pernicious contentions for the Crown between the red rose and the white (which were, to say the truth, long, ruthful, and pitiful), and at length pacified in the person of King Henry the Seventh, both families, by his marriage with King Edward's daughter, being united and knit together. But for the unkindness of King Henry, his son, toward God, in not thankfully remembering such a great benefit employed upon him and his family, and for breaking God's blessed will, first in violating the sacrament of wedlock by divorce from his lawful wife, and then the unity of Christ's Catholic Church by his new and worse divorce from the same, and for his other great enormities, and for lack of due repentance, God sent him such a son as should plague England more, in less than seven years, than it was plagued before in all the other long tumultuous time of blood. And yet do I not speak this principally for such dangerous events as chanced to the realm in civil and politic matters, as for the notable abasing of the coin, for the great tumults and bloodshedding in the seditions rising in Norfolk and Suffolk, and divers other parts of the realm, nor for the strange bloody spectacle wherein the one brother was butcher to the other, both being the King's uncles, and the supervivant (I mean the Lord Protector) beheaded not long after ; neither yet for the strange and unnatural dealing of the King himself, that was so far abused that he was content to spoil both his sisters of the succession of the [p. 109] Crown due unto them by his father's will, and by Act of Parliament, and to substitute another that had no right thereto. These things and like, though of most great weight, I do not principally rest upon. It is another thing of greater weight than all this that I ground myself upon. King Henry his father, though he broke the unity of the Church and abolished the Pope's authority to serve his fleshly lust, and all the monasteries to serve his covetous appetite, yet had he great respect and regard to the residue of the Christian Catholic religion, and especially to the Blessed Sacrament, and by divers statutes provided great and sharp punishments for the contemners, breakers, and violators of the same, and commanded in his last will that there should be certain chantries erected that he might be continually prayed for. But his son was not so soon crowned but that he began to impugn and evert his father's said testament, and the prayers for the dead, whereof his father (God knoweth) had great need ; he suppressed and abolished also all the colleges, chantries, and free chapels in England which his father (though they were given to him by Act of Parliament) did spare ; yea, he defaced, suppressed [p. 110], and extinguished one of the most noble and most ancient bishoprics of all England ; I mean the bishopric of Durham. He everted, extinguished, and abolished, not only the rightes and ceremonies of the Catholic Church, but divers articles of our faith, and the chief sacraments withal. Then our churches were more like to the Jews' synagogues (the image and cross of Christ, with the image of his blessed mother and all his holy saints, being defaced and broken, the altars overthrown, and the precious body of Christ villanously profaned) than to Christian churches; the walls all bepainted, like the Jews' temples, with places of holy Scripture; and yet worse than the Jews' temples, for that the meaning of these authorities was to make the world believe that to pray to the saints, to pray for the dead, to worship Christ's body in the blessed sacrament, was nothing but plain superstition and idolatry.

Then should you have seen in the place where Christ's precious body was reposed over the altar, and instead of Christ his crucifix, the arms of a mortal King set up on high with a dogg and a lyon, which a man might well call the abomination of desolation standing in the temple [p. 111] that Daniell speaketh of; so that the reign of the good blessed child King Josias that commenced his reign about the same age that King Edward did was not more pleasant and acceptable to God or more profitable to the people than was King Edward's displeasing and disliking to God and unprofitable and noyfull to the realm. For, as Josias, being a child, reformed the errors, superstitions, and idolatries wherewith his forefathers had corrupted and depraved God's true religion, and reformed the temple and brought thereinto the ark, which was but a figure of Christ's body, so this young King increased and amplified the errors and abuses that his father began, so far and so excessively that in a manner the whole face of Christ's Catholic religion was altered and changed, and (the daily sacrifice of the Church being abolished) that time seemed to be nothing else but the very forerunning and foreshowing of Antichrist. Oh, what a detestable and ugly sight was it to see the blessed body of Christ taken from the altar;* yea, in an university before the whole company of a

---

* This detestable and heinous impiety was committed at St. Mary Magdalen's College in Oxford, upon Whitson eve, in the year 1547, by one Thomas Bickley, then

college (I tremble and shake to tell it), and to be villanously and wretchedly conculcated and trodden under foot. Finally, as the said Julius Caesar utterly oppressed [p. 112] and extincted the ancient liberty and freedom and the good government of the people of Rome, so was Christ's Catholic religion quite overthrown by this and in this King's reign. So that we might well say with the Prophet Joell—*capite primo*—as well for the temporal as spiritual plague,—That which the palmer worm left the grasshopper did eat, and that which the grasshopper left the canker worm did eat, and that which remained from the canker worm the caterpillar did eat. Thus seemed Joell to cry out rather to us than to the Jews,— O, you priests, gird yourselves and lament ; cry out and howl, you that are ministers of the altar ; come you the ministers of my God, and lie all night in sackcloth, for the meat-offering and the drink-offering (the sacrifice of the body and blood of Christ) is taken away from the house of our God. The profound depth and greatness of these mysteries and calamities, if they should be penned and set forth as the matter craveth, would require a long time and an excellent orator. But, as I began to say, I constantly affirm that, the premisses and all other circumstances duly considered, with the infinite number of souls that with these and other pestiferous heresies were in this short time utterly destroyed, and shall be (God knoweth how long) by the evil example of that time and by [p. 113] the naughty books then made daily (though not so openly) undone, that there was much more hurt done in this little season by the destruction of [so] many souls than there was in the other long wretched time for the destruction of men's bodies. And, notwithstanding the great consideration of the said English dialogue

---

a junior fellow of that house, but shortly after preferred to be chaplain or preacher to King Edward the Sixth, and in the year 1585 promoted to the bishopric of Chichester by Queen Elizabeth. See more of this man, and the disorders committed at Oxford, in Wood's Historia et Antiquitates Universitatis Oxoniensis, lib. 1mo p. 271, and his Athenæ Oxonienses, volume the first, p. 613.—Charles Eyston.

that there must needs be a divorce with Queen Katherine that the realm might be provided of a male child that should enjoy the crown, it had been, I say, much better for the realm that the King should have had no male child at all. And all these enormities, introduced, as well in the time of the said young king as by his father, were reformed and redressed, not by a man King, but by a woman, our gracious Mistress and Queen that now is. Surely, I suppose, if King Henry might have known that his son Edward would have come to such proof that as Augustus the Emperor (being a most fortunate and lucky man) was wont to call himself most unfortunate and unhappy, for nothing else but for that he had children (he did so highly dislike of them), so King Henry the Eighth, among all his other misfortunes in marriages, would (as he well might) have said that this was the greatest that ever he had, to have such a male child. Yea, I think, verily [p. 114] he would have beaten him out of his sight, as I credibly understand himself was beaten of his father, saying to Alcock Bishop of Ely then present and entreating for him—" Never entreat for him, for this child shall be the undoing of England."[a] And thus have we now done at length with all his marriages, and so might we now finish and make up this our treatise, saving that we think it convenient that, as we have declared how God suffered the King and the realm to fall after this divorce into divers errors in matters matrimonial, and grievously to be plagued by the King's marriages following (wherein as the King diversly offended and sinned so were the said marriages to him both sin and pain of sin), to declare also three branches more ; the one what other plagues fell upon the King by reason of the said divorce, the other what plagues fell upon the chief procurers and contrivers of the said divorce; the third and last what plagues fell also upon the whole realm for and after the said divorce; which narration accordingly to accomplish would require a long process and a cunning eloquent workman. But it shall be enough for me at this time, according to my poor skill, shortly and briefly to touch some principal parts of the [p. 115]

[a] King Henry the Seventh is said to have beaten his son Henry, and to have foretold of him that he should be the undoing of England.

same. For the King, I find him chiefly in four points after this divorce wonderfully changed and altered to the worse;
1, that is in sensual and fleshly carnality;
2, in schism and heresy;
3, in cruelty; and
4, in covetousness.

For the first, we have said so much as we need not now repeat any part again.

For the second, we say that, whereas before this divorce the King was highly renowned throughout all Christendom, as well for many other princely qualities, as especially for his purity and constancy in the Catholic religion, for the defence whereof he wrote a notable learned book against Luther; after this divorce he was most ugly, deformed, and transformed into a quite contrary monstrous shape; so far forth that he took upon himself (the first pestilent pernicious precedent that ever was before or since shewed in any realm of Christendom, and wherein he is yet alone)—he took upon him, I say, to be [the] supreme head of the Church of England in all causes, as well ecclesiastical as temporal. Neither is it to be marvelled if he thus fell into schism and heresy, and forsook the unity of the Catholic Church. For, as St. Paul (ad Ephesios, cap. quinto) writeth,—Matrimony is a great sacrament [p. 116] in Christ and his Church. [Matrimony signifieth the unity between Christ and the said Church.] Wherefore, after the King had once broken this unity [of matrimony], dividing and parting his body to divers wives (which unity is the sign), the Devil the more facilely brought him to break also the unity with Christ and his Church, which is by the same sacrament signified, dividing and parting his faith also (which should be but one) into sundry schisms and heresies. Now, as this carnal sensuality drowned and defaced the sincerity of his faith, so did it also all his other commendable ornaments. And whereas for twenty years and more he had been a benign, gentle, and mild prince, he was now turned to a tiger or ramping lion, raging and roaring

after blood, sparing neither kinsman—no, not the worthy Marquess
of Exeter, nor the good lady the Countess of Salisbury, nor any
others ; no, not those that, I trowe, the very Turk would have rever·
enced, I mean the angelical Carthusians, and the most notable,
virtuous, learned men, the Bishop of Rochester and Sir Thomas
Moore, which had been his lord chancellor and his most worthy, true
and faithful counsellor above twenty years. I [p. 117] speak not
against doing of justice, neither intend narrowly to sift his doings,
but I speak against his outrageous, raging, notorious cruelty upon
them that were innocent and worthy of high favour and advancement for their truth and fidelity to God and him. Now, as his cruelty
had no measure, so neither had his insatiable covetousness, which
never ceased until it had eaten up and devoured all the monasteries
and religious houses in England (which amounted to the number of
8,000 or thereabouts), with their lands, goods, jewels, plate, and
other moveables, with the timber and lead, and all, for the which
he hath run into so many curses and excommunications, as were
either kings of England, from the first Christened King Ethelberte,[a]
which builded the monasteries of St. Austine's and of Christ his
Church in Canterbury, and forbade the destruction and spoil of the
same upon his and St. Gregory our Apostle's curse), or noble men
in this realm, or bishops, or any other that erected any religious
houses, and most [p. 118] of all his own father's. And by this and
his other doings he brought to pass indeed that which his father (I
cannot tell upon what forejudgment) did, as I have said, fear
of him.

[a] The words of the original charter of King Ethelbert, given to the monastery of
St. Augustine, are these : In nomine domini nostri Jesu Christi notum sit omnibus
tam praesentibus quam futuris Quod Ego Ethelbertus Dei Gratia Rex Anglorum per
evangelicum genitorem meum Augustinum de Idolatra factus Christicola tradidi
Deo per ipsum antistitem aliquam partem terrae Juris mei sub orientali muro civitatis Doroberniae, ubi scilicet per eundem in Christo institutorem Monasterium in honore
principum Apostolorum Petri et Pauli condidi et cum ipsa terra et cum omnibus quae
ad ipsum monasterium pertinent perpetua libertate donavi, adeo ut nec mihi nec alicui
successorum meorum regum nec ulli unquam potestati sive ecclesiasticae sive seculari

Surely many ancient [old] grave persons, and among other William Warham, Archbishop of Canterbury, of whom we have spoken, were wont to foretel of this wretched world; yea, there have been many bodings and prognostications of the same: myself have talked with men of good honesty and credit that most constantly affirmed, as a thing most certain, that before the suppression of the said abbeys, divers men in Kent saw in the day time, as it seemed to them, the tower and church of St. Austine's[a] in Canterbury lift up on high in the air, and suddenly falling down to the ground. But to return where we left. This insatiable glutting Charibdis and Sylla, not content to swallow up the said monasteries, with the tombs and shrines of the blessed saints, and to thrust out the virtuous and godly men that daily and nightly prayed for him and the realm [and that [fol. 119] by their virtue and prayer defended the realm] from the inward enemy, suppressed and destroyed also the noble houses called the hospitals of St. John['s in England and Ireland, with the whole order of the brethren called the Knights of St. John's] and Knights of the Rhodes which defended Christendom against our open enemy the Turk. O, how far unlike were the facts and doings of King Henry to his predecessors, especially [to] King Edward the Second, who at what time the order of the Templars was by a general council for certain causes suppressed and extinguished, and that thereupon the lawyers determined that the said lands were devolved to the King's and other the chief lords' use and dominion, would for all that enjoy no part thereof, nor the said chief lords, but caused the said lands wholly to be conserved and converted to the use of the said knights, to whom the said lands were also confirmed by Act of Parliament. The revenues, goods, and moveables of the said abbeys, with the said hospitals,

[a] The tower of St. Austin's in Canterbury, a little before its dissolution, was seen lift up in the air.

quicquam inde liceat usurpare sed in ipsius Abbatis sint omnia libera ditione. Si quis vero de hac donatione nostra aliquid minuerit aut irritum facere temptaverit, auctoritate beati Episcopi Gregorii nostrique Apostoli Augustini simul et nostra imprecatione sit hic segregatus ab omni sanctæ ecclesiæ communione et in die judicii ab omni electorum societate, etc. Actum est hoc in civitate Dorobernhe Anno ab Incarnatione Christi 605. *Vide* etiam Monasticon Anglicanum, tom. 1, p. 24.

with the great treasure that was made of the timbers, bells, and leads, and the ornaments of the church, and other furniture of the said houses, were so great that the commodity thereof seemed able and sufficient to have defended and maintained the realm [p. 120] against all outward and inward enemies many Kings' days. And yet was the King brought within [a very] few years to great need and debt, and borrowed great sums of the merchants beyond the seas upon interest, whereof some part is yet unpaid, and the Queen that now is, fain to take order for it. Yea, beside the said monasteries he levied within a fourteen or fifteen years and laid such exactions upon the people of subsidies, contributions, and benevolencies when they gave it with an evil will; beside many loans and beside the immeasurable abasing of the coin to his inestimable advantage, that I trowe never any one King did for the rate of the time ever before. But in this a man may see that to be verified that Solomon writeth,[a] "There be some (saith he) that bestow their own liberally and wax rich; other there be that catch and rape all that ever they can from other, and yet are ever needy." These and many other vices and enormities grew in King Henry after this divorce, which (beside God's high displeasure) brought him to as much dishonour and obloquy in the world that ever he had honour and commendation before.

We will [p. 121] now consequently show what evil success happened to them that were the principal devisers and workers of the said unhappy divorce, and, namely, of two, the one Thomas Woolsey Lord Cardinal and Archbishop of York, the other Thomas Cranmer Archbishop of Canterbury. Touching the said Cardinal, we have declared before what fervent suit the King made to have made him Pope, being ready to rear a schism in the whole Church, and to set up an Antipape against the true Pope rather than he would have been defeated of his purpose. And all was by his authority (being once made Pope) to bring to effect the divorce that

[a] Proverb. 11° Alii dividunt propria et ditiores fiunt, alii rapiunt aliena et semper sunt in egestate.

he so long sought for. But what was the end either of the King's unlawful and ungodly suit or of the Cardinal's importunate [and immoderate] ambition? Truly, the Papacy that the King would have conveyed to him, and that he so sore looked for, he never obtained. But the King's high favour, wherein he had so many years continued, 'ere that year went about wherein this hot suit was commenced, he utterly lost, and ran into the King's extreme displeasure and indignation (being spoiled of his authority and dignity of the Lord Chancellorship, and cast into a præmunire), was at [p. 122] length arrested and commandment given that he should be brought to London.[a] And being thus arrested in Yorkshire and being in his journey towards London, either from sickness or feebleness, or (that is most likely) for grief of mind, he died in the way.

[a] Cardinal Wolsey's fall and death.

Concerning the Archbishop of Canterbury, as he was much worse than the Cardinal, so had he a worse end. He was a scholar and student in the University of Cambridge; and there, being cast in love with a wanton maid at the sign of the Dolphin, that was wont to sell young scholars their breakfasts, married her.[b] It chanced not long after that she died, and then became he a priest, and afterwards chaplain to Thomas Earl of Wiltshire, father to the Lady Anne Bulleyne, at that time that the King went about to make a divorce with Queen Katherine; of the which matter the Earl had oft talk with the said Cranmer, who was very forward to help forth the said divorce, and found much fault with the King that he delayed the matter so long. To whom the Earl answered that all the stay was to see if the King could possibly win the Pope's aid and favour to pronounce a sentence definitive for the said divorce, much fearing the event of matters if he should put away his former wife without [p. 123] his consent. Why, saith Cranmer, is this all the stay? Surely, if I were King, I would with all speed reject this barren Katherine and take another, and never tarry for any advice to come from Rome; neither would I more regard the Pope's judgment and censure in this matter than the bishop's of Alexandria; for as great

[b] A short account of Cranmer's education, marriage, promotion, fall, and death.

authority hath the one as the other in England. And, while the King thus hangeth upon the Pope's answer as upon a divine oracle, he seemeth to make himself and his realm as slaves to the Pope, and to hang all upon his will and pleasure. When the King understood by the Earl the great towardness of Cranmer to advance so much his desired purpose, little caring whether it were by right or wrong, and done by lawful authority or no, he thought him a very meet man to serve his turn, and began daily more and more to be advised by him, being desirous to advance him to some high dignity ecclesiastical, that he might the better work his purpose by him. And shortly after, Doctor Warham being dead, he bestowed upon him the archbishopric of Canterbury. Then loe had Cranmer the sweet soppe he looked for, that made him [p. 124] so drunk that he wist not nor cared what he did so he might serve the King's pleasure and appetite. You have now heard that the King gave him the said archbishopric, and you see withal to what end and purpose. But yet it is to be observed when, and where, and after what sort it was given him. Whereas then in the bestowing of such high rooms good kings and princes were wont to have grave and mature deliberation with the Bishops and their Council, and then, after devout prayers made unto God to direct their choice, to appoint such as the consent of the most part of the best concurred withal, King Henry took no other counsel but his will and pleasure, and his disordinate affection to the setting forth of his divorce. And thereupon accordingly (being at a bear-baiting[a] and Cranmer also), called the said Cranmer unto him, and there told him that he gave him the archbishopric of Canterbury, which thing being heard abroad was an heavy boding to good and wise men of some great and civil mishap hanging upon the Church and realm of England. This pernicious pestilent prelate, as in Cambridge he began with the flesh, so afterward [p. 125] also (being once inured) he still smelt of the smock. And I have already told you how he carried about with him (like a worthy Archbishop) his darling in a chest, neither yet durst he abide by his filthy incestuous doctrine of mar-

[a] King Henry gives Cranmer the archbishopric of Canterbury at a bear-baiting.

rying of priests ; but with the residue of the bishops, and with the parliament, he consented to the contrary in words, though in heart he thought otherwise, and in fact did also privily otherwise; whereby you may see the constancy of this worthy prelate, and the deep dissimulation of a man of such vocation. If his doctrine were good, why did he give it over? if his doctrine was naught (as indeed it was, as well for his incestuous marriage as against the presence of Christ his holy body in the sacrament of the altar and for other articles), why did he, contrary to the true doctrine of the Church, under the pretence and color of marriage, keep an harlot? Surely he was the first of all Bishops of Canterbury, and of all Bishops in England before our time, that either gave such a filthy precedent and example or sowed such pestilent doctrine.

Hear now, I pray you, another pretty point and gay pageant of the dissimulation of [p. 126] this worthy prelate. When he should be consecrated Archbishop by the Pope's Bulls, he took (according to the use of the Church) his oath of due obedience to the see Apostolic. But before he took the said oath, early in the morning, he called to him certain of his friends, and among other Master Goodricke, that was afterward Bishop of Elye, and said to them, Sirs, bear me witness that, albeit I shall swear this day to be obedient to the see Apostolic of Rome, yet I shall swear but with my outward lips, and not with my inward heart and mind, neither do I intend to keep promise with the Pope that is absent, but to blind and bleare the eyes of the people here present.ᵃ And this his protestation he required might be (doubtless to his perpetual shame) enacted and registered. Such an archbishop so nominated, and in such a place, so and in such wise consecrated, was a meet instrument for the King to work by,—a meet instrument to make such a divorce by,—a meet cover for such a cup; neither was there ever bearward that might more command his bears than the King might command him. Neither was there ever any bearwards Jackanapes that made more pastime [p. 127] and toys to the people, than this the Divell's Jackanapes made pastime to Lucifer and all his angels,

ᵃ Cranmer's hypocrisy in taking his oath of canonical obedience to the Pope.

whom they saw so serviceable to his worldly king, to recompense the benefit he received at his hands at the bear-baiting, that he nothing passed for right or justice, or for the high King of all Kings' will and pleasure. This prelate, when the King went about to suppress the monasteries, was his chief instrument and worker.[a] And, to bring the people asleep and cause them to have better contentation that (as it was doubted) would not patiently and quietly bear the suppression (as it proved afterward by the rebellion of Lincolnshire and Yorkshire), came and preached at Paule's Crosse, and to sweet the people's ears with pleasant words told them, among other things, that they had no cause to be grieved with the evertion of the abbeys, but should rather be very glad thereof, for the singular benefit that should redound to the whole realm thereby. And then as he had and did many times afterward wrongfully persuade the people in many matters, by his lewd lying divinity, so now he telleth them by his vain lying rhetoric many proper imagined toys, and, among other, that the King should by the [p. 128] suppression of the abbeys gather such an infinite treasure that from that time he should have no need, nor would not put the people to any manner of payment or charge for his or the realm's affairs. This sermon, as no wise man did believe, so myself, that chanced to be there present, have known, and the whole realm beside to their smart have felt, that the exactions taken by the King after this jolly gay preaching were intolerable, and no less than such as I have before told you of. Now if you will see and hear his other marvellous dissimulations and contrarious proceedings; if you will call to remembrance divers things contained in the said book made for the King's divorce (wherein and whereof this man was one of the chiefest workers) and compare these sayings and doings with the contrary sayings and doings of the Parliament and [of] the clergy, wherein this man was a principal doer, which contrarieties I have before specified, then shall you plainly see that this man played the principal part and pageant in all these contrarieties and contradictions, whereof you shall now hear, before we quite leave

---

[a] Cranmer was a great instrument in the pulling down religious houses.

off his foresaid sermon, another notable [p. 129] demonstration. You must then remember that in the foresaid book, made for the divorce, one of the principal arguments whereby they would prove that the King might divert and divorce himself from Queen Katherine, and never expect the Pope's sentence or order therein, resteth upon this point following, which is, that, though a priest cannot depart out of the diocese without the bishop's licence, yet if he will be a regular canon, or enter into any [other] monastery, he may lawfully do it, and is not bound to expect and tarry for his ordinary's consent. For this man that leaveth the secular priest's life, and professeth straightly religion to save his soul, is led by the law of God and by the spirit of God. We speak nothing here what a feeble and weak reason this is, that, because a man may without the bishop's licence lead a sharp straight life in hard religion, therefore the King without the Pope's licence might lead an incontinent and dissolute life, forsaking his lawful wife. We will speak nothing of this now, and we have already shewed also the Bishop of Rochester's answer to the said reason; but we will rather return again to the said prelate's sermon, who, after he had once given the said sentence [p. 130] of divorce, was changed into a new man, not as Saul was when he was made king, but as Saul was afterward, when he was taken with an evil spirit and became every day worse and worse. You have heard how well and godly he and his fellows preached in the said book touching monasteries, though the place were very evily applied. Now shall you hear how [conformable] his said sermon was made afterward at Paule's Cross, which in effect was nothing else but a plain invective against all monasteries, as the places and dens of all error and superstition, and such as the commonwealth could not stand unless they were overthrown. I should enlarge my narration of him far and too long if I would go forward in opening unto you many like parts of this prelate's lewd life and marvellous inconstancy. Now to what end he came, it is so late done and so notorious that I need say nothing in it. Only this I will tell you, that in all his life he never shewed more inconstancy and mutability, nor more dangerous to his soul, than at his very end; for whereas he had by writing recanted and revoked his heresies and given out many copies thereof signed with his own hand, whereby if he had continued he might have saved [p. 131] his poor soul, loe, suddenly that same day that he saw he should needs die he revolted and reverted with the dog to his pestilent vomit. So this revocation was only for an outward show while he was yet in some hope to get thereby pardon for his temporal life, whereof when he was in despair he discovered his cloaked dissimulation and desperately cast away both his body and soul. And as he entered his first preferment (as you have heard) with devilish dissimulation, so he ended his wretched life in the same. This, loe, is the pillar of this divorce. This is he that adventured to take upon him the Pope's authority and to give judgment against the lawful marriage, which, though it had been unlawful, yet had his sentence been unlawful for lack of competent jurisdiction. And yet, if his jurisdiction had been competent, there is no godly wise man that might justly think [him] a meet person to commit such a weighty matter unto.

And thus end we with this prelate, made at the bear stake, to whose poor soul it had been much better if he had followed the steps of the said Cardinal Poole,[a] [and especially] the grave, godly, learned counsel he gave him to forsake his heresies (namely, against the blessed sacrament of the altar) for the [p. 132] verity whereof and of Christ's bodily presence therein he wrate him a long learned discourse, not yet printed as far as I know. Yea, it had been better for his poor soul if he had been a layman all his life (as he was at the time of his death), being despoiled and degraded of all his priestly and episcopal dignity, and a bargeman's coat set on his back. Better, I say, for him if the King that day had given him a silver bawdericke and made him his bearward than to have given him the chiefest bishopric of England to the utter undoing of his soul and of the King's soul, and of many a thousand beside. And, if there were nothing else to consider in this divorce but the

<small>a Cardinal Poole's character.</small>

great disparity and odds in all worthiness of this prelate (who, to
advance his worldly preferment, fervently at all times set forth the
divorce, and at length gave definitive sentence for the same), and
of the Lord Cardinal Poole, his successor, who refused the bishop-
ricks of Winton and Yorke, as I have said, the election whereof he
might have had if he would have satisfied the King's will and
pleasure for his new marriage; this only, I say, were enough for
a godly wise man to cause him to misdeem and mistrust the justice
of this divorce. I add here that the [p. 133] great integrity and
modesty of the said Cardinal,[a] free from all importunate ambition of   [a] Cardinal Poole's
all worldly honour, wherewith the other prelate was overwhelmed   character.
and drowned, is otherwise also more notable as for one that refused
the very high and supreme dignity of the Papacy of Rome, whereto
he was by the Cardinals lawfully elected, for whose consent they
stayed their election of any other person two whole months; a
thing that was never read or heard of, I trowe, before in any Pope's
election, and yet could they not win his consent. This thing, as it
is of itself most notable, so it should be to us Englishmen most
comfortable; for, unless I be greatly deceived, one of the greatest
causes of his refusal proceeded from the fatherly, tender love he
bare to this his native country, whose reformation he desired of all
other things, and would reserve himself free (if ever God did send
a meet time) to help forward in his own person that holy work and
business of our reformation; whereof it seemed he was not out of
hope, but looked and longed for it, and hoped to be a worker
therein. Surely, after the time that he refused the Papacy and
that many of his friends were discontented with him for it, and laid
the matter hard to his charge [p. 134] as foreslowing and pretermitting the vocation that God himself did call him unto, thereby
to do acceptable service to his Universal Church, these complaints
the Cardinal satisfied, partly in talk with his friends present and
partly by his letters sent to such as were absent; of the which, one, a
long godly learned letter (not yet printed), it hath been my chance
to see, wherein he laid many things for his excuse, and among other

he hath one clause in this sense—*Quid si dominus meus velit dilectum meum introduci in domum genitricis suæ per me*—What if it be God's pleasure [that] I shall bring in my beloved into his mother's house, which he meant by the reconciliation of this realm of England to our mother the Catholic Church. And, loe, not long after he had refused the Papacy and written this letter, tidings came to Rome that King Edward was dead and that our gracious Queen sat in the throne royal, and in short space after we were, by the said virtuous Cardinal's pain and travell, reduced to our mother's house again, from the which we had long run astray, and with the prodigal son riotously and wantonly lost and spent all the substance of our Catholic faith which our Celestial Father [p. 135] had given us, and were brought to such penury and famine that we were fain to feed upon the husks with hogs, and upon the draffe of filthy errors and heresies. Well, this shall suffice for the first two branches.

Let us now consider the third, which is the vengeance of God that happened even to the whole realm after and for the said divorce, the smart whereof there is no man lightly but hath one way or other felt, and many yet do feel, especially in the irreparable loss of the monasteries, and in dangerous, pestilent, cankered heresies, which, though by the goodness of God and our princess, the open face of the true Catholic Church sheweth itself everywhere, do yet lie lurking and festering in the hearts of many people, and will do, God knoweth how many years, beside the loss of innumerable souls already departed out of this life that were poisoned with the [said] pestilent heresies. What more mischief could our most enemy have wished to this realm than that the nobility and the clergy should consent to such statutes as passed in the said King Henry's days; whereby they were, after they had once renounced the obedience of the Apostolic see, made in a manner bondmen to the King's inconstant, wavering, carnal sensuality [p. 136], and to his immoderate and excessive covetousness, for the which great change, decay, and ruin of the prelates and nobility we have cause to lament and cry out with the prophet Jeremiah : *Quomodo obscuratum est aurum, mutatus est color optimus, dispersi sunt lapides Sanctuarii in capite omnium platearum. Filii Syon inclyti et amicti auro primo, quomodo reputati sunt in vasa testea, opus manuum figuli.*[a] What a pitiful hearing and sight was it when the Bishops could not freely do their pastoral duty in reforming the notable dissolute vicious living of the people and the errors and heresies that daily sprang more and more; of the lack of [the] which reformation it chanced that the virtuous learned physician Dr. Clement complained to Dr. Stokesley, Bishop of London, to whom he made this answer—*Vendidimus primogenita,* We have sold the right of our primogeniture, meaning of the renouncing of the obedience of the See Apostolic. This Stokesley was one of the great favourers of the divorce. King Henry himself, seeing errors and heresies to rise daily thicker and thicker, made many strait laws to repress and extinguish the same. But after that himself had once renounced first his true marriage and then his obedience [p. 137] to the See Apostolic, and took upon him St. Peter's authority and suffered the people, or rather compelled them, to a schism and to some heresies, he could no more stay and bridle them from other heresies that they were inclined unto than it is possible for a man to roll [down] a millstone from the top of a high hill and afterward to stay it in the midst of its course. He was like, I say, to one that would throw down a man headlong from the top of a high tower and bid him stay when he was half way down. The King had his subjects in reasonable good obedience before the said divorce and his new supremacy. But, as Adam had the power of all his sensual parts in good order and dutiful obedience to his soul and to reason as long as himself obeyed God's commandment, and afterward when he brake the same then did all the sensual parts rebel against the soul and reason, even so it fell between the King and his subjects; and as he withdrew his obedience from God and his Church so his people began by-and-by to fall to sedition and rebel-

[a] Lament. Jeremiæ, cap. 4°.

lion against him, as appeareth in the great commotion and rebellion of Lincolnshire and Yorkshire. Then began they to fall to divers errors and heresies, notwithstanding his laws and ordinances to the [p. 138] contrary. And as this most grievous plague of schism and heresy fell upon the realm after this divorce, so was the realm many ways plagued otherwise, as by the inestimable loss it suffered by the decay and abasing of money, by outward and domestical wars, by manifold grievous exactions and payments, laid as well upon the clergy as the temporalty, the said clergy being onerated and charged also with the payment of the first fruits and tenths of their ecclesiastical livings, wherein such haste was made that they were even in one year charged with both, and so with that which they did not receive, which oversight was afterwards seen and redressed. What shall I now speak of the notable decay of prayer, fasting, and alms, and universally of all virtuous living, of the disobedience of children to their parents, of servants to their masters, of fraud, deceit, circumvention, more practised than ever before in all contracts and bargains, of rarity of trusty true friends, and of decay of obedience to public laws and magistrates, and finally of all good order and public discipline; yea I will now add and conclude withall that the only loss of the monasteries was not only for the decay of [p. 139] virtue, prayer, and religion, but also of the politic commonwealth inestimable and importable. I say they were the very nurseries not only of piety and devotion, but also of the happy flourishing of the commonwealth. Where were the blind and lame and other impotent poor people fed and succoured, but there? I have heard that there were more such holpen in the city of Canterbury in one day than be now in all Kent; more in Winchester in one day than be now in all Hampshire; and the like may be said of other places. Where were noblemen's, gentlemen's, and other men's sons so well, so virtuously, and so mannerly brought up as they were there? Where had the younger brothers of noblemen and gentlemen better entertainment than there? Who found so many needy scholars and poor men's sons at the universities as they did? Whereby were the rents and the price of other things so excessively enhanced but by the suppression of the abbeys? Yet were there some ignorant people that would talk, and some fond foolish preachers that would preach, before the suppression of the said abbeys, eggs then being at twelve or more a penny and fish at a very reasonable [p. 140] price,[a] that the religious people by reason of their fasting in Advent and at other times made these victuals dear. But since, we have been fain and glad to buy three or four eggs a penny and to pay three times or four times so much for fish as we did before; yea, I have credibly heard that our sea and our waters in many places have not so plentifully yielded fish as they did before. Whereby is it come to pass that where before there dwelt many a good yeoman able to do the King and the realm good service, there is nobody now dwelling but a shepherd with his dog, but by the suppression of the abbeys? Whereby is it that whereas men were wont to eat sheep, now sheep eat up houses, whole towns, yea, men and all, but by the suppression of the abbeys? What is the decay of tillage but the suppression of abbeys? What is the decay of woods and the cause of the excessive price of wood but the suppression of the said abbeys, which did carefully nourish, supply, and husband the same? What is one of the causes that the people is now more charged than they were wont to be with subsidies, loans, and other payments but the suppression of the said abbeys, out of the which was wont the Prince to be furnished [p. 141] of money when occasion of his sudden and weighty affairs required present help?[b] Again, what is one of the causes of the great poverty and beggary of the people but the suppression of the said abbeys? For whereas, in times past, a great number of both sex and kind entered yearly into religion and there led a single chaste life, now all such being since married, and they, their children, and their children's children being multiplied in such an infinite number, neither farms sufficient for such a number can be conveniently provided, nor yet can they live by the way of merchandize or by occupying, but with the great hindrance of other occupiers and

[a] Prices of eggs and fish.

[b] Inconveniences that arose from the suppression of religious houses.

merchants. Nor yet can they by service and retainment with noblemen and other gentlemen conveniently in such a huge number be provided for. I talk nothing here of divers other intolerable and importable detriments, whereof one among other is the defacing, destruction, and loss of the old worthy chronicles and other rare monuments (as yet unprinted) that were carefully and tenderly kept and preserved in the said monasteries, which loss, if it be well valued as it ought to be [p. 142], is greater than I can well express, and will be felt by the whole realm and our posterity many years after our deaths. Woe, therefore, even for very civil and politic causes to the said prelate that made the lewd, lying sermon for the destruction of the said abbeys. Woe be, therefore, to them that procured the spoil and evertion of them. Woe be even to the great Abbots themselves that winked at the matter; yea, and gave their consent to the suppressing of the lesser, thinking to keep and preserve their own still, which they could not do long after, for all the fair and flattering promises made unto them, and for all that many of them had to their great charges and impoverishment procured and purchased the continuance of their houses under the great seal, as I have heard some of them report; only they got that benefit that Poliphemus promised to Ulysses, that is, that he would be so gracious and favourable to him that he would spare him and eat him last of all his fellows. But yet Ulysses got himself by policy out of danger. But these men could by no means provide, but that their abbeys were at length eaten and devoured as well as the lesser. All those which being under the clear value of [p. 143] two hundred pounds or not above were given to the King by Act of Parliament; but, as for the residue, they came to the King's hands by one means or other, and that without any Act of Parliament at all. Such as would voluntarily give over were rewarded with large annual pensions and with other pleasures. Against some other there were found quarrels, as against Hugh Farindon, Abbot of Reading, which was there hanged, drawn, and quartered; against Richard Whiting, Abbot of Glassenbury, that was hanged on the Torr Hill beside his monastery; against John Beche, Abbot of Colchester, put also to death, which dreadful sight and hearing made some other [abbots] so sore afraid that they were soon entreated to yield over all to the King's hands; and some thought they escaped fayer when they escaped with their lives. So that, after a few years, there needed no parliament at all for the great abbeys; they came in otherwise so thick and so roundly, but only to confirm such as had been already relinquished and such other as should afterward be so relinquished and yielded up to the King.

So much have I the more said that you may (gentle reader) see the just hand and plague of God upon these great [and] rich abbots, and their marvellous strange overthrow [p. 144], which so lightly and unadvisedly gave their consent to the overthrowing of the houses of their poor brethren. These, then, and many other great inconveniences, misfortunes, and calamities, did light upon the King and the whole realm, and especially upon the workers and contrivers of the said divorce; whereby a wise godly man may easily perceive how highly it disliked Almighty God, and that Sir Thomas Moore did rightfully stand against it, and had good cause to refuse the oath made for the confirmation of the same. God, I say, disliked with the divorce, and liked well of the marriage with Queen Katherine, adorning and blessing the same with issue of a noble virtuous lady, whom God, by his marvellous providence, notwithstanding the said divorce and illegitimation pretended thereupon, notwithstanding the great huge conspiracy made against her at the death of King Edward to spoil her of the right of the Crown due unto her, notwithstanding she was left destitute and desolate of all man's help, did yet so shield and protect her, that, maugre all their malicious conspiracies, against all man's expectation, and without any bloodshedding, he marvellously discomfited her enemies, and placed her in the royal seat wherein she most graciously sitteth as the right heir of King Henry the Eight, born in good and lawful [p. 145] matrimony, as the Parliament and the whole realm hath lately acknowledged, and the whole world beside believeth, whose Grace Almighty God long preserve to his glory, to the advancing of the Catholic faith, and to the comfort of all her true loving subjects. Amen.

At the end of the copy from which this was transcribed there is this note following :—

> This Coppy was taken from the Originall, which was found by Mr. Topliffe, in the house of William Carter, sometime servant to the said Doctor Nicholas Harpesfield, who confessed that the two leaves of the said original were of his said master's own handwritinge.

NOTES.

NOTES.

P. 4 l. 8. It is evident that Wood was quoting from an inaccurate copy of the passage, for neither the beginning of the epistle to the reader, nor the note at the end, agrees with either of the copies in New College Library. That with the pressmark 311 A begins:
It is an old true saide saying.
The copy numbered 311 B begins as follows:
It is an old true said sawe,
corrected into,
It is an old and true saing.
In the note at the end they both agree in reading *leaves* for *lines*, and the insertion of the Christian name *Nicholas*; but 311 B omits the surname of the servant *Carter*, and in this respect agrees, as 311 A does not, with Wood's account. It is probable, therefore, that 311 B is the copy which Antony Wood had seen at New College.
That this is so, is further evidenced by the next quotation from Antony Wood, made by Mr. Eyston. Here again the words of Wood are not an exact copy, and probably were not intended to be exact. For, whereas the words as copied from the Eyston copy agree precisely with those in 311 A, it is plain, from the use of the word *benefit* for *beautify*, that the copy seen by Antony Wood must have been 311 B and not 311 A, though Wood's words materially differ in other respects from both copies. Mr. Eyston's references in the next line of page 4 and in subsequent pages are, of course, to the first edition of the *Athenæ Oxonienses*, the only one published at the date of his writing, A.D. 1707.

P. 10, last line but 8. The date of Harpsfield's death is incorrectly given. He died December 18, 1575, as appears from a notice in The Academy for April 15, 1876.

P. 10, last line but 5. The passage is somewhat incorrectly copied. The original is as follows:—
Nicolaus Harpesfeldns natione Anglus, Juris utriusque doctor, Oxoniensis, Adolescens in celebri schola Wiccamicâ litteras humaniores didicit. Deinde ad Oxoniense Collegium etiam Wiccamicum missus, decurso Philosophiæ studio operam dedit jurisprudentiæ, susceptisque supremis in ea facultate insignibus successu temporis vocatus Cantuariam, factus est ibi Archidiaconus. Erat vir gravis et prudens,

moribus candidissimis, integerrimæ vitæ, multiplicis doctrinæ et Catholicæ fidei Confessor constantissimus. Primum sub Edvardo sexto Rege conscientiæ causâ, in exilium voluntarium profectus est anno Domini 1550. Deinde regnantibus Maria et Philippo, et reflorescente vera religione, domum reversus est. Sed mutato denuo rerum statu sub Elizabethâ anno salutis 1559, eo quod primatum ejus Ecclesiasticum agnoscere nollet, cum aliis multis in carcerem conjectus est, ubi ad scribendum animum appulit. Erat enim Poeta ingeniosissimus, orator disertus, historiarum peritissimus, linguarum scientissimus, in utroque jure optime, in Theologiâ non vulgariter versatus, solide fundatus, omnium denique optimarum scientiarum panopliâ ubertim instructus. In carcere igitur constitutus scripsit egregium opus sex doctissimis dialogis comprehensum contra Magdeburgenses et Pseudomartyrologium Joannis Foxii Angli. Quod opus quia sub nomine proprio in lucem emittere non est ausus, intimo amico suo Alano Copo, in exilio tum agenti, edendum commisit, suppresso auctoris nomine ne captivo capitis periculum crearet. Edidit igitur Alanus hoc opus suo nomine. Tamen ne veritas posteritatem lateret, et amicus amicum debita sua laude fraudaret, in calce voluminis, id est, finito sexto dialogo, majusculas quasdam litteras imprimi curavit, earumque explicationem amico uni forsan et alteri communicavit, in hunc modum qui sequitur,

Majusculæ litteræ
A. H. L. N. H. F. V. E. A. C.
Explicatio characterum.

Auctor hujus libri Nicolaus Harpesfeldus, Edidit vero eum Alanus Copus.
Igitur Alanus Copus erat qui librum sex dialogorum suo nomine edidit, sed Harpesfeldus erat qui composuit. Scripsit igitur *Sex dialogorum Librum unum.*

Historiam Angliæ Librum i. Opus egregium, nunquam tamen excusum. MS. habentur Romæ in Collegio Anglorum.

Historiam hæresis Wickleffianæ Librum unum MS. ibidem.

Epigrammatum et aliorum carminum Librum unum.

Ex quibus varia vidi. Quorum unum sic incipit:

Flumina ab Oceano primum decurrere vasto.
Inque illum rursus cuncta redire ferunt.

Obiit tandem Londini Confessor in carcere post vicesimum captivitatis annum, qui fuit partus virginei plus minus 1583, sub duro Catholicis Elizabethæ regno.

P. 18, l. 2. It will be seen, by referring to p. 149 of this treatise, that Robert Wakefeild, whose name is variously spelt Wakfeld, Wakefelde, &c., had written two books on the subject, one of which the author had not seen. That which he refers to so often in this work is much the rarest of the two. It is described in Wood's *Athenæ Oxonienses* under the heading Robert Wakfeld, an. 1537, as "*Syntagma de Hebræorum codicum incorruptione.* Printed in qu. [Bodl. 4to. F. 21, Th. Seld.] In which book are several things against Joh. Fisher, B. of Rochester, concerning matrimony, and the unlawfulness of the king's marrying with his brother's wife.

"*Oratio Oxoniæ habita in Coll. Regio.* Printed with the former in qu."—Vol. i. p. 104, ed. Bliss.

In a note at the foot of the page is added by Dr. Bliss :

"This rare volume has been omitted by Ames, Herbert, and Dibdin in their lists of De Worde's books, although it was undoubtedly printed by him. The Bodleian copy referred to above was formerly in the possession of Sir Thomas Elyot."

The whole title of the work, as taken from the copy in the Bodleian, which is the only one the present editor has ever seen, is as follows :

Roberti Wakfeldi sacrarum literarum professoris eximii Regiique sacellani syntagma de Hebræorum codicum incorruptione. Item ejusdem Oratio Oxonii habita una cum quibusdam aliis lectu ac annotatu non indignis.

The book is not paged or foliated. The sheets are in fours from A I to L II.

That it was written subsequently to the *Kotser Codicis* is evident from the words on signat. B 1, *quemadmodum in Kotser meo scripsi.* It is therefore wrongly ascribed conjecturally in the Bodleian Catalogue to the year 1526. From the first page, moreover, it appears that the Kotser had been written about seven years before this, as appears from the following extract from the back of the title, which runs as follows :—

"Quoniam ipsum totum Regis ac Reginæ negocium ex autoritate solum scripturæ divinæ pendet, nihilque roboris aut virium in eorum connubio habet dispensatio vel verius dissipatio pontificis Romani; ad probandum ejus scripturæ veritatem certam et infallibilem esse in codicibus hebræis ceu fonte ex quo omnes aliæ translationes tam lxx. interpretum et aliorum græcæ quam Hieronymi et ceterorum latinæ emanarunt, argumenta non pauca eaque solida, firma, ac irrevincibilia in syntagmate hoc adducam, quæ illam diffuse satis declarabunt, atque palam et ob oculos ponent. Primum tamen quæstionem per reverendum in Christo patrem dominum Johannem Fisshcrium episcopum Roffensem propositam atque responsionem quam illi in codice meo adhibui annos antehac fere septem in medium hic afferam. *Julii secundi pontificis Romani dispensatio in conjugio Regis et Reginæ dissipatio fuit.*

Quæstio episcopi Roffensis. An matrimonium in quo dispensavit pontifex ut frater fratris uxorem duceret firmum sit et indissolubile ?

Responsio Roberti Wakfeldi. Hujusmodi conjugium siquidem ea a defuncto fratre prius cognita fuit, nullum est neque constare potest. Nam juxta divinæ legis dispositionem illegitimum est et per personas illegitimas atque illicite contrahentes factum fuit. Quin potius *aserima* et impietas seu abhominatio contra naturam est incestusque execrabilis et immundicia ac fœditas deo abominabilis atque detestabilis, et fornicatio seu scortatio, quam velut culpam letiferam, Christiani omnes juxta Pauli præceptum, quod et a Moyse desumptum est fugere debent ac tenentur. Imo Julius pontifex Romanus juxta Apostolum anathemati (quod hebræorum proprie est verbum) obnoxius fuit, ac execrabilis omnibus factus qui deum diligunt." *Epistolæ ad Galatas cap. primo.*

The reason assigned is that the precept is moral and of eternal obligation, and only dispensable by God, who made it so, or by one inspired by Him with a divine commission and secret inspiration.

This part of the treatise, from which some extracts are given in the following

PRETENDED DIVORCE OF HENRY VIII. AND KATHERINE.

notes, ends on signat. D IV, and is followed by Pace's letter to the King translated into Latin. After which comes the *Oratio Oxonii habita in Collegio Regio*. Then the *Exemplum Literarum Universitatis Oxoniensis quarum in oratione meminit Autor*, dated 14 Kal. Oct. After which follows the *Syntagma de Hebræorum codicum incorruptione* beginning on signat. E III and ending on L. II.

The other treatise, which Harpsfield had not seen, is the more celebrated *Kotser Codicis*, which is correctly described in Wood's *Athenæ Oxonienses* as the same book as that described by Bale and Pits under the title *De non ducenda Fratria*. In the reference to Bale in the note in Bliss's edition, Cent. 9 has been wrongly reprinted for Cent. 8.

There are copies of this book in the Grenville Library and in the Bodleian. Its title is " Kotser Codicis R. Wakfeldi, quo prætor ecclesiæ sacrosanctæ decretum, probatur conjugium cum fratria carnaliter cognita, illicitum omnino, inhibitum interdictumque esse tum naturæ jure, tum jure divino, legeque evangelica atque consuetudine catholica ecclesiæ orthodoxæ."

It is not paged or foliated. The sheets are in fours, A to P, making 120 pages in small 4to.

The treatise ends on O 4, after which follow a letter to Thomas Boleyn, Earl of Wiltshire, another to John Fisher, Bishop of Rochester, and " The copie of a lettre wrytten unto the Kinges highnesse by mayster R. Payce deane of Poules, the yere of our lorde M.CCCCC.XXVII." and " The copie of a letter wrytten unto the kinges hyhnes by mayster R. Wakfelde, chapeleyne unto his grace, the yere of our lorde M.CCCCC.XXVII.;" these last two letters being in black letter, the rest of the book in Roman character. Pace's letter, signed R. Paice, is dated " from Syon this present fryday," Wakefield's " from Syon this present morning." Otherwise there is no date, the colophon being—

𝕮𝖍𝖔. 𝕭𝖊𝖗𝖙𝖍𝖊𝖑𝖊𝖙 𝖗𝖊𝖌𝖎𝖚𝖘 𝖎𝖒𝖕𝖗𝖊𝖘𝖘𝖔𝖗 𝖊𝖗𝖈𝖚𝖉𝖊𝖇𝖆𝖙.

CUM PRIVILEGIO.

Wakefield requests the King to keep the whole matter secret, saying, " for if the people should know that I, which began to defend the Queen's cause not knowing that she was carnally known of prince Arthur your brother, should now write against it, surely I should be stoned of them to death or else have such a slander and obloquy raised upon me that I had rather to die a thousand times or suffer it."

In the letter to Fisher he says, that Fox, " *Belo comitatus*," came to him seven years ago at Sion to establish that—1. The Levitical prohibitions were not about incestuous intercourse so much as unlawful marriages, 2. That they were moral. 3. That they referred not so much to living as to dead relatives. The King had been informed that this had been done by Stokesley, Bishop of London, but Wakefield asserts and Stokesley confirms that they are wholly his own. Pace had formerly written a book for the Queen's side, in which Wakefield had helped him, at a time when he believed that the Queen had not been carnally known by Prince Arthur, which was asserted by the King and unimpeachable witnesses.

The Bodleian copy is bound up with a copy of the "Italiæ et Galliæ Academiarum censuræ."

The end of the treatise just preceding the letter to the Earl of Wiltshire is as follows :—

"Fragmentum codicis R. Wakfeldi sacrarum literarum professoris eximii, regiique sacellani super quæstione de non ducenda fratria prius a fratre præmortuo cognita. HIC FINIT."

This book is attributed by bibliographers to the year 1528, but that date is impossible, because Wakefield could not have spoken of Fox's consulting him seven years earlier on the subject of the divorce. The date is settled to be later than the 8th of December, 1529, because of the letter addressed to Thomas Boleyn, Earl of Wiltshire, who was not created earl till that day.

P. 27, last line but one. The title, which is incorrectly given here in an abridged form, is as follows:—

Gravissimæ atque exactissimæ illustrissimarum totius Italiæ ac Galliæ Academiarum Censuræ efficacissimis etiam quorundam doctissimorum virorum argumentationibus explicatæ de Veritate illius Propositionis, Videlicet, quod ducere Relictam Fratris mortui sine Liberis ita sit de Jure divino et naturali prohibitum, ut nullus Pontifex super hujusmodi Matrimoniis contractis sive contrahendis dispensare possit.

The two preliminary sheets, which are numbered *a* 1 to *a* 4, and *b* 1 to *b* 4, contain the sentences of the Universities, and were certainly printed after the rest of the book, which consists of seven chapters, numbered from A 1 to Q 4, on the second page of which the book ends with this colophon :

Impress. Londini in officina Thomæ Bertheleti
Regii Impress. Mense Aprili An.
Dñi M.D.XXX.

The only one of the Determinations given at an earlier date is that of the University of Orleans, which was given on the 5th of April, 1529, *ante Pascha*. This means April 5, 1530, the year being reckoned to commence from Easter. This is plain from the fact that in 1529 April 5 was the Monday after Low Sunday, whereas in 1530 it was Tuesday after the 5th Sunday in Lent. The latest opinion given is that of the University of Toulouse, which is dated 5 Kal. Oct. 1530. The Latin copy consists of 80 leaves, neither paged nor foliated. The English book is foliated to fol. 154. It is entitled—

"The determinations of the moste famous and moste excellent universities of Italy and Fraunce that it is so unlefull for a man to marie his brother's wyfe that the Pope hath no power to dispence therewith." The colophon is—

Imprinted at London, in the house of Thomas Berthelet, printer to the Kinges moste noble grace, the 7 daye of Novembre. CUM PRIVILEGIO.

P. 46, l. 9. Emanuel, King of Portugal, married in 1497 Isabella, the widow of Alphonso of Portugal, the younger sister of Juana, the Queen of Castile and daughter of Ferdinand and Isabella. She died in 1498, and in 1500 he married Maria the third daughter of Ferdinand and Isabella, who died in 1517. In the following year Emanuel married her niece Eleonora, the daughter of Philip and Juana, who was left a widow in 1521, and in 1530 was married to Francis I. King of France. See below, p. 136.

P. 49, l. 12. The whole passage is as follows:—
Turpitudinem uxoris fratris tui non revelabis; turpitudo fratris tui est.
Quaeritur utrum hoc vivo fratre, an mortuo sit prohibitum, et non parva quaestio est. Si enim dixerimus de vivi fratris uxore locutam Scripturam, uno generali praecepto, quo prohibetur homo ad uxorem accedere alienam, etiam hoc utique continetur. Quid est ergo quod tam diligenter has personas quas appellat domesticas, propriis prohibitionibus distinguit a ceteris? Non enim et quod prohibet de uxore patris, hoc est de noverca, vivo patre accipiendum est, et non potius mortuo. Nam vivo patre quis non videat multo maxime prohibitum, si cujuslibet hominis uxor aliena prohibita est maculari adulterio? De his ergo personis videtur loqui, quae possent non habentes viros in matrimonium convenire, nisi lege prohiberentur, sicut fertur esse consuetudo Persarum. Sed rursus, si fratre mortuo intellexerimus prohibitum esse ducere fratris uxorem, occurrit illud, (quod excitandi seminis causa, si ille sine filiis defunctus esset, jubet Scriptura esse faciendum, ac per hoc collata ista prohibitione cum illa jussione, ne invicem adversentur, intelligenda est exceptio, id est, non licere cuiquam defuncti fratris ducere uxorem, si defunctus posteros dereliquit; aut etiam illud esse prohibitum ne liceret ducere fratris uxorem, etiam quae a fratre vivo per repudium recessisset. Tunc enim, sicut Dominus dicit, ad duritiam Judaeorum Moyses permiserat dare libellum repudii, et per hanc dimissionem potuit putari quod licite quisquam sibi uxorem copularet fratris, ubi adulterium non timeret, quoniam repudio discessisset. S. Aug. Quaest. in Levit. iii. 61.

P. 58, last line. *Filia spiritualis carnali filio nullo modo nubere potest.*
Pitacium nobis tua veneranda fraternitas obtulit, per quod sciscitari curasti, si liceat filio cujus pater alterius filiam ex sacro baptismate susceperit, susceptam, id est spiritualem ejus filiam (quod dici crudele est) in matrimonio accipere; quod apud te enormiter asseruisti contigisse. Sed bene tua sancta fraternitas compertum habet, quod dominus praeceperit per Moysem, dicens, Turpitudinem patris tui vel matris vel sororis non revelabis; turpitudo enim tua est. Cum ergo a propria consanguinitate jubemur abstinere, multo magis a spirituali nostri patris filia, omni excusatione aut argumento seposito, sub nimia districtione nos cavere convenit; ne in iram divini examinis incidat, si quis tali facinore mistus minime restrinxerit fraena luxuriae. Unde et omnes omnino cavendi sunt a tali sceleris commistione ne in perpetuum pereant; sed hunc qui hujus perniciosae temeritatis auctor, animae suae salutem despiciens, impiissimo se miscuit matrimonio per omnia tua fraternitas studeat separare et poenitentiae dignae submittere; quatenus ab aeterna erutam damnatione animam ejus lucreris. Decreti 2 Par. Causa xxx. q. 5. c. 2.

P. 59, 1. 13. The case alluded to is an accusation by the King of Hungary to Innocent III. against a bishop of incest with his niece, of which the Pope writes, Cum etiam secundum sententias ethnicorum naturale fœdus inter tales personas nihil permittat sævi criminis suspicari. On investigation the Pope speaks of the investigators as follows: Qui nobis postmodum rescripserunt quod cum virum honestæ conversationis esse credebant personam illius multipliciter commendantes.

P. 59, last line but three. *Infideles conjuncti in gradu prohibito a lege canonica, post baptismum non separantur,* cap. 4.

De infidelibus ad fidem conversis, utrum si ante conversionem suam secundum legis veteris instituta, circa gradus consanguinitatis a canone denotatos conjuncti fuerint, separari debeant post baptismum. Consul. t. duximus respondendum quod matrimonium sic contractum non est post baptismi lavacrum separandum, cum a Judæis Dominus requisitus, si liceret uxorem ex quacunque causa dimittere ipsis respondit, *Quos Deus conjunxit homo non separet;* per hoc innuens esse matrimonium inter eos.—Decret. Greg. lib. iv. tit. xiv. De Consang.

P. 63, l. 18. Καὶ ἐξ εὐθείας μὲν οὐδὲν οὗτοι περὶ ἀναστάσεως λέγουσι· λόγον δέ τινα πλάττουσι, καὶ πρᾶγμα συντιθέασιν, ὡς ἔγωγε οἶμαι, οὐδὲ γεγενημένον, οἰόμενοι εἰς ἀπορίαν αὐτὸν ἐμβαλεῖν, καὶ θέλοντες ἀνατρέψαι ἀμφότερα, καὶ τὸ ἀνάστασιν εἶναι, καὶ τὸ τοιαύτην ἀνάστασιν. Hom. xx. in S. Matth.

P. 67, last line but 6. Cum ergo tale aliquid legitur in instrumento veteris Testamenti, quale a nobis observari vel jussum non est in novo Testamento, vel etiam prohibitum, quid significet quærendum est, non reprehendendum; quia eo ipso, quo jam non observatur, non damnatum sed impletum probatur; unde multa et sæpe jam diximus.

Velut hoc ipsum quod modo non intelligens Faustus mandatis veteris Testamenti pro crimine objecit, quod uxorem fratris ad hoc frater jussus est ducere, ut non sibi sed illi sobolem suscitaret, ejusque vocaret nomine, quod inde nasceretur, quid aliud in figura præmonstrat, nisi quia unusquisque Evangelii prædicator ita debet in Ecclesia laborare, ut defuncto fratri, hoc est Christo suscitet semen, qui pro nobis mortuus est, et quod suscitatum fuerit ejus nomen accipiat? S. Aug. Contra Faustum, lib. xxxii. cap. 9, 10.

P. 69, l. 8. The original is as follows:—

Cetera certe quæ ad pietatem bonosque mores pertinentia, non ad aliquam significationem ulla interpretatione referenda, sed prorsus ut sunt dicta, facienda sunt; profecto illam Dei legem, non solum illi tunc populo, verum etiam nunc nobis ad instituendam recte vitam necessariam nemo dubitaverit.

P. 69, line 8 from bottom. The passages in the chapter referred to which bear upon the point are as follows:—

Cum igitur genus humanum post primam copulam viri facti ex pulvere, et conjugis ejus ex viri latere, marium feminarumque conjunctione opus haberet, ut gignendo multiplicaretur; nec essent ulli homines nisi qui ex illis duobus, nati fuissent, viri sorores suas conjuges acceperunt; quod profecto quanto est antiquius compellente necessitate, tanto postea factum est damnabilius religione prohibente.

He continues, that, when the necessity for such marriages ceased, the law of charity prevailed, which discountenanced and disapproved such marriages, so extending the affection of men and women over a larger sphere of relatives. And for the same reason he disapproves of the marriage of cousins, saying :—

Experti autem sumus in connubiis consobrinorum etiam nostris temporibus propter gradum propinquitatis fraterno gradui proximum, quam raro per mores fiebat, quod fieri per leges licebat; quia id nec divina prohibuit et nondum prohibuerat lex humana. Veruntamen factum etiam licitum propter vicinitatem horrebatur illicite; et quod fiebat cum consobrina pene cum sorore fieri videbatur; quia et ipsi inter se propter tam propinquam consanguinitatem fratres vocantur, et pene germani sunt....
Verum quis dubitet honestius hoc tempore etiam consobrinorum prohibita esse conjugia? Non solum secundum ea quæ disputavimus, propter multiplicandas affinitates, ne habeat duas necessitudines una persona cum duæ possint eas habere, et numerus propinquitatis augeri; sed etiam quia nescio quomodo inest humanæ verecundiæ quiddam naturale atque laudabile ut cui debet causa propinquitatis reverendum honorem, ab ea contineat quamvis generatricem tamen libidinem, de qua erubescere videmus et ipsam pudicitiam conjugalem. S. Aug. de Civitate Dei, lib. xv. cap. 16.

P. 76, l. 10 from bottom. The two passages in the Canon Law are as follows:
Infamia notentur qui consanguineas ducunt uxores. c. ii.

Conjunctiones consanguineorum fieri prohibete; quando has et divinæ et sæculi prohibent leges. Leges ergo divinæ hoc agentes et eos qui ex his prodeunt, non solum ejiciunt sed et maledictos appellant. Leges vero sæculi infames tales vocant et ab hæreditate repellunt. Nos vero sequentes patres nostros et eorum vestigiis inhærentes infamia eos notamus, et infames esse censemus, quia infamiæ maculis sunt aspersi; nec eos viros, nec accusationes eorum quos leges sæculi rejiciunt, suscipere debemus. Et infra—Eos autem consanguineos dicimus, quos divinæ, et Imperatorum, ac Romanorum, ante Græcorum leges consanguineos appellant, et in hæreditate suscipiunt, nec repellere possunt.

Affines in quinta generatione copulari possunt; in quarta si fuerint inventi, non separentur. c. iii.

De propinquis, qui ad affinitatem per virum et uxorem veniunt, defuncta uxore vel viro, in quinta generatione conjungantur; in quarta si inventi fuerint, non separentur. In tertia vero propinquitate non licet uxorem alterius accipere post obitum ejus. Æqualiter vir conjungatur in matrimonio eis, quæ sibi consanguineæ sunt, et uxoris suæ consanguineis post mortem suæ uxoris.

P. 80, last line but two.
The heading of this chapter, which is too long to be inserted here, runs as follows:—
In terris ecclesiæ Papa potest libere illegitimos legitimare, in terris vero alienis

NOTES.

non nisi ex causis multum arduis, vel nisi in spiritualibus; tunc tamen indirecte et per quandam consequentiam intelligitur legitimare etiam quoad temporalia: hoc tamen ultimum non est sine scrupulo. h. d. secundum intellectum qui placet Panor. et est cap. difficile et multum famosum.

P. 83, last line.
The passage referred to is at the beginning of the prologue of S. Thomas Aquinas to his treatise, entitled
In duo præcepta caritatis et in decem legis præcepta Expositio. It commences as follows:—
Tria sunt homini necessaria ad salutem, scilicet scientia credendorum, scientia desiderandorum, et scientia operandorum. Primum docetur in symbolo, ubi traditur scientia de articulis fidei; secundum in oratione dominica; tertium autem in lege. Nunc autem de scientia operandorum intendimus: ad quam tractandam quadruplex lex invenitur. Prima dicitur lex naturæ; et hæc nihil aliud est nisi lumen intellectus insitum nobis a Deo, per quod cognoscimus quid agendum et quid vitandum. Hoc lumen, et hanc legem dedit Deus homini in creatione.
The other reference is probably a mistake of dist. 37 for dist. 17, q. 3, art. 1. Perhaps the passage alluded to is the following:—
Et quandoque etiam naturale dicitur secundum quod cuilibet rei illud est naturale quod ei a suo Creatore imponitur, tamen proprie naturalia dicuntur, quæ ex principiis naturæ causantur.

P. 96, last line but two.
¶ *Ex propinquitate sui sanguinis usque ad septimum gradum nullus ducat uxorem.* C. xix.
Nulli ex propinquitate sui sanguinis, usque ad septimum gradum uxores ducant; neque sine benedictione sacerdotis. Qui autem nupturi erunt a sacerdote benedicti nubere audeant, nec aliter præsumant.
¶ *Anglis permittitur, ut in quarta vel in quinta generatione copulentur.* C. xx.
Quædam lex terrena in Romana republica permittit ut sive fratris et sororis, seu duorum fratrum germanorum seu duarum sororum filius et filia misceantur. Sed experimento didicimus ex tali conjugio sobolem non posse succrescere; et sacra lex prohibet cognationis turpitudinem revelare. Unde necesse est ut in quarta vel quinta generatione fidelium licenter sibi conjungantur. Sed idem humillimus pater Gregorius post multum temporis a Felice Messanæ Siciliæ civitatis præsule requisitus, utrum Augustino scripserit ut Anglorum in quarta generatione contracta matrimonia minime solverentur, inter cætera talem responsionem reddidit. Quod scripsi Augustino Anglorum gentis episcopo, alumno videlicet ut recordaris tuo, de sanguinis conjunctione ipsi, et Anglorum genti, quæ nuper ad fidem, venerat ne a bono quod cœperat metuendo austeriora recederet, specialiter et generaliter cæteris me

certissime scripsisse cognoscas. Unde et mihi omnis Romana civitas testis existit. Nec ea intentione hæc illis scripta mandavi ut postquam firma radice in fide fuerint solidati, si infra propriam consanguinitatem inventi fuerint, non separentur aut infra affinitatis lineam, id est, usque ad septimam generationem jungantur. Sed adhuc illos neophytos existentes, sæpissime eos prius illicita docere [vitare], et verbis ac exemplis instruere, et quæ post de talibus egerint, rationabiliter et fideliter excludere oportet. Nam juxta Apostolum qui ait—Lac dedi vobis potum non escam—ista illis modo, non posteris, ut præfixum est temporibus tenenda indulsimus, ne bonum quod infirma adhuc radice plantatum erat, crueretur, sed aliquantulum firmaretur et usque ad perfectionem custodiretur.

¶ *Nurus non est aliter deputanda quam filia.* C. xv.

Si vir et uxor non jam duo, sed una caro sunt, non aliter est nurus deputanda quam filia.

¶ *In parentela propria conjugis eadem consanguinitate est observanda.* C. xiiii.

Sane consanguinitas quæ in proprio viro observanda est, hæc nimirum in uxoris parentela de lege nuptiarum custodienda est. Quia enim constat eos duos esse in carne una, communis illis utraque parentela censenda est sicut scriptum est—Erunt duo in carne una.

¶ *Quare consanguinitas uxoris ad virum pertinere dicitur, et quomodo affinitas sit computanda.* C. iii.

¶ Porro de affinitate quam dicitis parentelam esse, quæ ad virum ex parte uxoris, seu quæ ex parte viri ad uxorem pertinet, manifestissima ratio est: quia si secundum divinam sententiam, ego et uxor mea sumus una caro, profecto mihi et illi mea, suaque parentela propinquitas una efficitur. Quocirca ego et soror uxoris meæ in uno et primo gradu erimus; filius vero ejus in secundo gradu erit a me, neptis vero tertio, idque utrinque in cæteris agendum est successionibus. Uxorem vero propinqui mei cujuscunque gradus sit, ita me oportet attendere, quemadmodum ipsius quoque gradus aliqua fœmina propriæ propinquitatis sit. Quod nimirum uxori de propinquitate viri sui in cunctis cognationis gradibus convenit observari. Qui vero aliorsum sentiunt, Antichristi sunt; a quibus tanto fortius vos oportet cavere quanto apertius deprehenditis illos divinis legibus repugnare.

¶ *In quarto et quinto gradu qui conjuncti inventi fuerint separentur.* C. ii.

Hæc salubriter præcavenda sancimus, nequis fidelium propinquam sanguinis sui usque quo affinitatis lineamenta generis successione cognoscuntur, matrimonio sibi desideret copulare, sed sicut a majoribus nostris definitum est, ita modis omnibus observetur; quoniam usque ad septenarium numerum parentelæ nulli unquam copulam contrahere licentiam damus, his videlicet qui ex patre et matre consanguinitatis parentela descendunt. Qui autem et quæ in quarto vel in quinto gradu conjuncti inventi fuerint separentur; quoniam scriptum est—Omnis homo ad proximam sanguinis sui non accedet ut revelet turpitudinem ejus—et iterum—Anima quæ fecerit quippiam ex istis peribit de medio populi sui. Sane quibus conjunctio interdicitur illicita, habebunt incundi conjugii melioris libertatem.

P. 103, l. 12. The whole passage is as follows:—
Et quia Dominus naturalia Legis, per quæ homo justificatur, quæ etiam ante legisdationem custodiebant, qui fide justificabantur et placebant Deo non dissolvit, sed extendit, sed et implevit, ex sermonibus ejus ostenditur. *Dictum est enim,* inquit *antiquis, Non mœchaberis. Ego autem dico vobis, quoniam omnes qui vident mulierem ad concupiscendum eam jam mœchatus est eam in corde suo. Et iterum: Dictum est, Non occides. Ego autem dico vobis, omnis qui irascitur fratri suo, sine causa reus erit judicio. Et, Dictum, Non perjurabis. Ego autem dico vobis non jurare in totum. Sit autem vobis sermo etiam etiam, et non non.* Et quæcunque sunt talia. Omnia enim hæc non contrarietatem et dissolutionem præteritorum continent, sicut qui a Marcione sunt, vociferantur, sed plenitudinem et extensionem, &c.

P. 107, last line but two. *Non jubet aliquid injustum, qui Deum timere probatur.* C. xcv.
Qui omnipotentem Deum metuit, nec contra Evangelium, nec contra Apostolos, nec contra prophetas, vel sanctorum Patrum instituta aliquid ullo modo agere consentit.

P. 107, last line but one. *In quibus Romano Pontifici licet novas condere leges.* C. vi.
Sunt quidam dicentes Romano Pontifici semper licuisse novas condere leges. Quod et nos non solum non negamus, sed etiam valde affirmamus. Sciendum vero summopere est, quia inde novas leges condere potest, unde Evangelistæ aliquid et prophetæ nequaquam dixerunt. Ubi vero aperte Dominus vel ejus Apostoli, et eos sequentes, sancti patres sententialiter aliquid definierunt, ibi non novam legem Romanus Pontifex dare, sed potius quod prædicatum est, usque ad animam et sanguinem confirmare debet. Si enim quod docuerunt Apostoli et prophetæ destruere (quod absit) niteretur, non sententiam dare sed magis errare convinceretur. Sed hoc procul sit ab eis, qui semper domini ecclesiam contra luporum insidias optime custodierunt.

P. 107, last line. *Non licet alieni episcopo contra Romanorum Pontificum decreta aliquid agere.* C. xii.
Omnia decretalia et cunctorum decessorum nostrorum constituta, quæ de ecclesiasticis ordinibus et canonum promulgata sunt disciplinis, ita a vobis et ab omnibus episcopis ac cunctis generaliter sacerdotibus custodiri debere mandamus, ut si quis in illa commiserit, veniam sibi deinceps noverit denegari.
This is a letter not of Pope Marcellus but of Damasus to Prosper.

P. 108, l. 7. Præterea, Dominus in uxoribus ducendis quosdam consanguinitatis et affinitatis gradus præcepit esse vitandos ut patet Lev. xviii. Inconvenienter igitur mandatur Deut. xxv. quod si aliquis esset mortuus absque liberis, uxorem ipsius frater ejus acciperet.
Ad septimum dicendum, quod, sicut Chrysostomus dicit super Matth. (Hom. 49,

circa med.) *quia immitigabile malum erat mors apud Judæos, qui omnia pro præsenti vita faciebant, statutum fuit ut defuncto filius nasceretur ex fratre, quod erat quædam mortis mitigatio.* Non autem alius quam frater vel propinquus jubebatur accipere uxorem defuncti, quia non ita crederetur, qui ex tali conjunctione erat nasciturus esse ejus filius qui obiit; et iterum extraneus non ita haberet necessitatem statuere domum ejus qui obierat, sicut frater, cui etiam ex cognatione hoc facere justum erat. Ex quo patet quod frater in accipiendo uxorem fratris sui, persona fratris sui defuncti fungebatur. Quæst. cv. art. 4.

P. 111, l. 18. Videtur quod Papa non possit dispensare in bigamiæ irregularitate..... Respondeo dicendum quod Papa habet plenitudinem potestatis in Ecclesia, ita scilicet quod quæcunque sunt instituta per Ecclesiam vel Ecclesiæ prælatos sunt dispensabilia a Papa..... In solis vero his quæ sunt de lege naturæ, et in articulis fidei, et sacramentis novæ legis dispensare non potest.... Manifestum est autem quod bigamum non promoveri neque est de lege naturæ, neque pertinet ad articulos fidei, neque est de necessitate sacramenti..... Unde circa hoc potest Papa dispensare. Quodlib. iv. art. 13.

P. 113, l. 7. The passages referred to in the Canon Law are as follows:—
Qui clericum percusserit excommunicetur, et non nisi a Romano Pontifice absolvatur. C. xxix.

Si quis suadente diabolo hujus sacrilegii reatum incurrerit quod in clericum vel monachum violentas manus injecerit, anathematis vinculo subjaceat; et nullus episcoporum illum præsumat absolvere (nisi mortis urgente periculo) donec Apostolico conspectui præsentetur, et ejus mandatum suscipiat.

Nemini est permissum de eo quod Papa statuit judicare, vel ejus sententiam retractare. C. xxx.

Nemini est de sedis Apostolicæ judicio judicare; aut illius sententiam retractare permissum; videlicet propter Romanæ ecclesiæ primatum, Christi munere in beato Petro Apostolo divinitus collatum.

P. 115, l. 19. The passage in the Canon Law is as follows:
Qui monachorum propositum appetit etiam invito episcopo suscipiendus est. C. ii.

Duæ sunt, inquit leges, una publica, altera privata. Publica lex est quæ a sanctis patribus scriptis est confirmata ut est lex canonum quæ quidem propter transgressiones est tradita. Verbi gratia: Decretum est in canonibus clericum non debere de suo episcopatu ad alium transire sine commendatitiis litteris sui episcopi; quod propter criminosos constitutum est; ne videlicet infames ab aliquo episcopo suscipiantur personæ. Solebant enim officia sua cum non poterant in suo episcopatu in alieno celebrare; quod jure præceptis et scriptis detestatum est.

Lex vero privata est quæ instinctu sancti Spiritus in corde scribitur; sicut de quibusdam dicit Apostolus, *Qui habent legem Dei scriptam in cordibus suis,* et alibi, *Cum gentes legem non habeant, si naturaliter ea quæ legis sunt faciunt, ipsi sibi sunt lex.* Si quis horum in ecclesia sua sub episcopo populum retinet, et sæculariter vivit, si afflatus Spiritu Sancto, in aliquo monasterio, vel regulari canonia salvare se voluerit, quia lege privata ducitur, nulla ratio exigit ut a lege publica constringatur. Dignior est enim lex privata quam publica. Spiritus quidem Dei lex est, et qui spiritu Dei aguntur, lege Dei ducuntur; et quis est qui Spiritui Sancto possit [digne resistere. Quisquis igitur hoc Spiritu ducitur, etiam episcopo suo contradicente, eat liber nostra auctoritate. Justo enim lex non est posita; sed ubi Spiritus Dei, ibi libertas; et si Spiritu Dei ducimini, non estis sub lege.

Decreti 2 pars, causa xix., quæstio 2.

Page 120, last line but five.

Wood, who spells the name Wakfeld, says that he was the greatest linguist of his time. After taking his degree at Cambridge in 1514, he travelled with the view of learning languages, and obtained a considerable knowledge of Greek, Hebrew, Arabic, Chaldee, and Syriac. After teaching these languages at Tubingen and Paris, he went to Louvaine, where in 1519 he succeeded Matthew Adrian as professor of Hebrew, but remained there only four months, being succeeded in the office in that year by Robert Shirwode, another Englishman. About 1520 he returned to England, and lectured at Cambridge in 1524. He was brought to the King's notice by Richard Pace, dean of St. Paul's. He became chaplain to the king, and was patronized by Sir Thomas Boleyn, the father of Anne Boleyn. He at first took up the Queen's cause, and gained some popularity by so doing. He was offered much by the King to change his side, because of his great skill both in language and divinity, and incurred considerable odium by his adopting the King's cause against the Queen. He was sent by the King to Oxford in 1530, and lectured there in Hebrew. In 1532, he was made canon of Christ Church at Oxford, and he died in London, Oct. 8, 1537. Pits says of him that he was present at the demolition of Ramsey abbey in 1536, and stole from it several books, and, amongst others, Laurence Holbeche's Hebrew Dictionary.

The letter which he wrote to the King on signifying his adhesion to his side in the controversy is as follows:—

Please it your grace—

I as your true and faithful subject will and can defend your cause or question in all the universities of Christendom against all men by good and sufficient authority of the scripture of God, and the words of the best learned and most excellent authors of the interpreters of the Hebrews and the holy doctors both Greek and Latin in Christ's faith; humbly beseeching your grace to keep the thing secret from all persons living, both man and woman, unto such time as I shall shew unto you the time of publication thereof, or else Maister Paice, signifying unto your highness that it shall make much for the furtherance of your cause; and that otherwise I ne will ne can do anything therein; for if the people should know that I which began to defend the queen's cause, not knowing that she was carnally known of

318   PRETENDED DIVORCE OF HENRY VIII. AND KATHERINE.

Prince Arthure your brother, should now write against it, surely I should be stoned of them to death or else have such a slander and obloquy raised upon me that I had rather to die a thousand times or suffer it. I have and will in such manner answer the bishop of Rochester's book that I trust he shall be ashamed to wade or meddle any further in the matter. The thing which I am making will be *ingens volumen*, and I shall take no rest to I have brought it by the grace of God, who always helpeth the truth, to a perfect end. I have shewed somewhat of my book to Maister Paice, and I trust he will confirm the same unto your grace. No more to your highness at this time, but Jesu preserve you.
From Syon this present morning.
By your grace's faithful subject and scholar,
R. WAKFELDE.

This letter was printed in the Kotser Codicis together with a letter from Pace to the King, apparently written on the same day from the same place. Both are analysed in Mr. Brewer's Calendar, and are assigned to the date of July 5, 1527, the date of Pace's letter being simply Friday. Pace's letter in a Latin version appears in Le Grand, vol. iii. p. 1, and is there wrongly ascribed to the year 1526.

Page 120, line 5 from bottom.
The Glasse of Truth.
This dialogue is entitled *A Glasse of the Truthe*. There were two different editions of it, copies of which exist in the Bodleian Library. Both have been collated for the reprint which appears in Pocock's Records of the Reformation, vol. ii. pp. 385-421. Some account of it is given in the Editor's Preface to that work, p. xxi. It was probably published early in September, 1532.

P. 122, l. 15. The whole chapter is as follows:
Non licet relictam fratris in uxorem accipere; et de facto ducta separanda est, nisi aliter ecclesia dispenset.
Deus qui ecclesiam suam; et infra. Quia dispar est ritus in Livoniensi ecclesia de novo ad fidem Catholicam conversorum a nostro; propter infirmitatem gentis ejusdem concedimus ut matrimoniis contractis cum relictis fratrum utantur, si tamen (fratribus decedentibus sine prole, ut semen defuncti juxta legem Mosaicam suscitarent) cum talibus contraxerunt; ne tales sibi de cætero postquam ad fidem venerint copulent prohibentes. Decret. Greg. lib. iv. tit. xix. c. 9.

P. 122, l. 25. Decret. Greg. lib. ii. tit. xiii. cap. 13. De rest. spol.

P. 122, last line but three.
See the note at p. 107, last line but one.

P. 141, l. 5. S. Gregory's words are—
Quia vero sunt multi in Anglorum gente qui dum adhuc in infidelitate essent, huic nefando conjugio dicuntur admixti, ad fidem venientes admonendi sunt ut

se abstineant et grave hoc esse peccatum cognoscant. Tremendum Dei judicium timeant, ne pro carnali dilectione tormenta æterni cruciatus incurrant. Non tamen pro hac re, sacri corporis ac sanguinis Domini communione privandi sunt, ne in eis, illa ulcisci videantur, in quibus se per ignorantiam ante lavacrum baptismatis adstrinxerunt. In hoc enim tempore sancta Ecclesia quædam per fervorem corrigit, quædam per mansuetudinem tolerat, quædam per considerationem dissimulat, atque ita portat et dissimulat ut sæpe malum quod adversatur portando et dissimulando compescat. Omnes autem qui ad fidem veniunt, admonendi sunt ne tale aliquid audeant perpetrare. Si qui autem perpetraverint, corporis et sanguinis Domini communione privandi sunt; quia sicut in his qui per ignorantiam fecerunt, culpa aliquatenus toleranda est, ita in his fortiter insequenda qui non metuunt sciendo peccare. Bedæ Hist. Eccles. lib. i. cap. 27.

P. 148, l. 7. This word *hoverly* occurs again at p. 170. It is used in a letter of Paget's to the King printed in State Papers, ix. 60. It means *crasively*.

P. 149, l. 9. See the previous notes at p. 307 and p. 317 for an account of the writer and his works.

P. 149, l. 16. See A I.

P. 149, last line but three. See A II.

P. 149, last line but one.

Uxorem fratris nullus accipiat. Verum huic in codice tuo sic ipse respondes. Episcopus Roffensis. Hoc non habetur in hebraica veritate neque in traditione chaldaica neque iu lxx. interpretibus græce. Sed (quod non raro fit) ex imperitia scriptoris id quod a quopiam in margine pro notula descriptum, intersertum fuit textui. Et quum hoc ipsum nec in lxx. nec in hebræo nec in chaldæo repertum sit, palam est pro sacra scriptura minime recipi debere. A III.

The author replies to this saying that he had eighteen years ago taught Hebrew to both Fisher and Thomas Hurskey, the præfect of the whole Gilbertine Order, and after Fisher the light and glory of the country, and adding that they are virtually in the original, and that if this were not so, and the meaning of Leviticus were not that the wife had only been espoused to the first brother, one law would be opposed to another, idemque quemadmodum in Kotser meo scripsi pro uno ac eodem tempore et populo præceptum esset et prohibitum, licitum ac illicitum,

P. 150, l. 1. See A III.

P. 150, l. 5. See B III.

P. 150, l. 9. See C IV.

P. 150, l. 14. See D I.

P. 150, l. 16. See D II.

P. 151, l. 9.
The decree was made in the fourth Session of the Council, April 8, 1546. After naming the books included in the canon of Scripture, it continues:—

Si quis autem libros ipsos integros cum omnibus suis partibus, prout in ecclesia catholica legi consueverunt, et in veteri vulgata Latina editione habentur, pro sacris et canonicis non susceperit, et traditiones prædictas sciens et prudens contempserit, anathema sit. Omnes itaque intelligant, quo ordine et via ipsa synodus post jactum fidei confessionis fundamentum sit progressura, et quibus potissimum testimoniis ac præsidiis in confirmandis dogmatibus et instaurandis in ecclesia moribus sit usura.

Then follows the *Decretum de editione et usu sacrorum librorum.* Insuper eadem sacrosancta synodus considerans, non parum utilitatis accedere posse ecclesiæ Dei, si ex omnibus Latinis editionibus, quæ circumferuntur, sacrorum librorum, quænam pro authentica habenda sit, innotescat, statuit et declarat, ut hæc ipsa vetus et vulgata editio, quæ longo tot sæculorum usu in ipsa ecclesia probata est, in publicis lectionibus, disputationibus, prædicationibus et expositionibus pro authentica habeatur, et ut nemo illam rejicere quovis prætextu audeat vel præsumat.

Præterea ad coercenda petulantia ingenia decernit ut nemo suæ prudentiæ innixus, in rebus fidei et morum ad ædificationem doctrinæ Christianæ pertinentium, sacram scripturam ad suos sensus contorquens, contra eum sensum quem tenuit et tenet sancta mater ecclesia, cujus est judicare de vero sensu et interpretatione scripturarum sanctarum, aut etiam contra unanimem consensum Patrum ipsam scripturam sacram interpretari audeat, etiamsi hujusmodi interpretationes nullo unquam tempore in lucem edendæ forent.

P. 153, l. 12. See B I.

P. 154, l. 18. See B I.

P. 155, last line:
The reference is to *La Mer des Histoires.* The passage occurs at tom. ii. fol. 108 verso of the Paris edition circa 1507. The text is—

Item en ung lieu ou le fleuve de moselle entre dedans le rin une fille aagee de neuf ans fut enceinte et engrossie par le cuisinier de son pere dont enfant a ung beau filz, laquelle chose consideree la nge estoit a nature fort monstrueuse.

P. 160, last line but three.
See Records of the Reformation, vol. ii. p. 386, where the argument is made to rest on the difficulty of finding a husband for the female heir who would be acquiesced in by the people.

P. 170, l. 17. See the note at p. 148, l. 7.

P. 170, l. 20. See Records of the Reformation, pp. 402—410.

P. 170, l. 22. See *ibid.* pp. 413—417.

P. 170, last line but three. These words—
I think there cannot be a better exhortation than you have here given us all, are attributed in the dialogue to the Divine, p. 399.

The answer given by the Divine, *Wherefore now using the saying of Saint Poule, I do exhort you in our Lord God that you his subjects do exonerate yourselves of all manner of grounds or occasions that might bind any unkindness in his heart toward you*, appears at p. 401.

P. 171, last line but one. See *ibid.* p. 392.

P. 172, l. 9. See *ibid.* p. 393.

P. 172, l. 16. See *ibid.* p. 394.

P. 174, l. 4. See *ibid.* p. 394.

P. 175, line 14.
The whole passage referred to is in the 10th chapter as the book is now divided §. LXIX, LXX, and is as follows:—

Unde quod Ruth, licet ipsa alienigena, tamen quia maritum habuerat ex Judæis, qui reliquerat superstitem proximum, eamque colligentem manipulos suæ messis, quibus alebat et se et socrum, Booz vidit et amavit; non aliter eam accipit uxorem, nisi calceamentum ejus ante solvisset, cui uxor debebatur ex lege.

Historia simplex, sed alta mysteria; aliud enim gerebatur, aliud figurabatur. Nam si secundum litteram sensum torqueamus; prope quidam pudor et horror in verbo est, si ad commixtionis corporeæ consuetudinem sententiam intellectumque referamus. Designabatur autem futurus ex Judæis, ex quibus Christus secundum carnem, qui proximi sui, hoc est populi mortui semen doctrinæ cælestis semine suscitaret, cui calceamentum nuptiale Ecclesiæ copulandæ præscripta Legis spiritalia deferebant.—S. Ambros. de fide, tom. 6, p. 118, ed. Caillau, Par. 1842.

P. 175, last line but four.
Sanders gives nearly the same account, but he more definitely states that Wolsey called Longland the King's confessor, and persuaded him that he had real doubts as to the validity of the King's marriage; that Longland, believing him to be in earnest, advised that Wolsey himself should lay the matter before the King, This, he says, Wolsey did, and was bidden by the King to take care how he opened a controversy on a thing already judged. Three days afterwards the Cardinal and Longland are represented as petitioning the King to have the matter investigated, and, upon the King consenting, Wolsey suggested Margaret Duchess of Alençon as a suitable

person, upon which Henry replied that that could be treated of at a future time, but that for the present secrecy was above all things to be observed. Sanders attributes to Wolsey the motive of disappointment at his failure of obtaining the Papal see when Adrian VI. and Clement VII. were elected, and the desire to revenge himself upon the Emperor. Polydore Vergil, Wolsey's greatest enemy, tells substantially the same story. He speaks of the interval of three days between the two interviews, and puts the same words into the King's mouth about the virginity of Katherine at the time of her second marriage, and the same reply to the suggestion about the Duchess of Alençon. A third contemporary and independent account is given by Tyndale in his "Practise of Prelates," published in 1530 as follows:—

"He inspired the King that the Queen was not his wife, by the bishop of Lincoln his confessor as the saying was; by whom he hath breathed many things into his grace, and by whom he hath heard his confession, and by whom and like hypocrites he hath long betrayed him to have married him unto the King's sister of France as the fame went, by that means at the last to make us French. And then the cardinal's doctors laid their heads together to seek subtle arguments and riddles to prove his divorcement." Tyndale's Practice of Prelates, p. 320.

P. 177, l. 20.

Harpsfield has omitted the earlier steps taken in the matter of the divorce; which began with the judicial proceedings before Wolsey at his house at Westminster, May 17, 1527. Considerable secrecy was at first observed, as may be seen by Sampson's Letter to Wolsey (Brewer's Calendar, 3302); but Don Inigo de Mendoza had informed the Emperor early in July of the King's intention (*ibid.* 3312), and intelligence had also reached him from the Queen. Later in the year the Pope had been applied to by Wolsey to issue a commission to Wolsey to decide the cause, and a dispensation to Henry to marry any woman, even though related to him within the first degree of affinity by illicit intercourse. It was not till the next year, 1528, that application was made for a legate to be sent to act with Wolsey. The appointment was delayed for some months, and Campeggio did not arrive in England till October 1528. The object of having Campeggio associated with Wolsey was to avoid any objection which might be taken by the Queen to Wolsey as the King's subject. The attempt to get the judgment of the universities belongs to the following year, October 1529. The mission of Foxe Bishop of Hereford into Germany was altogether later, being in the autumn of 1535. He was consecrated Bishop of Hereford in succession to Charles Booth, September 26, 1535, and died May 8, 1538. He had been sent to Rome with Gardiner in 1528, and he was afterwards employed in 1531 in France to obtain the determinations of Paris and Orleans that the King is not bound to appear in a court held out of his dominions, either in person or by proxy. See Records of the Reformation, vol. ii. p. 135, no. ccxlv.; also p. 139, no. ccxlvi.

Stokesley had been sent to France in October 1529 to get the opinions of the divines of Paris in favour of the divorce, and was nominated ambassador to the

NOTES. 323

Emperor. He was at Bologna, where he obtained the Decree of the theligians of that university for the divorce in June 1530, and returned through France in the autumn of that year.

P. 179, l. 6.
Campeggio crossed from Calais Sept. 29, 1528; but this was not the twenty-first year, but the twentieth, of the reign of Henry VIII. He was at Canterbury Oct. 1, but did not arrive in London till Oct. 8. The meeting of the King at Bridewell was on Thursday, Oct. 22.

P. 179, l. 12 from bottom.
The assembly at Bridewell was held on the 8th of November.

P. 180, l. 11.
This interview with the Queen took place October 27, a few days before the assembly at Bridewell.

P. 180, last line but 5.
This took place on the 31st of May. Hall speaks of May 28th as the day on which proclamation was made for the Court to be held. Herbert says that the Chronicles with one consent say that on the 31st the King was called and appeared personally, and that the Queen prostrated herself at his feet, demanding justice, &c. In this he is confusing a subsequent appearance. Harpsfield is right in saying that the King appeared by his two proctors, and that the Queen appeared personally with the four Bishops, refusing the jurisdiction of the Court. On the 1st of June the citation to the King and Queen to appear on the 18th was delivered by Longland and Clerk at Windsor. (See Brewer's Calendar 5613 and 5636.) On the 15th of June the Queen paid a visit to Campeggio, who was in bed owing to his gout (Brewer, 5681), but left him in doubt as to the course she would pursue. The next day she drew up her appeal to the Pope and protestation against the jurisdiction of the Legates. (Records of the Reformation, ii. 609.)

P. 181, l. 1.
Here the author confuses the first day of the trial, June 18, with the second, June 21. On the 18th for the King Richard Sampson Dean of the Chapel Royal appeared with letters of proxy for himself and Dr. John Bell. The Queen was present in person, protesting against the jurisdiction of the Court. See Brewer's Calendar, Nos. 5,694 and 5,702. The directions for the process of the 21st are still in existence, and are printed in the Records of the Reformation, vol. i. p. 206, no. lxxvii. They provide for the event of both parties appearing and one not appearing, and for the case of the Queen appearing only to protest. On Monday, June 21, both were present, and this is the date of the scene described by the author.

324 PRETENDED DIVORCE OF HENRY VIII. AND KATHERINE.

P. 181, l. 9. The words from this point to *further discern* are almost word for word taken from the King's letter printed in Burnet, I. ii. Number xxviii.

The words from *thrice preconisate* to *objected unto her* are almost verbatim from the same letter.

P. 181, l. 14. This is correctly described, as it is also by Cavendish and Sanders.

P. 182, l. 5.
This letter is analysed in Brewer's Calendar, 5707, and printed at length in Burnet, vol. i. part 2, no xxviii.

The passage from *special care* to *into the same*, p. 183, is extracted almost word for word.

P. 184, l. 4. The King was at Grafton from the 10th to the 24th of September, 1529. (Brewer, **5965**.)

In a letter from Thomas Alward to Cromwell written from St. Alban's, September 23rd, he says that on Sunday last (*i.e.*, September 19th) he (*i.e.*, Wolsey) and Campeggio were received at Greenwich by the King with his usual favour, "and the King talked a great while with my lord, and, immediately after dinner, he went into the King's privy chamber for the space at least of two hours. Afterwards my lord and the legate returned to their lodgings at Empson's place. Monday morning he went again to the King and with him sat at the Council all the forenoon, and in the afternoon they both took their leave, the King going a hunting. My lord sat with the Council till it was dark night. Suffolk, Rochford, Tuke, and Stevyns shewed as much observance to him as before. What they bear in their hearts I know not. If you could mark the chief movers of these reports you would do his Grace a pleasure. My lord, who will be at London on Monday next, will be glad of your return. Campeggio leaves shortly." (Brewer, **5953**.) Campeggio left London October 5. (Brewer, 5955.)

P. 185, l. 10 from bottom. See Brewer' Calendar, 4977.

P. 186, l. 18. See Brewer's Calendar, 5050, 5179.

P. 187, l. 1. The passage is in cypher, and runs as follows in the decypher given by Mr. Brewer, p. 2278:—

And as ye know and was declared to you in counsel, one of the things noted to be much to the avancement of the King's cause was, that the Pope's Holiness, taking this presidy, should thereby be brought to have as much fear and respect towards the King's highness as he now hath towards the Emperor, and consequently be the gladder to grant and condescend unto the King's desire, though ye were ordered to shew the French King it was devised chiefly for his sake, and to tee . . . the Pope that it was invented principally for his surety, and yet it forseth not though they both think [that it were] don partly for the benefit of the King's cause.

P. 187, l. 8 from bottom.

The reading in (G) is *the lappe of religion*, which is an attempt to make sense of a phrase which the transcriber did not understand. (E) and (N$_2$) have *enter lape religion*, which is accounted for by the resemblance of the *p* to an *x*, which was written with a long tail to it. (N$_1$) has *enter in lape religion*. It is plain, therefore, that the original had the words *lape religion*, and that it was directly copied from the instructions to Bryan and Vannes, part of which is quoted in State Papers, vii. 136, and which has the words *la pe religion*, where Mr. Brewer suggests the correction *laxe*. That this is the true reading intended is manifest from another set of instructions apparently issued at the same time to Kuight, Bennet, Cassali, and Vannes, where the words are, "to enter lax religion." Harpsfield's extreme accuracy of quotation is here shewn. There is scarcely a word of variation between his copy and that in the State Papers. In fact he supplies some words which are wanting in the copy in the Record Office.

P. 189, l. 14. There is a copy of this address to be made by Vannes to the Pope in Vitellius, B. x. 146. See Brewer's Calendar, 4977, p. 2159. It forms the seventh of the *Capita rerum expediendarum*.

Verba dicenda Pontifici per Petrum Vannem de periculis futuris, casu quo non sit satisfactum Regi et Regno.

In the same Instructions, the 18th is—De Commissione pacis *pro præsidio circa personam sanctissimi Domini nostri et pro defensione personæ suæ*—where the words in Italics are added in Wolsey's hand. See the copy of these Heads of Instructions in Pocock's Records of the Reformation, vol. i. p. 819, no. lxix.

P. 190, l. 6. Harpsfield had evidently seen a letter which has not been preserved. That there was such a letter appears from the answer of Sir Gregory and Vannes, printed in State Papers, vii. p. 184. The letter was written June 6, 1529, and alludes in cypher to this protestation, which is also spoken of in Gardiner's letter to Vannes of the 25th of June, as follows:—

And whereas by the King's letters to you, directed since my departing thence, ye were advertised and instructed to make an appellation and protestation *tanquam a non vicario ad rerum vicarium Jhesu Christi*, because the King's grace perceiveth by your letters written in cypher to his grace that the said appellation might irritate the Pope's holiness and rather hinder his cause than do good, his pleasure therefore is that ye shall forbear to make any such protestation or appellation, notwithstanding any clause contained in his said letters to the contrary, but that ye shall by all dulce and pleasant means entertain the Pope's holiness in good benevolence and favour towards the King's highness, so that by exasperating him he do none act anew to the derogation of his commission and process to be made thereupon here.

P. 190, l. 11. The author here goes back six months in the history to the beginning of the year 1529. The Pope's illness was in January of that year.

P. 190, l. 13. This letter is analysed in Brewer's Calendar, 5270, and is printed at length in Pocock's Records of the Reformation, vol. ii. p. 590. It had previously been published by Foxe, p. 1126, ed. 2.

The passage, *And in case the election*, to *entertainment*, is almost verbatim from the letters, as in p. 598.

P. 191, l. 5. This letter, dated Feb. 7, 1529, is analysed in Brewer's Calendar, 5272, and printed at length in Fiddes's Wolsey, p. 211.

P. 191, l. 11. See Wolsey's letter of Feb. 20, 1529, to Gardiner, Brian, Cassali, and Vannes in Brewer's Calendar, 5314. See also 5375.

P. 191, l. 17. See Wolsey's letter of April 6, 1529, in Brewer's Calendar, 5428, and in Burnet's Reformation, iv. 79.

P. 192, l. 13, King of Spaine. This must have been the reading of the original manuscript, for thus it is copied in (E), (N$_1$) and (N$_2$). (G) alone has altered it into *England*, which Harpsfield meant; though he carelessly wrote *Spaine*.

P. 192, l. 7 from bottom. For innumerable allusions to the Breve and its defects, see Brewer's Calendar, vol. iv. parts ii. and iii. *passim*.

P. 193, l. 2. A draft of the letter alluded to was printed by Burnet, vol. i. part ii. no. xxiv. It is in Vannes's hand, and has been analysed in Brewer's Calendar, 4980, with the following very necessary note of caution:—

"The reader must be upon his guard against supposing that any of these drafts were really sent or submitted to the persons to whom they are addressed. They are probably, like other papers on the great question of the Divorce, devices which occurred to the King or Wolsey from time to time, and might or might not be used as occasion served."

Upon comparing Harpsfield's account of this letter with the draft, there seems reason to believe that the order of the contents was altered, and probably some additions made in the actual letter sent. It is not dated, but evidently is of Nov. 28, 1528. It begins also with a reference to a previous letter of the two legates to the Pope which is not known now to exist, but which perhaps Harpsfield had seen at Rome.

P. 195, l. 1. See Brewer's Calendar, 4977.

P. 195, last line. Sir Thomas Boleyn was made earl of Wiltshire, Dec. 8, 1529, when he was sent to Bologna with Stokesley and Lee. The King wrote commending them to Ghinucci and Sir Gregory Cassali at Bologna, Jan. 20, 1530 (Brewer's Calendar, 6154). Their commission is dated the following day (*ibid.*

NOTES. 327

6155). What the author says of the opinions of the Universities being shown to the Pope can scarcely be true, for it does not appear that any had as yet been ascertained.

P. 196, l. 15. The date of this proclamation is Sept. 12, an. 22, i. e. 1530. It has been printed from the MS. copy in possession of the Society of Antiquaries in the Records of the Reformation, vol. ii. p. 49, no. ccxxiv.

P. 196, l. 9 from bottom. This parliament was summoned for January 16, 1530-1, the twenty-second year of the reign, not, as the chroniclers say, January 6. The reading of the sentences of the universities translated into English was March 30 1531. The interview of the Lords of the Council with the Queen took place at Greenwich May 31, Wednesday in Whitsun week. After this the King and Queen went to Windsor and lived there till July 14, 1531, when the King went to Woodstock, leaving the Queen at Windsor, from which she removed to the More, and thence to Easthampstead.

P. 197, last line but one. Anne Boleyn was created Marchioness of Pembroke at Windsor, on Sunday, Sept. 1, 1532, which is, as the author describes it, the 24th year of the King's reign. See Stow, p. 560, who mentions the pension of 1,000*l.* a year. Henry crossed over to Calais Oct. 11. See Herbert, p. 339. They returned Nov. 14, St. Erkenwald's day, on which day the marriage took place, as Sanders says. The expression used by Cranmer describing the marriage as having taken place "much about St. Paul's day last" has been quoted as showing that it took place Jan. 25, 1533, but Cranmer's meaning is St. Erkenwald's day, on which there was a grand function performed at St. Paul's. Harpsfield states that there was a private marriage in April 1533, *i.e.*, immediately after the decisions of the two Convocations of Canterbury and York, which is most probably true, and which preceded her public acknowledgment as Queen on Whit Sunday, the 1st of June. On the 28th of May Cranmer held a court at Lambeth, in which he pronounced that Henry and Anne had been joined in lawful matrimony. Dr. Lingard thinks this marriage must have been after the pronouncement of the Court at Dunstable towards the end of May. It may be taken for granted that the ceremony was performed for a second time in May this year, in order to avoid any objections being urged against the previous marriage of Nov. 14, 1532. Harpsfield has, however, made a mistake of a year in saying that "about a year after, perceiving her to be great with child, he caused her to be proclaimed Queen, and at Whitsuntide following caused her to be crowned," for this took place in 1533, and Elizabeth was born Sept. 7 of that year.

P. 198, last line but five. Cromwell was kept informed of the proceedings from time to time by Thomas Bedell, who wrote, May 10, to say that the process began that day before Cranmer, the Bishops of Winchester and Lincoln being present. On this day the Queen was declared *contumax*. (Records of the Reformation,

328 PRETENDED DIVORCE OF HENRY VIII. AND KATHERINE.

no. cccxxxii.) The proceedings of the 17th were detailed beforehand in another communication from Bedell to Cromwell. He wrote again on the 23rd, the day when the sentence was pronounced. These letters are printed in the Records of the Reformation, no. cccxxxiii. and cccxxxiv., and complete the history of the transaction, of which there had been previously printed in State Papers, vol. i. pp. 394-397, three letters from Cranmer to the King, of the 12th, 17th, and 23rd of May, and one other from Bedell to Cromwell of the 12th of May, and one in Ellis, 2, ii. p. 42.

Cranmer, in his last letter, asks for instructions as regards the second matrimony, which it was necessary should be settled before June 1, 1533, the day fixed for the coronation of Anne Boleyn.

P. 197, l. 9. This year began April 22, 1531.

P. 198, l. 6. The Parliament met Feb. 4, 1532-3. The Act referred to is (chap. xii.) " An Acte that the appeles in suche cases as have been used to be pursued to the See of Rome shall not be from hensforth had ne used but wythin this Realme." The passage referred to is the last clause of the Act.

P. 198, last line. Cranmer wrote his letter to the King for permission to try the case April 11, 1533, which permission was given on the same day. Katherine was pronounced contumacious May 10, and the decree for the divorce was pronounced Friday May 23rd.

P. 199, l. 4. The date of their mission is Aug. 8, 1533.

P. 199, l. 18. This interview was Dec. 18, 1533, an. xxv.

P. 199, l. 22.
Queen Katherine died Jan. 7, 1536. The letter which follows is like that given in Herbert's History, for which he refers to Polydore Vergil, who has given it in Latin. There is a different Latin version in Sanders.

P. 201, l. 2. This Parliament met Jan. 1533-4. The Act referred to is (chap. xxii.) entitled " An Acte for the establishement of the Kynges succession."

P. 201, l. 8. The preamble of the Bill states first that the Lady Katheryne, the lawful wife of Prince Arthure, " by hym was carnally knowen as doth duely appere by sufficient prove in a lawful proces had and made before Thomas by the sufferaunce of God now Archebisshopp of Canterbury and Metropolitane and Prymate of all this Realme," who had judged the marriage with Queen Anne to be lawful. It goes on to say that this judgment had been confirmed by both Convocations, both Universities, as well as by the Universities of Bologna, Padua, Paris,

NOTES.   329

Orleans, Toulouse, Angers, and others, and also by the private writings of many right excellent well learned men. It then proceeds to enumerate the prohibited degrees of marriages, amongst which appears the marriage with a brother's wife, which are plainly prohibited by God's law, yet had been dispensed with by the dispensation of man's power, which is but usurped, as no man has power to dispense with God's law, as was affirmed by the Clergy and the Universities. Statutes, 25 an. Hen. VIII. cap. 22, p. 472.

P. 202, last line but nine. Little is known of these individuals excepting of Holyman, who was Bishop of Bristol in 1554.

Bayne is probably the same with Ralph Baynes, afterwards Bishop of Lichfield and Coventry, who was deprived and imprisoned by Elizabeth.

Moreman is Dr. John Moreman of Exeter College, Oxford, whose name appears in the demands of the insurgents in Cornwall in 1549 upon the attempt to inforce the first Prayer Book of Edward VI.

Dr. Thomas Kyrkham was guardian of the College of Minorites at Doncaster, and appears by Boner's register to have been admitted to the church of St. Martin's Outwich, June 8, 1548, if the date of the quotation from Kennet in Bliss's edition of Wood's Fasti is correct.

P. 208, l. 15.
Barnes, Gerard, and Jerome were burned for heresy, condemned without trial by attainder. Powell, Fetherstone, and Abel were hanged for treason. All were drawn on hurdles from the Tower to Smithfield, July 30, 1540. See Wriothesley's Chronicle, p. 120.

P. 209, l. 6. The titles of these books are as follows:—
Cochlæus (Joh.), De Matrimonio Regis Angliæ Congratulatio Disputatoria. Lipsiæ, 1535, 4to.
Morysin (Ric.), Apomaxis Calumniarum J. Cochlæi contra Henricum VIII. Lond. Berthelet, 1537, 4to.
Cochlæus (Joh.), Scopa in Araneas Ricardi Morysini, Angli. Lipsiæ, 1538, 4to.

P. 209, l. 14 from bottom. See Seckendorf sub an. 1535, p. 111.

P. 210, l. 8. The sentence of the Canonists had been given May 23, 1530. That of the Divines was not secured till July 2. The letter of Francis to the Faculty of Theology at Angers has been preserved by Le Grand, and is dated April 30, 1530 (Brewer's Calendar, 6370); that to the Divines of Paris has not been preserved; but a letter of June 12 to the French King (Brewer's Calendar, 6449) shows that such a letter was written. According to Le Grand it was written May 27. They met June 8, but as they had come to no conclusion Francis I. wrote to the President of Paris June 17 to complain of their conduct. On the 18th of June, Norfolk, writing to Montmorency, complains that whereas he had had 56 on his side against 7 on the other he had now only 22 against 36.

CAMD. SOC.   2 U

P. 214, l. 3. These words are not literally quoted from the Dialogue. See Records of the Reformation, vol. ii. p. 415.

P. 214, l. 14. See *ibid.* p. 413.

P. 217, l. 7. The passage referring to these matters is as follows :—

Καί ποτε καὶ Φρύνην τὴν ἑταίραν ἐθελῆσαι πειράσαι αὐτόν, καὶ ζῆθεν διωκομένην ὑπὸ τινῶν καταφυγεῖν εἰς τὸ οἰκίδιον. Τὸν δὲ, ἕνεκα τοῦ ἀνθρωπίνου εἰςδέξασθαι, καὶ ἑνὸς ὄντος κλινιδίου δεομένῃ μεταδοῦναι τῆς κατακλίσεως· καὶ τέλος πολλὰ ἐκλιπαροῦσα, ἄπρακτος ἀναστῆναι, λέγειν τε πρὸς τοὺς πυνθανομένους, ὡς οὐκ ἀπ' ἀνδρὸς ἀλλ' ἀπ' ἀνδριάντος ἀνασταίη. Ἔνιοι δὲ Λαΐδα φασὶ παρακατακλῖναι αὐτῷ τοὺς μαθητάς. Τὸν δὲ οὕτως εἶναι ἐγκρατῆ, ὥστε καὶ τομὰς καὶ καύσεις πολλάκις ὑπομεῖναι περὶ τὸ αἰδοῖον.

The words *but with a stone* should have been rendered *but with a statue.*

P. 217, l. 12. It is not exactly accurate to say that Ammon " continued with his wife many a year." The story, as told by Socrates, is, that, having agreed to remain in virginity, they retired to a hut, where for a short time they occupied a common apartment as ascetics, but that afterwards they separated and lived the rest of their lives in abstinence.

P. 217, last line but 7. " And as for words, it is too open in law that the husband's attestation making for the marriage is to be preferred to the woman's denial in that case ; so that, if there were no more than Prince Arthur's own saying, the law willeth that credit should be given to him and not to her."—Records of the Reformation, p. 416.

P. 218, l. 8. See Records of the Reformation, p. 414.

P. 220, line 16 from bottom. This passage may be seen in the Latin draft of instructions to Benet in Vitellius, B. XI. 115, which has never been printed, though it is calendared at p. 2466 of Brewer's Calendar as " a draft of similar instructions," *i.e.* similar to the English copy analysed by him in No. 5575, as Instructions for Dr. Benet, which are printed at length in State Papers, vii. 171-177.

P. 220, l. 12 from bottom. These words are exactly transcribed from the Cardinal's despatch to Rome, printed by Burnet, part 1, book 2, no. xxv.; and they occur also with scarcely a variation in the Instructions printed in State Papers, vii. 171-177, bearing date May 21, 1529.

Nevertheless, after this date it appears that Lee wrote to Henry, May 31, that he

NOTES. 331

and Ghinucci were of opinion that the breve was forged, and accordingly Wolsey, in his cyphered despatch, addressed to Benet July 27, 1529, directs him to make further inquiries with a view to the "disproving the said breve." This is the last we hear of any attempt to prove the breve false. This is printed at length in State Papers, vii. 193.

P. 224, l. 16. See Records of the Reformation, ii. p. 402.

P. 228. See Records of the Reformation, ii. p. 404.

P. 230, l. 11. *Ibid.* p. 405.

P. 230, l. 11 from bottom. *Ibid.* p. 406.

P. 230, last line but one. See *Ibid.* p. 408.

P. 231, l. 3. *Ibid.* p. 396.

P. 232, l. 1. *Ibid.* p. 409. The allusion is to "The determination of the University of Orleans that the King is not bound to appear in a Court held out of his dominions, either in person or by proxy," which is dated June 22, 1531. This was printed for the first time by Rymer, and again in the Records of the Reformation, ii. 135, No. ccxliv. Also to the decree made at Paris of June 14 and August 19, to the same effect, also printed by Rymer.

P. 232, l. 15. See the Records of the Reformation, ii. p. 411.

P. 232, l. 19.
At vero post mortem Aedilbercti, cum filius ejus Eadbald regni gubernacula suscepisset, magno tenellis ibi adhuc ecclesiæ crementis detrimento fuit. Siquidem non solum fidem Christi recipere noluerat, sed et fornicatione pollutus est tali "qualem nec inter gentes auditam" apostolus testatur, "ita ut uxorem patris haberet." Quo utroque scelere occasionem dedit ad priorem vomitum revertendi, his qui sub imperio sui parentis, vel favore vel timore regio, fidei et castimoniæ jura susceperant. Nec supernæ flagella districtionis perfido regi castigando et corrigendo defuere; nam crebra mentis insania et spiritus immundi invasione premebatur.—Bædæ Hist. Eccles. lib. 2, cap. 5.

The following chapter narrates the conversion of the King to the Christian faith and his repudiation of his illegal marriage with the wife of his father.

P. 235, l. 1. The same story is more briefly told by Sanders, p. 91, ed. Rom. 1586.

332   PRETENDED DIVORCE OF HENRY VIII. AND KATHERINE.

P. 236, last line but eight.   For the evidence for the King's connexion with Mary Boleyn, see the Records of the Reformation, *passim*, and the Editor's preface.

P. 241, last line but three. S. Ambr. in expositione in Matth. Non defloratio virginitatis facit conjugium sed pactio conjugalis. Magister Sentent. lib. iv. dist. 27, cap. 4.

P. 241, last line. Add to Dist. 27, lib. iv. cap. 2.

P. 249, l. 13. The transcribers have blundered over this word *Licet*, copying in entire ignorance, one having *Licit*, another *Lices*. The Decretal alluded to is

Licet præter solitum [et infra]. Consultationi tuæ taliter respondemus, quòd si inter virum et mulierem legitimus consensus interveniat de præsenti, ita quidem, quòd unus alterum in suo mutuo consensu verbis consuetis expresse recipiat, utroque dicente: Ego te accipio in meam, et ego accipio te in meum ; sive sit juramentum interpositum sive non, non licet mulieri alii nubere: Et si nupserit, etiam si carnalis copula sit secuta, ab eo separari debet, et ut ad primum redeat, ecclesiastica districtione compelli: Quamvis aliter a quibusdam prædecessoribus nostris sit aliquando judicatum.—Decret. Greg. lib. 4, tit. v. cap. 3.

P. 253, l. 5. The story is told by Sanders in a different way, as if the confession of Wyatt had been made to the Council, through fear of the consequences, if it should afterwards be discovered that he had any connexion with Anne Boleyn. He says that Wyatt, so far from feeling any shame, offered, upon the King's expressing his entire disbelief in the charge, to give him ocular demonstration, and that the King, persisting in his determination, told the whole affair to Anne Boleyn, and that upon it Wyatt was dismissed from court. He adds that this confession saved his life, as otherwise he would with her other paramours have suffered the penalty of death.

Harpsfield's version of the story seems the more credible in itself, and his testimony is in general more to be relied on than that of Sanders. Moreover, he gives his authority for the story.

P. 253, last line but three. This Act is of 28 Hen. VIII. cap. 7, passed in the session of parliament which began June 8, 1536, and is entitled, An Act for the establishment of the Succession of the Imperial Crown of this Realm.

P. 259, last line but four. Herbert (p. 453) says that the match was fully concluded at the coming over of Frederic Duke of Baviere, Count Palatine of the Rhine, and the several ambassadors of the Dukes of Saxony and Cleves. Godwyn says, that for treating of the match in September came into England Frederick Duke and Elector of Saxony, Frederick Duke of Bavaria, Otho Henry Count Palatine of

NOTES. 333

Rhine, and the Chancellor of the Duke of Cleve, with some others, who were for eight days royally entertained by the King at Windsor.
Hall omits all notice of this arrival. Stow speaks of it as being in September. The most precise account is that given by Holinshed, p. 947, who says, "This year the 16th of Sept. came to London duke Frederike of Baviere, the Palsgrave of the Rhine, and the 18th of the same month came to London the marshall of Haus Frederike Prince Elector of Saxony and the Chancellor of William duke of Cleve, Gulicke, Gelderland, and Berghen. The Palsgrave was received and conducted to Windsore by the Duke of Suffolke, and the other were accompanied with other noble men; and the three and twentieth of the same month they all came to Windsore, where eight days together they were continually feasted, and had pastime shewed them in hunting and other pleasures so much as might be. The Palsgrave shortly after departed homewards, and was princely rewarded, and at that present was the marriage concluded betwixt the King and the Lady Anne sister unto duke William of Cleve, and great preparation was made for the receiving of her."

P. 260, l. 13. The following extract from the recently published Chronicle of Charles Wriothesley (p. 109), gives the following account of this private interview. "And on the New Year's Day, at afternoon, the King's grace, with five of his privy chamber, being disguised with clokes of marble with hoods, that they should not be known, came privily to Rochester, and so went up into the chamber where the said Lady Anne looked out at a window to see the bull-baiting that was that time in the court, and suddenly he embraced her, and kissed and showed her a token that the King had sent her for her New Year's gift, and she being abashed, not knowing who it was, thanked him, and so he communed with her; but she regarded him little, but always looked out of the window on the bull-baiting; and, when the King perceived she regarded his coming so little, he departed into another chamber and put off his cloke, and came in again in a coat of purple velvet; and when the lords and knights did see his grace they did him reverence; and then, she perceiving the lords doing their duties, humbled her grace lowly to the King's Majesty, and his grace saluted her again, and so talked together lovingly, and after took her by the hand and led her into another chamber, where they solaced their graces that night and till Friday at afternoon."
Where the stories begin to differ Harpsfield is the more to be relied on, for Anne could speak no language but Dutch, of which the King was entirely ignorant.

P. 260, last line but four. "This year the 8 day of August, being Sunday, the King was married to Katherin Hawarde, daughter of the late Edmond Haward deceased, and brother to the Duke of Norfolke, at his manor of Hampton Court, and that day she dined in her great chamber under the cloth of estate, and was there proclaimed Queen of Englande."—Stow.

P. 261, l. 1. This Act is cap. 38 of 32 Hen. VIII. The Bill was brought into the House of Lords on Friday July 2, 1540, and committed to the archbishop of

334 PRETENDED DIVORCE OF HENRY VIII. AND KATHERINE.

Canterbury, the bishops of Durham, Winchester, and Rochester, to be examined and corrected. It was read a third time the next day, and finally was brought up from the Commons and passed on the fifth of July, the day before the divorce of Anne of Cleves was mooted in the upper house.

P. 263, last line but fourteen.

Catherine Howard and Anne Boleyn were first cousins, having a common grandfather, Thomas Howard second Duke of Norfolk. Catherine was the daughter of Lord Edmund Howard, the third son of the Duke, and Anne was daughter of Elizabeth, his eldest daughter, who was married to Sir Thomas Boleyn, Viscount Rochford, afterwards Earl of Wiltshire.

P. 266, last line but two. This word is spelt Cyren both in the Eyston MS. and (N_1). In the Canon Law he is styled *Theodorus episcopus ecclesiæ Ticinensis*. The decree is as printed at p. 310.

P. 272, line 11. The story is told by Valerius Maximus, lib. v. cap. 7, De patrum amore et indulgentia in liberos. It is as follows:—

Cæterum ut ad jucundiora cognitu veniamus. Seleuci regis filius Antiochus novercæ Stratonices infinito amore correptus memor quam improbis facibus arderet, impium pectoris vulnus pia dissimulatione contegebat. Itaque diversi affectus iisdem visceribus ac medullis inclusi, summa cupiditas et maxima verecundia ad ultimam tabem corpus ejus redegerunt. Jacebat ipse in lectulo, moribundo similis; lamentabantur necessarii; frater mœrore prostratus de obitu unici filii deque sua miserrima orbitate cogitabat; totius domus funebris magis quam regius erat vultus. Sed hanc tristitiæ nubem Leptinis mathematici vel, ut quidam tradunt, Erasistrati medici providentia discussit. Juxta enim Antiochum sedens, ut eum ad introitum Stratonices rubore perfundi et spiritu increbrescere, eaque egrediente pallere et excitatiorem anhelitum subinde recuperare animadvertit, curiosiore observatione ad ipsam veritatem penetravit. Intrante enim Stratonice et rursus abeunte, brachium adolescentis dissimulanter apprehendendo, modo vegetiore, modo languidiore pulsu venarum comperit cujus morbi æger esset, protinusque id Seleuco exposuit. Qui charissima sibi conjuge filio cedere non dubitavit, quod in amorem incidisset, fortunæ acceptum referens, quod dissimulare cum usque ad mortem paratus esset, ipsius pudori imputans. Subjiciatur animis senex, rex, amans; jam patebit quam multa, quamque difficilia paterni affectus indulgentia superavit. Valer. Max. lib. v. cap. 7.

The story is told more fully by Plutarch in his Life of Demetrius Poliorcetes, cap. 38 ; by Appian, De rebus Syr. cap. 59—61 ; and by others.

Another reference is given in all the MSS. to Suetonius, lib. i. cap. 24, but this is a mistake for lib. iv. cap. 24, and ought to have been placed opposite the word Caligula in the text below. The passage referred to evidently is the following :—

Cum omnibus sororibus suis stupri consuetudinem fecit, plenoque convivio singulas infra se vicissim collocabat, uxore supra cubante. Ex his Drusillam vitiàsse virginem, prætextatus adhuc, creditur. Atque etiam in concubitu ejus quondam deprehensus ab avia Antonia, apud quam simul educabantur. Mox Lucio Cassio Longino consulari collocatam abduxit, et in modum justæ uxoris propalam habuit. Eadem defuncta, justitium indixit, in quo risisse, lavisse, cœnâsse cum parentibus aut conjuge, liberisve, capitis fuit.

P. 274, l. 5.

This was sanctioned in the *Reformatio Legum Ecclesiasticarum*, which was first printed in 1571, in the section De adulteriis et divortiis, cap. 8, which runs as follows :—

Cum autem conjunx non possit absens investigari nec erui, ne locus ullus in hoc crimine levitati vel temeritati relinquatur, primum absentem personam nominatim requiri volumus illa juris formula quam viis et modis appellant; quo tempore si se non ostenderit aut ejus aliquis vicarius qui causam ejus velit agere, judex illi biennium vel triennium indulgebit, in quo persona possit absens se repræsentare. Quo tempore consumpto, si se ipse non sistat et justas afferat absentiæ tam diuturnæ causas, destituta persona nuptiarum vinculis liberabitur et novum sibi conjugem (si velit) assumet. Desertrix autem persona, si, judicio jam peracto, novisque consecutis nuptiis, sero post biennii vel triennii spatium expletum sui potestatem fecerit, in æternas carceris tenebras detrudatur et secundum matrimonium plenissimo jure valeat.

This chapter is entitled *Divortium propter desertum matrimonium.* A still more remarkable permission is conceded in the following chapter, cap. 9, headed Divortium propter nimis longam conjugis absentiam. The chapter runs as follows:—

Quando non aufugerit conjunx, sed militiam aut mercaturam aut aliquam habet hujusmodi legitimam et honestam peregrinationis suæ causam, et abfuerit diu domo, nec illius vel de vita vel de morte quicquam certo sciatur, largientur alteri conjugi, judices (siquidem hoc ab illis requirat) biennii vel triennii spatium, in quo mariti reditum expectet. Quo tempore toto, si non revertatur, nec de vitâ possit illius aliquid esse explorati, cum diligentissime de ea fuerit interim perquisitum, alteri conjugi novas concedi nuptias æquum est; cum hâc tamen conditione, prior ut maritus si tandem se repræsentet, uxor illum rursus ad se recipiat, siquidem ostendere possit culpa sua factum non esse, quod foras tamdiu peregrinatus sit. Tantum enim et tam longi temporis absentiam nisi plene magnaque cum ratione possit excusare, custodiam in perpetuam carceris dimittatur, nullum ad uxorem reditum habeat, et illa secundis in nuptiis rite permaneat.

Various other occasions of divorce are allowed in other chapters of this section.

P. 275, l. 15. The date of this event is fixed by the following extract from Stow quoted by Holingshed, p. 961. "The 18th of December [1543] the Archbishop of Canterbury's palace at Canterbury was burned, and therein was burnt his brother-in-law and other men." This particular incident is not narrated by Sanders, who, however, confirms the statement of Mrs. Thomas Cranmer being carried about in a chest.

P. 275, last line but 11. This was Edmund Cranmer, who was appointed Archdeacon of Canterbury, March 9, 1534, and on his deprivation in 1554 was succeeded by the author Nicolas Harpsfield.

P. 275, last line but three. The case was brought before the Council, Nov. 23, 1551, and was directed to be inquired into, but seems to have been hushed up, as the council books make no further mention of it. He himself alleged that he married to please the Duke of Somerset.

P. 278, l. 2. Catherine Howard was married to the King, Aug. 8, 1540, and put to death, Feb. 13, 1542.

The marriage with Catherine Parr was at Hampton Court, July 12, 1543.

P. 278, l. 13. The author appears to place the suit to the Duchess of Milan after the execution of Catherine Howard, whereas it preceded the marriage with Anne of Cleves, as, of course, he knew very well, and so expresses his meaning a few lines further on.

P. 278, l. 14. This was Christina, youngest daughter of Christian II., King of Denmark, who was married in 1533 to Francis Duke of Milan, who left her a widow in 1535. She was afterwards married in 1541 to Francis Duke of Lorraine and Bar. Her mother was Isabella of Spain, a sister of the Emperor, and niece of Catharine of Aragon. She would therefore have been within the prohibited degrees, they having a common descent from Ferdinand and Isabella.

Jane Seymour died Oct. 24, 1537. The story of her death has been treated as the invention of Sanders. But Harpsfield's testimony is independent. The Editor of the State Papers assigns this same date to the letter which was written by Cromwell or Wriothesley to Gardiner and Lord William Howard to look out for another wife, stating that the King was willing to marry again for the content of his subjects. The Duchess of Milan was suggested by Hutton to Cromwell on the 4th of December. She was at this time only sixteen, and was reported to be both widow and maid. Wriothesley had been entrusted with the affair of the contemplated marriage, for he wrote instructions to Peter Mewtas how to manage the King's suit with Mary de Guise, widow of the Duke of Longueville, who in 1538 became the wife of James V. of Scotland. In Wriothesley's Instructions of Sept. 25, 1538, it is stated that the overture now renewed for the marriage with the Duchess of Milan had been made immediately upon the decease of the late Queen Jane.

P. 279, l. 1. No mention is made of Wriothesley's brother-in-law, Mr. Knight, in the State Papers, unless he is the same person with Thomas Knight, who appears to have been employed by Cromwell, and who carried a letter from Cromwell to Wriothesley which he delivered to him at Brussels, Feb. 26, 1539. Vaughan and Carne were associated with him in the matter. From a despatch from the three to Henry VIII., dated from Brussels, Feb. 1, 1539, it appears that they had heard that the Duchess of Milan did not much affect the marriage, though she had apparently acquiesced in the negociations for it during the year, but had been reassured on the subject at an interview which Wriothesley had had with the Duchess of Milan. The difficulty about obtaining the requisite dispensation does not appear to have been represented till the following year, when the negociations were about to be broken off.

P. 279, l. 8. The Emperor Leo, after the death of his third wife Eudocia in childbirth, married a fourth, but she was not crowned till after the birth of his son Constantine, who was baptized by the Patriarch Nicolas. After relating this Zonaras, lib. xvi. cap. 13, adds:—

Διὰ γοῦν τὸν τέταρτον γάμον ἀφώριστο παρὰ τοῦ Πατριάρχου ὁ Λέων.

P. 281, l. 8. Thomas Seymour, Lord Sudeley, was beheaded March 20, 1549, and his brother the Protector on Friday, January 22, 1552.

INDEX.

Abell, Master Thomas, Chaplain to Queen Katherine, 197; executed 208, 329
* Abraham, marries Sarah his niece or sister, 33, 66, 72, 82
Accursius, 214
Acton, lord, i. ii.
Adonias, put to death by Solomon for wishing to marry Abisaig, his father David's widow, 242
Adrian, Matthew, 317
Adrian, Pope, 17, 195, 322
Africk, Council of, 198
Agathen, Council, Author's answer to, 60, 92, 238, 264
* Ahab, King, 153
Albertus Magnus, 52, 84, 108, 128, 156
* Alcinous, King of the Phæcenses, marries his brother's daughter, 32
Alcock, Bishop of Ely, 284
Alençon, Duke of, 176; Margaret duchess of, 321
Alexander, Emperor, 239
Alexander, King of Epirus, marries his niece Cleopatra, 31
Alexander III. Pope, 243
Alexander VI. Pope, 46, 136
Alexander's Decretal, 119
Alphonsus, 128
Altisiodorensis, Author's answer to, 75, 118
Alward, Thomas, 324
Ambrose, St., 15, 20, 20, 28; Author's answer to, 65-67, 107, 118, 175, 241, 264, 321, 332
* Amram, Father of Moses, marries Jochebed his aunt, 32
Anatholius, 110
* Anaxandrides, King of Sparta, marries his sister's daughter, 32
Andreas, Johannes, Author's answer to, 79, 119, 134
Angell, General of the Observants, 186

Anjou, Doctors of Law of university of, 210, 329
Anselmus, St., Archbishop of Canterbury, Author's answer to, 70, 118
Antioch, Council of, 22
Antiochus, son of Seleuchus King of Syria, marries his step-mother Stratonice, 272, 334
Antonine, Archbishop of Florence, Author's answer to, 77, 118
Antonio Caracalla, Emperor, marries his * step-mother, 272
Antonius, 108
Aretas, King of the Arabians, 251
Aristarchus, 34
Arminach, Bernard Earl of, 76, 121
Arthur, Prince, 170, 176, 192, 195, 201, 210, 215, 217, 223, 237, 308, 318, 330
Ascalonta, Herodes, 53
Astexanus, Author's answer to, 78, 118
Audeley, Speaker of the Parliament of Henry VIII. 197
Audrey, St. (Etheldreda), 217
Augustine, St., 19, 22, 28, 36, 49, 55; Author's answer to, 67, 84, 94, 98, 101, 103, 113, 118, 128, 132, 142, 152, 160, 164, 226, 242, 245, 248, 264, 274, 311
Augustus, Emperor, 284
Azolinus de Romano, 134

Bacon, Sir Nicholas, 8; John, 19, 21; Author's answer to, 78, 118, 123, 126, 131
Barkeley, the Lady, 234
Barnes, burnt for heresy, 208, 329
Barton, Elizabeth, a nun, 178
Basil, St., Author's answer to, 63, 107, 117, 163
Bath, Bishop of, 198
Bavaria Duke Frederick of, 259
Bayne, Dr. Bishop of Lichfield, 9, 202, 329

INDEX.   339

Beeche, John, Abbot of Colchester, put to death, 301
Beda, 52
Bedell, Thomas, 327
Bell, Dr. John, 323
Bennett, Dr. Ambassador of Henry VIII. at the Court of Rome, 182, 186, 220, 325, 330
Bernard de Trilla, 108
Bernard, St., 107, 108
Berthelet, Thomas, 308, 318, 329
Bickley, Thomas, made Bishop of Chichester by Elizabeth, 283
Biturs, Divines of University of, 50, 210
Blesensis, Petrus, 84
Bliss, Dr. 307
Boleyne, Anne, 24, 26, 171, 184; created Marchioness of Pembroke, 197, 200, 234, 236, 253, 255, 260, 263, 268, 277, 289, 317, 327; Mary, 332
Boleyne, Thomas, Earl of Wiltshire, 195, 308, 326, 334
Bologna, University of, 210, 329
Bonaventura, 85, 98
Bonvise, Anthony, 253
Booth, Charles, Bishop of Hereford, 322
Bowles, rev. Thomas, ii.
Brewer's Calendar, references to, 318, 322, 324, 325, 329, viii.
Browne, Archbishop of Dublin, 276; Sir Anthony, 199, 276
Burnet's Reformation, Reference to, 326, 330, 331
Bryan, sir Francis, 185, 187, 190, 199, 325

Cæsar, Julius, the Emperor, 280, 283
Caligula, Emperor, marries his own sister, 272
Calixtus, Pope, Author's answer to, 58
Campeggio, Cardinal Laurentius, 177, 179, 183, 229, 322, 324
Capua, council of, 110
Carbilius, Spurius, 279
Carne, 337
Carter, William, 1, 4, 5; executed 6, 302, 305
Carthage, council of, 229
Cassalis, sir Gregory de, ambassador to Henry VIII. at the court of Rome, 182, 186, 190, 325, 326
Caunus, 93
Celestine, Pope, 229

Celsus, 156, 158
Chadsey, Dr., Archdeacon of Middlesex, 9
Chalcedon, council of, 198
Chapter 11. Author's answer to conclusion of, 62; 111. Epilogue of, Author's answer to, 69; V. Author's answer to, 81; VI. Author's answer to, 89; VII. Author's answer to, 105
Charles, Emperor, 278
Christian II. King of Denmark, 336
Chrysostom, St., 21, 51; Author's answer to, 63, 117, 143, 153, 241, 315
Clement, Pope, 41, 121, 177, 184, 195, 232
Clement, Dr. 297
Cleves, Anne of, 24, 175, 260, 268, 278, 333
Cleves, Duke of, 259. 333
Clodius, P. 93
Cole, Dr., Dean of St. Paul's, 9
Consell, William, 204
Constance, Council of, 19, 23; Author's answer to, 61, 231, 274
Constantinople, Council of, 22
Cope, Dr. Alan, Canon of S. Peter's, Rome, 10
Courrant, one of the chaplains of Henry VIII. 204
Cranmer, Thomas, Archbishop of Canterbury, 4, 198, 223, 234, 254, 259, 275, 288; short account of, 289, 294, 327, 328; Mrs., i.
Cranmer, Edmund, Archdeacon of Canterbury, 8, 275
Cromwell, Thomas, Lord, 178, 260, 324, 327, 336, 337
Culpeper, Thomas, 278
Cyprian, St., 107

Damasus, Pope, 228, 315
Darius (Ahasuerus), marries his father's concubine Aspasia, 272
D'Aubigné, M. Merle, ii.
Deiphobus, son of Priam, marries Helen, wife of Paris, 32
Demetrius, King, marries Cleopatra, his brother's wife, 32
Dido, Queen, marries her uncle Sychæus, 31
Dion Prusieus, historiographer, 16
Drusilla, 335
Druthmarus, Christianus, 14

Dunce, 85
Dunstan, St., 20, 114, 232
Durandus, 4
Durham, Bp. of, 334
Dyoscorus, heretical bishop, 225
Dyreham, Francis, 278

Edbald, King, 113
Edward the Confessor, 217, 262, 279, 296, 301
Edward II. 287
Edwin, Earl, 114
Egfride, King, 217
Eggs and fish, high prices of, consequent upon the Reformation, 299
Egidius de Bellamera, 17, 21, 24, 120, 124, 130
Eleutherius, Pope, 262
Elizabeth, Queen, 5, 8
Elmer, Protestant Bishop of London, 6
Elstowe, Friar, 204
Elyot, sir Thomas, 307
Emanuel, King of Portugal, marries two sisters, 46, 136, 310
Erasmus, 154, 211
Ethelbert, King, 262, 286
Eugenins, Pope, 76
Eumenes, King of Pergamos, leaves both wife and kingdom to his brother Attalus, 32
Eusebius, Bishop of Constantinople, 52, 228
Exeter, Marquis of, 286
Eyston, William, 1; Charles, dedication of Treatise to his son, 3-6, 302, 305, i., ii., iv., vi., viii.

Fabian, Pope, 107
Farindon, Hugh, Abbot of Reading, executed, 300
Faustus, the Manichean heretic, 68, 118, 311
Feckenham, Dr., Abbot of Westminster, 9
Ferdinand and Isabella of Spain, 29, 30, 42, 136, 192, 250, 310, 386
Ferrara, University of, 210
Fetherston, executed, 208, 329
Fisher, John, Bishop of Rochester, 15, 23, imprisoned in Tower, 27, 36, 39, 48, 119, 149, 160, 170, 177, 205, 223, 231, 249, 254, 256, 286, 293, 306, 508, 318, 334

Fitzwilliam, Lord, 260
Florence, University of, 210
Franciscus de Maaso, 84
Franciscus Maro, 108
Fox's Acts and Monuments, references to, 8, 9
Fox, Dr., King's Almoner, 28, 177, 306, 308, made Bishop of Hereford. 322, 326
Francis I., King of France, 310, 329

Gabriel, 108
Gardiner, Stephen Bishop of Winchester, 184, 190, 198, 220, 322, 324, 336
Gerat, burnt for heresy, 208, 329
Ghinucci, 326, 331
Gibbon, father Richard, 10
Glass of Truth, allusions to the, 18; Answer to English dialogue called, 168, 318
Glossa interlinearis, 51
God's Law, Author's definition of, 81
God's Law, Judicial, Author's definition of, 82
Godwin, 332
Goodricke, Bishop of Ely, 291
Goriam, Nicholaus, 51
Gratian, 245
Gregory, St., 19, 28, 34; Author's answer to, 55-58, 100, 135, 141, 153, 223, 228, 238, 245, 249, 262, 268, 286, 313, 318
Gregory the Younger, St., Council under, Author's answer to, 61
Grenville MS. reference to, i. ii.
Grosshead or Grosthead, Bishop of Lincoln, 115
Guise, Mary de, 336
Gulielmus Parisiensis, 92
Guntherius, Archbishop of Cologne, 16

Hahmo, Halberstatensis, Bishop, 84
Hales, Halis, Alexander de, 84, 108
Hall, 333
Harpsfield, Dr. Nicholas, last Catholic Archdeacon of Canterbury 1; Life and Character of, 7; admitted Principal of White Hall in Oxford, *ib.*; made King's Professor of Greek tongue in Oxford, 1546, *ib.*; went into voluntary exile, 1550, *ib.*; returned on Queen Mary's Accession, made Archdeacon of Canterbury, 1554, 8; Prolocutor in first Convoca-

tion of Clergy in Elizabeth's reign, *ib.*; deprived of his Ecclesiastical Preferments and imprisoned, 9; author of several works against heresy, *ib.*; died 1583 after an imprisonment of nearly 24 years, 10; his epistle to the reader, 12 to 24; his answers to, Tertullian, 53; S. Gregory, 55; Pope Calixtus, 58; Pope Zacharias, *ib.*; Pope Innocent III. 59; second Council of Toledo, *ib.*; Agathen Council, 60; Neocesarien Council, *ib.*; Council of Gregory the Younger, 61; Council of Constance, *ib.*; to conclusion of second chapter, 62; Origen, *ib.*; St. Chrysostom, 63; St. Basil, *ib.*; Isichias, 64; St. Ambrose, 65; St. Jerome, 69; St. Augustine, *ib.*; the epilogue of third chapter, 69; St. Anselm, 70; Hugo Cardinalis, 71; Rodolphus Flaviacensis, *ib.*; Rupertus Tuitiensis, *ib.*; Hugo de Sancto Victore, 72; Hildebert, *ib.*; Ivo Carnotensis, 73; Walterus de Constantia, *ib.*; St. Thomas Aquinas, 74; Altisiodorensis, 75; Petrus de Palude, *ib.*; Johannes de Turre Chremata, 76; Antonine Archbishop of Florence, 77; Jacobus de Lausania, *ib.*; Johannes de Tabiena, *ib.*; Astexanus, 78; John Bacon, *ib.*; Waldensis, *ib.*; the residue of the Scholastical doctors, 79; Johannes Andreas et Johannes de Imola, *ib.*; Abbot Panormitane and others, 80; the fifth chapter, 81; sixth chapter, 89; to seventh chapter, 105; Marcus Mantua, 133; Robert Wakefeild, 149; a dialogue called the Glass of Truth, 169, 305, 306, 308, 322, 326, 327, 332, 335, i. ii. ix.

Harpsfield, John, Archdeacon of London and Dean of Norwich, 7

Helenus, Hector's brother, marries Andromache after the death of Pyrrhus, 32

Helvidius the heretic, 118

Henage, Mr., 234

Henry I. the Emperor, and Cunigundis his wife, 217

Henry VII., 42, 207, 280, foretells that Henry VIII. shall be the undoing of England, 284

Herbert, 332

Herod, King, 18, 39, 52, 249
Herodias, 249
Herveus, 108
Hierome burnt for heresy, 208, 329
Hilary, Pope, 110
Hildebert, Author's answer to, 72, 118, 243
Hildesley, Francis, 1, Thomas, 6
Holgate, Archbishop of York; Gilbertine, Prior of Wotton and Master of the Order of Sempringham, 275
Holinshed, 333, 335
Holyman, Dr., 202
Hostiensis, 123
Howard, Katherine, 260, 263, 268, 277, 333; Edmund, *ib.*; Lord William, 336
Hugo, Cardinal, 19, 49, 51; Author's answer to, 71, 84, 118, 246, 248
Hugo de Sancto Victore, Author's answer to, 72, 118
Hungary, King of, 311
Huntingdon, Henry Earl of, 113
Hurskey, Thomas, Prefect of the whole Gilbertine Order, 319
Hutton, 336

Imola, Johannes de, Author's answer to, 79
Inigo de Mendoza, Don, 322
Innocent III., Pope, 24, 46; Author's answer to, 59, 80, 112, 125, 135, 137, 226, 311
Irenæus, 19, 103
Isichius, 19, Author's answer to, 64, 92, 117, 128
Isidore, St., 107, 227, 241
Ivo Carnotensis, Author's answer to, 73, 118

Jacob, the Patriarch marries two sisters, 33, 82
Jacobus de Lausania, Author's answer to, 77
Jacobus Almaine, 108
James V. of Scotland, 336
Jerome, St., 19, 22, 51; Author's answer to, 67, 94, 118, 149, 151, 155, 168, 245, 249, 274
Jerusalem, council of the Apostles at, 38
Johannes, de Savo, 123
Johannes Knappius, 133

Johannes de Andreas, 136
Johannes Cochleus, 209, 211
John Baptist, St., 52, 55, 71, 76, 249, 251, 255
Josephus, 52, 128, 160
Josias, King, 282
Jovinian, 274
Julius, Pope, 41, 144, 149, 193, 215, 225, 230, 307
Justinian, Emperor, 267

Kirkham, Dr., 202, 329
Knight, principal secretary to Henry VIII., 187, 279, 325, 336
Kotser Codicis, 308, 318

Lais, 217
La Mer des Histoires, reference to, 320
Langdale, Dr., Archdeacon of Lewes, 9
Langlond, John, Bishop of Lincoln, King's Confessor, 175, 198, 321, 323, 327
Lateran, Council of, 47, 233, 269
Laurence, St., 114, 232
Lanrentius. Archbishop of Canterbury, 113
Law of Nature, Author's definition of, 83
Law, Moral, Author's definition of, 85
Lee, Dr., Bishop of Hereford, 177, 209, 326, 330
Lee, Rowland, Chaplain to Henry VIII., 2, 34, made Bishop of Coventry and Lichfield, *ib.*
Leo, Emperor, 279, 337
Leo, Pope, 110, 225
Leo, St., 245, 248
Lincoln, Robert, Bishop of, 232
Lingard, Dr., 327
Longueville, Duke of, 336
Lotharius and Thietburga, 16
Lucius, King, 262
Luther, Martin, 285

Macharcus, 93
Mantua, Marcus, of Padua, 17, 21, 24, 120, 122, 125; Author's answer to, 133-149, 213, 232
Marcellus, 107
Marcus Crassus marries his brother's wife, 32
Martinus de Salva, 123
Martyn, Pope, 46, 79
Mary, Queen, 6, 7, 13, 197, 200

Methodius, 93
Mewtas, Peter, 336
Milan and Lorraine, Duchess of, Duke of, 278, 336, 337
Milevitane, Council of, 229
More, Sir Thomas, 15, 25, 28, 36, 47, 119, 175, 201, 205, 207, 221, 234, 237, 249, 254, 256, 286, 301
Moreman, Master, 202, 329
Morison, Master, 209
Moses, Rabbi Neclimanides Gerundensis. 154

Nachor, Abraham's brother, marries Sarah's sister, 53
Neocesarea, Council of, Author's answer to, 60
Nero, Emperor, 249
Nerva, Emperor, 32
Nice, Council of, 110, 227
Nicholas, Pope, 16
Nicholas, Dr. Italian friar, 28
Nicholaus de Lyra, 33, 66, 119, 128, 152, 154, 166, 243
Nicholaus, Patriarch of Constantinople, 279, 337
Norfolk, Duke of, 183, 199, 333, 334
Norris, Mr. 234
Northumberland, Earl of, 236, 259
Norton, Judge, 6

Oglethorpe, Dr. Bishop of Carlisle, 9
Origen, 19, 21, 52; Author's answer to, 62, 150, 245, 249
Orleans, Council of, 34, 139. 210, 232, 329
Orleans, Earl of, 180
Othoniel marries his brother Caleb's daughter, 33, 66

Pace, R. Dean of S. Paul's, 308, 317
Padua, University of, 210, 329
Pampilona, Cardinal of, 123
Panormitane, abbot, and others, Author's answer to, 80, 110, 119
Paris, Divines and Canonists of University of, 50, 210, 232, 329
Paris, son of Priam, 16
Parr, Katherine, 280
Patavium, 128
Paul, St., 33, 51, 99, 111, 142, 165, 170, 242, 321
Paulette, Sir William, Controller of the King's House, 199

INDEX. 343

Paul Flavianus, Bishop of Constantinople, 225
Paulus Burgensis, 33, 66, 92, 156, 164, 166
Paulus Pansa, 132
Peter, St., 109, 212, 266, 316
Peto, one of the Greenwich Observant Friars, 202; preached sermon on King Ahab to Henry VIII. 203
Petrus de Anchorano, 46
Petrus de Palude, Author's answer to, 75, 77, 83, 100, 118, 121
Philip and Juana of Castile, 310
Philip Augustus, King, 17
Philip I. King of France, 17
Philip, Herod's brother, 54
Philo, 160
Phryne, 217
Pisa, University of, 210
Pits, Dr. 10
Pius, Pope, 76
Pole, Cardinal, 202, 205, 207, 218, 236, 258; his character, 294
Pomponius, 156
Powell, executed, 208, 329
Prosper, 315

Rabanus, 52
Rhine, the Palgrave of the, 259, 332
Rochford, George Boleyne, Lord, 199, 254, 324
Roper, Dr. 202
——— Margaret, 223
Rouen, Bishop of, 72
Rupertus Tuitiensis, Author's answer to, 71, 118
Ruth, allusions to Book of, 173, 174, 227, 321
Rymer, 331

Salamanca, University of, 210
Salisbury, Countess of, 286
Sampson, Richard, Dean of the Chapel Royal, 322
Sanders, 321, 324, 328, 331, 335, i.
Sardis, Council of, 229
Saxony, Duke, John Frederick, of, 259, 332
Scholastical Doctors, residue of, Author's answer to, 79
Scot. Dr., Bishop of Chester, 9, 61, 98, 103, 108
Seckendorf, 329

Sedulius, 51
Seymour, Jane, 280, 336
Sherwood, Robert, 317
Sienna, University of, 210
Simon de Cassia, 84
Solomon, King, 155
Somerset, Duke of, 336
Standish, Henry, Bishop of St. Asaph, 177
Stevens, 324
Stevenson, Rev. Joseph, i.
Stocksley, Dr., Bishop of London, 177, 195, 198, 297, 308, 322, 326
Stow, 333, 335
Sudeley, Thomas Seymour, Lord, 337
Suffolk, Duke of, 183, 324

Tabiena, Johannes de, Author's answer to, 77
Tancredus the Glosse, 123
Tarvisana, Marchia, 134
Temses, a Member of the House of Commons, 197
Tereus, 93
Tertullian, 19; Author's answer to, 53-55, 128, 159
Thamar, marries the three sons of Judas, 21, 49, 82, 98, 117, 153
Theodore, Bishop of Pavia, 266
Theodosius, Emperor, 15, 17, 66, 225
Theophilact, 51
Thiestes, 93
Thietgandus, Archbishop of Trèves, 16
Thomas Aquinas, St., 5, 19, 103, 108; Author's answer to, 74, 75, 83, 111, 118, 128, 178, 313
Thurlby, Dr. Bishop of Ely, 275
Toledo, Second Council of, Author's answer to, 59, 92; Council of, 198; University of, 210
Topliffe, a priest catcher, 1, 5, 302
Toulouse, University of, 210, 329
Touraine, Viscount of, 186
Treatise of Dr. Nicholas Harpesfield concerning the marriage occasioned by the pretended divorce between King Henry VIII. and Queen Katherine, first book, 25; second book, 121; third book, 222; Epistle to the reader, 12-24
Trent, Council of, 151
Tuke, 324
Turre Chremata, Johannes de, Author's answer to, 76, 109, 111

INDEX.

Tyndale's Practice of Prelates, allusion to, 322

Ulpian, 31, 240
Ulysses Polyphemus, 300
Urbanus, Pope, 107, 115

Valentia, University of, 210
Valentinian, Emperor, 271; Justina his wife, 272
Vannes, Peter, Ambassador of Henry VIII. at the Court of Rome, 182, 185, 187, 189, 325
Vaughan, 337
Vaux, M. de, 190
Vergil, Polydore, 322, 328
Victritius Rathmagensis, Bishop, 226
Vincentius, 80, 123

Wakefield, Robert, 18, 21, 24; Author's answer to, 149, 244, 306, 307, 309; his letter to Henry VIII. 317
Waldensis, 61; Author's answer to, 73, 118
Waldrada, 16, vii.
Walterus de Constantia, Author's answer to, 73, 118
Warham, Dr. William, Archbishop of Canterbury, 4, 175, 287, 290; Sir William, 4, 178
Warwick, Edward Earl of, 207

Watson, Dr., Bishop of Lincoln, 9
West, Nicholas, Bishop of Ely, 177
White, Dr., Bishop of Winchester, 9
Whiting, Richard, Abbot of Glastonbury, hanged beside his monastery on Torr Hill, 301
Wickliffe, Thomas, 19, 23, 61, 78, 231, 274
William of Malmesbury, 113
Wilson, Dr., 28, 223, 237
Wolsey, Cardinal, 24, 180, 184, 186, 189, 195, 201, 288, his fall and death, 289, 321, 322, 324, 326, 331
Wood, Antony, 305, 317, iii.
Wood's Athenæ Oxonienses, references to, 4, 5, 7, 9, 255, 283, 305, 308
Woodford, 61, 118
Worcester, Bishop of, ambassador of Henry VIII. in Spain, 195
Wriothsley, Lord Chancellor of the realm, 278
Wriothesley, Charles, his Chronicle, 329, 333, 336, 337
Wyatt, Sir Thomas, 253, 332

Xenocrates, 217

Zacharias, Pope, Author's answer to, 58, 266
Zasius, 133
Zosimus, Pope, 109

www.ingramcontent.com/pod-product-compliance
Lightning Source LLC
Chambersburg PA
CBHW020238240426
43672CB00006B/571